Ideal
298

Sparks

59-13586

3-12-62

J. C. Furnas

1959

WILLIAM SLOANE ASSOCIATES

NEW YORK

THE ROAD TO

HARPERS FERRY

FOR C. B.

WHO WANTED MORE AFRICA LAST TIME.

Acknowledgments

Thanking individuals for help on books that range as widely as this one is risky. Somebody always gets left out. Will all who gave me advice or information—and there are some hundreds of them—take this, please, as personal and hearty thanks?

Institutions that generously put materials at the author's disposal include first and foremost the Princeton University Library; then the New York Public Library, the Harvard College Library, the library of the Harvard Club of New York City, the Library of Congress, the National Archives, the Flemington (N.J.) Free Library, the Hunterdon County Library, the Institute of Jamaica, the Kansas State Historical Society, the New York State Library, the Royal Empire Society, the Royal Naval College, the National Maritime Museum (of Greenwich, England), the Municipal Museums of Hull, England. Those supplying information or good offices include the American Museum of Natural History, the National Park Service, the Perkins School for the Blind, Mount

Auburn Cemetery (Cambridge, Mass.), the New York Yacht Club, H.M. Colonial Office, the Farrell Lines, the U.S. State Department . . .

Every page, as was said previously in respect to *Goodbye to Uncle Tom,* reflects my wife's skills as researcher, editor and whetstone to an extent that amounts practically to collaboration.

J. C. Furnas

CONTENTS

excessiveness *Accessories)*

PROLOGUE : *Immortality* 3

1 *The Blown Trumpet* 9

2 *Sunny Fountains* 52

3 *The Middle Passage* 105

4 *U.S.S. Frustration* 152

5 *The Curse of Cane* 182

6 *The Spartacus Complex* 206

7 *A Man and a Brother* 245

8 *Borrowed Plumage* 286

9 *The Secret Six* 327
    CADMUS INDICTED 327
    MOSS-TROOPERISM 332
    DR. GALAHAD 338
    PURITAN PROPHET 346
    LORD BOUNTIFUL 354
    BEARDED ANGEL 362
    THE YOUNGEST DISCIPLE 367
    THE SORCERER'S APPRENTICES 372

EPILOGUE : *The Most Dangerous -Ism* 383

NOTES 393

WORKS CONSULTED 437

APPENDIX 459

Prologue: *Immortality*

"Little of all we value here
Wakes on the morn of its hundredth year
Without both feeling and looking queer."
                              —HOLMES, The Deacon's Masterpiece

The great, sullen, black rock, humped and bulky as a whale, crops up in the middle of a plateau hemmed in by the high Adirondacks. Fourteen symbols cut in its iron-hard flank spell: "JOHN BROWN—1859."

The hero-worshipers who paid for that inscription took it for granted that further details were not needed: that that name and date would always send flashing across people's minds the basic story of the first American ever hanged for treason—at Charlestown, Virginia (now West Virginia), on December 2, 1859. For the Civil War generation and their children John Brown was as conspicuous as Abraham Lincoln or Robert E. Lee. John Jay Chapman called his story "an immortal legend—perhaps the only one in our history." Planning this book for publication round the centenary of the momentous raid on Harpers Ferry, I too assumed that potential readers would already know the outlines of the career that led to that extraordinary gesture. My concern was to be not so much with what John Brown did as with the ideas and emotions that culminated in anybody's attempting so strange a thing.

The assumption did not hold up. By his private war against slavery the gaunt man buried in the lee of that Adirondack outcrop confirmed the South in the frame of mind that precipitated the Civil War. But when asked "Who was John Brown and what did he do?" my literate acquaintances of 1958 under the age of sixty knew only that, though his body lies moldering in the grave, his soul goes marching on. Many had read Benét's *John Brown's Body*—which offers the best summary of the man ever written—but the facts had not stuck. Some thought of him as a mutinous Negro slave; others as a Confederate guerrilla. Some associated him with Harpers Ferry but were unsure where that is: Virginia? No, Kansas? Most thought that he did whatever it was he did during or after the Civil War.

If people know so little that is definite about him, obviously the legend was not immortal, the tense old warrior's soul does not go marching on. And it should. The more one knows of it, of the causes of its lost renown, of the strange "Secret Six" group of men who encouraged it to vaunt itself, and of the implications of such souls and such ideas and their origin, the clearer it is that this affair was highly significant. I cannot take such paucity of public knowledge as summons to write another biography of John Brown. There is little new material to explore. The target has never taken a salvo square amidships but it has been conscientiously bracketed, and modern inquirers, free from the glamor that clung round it in grandfather's time, usually conclude that John Brown was like the rabbit that dislodged the pebble that started the avalanche, far less important than what he helped to happen. But he was also an invaluably clear example of the right kind of man in the right place who serves exasperated people as catalyst. For millions both North and

South he made bad temper, poor judgment and eager self-deception feel righteous and valiant.

So his acquaintance is worth making: First the strange case of John Brown himself; then the far stranger case of the men and notions that sent him forth that damp fall night to rouse rebellion among people of whom he knew little; in a region of which he knew no more; with exactly one professional and seventeen amateur soldiers at his back, and world-wide fame just around the corner.

The countryfied county seat, Charlestown, where John Brown was tried for his life and hanged by the neck till he was dead, lies in full view of the Blue Ridge, the mountain range defining the Shenandoah Valley to the eastward. Among his last utterances were three opinions: that the countryside he saw as he rode to the gallows seated on his own coffin was beautiful; that, by making him a martyr, his being hanged would serve the antislavery cause better than would his living on; and that his country, North or South, could no longer avoid bloody catastrophe.

This disastrously accurate prophet even looked the part. The high, thick mane and almost sacrilegiously impressive beard of his best known portrait, taken a few months before he raided the Ferry, have ever since tempted artists to make him more and more resemble Michelangelo's Moses. The beard was actually a disguise grown in his last year when there were Federal and state rewards totaling $3250 for his apprehension; then, further to confuse officers of the law, he clipped it back fairly short at the time of the raid. During his previous career as antislavery guerrilla in "Bleeding Kansas" he had been clean-shaven. This minimized the whiteness of his beard but otherwise added to the im-

pression of age that he usually gave. Kansas called him "Old
John Brown" or "Old Man Brown," oftenest just "Old
Brown," to distinguish him from his sons and other Browns
involved in Kansas troubles. When he was only fifty-six he
called himself "an old man of nearly sixty years." A Kansas newspaper at the same time described him as "an aged
gentleman." But it was a wiry old age. His exalted energy
could outmarch, outwake, outfast men of half his actual
years.

Photographs of him clean-shaven show a thin-lipped ferocity, a pair of the most alarming eyes in American history
and a worn ruggedness like a long-weathered fence post.
The deservedly dead "science" of physiognomy never was a
science. Yet habitual reactions can do meaningful things
to the set of facial muscles. The beardless old man who sat
for those daguerreotypists in the mid-1850's was under ten-
sions not to be attributed to mere suffering under the ordeal
of prolonged time exposures.

The "Secret Six"—his backers, a striking group set aside
by frenetic aggressiveness from the bulk of those disliking
slavery, even from the bulk of professed Abolitionists—had
all seen this face before that benevolent beard left only
the imposing nose and brows patriarchally in view. Yet it did
not daunt them. They were too calamitously well prepared
for what they took to be its implications. Their frames of
reference were artificial and impertinent. Their attitude toward John Brown mingled the xenophobia of the Old Testament with the histrionics of Miniver Cheevy. Their approach to slavery derived too much from British experience
in the West Indian slave economy—which differed widely
from Dixie's[1]—and was further skewed by the contemporary
taste for casting West Africans as "noble savages," those il-
lusory chimeras. Yet they were no muttering little clique of

[1] Superior numbers as here, running consecutively chapter by chapter,
indicate notes of reference and definition to be found on page 393 and
following.

nonentities. They were Theodore Parker, great radical theologian-preacher; Dr. Samuel Gridley Howe, world-famous physician-psychologist; Gerrit Smith, greatest American landowner of his day; Thomas Wentworth Higginson, militant colleague of Parker's; George Luther Stearns, industrialist-inventor; Franklin Benjamin Sanborn, schoolmaster, editor and eventual biographer of great New Englanders. Their second echelon, not so close to Old Brown's plans but deeply impressed with him and giving him money and countenance, included such very illustrious persons as Ralph Waldo Emerson; Henry David Thoreau; John Murray Forbes, builder of the Michigan Central and Chicago, Burlington & Quincy Railroads; Thaddeus Hyatt, pioneer of reinforced concrete construction; and for a while Amos A. Lawrence of the prominent and wealthy textile family.

All these rallied round John Brown in his pre-beard phase not primarily because he promised to be an expendable Abolitionist propaganda tool—though that factor was present—but because he seemed to them a Yankee Greatheart, another Gray Champion. It can be embarrassingly difficult to distinguish between the genuine virtues of a worthy cause and the distortions that its misguided supporters inflict on it. The fanatic who loves blood and fire for their own sakes has always stood behind the barricade alongside peaceable men of good will finally pushed too far. John Brown did earnestly seek to eradicate slavery—as unlovely a growth as the world ever knew—but probably not so much to relieve the slave as to gratify his own hate-powered drives. And the nearer people came to sharing his emotional habits, the farther they were from the common sense badly needed when civil war was imminent, needed still more after the killing was over. John Brown's raid, so admirably playing into the hands of Dixie's hotheads, could never have occurred if a self-righteous minority of Northerners had not already worked themselves up into bloody-minded hatreds. Their sole excuse is that their opposite numbers in Dixie were just as extravagant and probably more numerous. Both groups exemplify a familiar situation that would be ludicrous if it were not always dangerous: the incredible results when, after the fashion of Marxists, Nazis and white supremacists, people start taking literally the extreme language and violent figures of speech into which mounting passion has betrayed them.

To account for the Secret Six as well as John Brown requires tortuous exploration by way of Kansas, Guinea and the West Indies to Westminster and Concord, Mass. But the longest way round is the truest way home.

1 *The blown trumpet*

"... *A stone eroded to a cutting edge*
By obstinacy, failure and cold prayers ...
And with a certain minor-prophet air
That fooled the world to thinking him half-great
When all he did consistently was fail."
—STEPHEN VINCENT BENÉT, John Brown's Body

Even Old Brown had, like us all, been young once—born in Torrington, Conn., of stern, respectable Yankee stock in 1800. Owen Brown, his sharp-faced father, was a tanner and farmer, anxiously pious, early hot antislavery, father of sixteen by three successive wives—none of which details, except the fervency of his Abolitionism, was unusual in the gnarly Berkshire foothills. Our John Brown was out of the first wife. Owen's father, Captain John Brown, had died in 1776 of camp disease soon after joining Washington's army above New York City. Eighty-three years later his grandson had Washington's great-grandnephew kidnaped. Old Brown set considerable store by his Revolutionary grandsire's memory. He moved Captain John's crumbly tombstone to the Adirondacks farm and stipulated that "no other monument be used to keep me in remembrance." Epitaphs for the Harpers Ferry captain and those of his sons killed while fighting under him were duly added, and the old slab still stands by the great rock by which he located just where he wished to lie. Later admirers disregarded his orders and put up some distance away a sentimental bronze of him freeing a slave.

In 1805 Owen Brown and family migrated to Connecticut's Western Reserve in northeastern Ohio where Yankee settlers were making a new New England. Like their neighbors the Browns went in for hard work, enough to eat but nothing fancy, and religion and schooling as two sides of the same coin. John learned the tanner's trade by watching his father and doing what he was shown. When father supplied beef to Hull's force in Michigan in the War of 1812, John went along to help drive the cattle. His firsthand glimpse of soldiering gave him a lifelong contempt for armies as such. In view of Hull's ineptitude and what passed for discipline on such expeditions, this is understandable. But his subsequent conviction that amateur soldiers do as well as professionals had untoward results.

In his late teens the boy decided to enter the ministry and returned to New England to prepare for Amherst College, where a close relative was on the faculty. "Inflammation of the eyes" ended his studies. This was probably just as well since, though already Bible-soaked, he was a clumsy, droning speaker. Back in Ohio again, he learned surveying, the most useful of frontier professions except midwifing, and became a typical chance-taking, land-greedy jack-of-all-trades restlessly pioneering among mud, stumps and promissory notes. Presently he had a tanyard in northwestern Pennsylvania and a plain but worthy wife of the right Yankee extraction—only she proved intermittently psychotic and died "insane"—to beget children on.

Old Brown probably did not plan to erect a patriarchal clan, but that was the way semipioneering conditions and his own rearing and impulses worked it out. He did come to regard his many sons and sometimes his daughters and daughters-in-law as instruments duty-bound to his projects. But for that day he was no notably harsh father. Disobedient children earned demerits. At a certain total whipping evened the score. Father sometimes puzzled them by making them give him as many cuts of the whip as he gave them. Each remembered being sung to on his knee, usually his favorite hymn, "Blow ye the trumpets, blow!" with its refrain "The year of Jubilee is come!" Nor did this gentleness altogether disappear as (in my view) he drew nearer to chronic mental disease. I find it touching that, even in his own fifties, he would get up in the night to make sure that his father, who lived well past the age of eighty, was snugly tucked in. His grandchildren too heard the old hymns on grandpa's knee. "The children always come to me," he told a Boston admirer who found him playing with a small child. He put up with his sons' imitating his prejudice against organized religion to the point of agnosticism; and when two of them refused to join the Harpers Ferry raiding party, he took their defection coldly in stride. Right up to his portentous end his letters home express a volubly temperate fondness. It was not a simple personality, but then few personalities are so. Only the *naïf* take real people as being like characters in fiction, consistently patterned between the ages of hopeful thirty and bitter fifty-five. Old Brown was real, though strange, and on occasion could hark back to the less bitter, less dedicated, emotionally healthier days before the sun was bloody and God's word was fatally unmistakable.

Tanning in Pennsylvania did not suit. His schemes seldom did. He returned to Ohio to farm and speculate in land. He and other Browns contested suits over land titles and note endorsements even oftener than was usual with our litigious forebears among whom the lawyer often beat the teacher and the preacher into new settlements. He and two of his sons once spent some days in jail—a mere formality maybe—for violently resisting a foreclosure. As often happened to his contemporaries too, he fell into bankruptcy with some flavor of dishonesty. Yet others might trust him with assets. He bred race horses with a borrowed stud until he developed scruples against encouraging gamblers. He retained an eye for a good horse, was a sound though grace-less rider able to break colts to saddle, and trained his boys to equal skill—all eventually useful in Kansas. A well-to-do Akron man named Perkins took him as shepherd-partner to handle a herd of 1500 sheep. Soon he persuaded Perkins that Eastern brokers were cheating Ohio woolgrowers, and that an astute, honest Ohioan could sell pregraded Ohio wool in the Eastern market at negotiated prices instead of the predatory brokers' arbitrary quotations. So for a while after 1846 Perkins & Brown operated in Springfield, Mass. The unforeseen flaw was that John Brown, the managing part-ner, though an Ohioan and maybe honest, was an eccentric and by no means astute negotiator.

To by-pass conniving brokers he had visited Europe in 1849 but found that well-graded, neatly bagged American wool brought even less there than in Springfield. All he brought home was tales of how his knowledge of wool had astounded Britons,[1] and strange ideas about European farm-ing and soldiering. Perkins was patient about the irksome lawsuits required to wind up the affairs of Perkins & Brown. Years later he described Old Brown as a clever wool grader but a stubbornly wrongheaded shepherd unable to admit that in sheepherding or anything else he had managed wrong. Contrast this with Emerson's account of him, reflect-ing Old Brown's talk about himself in some soul-to-soul in-terview at Concord:

"A shepherd and herdsman," Emerson wrote, "he learned the manners of the animals and knew the secret signals by which animals communicate. He made his hard bed on the mountains with them; he learned to drive his flock through thickets all but impassable; he had the skill of a shepherd by choice to breed and by wise industry to obtain the best wool . . ." Mountains in Summit County, Ohio, and the secret signals of animals—this is just a passage out of Words-worth. As years passed Old Brown spun more and more

THE BLOWN TRUMPET 13

such stuff to impress his backers and himself. "I noticed," wrote Thoreau with, for once, unconscious irony, "that he did not overstate anything but spoke within bounds." The scene is readily imagined: the old jayhawker[2] waxing stiffly confidential—for he could talk a streak when the subject was not his plans but himself—while Thoreau, Emerson or maybe Mrs. Lydia Maria Child eagerly made mental notes for the diary kept for posterity.

As Old Brown continued his search for something to get his teeth into, his second wife—married in 1833, giving him thirteen more children—saw him little more than if he had followed the sea. He would be away for months, then home for days or weeks ordering this cow sold, that field cleared, that shed reshingled . . . In 1840 a plan to move to the undeveloped western edge of Virginia came to nothing, partly because he dillydallied about the deal. In 1849 the clan shifted to the Adirondacks, where daughter Ruth expanded it by marrying into a local family named Thompson, whose young men came heavily under Old Brown's spell. Finding the Adirondacks unrewarding, Old Brown moved part of his entourage back to Ohio. In 1854 the explosive Kansas-Nebraska bill signalized the opening of Kansas to settlers. Government was buying out the Indians; the land was fertile; popular vote was to settle whether the new Territory would admit slavery; so antislavery people—and old Owen Brown had instilled fanatic Abolitionism into any of his children at all susceptible—would do both themselves and the great cause a good turn by taking up Kansas land. John Brown's half sister Florilla, an early alumna of Oberlin College, was already out there as wife of a missionary. Maybe her letters home determined certain of her nephews—John jr. (the eldest), Jason, Owen, Salmon and Frederick (already given to fits of "lunacy")—to try Kansas. Old Brown stayed behind, representing that he had other fish to fry—maybe an early phase of the Harpers Ferry scheme.

The boys found Kansas satisfactorily fertile, given the

right weather. But soon after locating land claims in the new-settling areas near the Missouri border and setting out the vines and fruit trees that had been fetched along, they encountered hostile pressures from proslavery Missourian immigrants bent on forcing Kansas to admit slavery. Seeking strength where they had always found it, they invited their father to join them with fresh supplies and better weapons than their original outfit had included. He dropped everything, went on a tour of antislavery meetings to pass the hat for money for rifles, revolvers and so forth, promising that, in his sons' hands, they would strengthen the antislavery cause. He obtained not only enough cash but also certain firearms "spirited away" from Ohio militia stores and a consignment of heavy Navy cutlasses—of these more later. Then he loaded a wagon with all this hardware and a new cookstove and set off in the summer of 1855 with son Oliver and Henry Thompson, his eldest son-in-law.

"On the lintels of Kansas
The blood shall not dry;
Henceforth the Bad Angel
Shall harmless go by;
Henceforth to the sunset,
Unchecked on her way,
Shall Liberty follow
The march of the day."

—WHITTIER, Le Marais du Cygne

"Hostile pressures" had implied masses of Missourian "Border Ruffians" voting illegally in the formative elections in Kansas and playing ever rougher as "Free-State" resistance stiffened. Up and down the border counties knots of proslavery settlers bullied Free Staters or, depending on the area, *vice versa.* Each faction sought to wear its opposition down by claim jumping, cattle and horse stealing, cabin burning, flogging and tar and cottoning—Kansas was still too primitive to have enough pillows and poultry for tar and feathers. Missourian intruders elected a proslavery Territorial legislature countenanced by a Federal executive "sound on the goose"—the local slang for "sympathetic to slavery." The Free Staters called the resulting government "bogus"—as indeed it largely was—and set up a rival governor, legislature and militia which, unfortunately, could have no legal standing at all. Federal troops on the scene ordered to assist law and order inevitably served the cause of the nominally legal proslaveryites.

Both braggart Southerners and militant Abolitionists back in the Northeast had early chosen to make this rivalry a show of strength. "Bleeding Kansas" was to our Civil War rather like what the Spanish Civil War was to World War II, an exacerbating dress rehearsal.[3] The North's "Emigrant Aid" societies and "Kansas Committees" organized parties of settlers and economic resources to add weight to the Free-State side of the scale. The Deep South sent counterweight gangs of proslaveryites, mostly young and many reckless, pledged to help the red-shirted, bowie-knived Missouri "Pukes" make Kansas too hot to hold Free Staters. Soon New England's support of her Kansas *protégés* extended beyond farm tools, provisions and sawmills into hundreds of the then famous long-range, wickedly accurate Sharp's rifled carbines. "Border Ruffians" closed the Missouri River, natural route into Kansas, against Free Staters and their equipment. Free Staters worked out a new approach through Iowa to supply their bristly little capital in Kansas, named Lawrence after Amos A., who contributed much time and money to Emigrant Aid.

The less militant bulk of the settlers would have sought to evade the problem of slavery if left unmolested. Pioneer Kansas wanted to be lily-white. "We want no slaves and no niggers," was the prevailing sentiment reported by an Abolitionist in 1854. Every fair show of local sentiment showed strong opposition to both admission of slavery and the presence of Negroes, slave or free. This illiberal cutting of the Gordian knot may well have been illegal. But nobody ever knew, for it was never seriously tested. Two factions of doctrinaire intruders, the Border Ruffians and the hot Abolitionists, insisted on playing pull-devil-pull-baker with the Territory and made it a chaotic paradise for horse thieves, shysters, bullies, self-elected crusaders, shoddy adventurers, screaming propagandists and brash egocentrics mingling the crassest and the most visionary motives with highly shattering emotions.

Old Brown found this atmosphere heady. He plunged into local affairs as eagerly and, since he was no legal resident, as illicitly as any Border Ruffian. When Free Staters mustered against a Missourian threat to Lawrence, the Brown clan turned up armed to the teeth with rifles, revolvers and cutlasses; even the bed of their wagon was fenced with poles carrying bayonets pike-fashion. The old man had got good value for his takings from antislavery meetings. John Brown jr. became captain of the Pottawatomie Rifles, a Free-State militia unit including his father, brothers and a few devoted admirers of Old Brown. On the next call to protect Lawrence this outfit was still on the way when the Missourians burned the local hotel—as much a Free-State fort as an inn —broke up Free-State printing presses and left for home. The frustrated Rifles bivouacked on the road. After nightfall Old Brown gathered a squad of seven, including three sons and a son-in-law, and rode away. Two nights and a day later they returned close-mouthed, leading some strange horses. The news was soon out: At dead of night five proslavery men had been taken from their cabins near the Browns' land on Pottawatomie Creek and clumsily butchered—with those Navy cutlasses.

This "Pottawatomie Massacre" was widely assumed to be

Old Brown's work and made his name in Kansas. To con-
fidants he casuistically denied that he had personally "raised
a hand" in it, though approving of it as warning against
such raids as that on Lawrence. At best this incriminated
his sons and made him accessory before and after the fact.
Long after the old man was hanged one son and another
participant admitted that he was present and in charge
throughout the whole gruesome affair, though maybe not
actually wielding a cutlass himself.[4] But between lies and
half-truths—natural enough, of course—he encouraged his
admirers to deny his guilt, as they had to do if he were to
retain archangel's wings.

True, frontier violence often culminated in such horrors
elsewhere than in Kansas. Local indignation was high but
local justice was ill organized and evasion was easy in that
thinly settled, spottily timbered country. The sequel was a
tragedy of errors. John jr., who had no hand in the killing—
may indeed have tried to dissuade the old man from it—
took to the woods in mumbling confusion. After some days
he gave himself up and was turned over to a detail of U.S.
dragoons who, assuming he was one of the killers, completed
his mental collapse by severe brutality—specifically, they
hitched him to a chain and made him keep pace with their
horses over a day-long march. Eventually released, he regained rationality, but a sister considered that he was never
quite the same again. Frederick Brown, the overtly psychotic son who had stood guard while the others cut the victims down, was killed weeks later by a proslavery gang. But
the law never caught up with those most actively involved.
Nine days after the massacre, in fact, the clan, led by Old
Brown, were brazenly conspicuous in an affray at Black Jack
in which Free Staters captured a Missourian force; and
again three months later in a fight at Osawatomie where Old
Brown's slowness on the tactical uptake nearly got them all
captured.

Between and after these shindies the Browns, using false

names, melted into the Kansan half-world of stolen horses, looted supplies, minatory arson and doctrinaire hatred. Some of Old Brown's detractors see cattle rustling and horse thieving gradually displacing antislaveryism as the gang's chief concern. This may have been true of certain members from without the clan but not of Old Brown. Instead of staying in Kansas to cash in on raiding, he now entered on a double life. West of the Missouri he was only one of several guerrilla leaders working with Free-State militia when they saw fit; more or less countenanced by militant antislaveryites in "liberating" and using or selling proslaveryites' cattle, horses, watches and provisions. Old Brown thought this a lawful spoiling of the Egyptians. His rules for his "Kansas Regulars" gang provided for regular division of the proceeds from the sale of loot much after the fashion of Caribbean pirates. It was all in the good cause, and another familiar text advised against muzzling the ox that treadeth out the corn.

In the Northeast, however, which he now frequented, Old Brown loomed up as the ranking Free-State hero privileged to raise funds from antislaveryites for his personal "secret service" schemes and eventually given custody of two hundred Sharp's rifles and two hundred revolvers procured for Free-State use. The exact nature of his "secret service" was never described in public, seldom described explicitly in private. "Our best people," wrote Bronson Alcott in mid-1859, ". . . contribute something in aid of his plans without asking particulars . . . such confidence does he inspire . . . I think him . . . the man to do the deed." For some years he thus beglamored antislavery groups in Chicago, Cleveland, New Haven, Worcester, as well as Alcott's Concord. He was called as featured witness before a committee of the Massachusetts legislature deliberating an appropriation in aid of Free-State Kansas. He owed much of this special renown among Abolitionists to the imagination of James Redpath,[5] a young Scottish-born journalist with "a total dis-

CONTRASTING ASPECTS OF JOHN BROWN
At left: without the beard, from a daguerreotype probably taken in the year of the Potawotamie Massacre, 1856. *Kansas State Historical Society*. *At right*: with the beard at its fullest, in early 1859; engraved from a photograph taken by T. H. Webb. Artists used this in creating the looks-like-Michelangelo's-Moses legend. *Harvard College Library*.

HARPERS FERRY IN 1859

Above: the scene of "the late insurrection." *Below*: the storming of the engine house by United States Marines. Drawings by "Porte Crayon," in *Harper's Weekly*.

regard of facts" whose heavily antislavery dispatches to eastern papers made Old Brown sound like an ascetic Robin Hood.

For these eastern forays the old man took care to look his chosen role of "Captain John Brown of Osawatomie," guerrilla hero. ("Captain" derived from six days under formal commission of the Free-State militia as commander of the twenty men of the "Liberty Guards" in 1855.) His was a striking figure—not really tall but so weasel-lean that his five-foot-ten-inches seemed so; a slow, springy walk; foxy-brown, bristly hair shot with gray, grass-thick down over his narrow forehead; and glaring blue eyes. Artemus Ward saw him in Cleveland in 1859 and said he looked as if "he could lick a yard full of wildcats before breakfast and without taking off his coat." For quasi-military flavor he wore a leather stock of the style that nicknamed the U.S. Marines "leathernecks"; a caped, fitted overcoat of soldierish cut and a peaked fur cap. Vaingloriously he had written to his devoted wife and Mrs. Child that at Osawatomie his command had killed or wounded eighty-odd Missourians, an exaggeration of some thousand per cent. Glibly he assured his backers and himself that he had exhaustively studied fortification and Napoleonic battlefields during his nineteen days on the Continent in 1849. Yet he remained scornful of professional brass. At dinner at the George L. Stearns' in 1857 he ticked off some of his Kansas colleagues:

"As a rule . . . the higher the officer, the less of a soldier. Now I am but a plain captain, and yet I am always ready to fight the enemy. Jim Lane is a colonel, but I have no doubt he would fight if Governor Robinson would let him. Pomeroy is a general and there is no fight in him at all." [6] He told Thoreau that "he must eat sparingly and fare hard, as became a soldier." These are curious pretensions in a hand-to-mouth sheep farmer of strong Abolitionist views. The likeliest explanation is that, all the while things had been failing to work out well for him, Old Brown had lived

a hidden inner life now coming to the surface in self-dramatizing, self-aggravating violence. He had become a megalo-
maniacal Walter Mitty who meant business.

> *"A fanatic is a man that does what he thinks th' Lord wud*
> *do if he knew th' facts iv' th' case."*
> —Mr. Dooley's Philosophy

Long after Harpers Ferry the Browns told in various versions how father had once made the boys kneel and swear to
back him in antislavery violence of some sort. The date was
set back as far as 1835. The story is probably apocryphal but
not implausible. John Brown had long considered slavery
something meriting his personal attention. William Lloyd
Garrison's frenzied Abolitionist paper, the *Liberator,* and
Horace Greeley's Reformist-Abolitionist New York *Tribune* were his and old Owen's favorite reading after the
Bible, and father and son had always done what they could
for fugitives using the Underground Railroad. In Pennsylvania John Brown had considered buying, freeing, and edu-
cating a Negro boy among his own sons as nucleus of a school
for Negroes far from the slums of Northern cities, where
so many free Negroes learned proletarian vice. This was a
worthy scheme, but after that his projects grew steadily more
visionary.

He confided to the Negro porter of Perkins & Brown's
warehouse a vague scheme called the "Subterranean Pass
Way" for Negro-rescuing raids into the South. During the
agitation over the Fugitive Slave Act of 1850 he inducted
thirty-odd Springfield Negroes, including a few women, into
a "United States League of Gileadites" pledged forcibly to
rescue any fugitives arrested in town. The basic tactics were

taken from rescues staged in Boston and Syracuse but Old Brown suggested improvements. "After effecting a rescue, if you are assailed, go into the houses of your most prominent and influential white friends with your wives, and that will effectually fasten on them the suspicion of their being connected with you, and will compel them to make common cause with you . . . A lasso might possibly be applied to a slave-catcher for once with good effect . . ." The Gileadites never had occasion to lasso any slave catchers, so the worth of these strange counsels was never tested.

An alternate plan hinted to the porter was "to occupy land at the South as a slaveholder, using trusty colored men as his nominal slaves, and through them indoctrinating the real slaves with the hope of freedom." He gave his sons another version: Settle in Louisiana, stir up a slave rebellion and march their body of rebels into Texas. In moving the clan to the Adirondacks he hoped to find among the Negro colony there recruits for such projects. Scheming very gradually, never quite thinking anything through, changing ground even as he discussed matters, he "deliberately determined to organize an armed party, go into a slave state, and liberate a large number of slaves. Soon after, surveying professionally in the mountains of Virginia, he chose the very ground for his purpose. Visiting Europe afterward, he studied military strategy . . . making designs . . . for a new style of forest fortification . . . There was always a sort of thrill in John Brown's voice when he spoke of mountains. I shall never forget," wrote Higginson, hardest-headed of his "Secret Six" backers, "the quiet way in which he once told me that 'God had established the Allegheny Mountains from the foundation of the world that they might one day be a refuge for fugitive slaves.'" Old Brown told Sanborn, least hard-headed of the Six: "A few men in the right, and knowing they are right, can overturn a mighty king. Fifty men, twenty men, in the Alleghenies, could break slavery to pieces in ten years."

Never publicly but for individual admirers he spun such fantasies disastrously well. He knew what critical errors had kept Spartacus' slave rebellion from breaking Republican Rome to bits. He had studied intensively the guerrilla methods used by ancient Iberians against Rome and Circassians against Russia; was "thoroughly acquainted with the wars in Hayti and the islands round about . . ." He firmly believed that "upon the first intimation of a plan formed for the liberation of the slaves, they would immediately rise all over the Southern States [and] come into the mountains to join him . . . and . . . enable him to act upon the plantations on the plains lying on each side of the [Appalachian] mountains." Attacks on this mountain fastness by first militia and then regulars would be repulsed; the regulars were to be psychologically softened up by an antislavery pamphlet hinting that they owed it to their consciences to mutiny when ordered to oppose a righteous cause. Then he would "organize the [freed] blacks under [a] provisional constitution" to govern the "mountainous region in which the blacks should be established . . . to be taught the useful and mechanical arts, and all the business of life." Sometimes he assured himself that both free Northern Negroes and slaveholder-hating Southern poor whites would also flock to his mountain Sparta.

That is the clearest available statement of what he had in mind when raising money and recruiting men.[7] While staying with Frederick Douglass, the fugitive slave-Abolitionist editor of Rochester, N. Y., Old Brown asked for two smooth boards on which to design mountain redoubts "to connect with one another by secret passages, so that if one was carried another could be easily fallen back on." This might be Tom Sawyer planning a picturesque rescue of Miss Watson's Jim. In 1857, when his plan was as well matured as it ever would be, he ordered in the famous cutlery village of Collinsville, Conn., a thousand pikeheads patterned on a fancy two-edged dirk that he had taken from a Missourian guerrilla.

Such a blade on the end of a long wooden shaft would, he represented, make "a cheap and effective weapon [with which] a resolute woman" could defend her cabin door against man or beast.[8] The actual purpose, of course, was to arm slave rebels unused to firearms. A few of these resultant pikes were handed to slaves "liberated" at Harpers Ferry, who dropped them and went home as soon as they could. The effective part of the raiders' armament consisted of the two hundred carbines and two hundred revolvers procured for use in Kansas and entrusted to Old Brown—who fetched them back east for his own purposes.[9] The principal function of the pikes turned out to be in anti-Abolitionist propaganda: After Harpers Ferry, Edmund Ruffin, the rabid Virginian publicist, sent specimens of them all over the South as tokens of the barbarity of Black Republican nigger-lovers; he himself carried one as he pulled the lanyard of the first gun fired on Fort Sumter.

With vain, cunning forethought Old Brown tinkered at his grand scheme. His surviving five sons, all veterans of Kansas scuffles, were to be the nucleus of his private army; two of them eventually had a sudden access of caution and declined to serve. The personnel of his Kansas gang had shifted as months passed, but it furnished a dozen or so other young men with the indicated hot antislavery feeling, ability to take the old man seriously, taste for violence and, in some cases, half-baked hopes of lucrative posts in the mountain government-to-be. Aaron Stevens was a strapping Yankee veteran of the Mexican War who had re-enlisted in the First U. S. Dragoons, received a death sentence for "a drunken riot and mutiny"—later commuted to three years at hard labor at Fort Leavenworth—and escaped and devoted his military skills to jayhawking under Old Brown and others. He shared tastes for versifying and spiritualism with several of the Harpers Ferry party. John Henry Kagi was a Swiss-descended lawyer and stenographer who had taught school in Virginia before coming west; when a proslavery Kansas judge began murderously beating him over the head with a heavy cane, he castrated His Honor with a lucky revolver shot. People said that his queer fits of abstracted gloom began after this. Richard Realf was a poetical lower-class English youth who came to Kansas as newspaper correspondent;[10] for reasons to be gone into later he did not show up at Harpers Ferry . . . It was unfair of Nicolay and Hay to call all Old Brown's men "mere Kansas adventurers . . . boys in years and waifs in society . . . reckless, drifting . . ." But there were odd fish in Kansas in those days and some of the odder ones greatly fancied Old Brown's kind of overweening schemes.

They trained for the foray into Dixie in a Quaker-flavored Iowa village in a sort of Y.M.C.A. atmosphere: reading the sermons of Henry Ward Beecher and Theodore Parker; debating and holding mock legislatures; renouncing liquor and tobacco; and, all things considered, getting into singularly little trouble with the local girls. To drill them Old Brown had enlisted another odd fish, "Colonel" Hugh Forbes, a British soldier of fortune who had quit the silk trade in Italy to turn guerrilla with Garibaldi. The old man had found him giving fencing lessons and doing newspaper translations in New York and hired him to write a manual of guerrilla warfare with which to instruct the boys and others joining up as the scheme gathered way. Always keeping things to himself when possible, he failed to mention this great find to the Six. Forbes and he parted probably because the Colonel held out too stubbornly against the mountain scheme, preferring a series of in-and-out slave-stampeding raids. Stevens took over as drill master, and Forbes returned east breathing flames because he had not received the salary that he understood to have been promised.

Assuming mistakenly that Republican leaders knew of Old Brown's plans—the old man had probably exaggerated the extent of his backing—Forbes went screaming to Senator

Henry Wilson of Massachusetts and Senator William H. Seward of New York, demanding his pay and proclaiming Old Brown unfit to be trusted with those Free-State carbines and revolvers. Rightly judging that this vitriolic stranger was a little cracked, Seward ignored him. Wilson at least warned members of the Six to make sure the arms were not improperly used. The Six were already much alarmed by threatening letters from Forbes which indicated that Old Brown had told this fly-by-night as much or more of his plans than he ever had any of them. After frantic mutual consultation they decided to snub Forbes. God was still looking after Old Brown, so the Colonel subsided and went back to Europe. His part in the story nicely illustrates the attraction that often causes cranks to adhere to one another, take each other's pretensions seriously and, for a while, until the egos get too uneasy, collaborate.

To the sharp inquiries of the Six, Old Brown returned only oracular assurances rather than explanation of why he had seen fit so rashly to confide in Forbes. They nevertheless insisted that he postpone his strike, then planned for July 4, 1858. Rather bitterly he returned to Kansas under instructions to support the Free-State cause. Interpreting this in his own turbulent way, he reorganized his old outfit as "Shubel Morgan's Company" and presently raided into Missouri, looting two slaveholding households of slaves, horses, cattle and about everything else movable, including watches, harness, staple provisions and clothing—a typical jayhawker foray. The principal purpose really was slave rescue, however. Old Brown and some of the boys managed to smuggle eleven slaves thus acquired to "Canada West" (now Ontario), which automatically freed them.

This success—the only time Old Brown ever completed a thing according to plan—probably helped to confirm his belief that his hand was in, his God was propitious, the time had come. Soon he was in Cleveland ignoring the price that this caper had put on his head—$3000 from Missouri, $250 from the Federal government—and publicly selling the "liberated" Missouri horses that had hauled the party east. His blatant impunity, result of Cleveland's being very anti-slavery, convinced some of his men that his plans could not entail maximum hazards—a judgment that some revised on the gallows.

The colonies of Negroes in Canada West, mostly alumni of the Underground Railroad, had long interested Old Brown as likely sources of recruits. He went among them twice in 1858 under the auspices of Frederick Douglass and Harriet Tubman, escaped slave and indomitable expert in guiding slaves to freedom. In Chatham, capital of Canadian Negrodom, he and his men held a "convention" of former fugitives to ratify a "Provisional Constitution" for his projected mountain colony. This astounding document begins with an extreme version of the strained Abolitionist doctrine that "Slavery . . . in the United States is none other than a most barbarous, unprovoked, and unjustifiable War, of one portion of its citizens upon another . . ." After forty-five articles on the machinery of an independent, treaty-making government, Article XLVI says that none of it shall be "construed so as in any way to encourage the overthrow of any State Government . . ." or Federal either. Even Villard, a solicitous biographer, called this evidence of "temporary aberration of a mind that in its other manifestations defies successful classification."

Scores of Ontario Negroes brave and clever enough to have escaped from slavery were pledged to rally to Old Brown's call. Of the five Negroes in the Harpers Ferry raid, however, only one came from Canada. This did not imply cowardice. Once the Federals accepted Negro recruits, hundreds recrossed the border to enlist in the Civil War. Dr. W. E. B. DuBois, eminent spokesman for the American Negro, surmises that the postponement that Forbes occasioned made them "doubt Brown's determination and wisdom." Maybe Douglass' denunciation of the Harpers Ferry plan after learning its details had something to do with it. Maybe it came of the Negro's chronic and usually all too well justified mistrust of white man's doings. Anyway, when John Brown jr. came to Canada with word that the old man was coiling to strike, come now or never, these underprivileged exiles showed better judgment than the well-placed and cultivated Six.

This might have struck a less confident plotter as ominous, since the plan depended on the eagerness of Negroes to rise against slavery. But Old Brown knew that God had things under control beyond interference from practicalities. And it did sometimes rather look so. Early in 1859 the voluble Redpath published a book dedicated to Old Brown in terms most injudiciously spelling out the fundamentals of his scheme.[11] Nobody heeded. Late in August, when the boys were already in Maryland, certain Iowans decided to head the scheme off for the participants' own good and wrote anonymously to Secretary of War John B. Floyd that "Old John Brown" of Kansas fame was about to strike Harpers Ferry in a slave-freeing raid that also involved an armory in Maryland. Had their geography been better, Old Brown might never have been famous. But Floyd, on vacation when he received this tip, knew there was no Federal armory in Maryland—Harpers Ferry being just across the Potomac in Virginia—and took this error as an excuse for ignoring it. I cannot think that any benevolent power so desired the attack to be made that it stayed Floyd's hand. No doubt it was the Devil arranging for the old man's luck to hold just long enough to make catastrophe for him—and for the nation—inevitable.

"We've had enough talk about 'bleeding Kansas.' I will make a bloody spot at another point to be talked about."
—John Brown to Jonas Jones

Harpers Ferry lies in the angle where the Shenandoah River and the Potomac join just before the Potomac emerges from the Blue Ridge fifty miles above Washington. Thomas Jefferson told a French correspondent that the view downstream from the Ferry is worth a trip across the Atlantic. George Washington, who knew the region well as a surveyor, chose the spot as site for a Federal armory because both rivers offer good industrial waterpower and it was near sources of iron ore and charcoal to smelt it with. By 1859 the installation included several gunmaking shops (the Armory proper) along the Virginia bank of the Potomac, an arms storage (the Arsenal) and a separate rifle works half a mile up the Shenandoah. A double-duty bridge served foot and wagon traffic from the Maryland side of the Potomac and also carried the main line of the Baltimore & Ohio Railroad. The station almost at the Armory gate was part hotel. Another bridge well upstream linked the town with the right bank of the Shenandoah.

Several changes of hands during the Civil War wrecked the Armory and made it clear that, though strategically important, the town is impossible to defend. Tremendous cliffs tower over it from across each river. Lower but still commanding heights lie behind it. Even so amateurish a soldier as Old Brown must have seen that guns on the surrounding heights would have at their mercy any force trying to hold the place. Many other considerations have always made it impossible for biographers to determine why he wanted to seize it. His point of attack should have been well isolated, so that gathering enemies would be slow to reach him; instead it was on a main-line railroad and near main highways up the Shenandoah Valley and north into Maryland. It was within sixty miles of both Baltimore and Washington and one hundred fifty miles from the only Southern mountains with which he was closely acquainted. The region was not well chosen for ready slave risings. It lacked the big plantations, gang-labor methods and heavy slave population indicated; the relatively few local slaves were relatively well treated farmhands and house servants. And Harpers Ferry was not only a tactical trap—occupying it would also put a wide river between the raiders and their base in Maryland.

Maybe precedent swayed his judgment toward a place containing an arsenal. At least three times during the Kansas troubles arms smuggled out of public arsenals had served one side or other,[12] and he was not the man always coolly to weigh what practical good arsenal seizing might imply. True, it meant a wealth of arms, but he already had plenty of the best. His crowning error was to strike in late autumn, at the start of "the season when the support of life is most difficult . . . Starvation would have met him at the threshold of his [mountain] eyrie," wrote a former chief of the U. S. War College. Nobody knows what he planned to do when the Armory was in his hands. One theory is that he meant the raid as a panic-rousing gesture to be followed by a rapid movement across the Shenandoah to set up that mountain hideaway in the rugged Blue Ridge, abandoning the Maryland base and taking along what hostages, loot and slaves could be quickly scooped in. The other is that he hoped thus to withdraw across the Potomac to the base and thence into the mountains of western Maryland. But much of what he did fitted neither formula. A queer mixture of stubbornness and vacillation betrayed him. His son Salmon called him "strongly fixed . . . It was always difficult for him to fit himself to circumstances; he wanted conditions to change for him." This was consistent at least with his underlying conviction that, with God on his side, inspiring his movements, it was unnecessary to think things through beyond a certain point. Jehovah would take care of the details and the continuity as he had for Joshua and Gideon.

True, neither fanatic heedlessness nor military incapacity necessarily implies mental illness. The guess that Old Brown's last few overrestless years saw him spiral ever nearer serious mental trouble and then succumb to it periodically, with intervals of more nearly normal behavior— and I see him thus—depends on second- and thirdhand data obviously unsatisfactory for clinical purposes. They are, however, the best available and rather striking cumulatively.

It is well established that a tendency toward grave mental trouble can "run in families." Psychosis is not inevitable for any given member but is significantly likely to occur, often in association with undue emotional or physical strain. When Old Brown was on trial for his life, certain well-wishers of his in Ohio secured and sent to his counsel a sheaf of affidavits showing that his mother's family had been riddled with overt mental disease. Among his sons Frederick was acknowledgedly "crazy" much of the time; John jr. broke down into temporary psychosis—under great stress, true, but no more than many others have taken without breaking. True also, these two came of Old Brown's first wife, who had off-and-on fits of mental illness and died insane after bearing her seventh child, so the boys' troubles may have been connected with poor genetic heritage there. But by itself their father's family history was indeed, as Villard reluctantly wrote, "a fearful record," [13] and made him too a bad genetic risk. Jeremiah Brown, his half brother, told of having warned him to his face that he had gone "insane on the subject of slavery," and not as a figure of speech either. This is anything but responsible diagnosis. But a hundred years later one can still say that certain details of Old Brown's career are of a sort that greatly interests psychiatrists.

In an autobiographical letter he dwelt morbidly on childish calamities. He lost a prized yellow marble; his pet bobtail squirrel disappeared, and for years thereafter he searched obsessively for both. His pet lamb flourished a while and then died, bringing "another protracted *mourning season* . . . so strong & earnest were his attachments." The emotion was genuine and movingly set down but still inordinately important to a man of fifty-seven with grand projects on his mind and blood on his gnarly hands.[14] He was sorry for himself and sulky about a world subjecting him to such undeserved griefs. For years, he told an admirer, he had had "a strong steady desire to die." After 1856 his self-aggrandizing became unmistakable. He usually withdrew from forays putting him under another's command. He boasted that he could make dinner for forty out of one oxhide; that, when the wind was right, he could smell doughnuts frying five miles away; that he could make a cat or dog leave the room merely by staring at it. When staying with admirers in Boston, he ostentatiously checked his revolvers and repeating rifle every night before going to bed, saying: "Here are eighteen lives," and advised his hostess to put the baby under the pillow if she heard queer noises at night. He did not explain how this would protect the child, but apologized in advance in case her carpets were spoiled: "You know I cannot be taken alive."

An appeal for funds that he asked Theodore Parker to read from the pulpit—"Old Brown's Farewell: to the Plymouth Rocks; Bunker Hill Monuments; Charter Oaks; and Uncle Tom's Cabbins"—has a shattery paranoid flavor fit for a textbook of psychiatry. This is even more marked in the "Declaration of Independence" that he drew up on behalf of the slaves he hoped to free. And it is notable that, whereas his spelling and punctuation were not bad in earlier years, in his final phase the spelling degenerates and the punctuation goes illogically explosive. In his critical year of 1857 he ends a letter to his wife: "I am much confused in mind and cannot remember what I wish to write," and complains frequently of a "gathering in my head." John A. Andrew, a Boston lawyer-politician who did Old Brown favors out of personal liking and antislavery conviction, commented trenchantly: ". . . when I hear a man talk upon great themes, touching which I think he must have deep feeling, in a tone perfectly level, without emphasis and without any exhibition of feeling . . . I . . . suspect something wrong in the man's brain . . . in conversation [Brown] scarcely regarded other people, was entirely self-poised, self-possessed, sufficient to himself . . . entirely absorbed in an idea . . ." Another interesting witness is George B. Gill, an adherent close enough to be Secretary of the Treasury in the Provisional Government but finally showing common sense enough to stay away from the Harpers Ferry operation:

"[Brown] was very human . . . Very superstitious, very selfish, and very intolerant, with great self-esteem. His immense egotism coupled with love of approbation and his God idea begot in him a feeling . . . that he was God's chosen instrument, and the *only one,* and that whatever methods he used, God would be his guard and shield, rendering the most illogical movements into a grand success . . . He could not brook a rival . . . was intolerant in little things . . . essentially vindictive . . . Just before we left Kansas [while] Brown and myself were some days away . . . the boys arrested a man . . . Montgomery gave him a trial and he was released by general consent as not meriting punishment. When he returned Brown was furious because the man had not been shot . . ."

It could so readily be that Old Brown had been intermittently "insane" like his aunts and uncles for years before Harpers Ferry, sometimes able to cope with practicalities

but eventually betrayed by his strange inconsistencies leading up to and during the raid—his disease then progressing
into the egocentric exaltation that so edified millions between his capture and death. Illness, whether mental or
physical, is never either ridiculous or admirable. That consideration is what saves Old Brown from being either the
knave, fool or hero that people variously said he was.

"If it was John Brown against the world, no matter."
—T. W. HIGGINSON

Assuming that Old Brown was right, that God and twenty
men[15] were enough, the tiny private army did well. For a year
John Cook, one of them, had lived in or near Harpers Ferry
spying out the land while supporting himself as map ped-
dler, schoolteacher and locktender on the Chesapeake & Ohio
Canal; he even married a local girl. In July, 1859, Old
Brown, posing as "Isaac Smith," cattle feeder and pros-
pector, rented a hill farm with a sizable two-story-and-garret
house and a separate log cabin some five miles into Maryland from the Ferry. By twos and threes those of the boys
who saw fit to report now that the chips were down dribbled
in to be hidden by day in the upper stories of the house.
There too came the Free-State carbines and revolvers, as
Forbes had warned the senators they would, and the pikeheads to be fitted to ash shafts by the boys as they awaited the
word. Son Oliver Brown's girl wife and the next-to-youngest
Brown daughter came down from North Elba to cook, clean,
stand watch and give the household a normal air to deceive
nosy neighbors.

Some of the boys learned only after arrival of the plan to
seize the town and Armory instead of striking straight into

the mountains with the ample arms already on hand. Spell-bound as the old man had them, this alarmed them. His own sons led a protest calling it the suicide it was. Old Brown resigned as commander, promising to obey any new leader elected but reserving the privilege of "advising." He was promptly re-elected and assured in writing that "many of us will adhere to your decisions as long as you will." Once again they had insisted on being taken in. Most of them died for it—a severe penalty inflicted probably by the Foolkiller, not God.

The firearms were cleaned and ready, the pikes were hafted by mid-September, the girls were sent home in an obvious deck-clearing gesture. But soon October was half over and still Old Brown made no move. Each day height-ened the risk of discovery, wasted good marching and fight-ing weather and used up money—and the last supply from the Six was almost gone. Then appeared a puny, unstable Boston youth named Meriam[16] bringing $600 of his own in gold and himself as unsolicited recruit. That was somehow what Old Brown had been waiting for. On a damp Sunday evening five days later, October 16, 1859, he picked up the reins of a one-horse wagon loaded with a crowbar, a sheaf of pikes and a large number of ready-prepared hickory-and-pine torches.[17] Most of the boys had in their pockets com-missions as officers of a cadre to organize Negro recruits into companies as they joined up. Two such "captains" went ahead to cut the telegraph wires east and west from the Ferry. The rest fell in behind the wagon armed to the teeth —carbine, revolver and sheathed butcher knife. Off they went to show how much God could accomplish with in-adequate tools and spotty planning.

They crossed the B. & O. bridge into the Ferry toward 11:00 P.M. Surprise, the only sound element in the plan, served them well. At first the night watchman of the bridge, who knew "Isaac Smith" and Cook by sight, took it for a clumsy joke when told at gunpoint that he was a prisoner, but he surrendered quietly. The unarmed gateman at the Armory—it had never had armed guard—jitterily refused to hand the keys through the bars, so the boys broke the padlock chain with the crowbar and took over without hurting him. According to plan two raiders broke into the unguarded Arsenal, three into the distant rifle works. Six more went upcountry toward Charlestown to liberate slaves and seize slaveowners as hostages—particularly Colonel Lewis Washington, great-grandnephew of the first President. Old Brown knew that the Colonel owned a pair of pistols given to Washington by Lafayette and a dress sword allegedly the gift of Frederick the Great. The boys were to fetch these prestigious heirlooms in along with the Colonel.

Not much noise so far: The relief bridge watchman, an Irishman of quick reflexes named Higgins, came on duty and, summoned to surrender by Oliver Brown, swung on him and ran, ignoring orders to halt. A bullet fired after him merely nicked his scalp, and the hollow of the covered bridge probably muffled the report. At 1:25 the Wheeling-to-Washington passenger train of the B. & O. came in on schedule and Higgins rushed to the conductor with the little he knew of what was going on. The conductor went toward the bridge to investigate, also drew a shot from the party of raiders holding it, and, duly cautious, ordered the train backed away a little to await developments. Among the passengers there was talk that the delay and firing meant an unexpected railroad strike.

It was all rather innocuous. Nobody had been really hurt and there was a certain rowdy comedy about the outraged Higgins; the flabbergasted train crew, who could hardly have been more taken aback if their locomotive had turned into a fire-snorting dragon; and the gabbly panic as the passengers began to learn that they were in the hands of Abolitionist desperadoes, numbers and intentions ominously uncertain. But now things went serious. The free Negro station porter, Heyward Shepherd, came down to meet the train all unaware, failed to heed an unexpected "Halt!" and got a bullet in the back and out again through the belly. Biographers usually note the irony of it: This self-respecting free Negro was, in effect, the first man killed when John Brown opened his crusade to free Negro slaves. And he didn't even die cleanly, lingering for twelve hours in great agony that Dr. Starry, the local physician, could not relieve.

Presently Old Brown was acting as if this unlucky accident had bewitched him. He lost what tactical judgment he had ever had just when he needed it most. Ample getaway time was essential to both the Blue Ridge and the western Maryland schemes. Yet about 3:00 A.M. he gave the train leave to proceed. The conductor, afraid that the bridge might have been treacherously weakened, insisted on waiting until daylight enabled him to inspect it. Then off she steamed. By 7:00 A.M. she had reached a station beyond the cut in the telegraph wire and the conductor had informed his superiors that Harpers Ferry was in the grip of Abolitionist marauders. Here was the fat in the fire hours sooner than necessary. Dr. Starry, roused by the shot that felled Shepherd and the ensuing scream of pain, had gone to treat him and then, after sizing up the situation for some hours, sent a messenger to Charlestown to get the militia called out. But that was necessarily a slow process. It was Old Brown's undeserved good luck that the B. & O. head office chose not to act on such a cock-and-bull story as came over the wire from Monocacy. Not until 10:30 A.M. did the president of the road override his staff and wire alarms to Federal and state authorities.

Toward daylight Colonel Washington's two-horse carriage containing him and two of his neighbors arrived at the Armory under convoy of the six raiders. Behind it was the Colonel's four-horse farm wagon with ten slaves "liberated" from the respective households. The whites were added to the bag of prisoners under guard in the watchman's room that made up a third of the Armory firehouse. The slaves were issued pikes, which they accepted gingerly because this mean-looking old white man told them to, and stalked about uncomfortably because he told them to guard the place. And Old Brown, always the self-dramatizer, girded on Frederick the Great's sword, wearing it throughout the ensuing fighting.

Round 5:00 A.M. he sent five men, including two slave pikemen, with the Washington wagon to shift the arms from the farm—not to the Ferry, which might fit the Blue Ridge theory, but to a log schoolhouse near the B. & O. bridge but still on the other side of the river. No doubt it was a memorable morning for the pupils when armed strangers burst in and caused an impromptu holiday by borrowing the place as temporary arsenal. The children, allowed to scatter home, also spread word of dire doings at the Ferry sooner than need have been.

The morning was rainy. As it advanced some Armory employees, unaware of the raid, came to work and were added to the little crowd of hostages. A gauge on their eventual number is suggested by Old Brown's ordering from the hotel forty-five breakfasts on credit. The order was filled but Old Brown refused to partake because the food might have been poisoned. Whether he allowed his men to eat is not known. If not, they went hungry, for their commander had failed to include provisions, not even iron rations in his plans. This was strange for an experienced guerrilla who fancied himself as a camp cook. It was stranger still how, as hours slipped by, all he did was to send word to son Owen in charge at the schoolhouse that all was going well. Messages from "Captain" Kagi at the rifle works begged him to get out while the getting was good. The raiders should have gathered up their two wagons' worth of loot, including money and provisions, what slaves they had and the pick of the hostages, and struck out for either the Blue Ridge or the farm, whichever was the core of the plan. But Old Brown waited on and on—nobody ever knew what for, maybe he

was just in another dallying mood. And by noon the delay
had ruinous consequences.

The Charlestown militia had come down by rail, boated
across the Potomac to the Maryland shore above town, and
now drove Old Brown's boys off the B. & O. bridge into the
Armory yard, cutting the raiders off from retreat into Maryland. A scratch outfit of Charlestowners armed with anything that would shoot entered town from the rear. Some
seized the Shenandoah bridge, cutting off advance into the
Blue Ridge, others took over buildings commanding the
Armory yard. Their first shot, fired by another Washington,
killed the first raider to die—Dangerfield Newby, a plucky
free Negro who had hoped to liberate his slave-wife and
children. Presently a scratch company of B. & O. employees
come by train from Martinsburg boiled into the upper end
of the Armory and forced the raiders to hole up in the main
room of the firehouse. This rescued the minor hostages from
the watchman's room, which was not connected with the
main part where the fire engines were. But ten of the most
important prisoners, Colonel Washington included, had
been sorted out and put behind the engines in the main
part—where the raiders, coolly aware they were now under
siege for fair, kept up a nastily accurate fire out of the half-
open doorway while beginning to take out bricks to make
loopholes in the firehouse's sides.

Old Brown now developed an illusion that he could make
a deal allowing his force to retire into Maryland on condition of setting the hostages free when they got there. With
this in view he twice sent flags of truce. Both were disregarded. The net result was capture unharmed for raider
William Thompson; capture severely wounded for Stevens,
the former dragoon; mortal wounds for son Watson Brown,
who nevertheless got back into the firehouse. Dr. Starry organized armed citizens who drove the raiders from the rifle
works, killing two and capturing the third—John A. Copeland, a free Negro student from Oberlin College. The doc-

tor—the hero of the whole affair if there was one—saved him from being lynched. He was tried and hanged in December.

Organized fighting now stopped until Federal troops arrived. The town's three bars were all doing roaring business. More and more militiamen and civilians were taking it out in drinking and desultory shooting. But sometimes they hit something. A bullet sang through the firehouse door and killed Stewart Taylor, a versatile Canadian who was both wagonmaker and shorthand expert and went in for spiritualism. Another mortally wounded son Oliver Brown. The two raiders in the Arsenal somehow managed to get back to the farm. But the only one trying to desert from the Armory garrison was shot dead about 1:00 P.M. after reaching a small island in the Potomac above the bridge. Tipsy militia marksmen used his exposed dead body as target the rest of the afternoon. The rest stuck it loyally. Old Brown's boys were mostly crackpots but they were also clean shots and brave men. "Captain" Cook, reconnoitering from the Maryland side, saw the Charlestown men firing into the Armory, climbed high on the cliff and unlimbered his carbine deliberately to divert their fire to him. A retaliatory bullet cut the branch he was holding to and gave him a nasty fall. But he escaped serious injury, eventually got away into the mountains—and was captured, and tried and hanged in December.

Early in the afternoon a shot from the firehouse killed the much respected mayor of the town. In retaliation the prisoner Thompson was taken out on the bridge, shot in cold blood and tumbled into the water, where his body too became a sportsmen's target. A Maryland militia captain named Sinn found several such types bullying the apparently dying Stevens. "If this man could stand on his feet with a pistol in his hand," said the captain, "you'd all jump out of the window." Thanks to his intervention Stevens was left to recover—and be tried and hanged in March.

Sinn's was one of several Maryland and Virginia militia units crowding in, raising the total under arms in the town to at least 600 by nightfall. The firehouse garrison was down to five effectives. Risk of injuring hostages was the militia's pretext for not using their one cannon to smash the doors and then storm the place. About dark a flag of truce—which was respected—summoned Old Brown to surrender. He still made conditions about retiring, still refused. The firehouse buttoned up for the night. Toward 11:00 P.M. Captain Sinn fulfilled an earlier promise to take his company surgeon into the place to tend the dying Watson Brown. He also brought news for the raiders. A detachment of U. S. Marines had arrived: commander, Lieutenant Israel Green, USMC; in charge of the operation, Colonel Robert E. Lee, USA; acting as the Colonel's aide, Lieutenant J. E. B. Stuart, USA. Lee had planned to storm the position immediately on arrival but was persuaded to wait until daylight to minimize risk to the hostages.

The drunken whoops and occasional gunshots went on. Inside the cold, dark firehouse—the stove was in the watchman's room—Old Brown talked and talked, seemingly trying to impress the hostages with his abilities as well as the justice of his cause. During this rambling conversation one of the guests mentioned that what the raiders had done was treason. Two of the boys, Thompson's brother and a Hoosier lad named Anderson, overheard and asked Old Brown if this were true. "Certainly," he said. They spoke up sharply: Then no more fighting for them. They were there to free slaves, not commit treason. But, though still unwounded, they made no effort to get away. Old Brown's loquaciousness had been broken in on now and then by the groans of son Oliver, wounded even worse than Watson. Often he begged his father to put him out of his agony. "You'll get over it," the old man said once; and again, "If you must die, die like a man." The boy's moans ceased after a while. His father called to him but got no reply. "I guess he's dead," said Old Brown.

So dawn through the high, broken windows showed two corpses already in the room. By their own officers' choice the militia were only spectators of the finale. Lee had duly offered what to him, as career soldier, was the honor of supplying a storming party to the Maryland colonel commanding, then to the Virginia one. Both declined—the Marylander said his men had families, and the Marines were paid for such work; the Virginian even used the term "mercenaries." Lee ordered Green to pick twelve men and sent Stuart to the firehouse with a courteous demand for surrender. The door was opened a few inches by a gaunt man whom, for all the disguise of a full, short beard, Stuart was amazed to recognize as Old Brown, the old jayhawker whom he had once held in custody while serving with the cavalry in Kansas. Until then nobody but the hostages had known who "Isaac Smith" really was.

The old man again held out for withdrawal terms. Stuart stepped aside and waved his cap, the signal for assault, and the door closed. To reduce the hazard of stray bullets Marines were instructed to use bayonets only. Green's weapon was a light dress sword as unsuited for serious fighting as the relic that Old Brown was wearing. Three leathernecks battered at the doors with sledges while Green and the twelve waited aside for something to give. But the doors were springily well roped together, and it took a long heavy ladder used as battering-ram to breach them.

Green was first into the ragged, waist-high gap. The next two after him stopped bullets, at least one probably fired by Old Brown, whose hand was on the reload lever of his carbine when Colonel Washington pointed him out to Green. The lieutenant's first thrust may have struck a buckle or bone—anyway his toy sword bent nearly double. He managed to beat Old Brown bleeding and senseless to the ground by two-handed blows with the hilt. Thompson and Anderson are said to have asked for quarter but finished their lesson in the meaning of treason by getting spitted on bayonets anyway. Edwin Coppoc, an Iowa boy whose mother had warned him that consorting with Old Brown would take him to the gallows, was captured unwounded—and tried and hanged in December. Shields Green, runaway slave from South Carolina, tried to pass himself off as one of the "liberated" local Negroes but was identified—and tried and hanged with Stevens in March. It was all over—ten raiders dead, taking four Harpers Ferry men and one Marine with them. Watson Brown died next morning. Old Brown was badly battered but had no vital hurts.

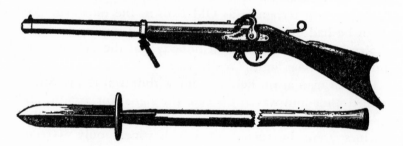

Above, swivel gun asserted by the Harper's Weekly *correspondent to have been found among the weapons of Old Brown's raiders. Below, one of the pikes the raiders prepared to arm rebel slaves. Sketched by "Porte Crayon" in* Harper's Weekly.

Within a week, in fact, he could stand on his own feet for arraignment in Charlestown. The indictment had three counts: murder; "advising and conspiring with slaves and others to rebel . . ."; and treason to Virginia, all capital offenses in the Old Dominion. On the first two a jury would hardly have had to leave the room. He was also convicted on the third, however—in spite of its being impossible for him to have committed that crime. Treason implies allegiance;

allegiance implies at least some sort of domicile; and Old Brown had neither been born in Virginia nor had anything like a domicile there.[18] He had committed flagrant treason against the United States, of course. The Constitution defines it as "levying war against the United States," and the Harpers Ferry Armory which he had captured by organized force of arms was as much pure Federal territory as the plot the White House stands on. But the Buchanan administration, aware how avidly Virginia craved the privilege of hanging Old Brown herself, neglected to pursue its probably superior claim.

Tried while still recovering from his beating, Old Brown was by turns silent and peevishly voluble—ascribing his failure to his tenderheartedness in allowing the train to leave and in special solicitude for the hostages; now rejecting able counsel provided for him, now denying that a fair trial was possible, now assuring the court of his confidence in its fairness. He utterly rejected efforts to raise the issue of his sanity. Governor Henry A. Wise of Virginia had asked the head of the Staunton Lunatic Asylum to examine Brown but soon withdrew the request, relying on his own lay opinion, arrived at in talking to the accused, that he was "remarkably sane." Examination might have been futile anyway, for the criteria of 1859 in such matters were cruder even than ours. For whatever twisty causes Old Brown was still lying blatantly and no doubt believing every word. He had admitted on the spot that his foray was treason; had held many people hostage in deadly peril for a day and a half; and had acknowledgedly encouraged slaves to mutiny. Yet his widely admired statement before being sentenced denied "any design against the liberty of any person, nor any disposition to commit treason or incite slaves to rebel . . ." Maybe he was confusedly recalling Forbes' and his long abandoned plan to lower the value of slave property by repeated slave-freeing incursions into Dixie. He was on better ground when, to justify whatever he thought he had intended, he eloquently referred the court to "the validity of the law of God":

". . . the New Testament . . . teaches me that all things whatsoever I would that men should do to me, I should do even so to them . . . to remember them that are in bonds as bound with them . . . I believe that to have interfered as . . . I have done in behalf of His despised poor, I did no wrong but right. Now if it is deemed necessary that I should forfeit my life for the furtherance of the ends of justice, and mingle my blood with the blood of my children and with the blood of millions in this slave country whose rights are disregarded by wicked, cruel and unjust enactments, I say, let it be done."

Old Brown alone had been prepared for the distance his sick soul would really carry him when the spring was released. Now he was confident that somehow the way he had finally applied his plan must be of God's proposing, else it could never have occurred to him—hence whatever came of it must suit God's purposes. In his need to grasp the Divine utility of his overthrow and capture he welcomed the suggestion soon made by, among others, Henry Ward Beecher: "Let Virginia make him a martyr . . . His soul was noble; his work miserable. But a cord and gibbet would redeem all that, and round up Brown's failure with a heroic success." Old Brown in prison read that in a spiritualist newspaper and noted "Good!" in the margin. He told a lady Abolitionist volunteering to nurse him, "I cannot now better serve the cause I love . . . than to die for it," and when she replied, " 'Then you will be our martyr!' . . . a pleasant smile came over his face." God's thus casting him as martyr was so deeply satisfying an occasion for self-dramatization that even hanging did not seem too high a price. Hence the impressive serenity of his last days . . . But let no such clinical analysis, however sound, distract from his stern loneliness as he stands blindfold on the trap at Charlestown, finally tricked by his own intolerance of reality to the brink

of the ultimate reality—and so self-dedicated that he does
not care.

It is a dreadful thing to know that eventually they will
come and deliberately take you out and hang you, and Old
Brown developed a dreadful dignity to match, more appropriate to his fate than the whininess of some of his utterances in court. It contributed greatly to his incipient canonization. He refused to let local ministers make "any mock;
or hypocritical prayers . . . over me, when I am publicly
murdered," requesting that instead "my only *religious at-
tendants* be poor *little, dirty, ragged, bareheaded & bare-
footed Slave boys & Girls* led by some *grayheaded Slave
Mother."* From this suggestion Redpath faked up the story
that as Old Brown left the jail on his way to execution, "a
black woman with a little child in her arms stood near . . .
He stopped for a moment . . . and with the tenderness of
one whose love is as broad as the brotherhood of man, kissed
it affectionately." Whittier, poet-laureate of Abolitionism,
soon had it in verses that epitomize what Old Brown soon
became for millions:

"John Brown of Ossawatomie spake on his dying day:
'I will not have to shrive my soul a priest in Slavery's pay;
But let some poor slave mother, whom I have striven to free,
With her children, from the gallows-stair, put up a prayer
    for me!'

"John Brown of Ossawatomie, they led him out to die;
And lo! a poor slave mother with her little child pressed nigh.
Then the bold, blue eye grew tender, and the old, harsh face
    grew mild,
As he stooped between the jeering ranks and kissed the
    Negro's child!

"The shadows of his stormy life that moment fell apart;
And they who blamed the bloody hand forgave the loving
    heart.

That kiss from all its guilty means redeemed the good intent,
And round the grisly fighter's hair the martyr's aureole bent!"

Such an incident was impossible. Armed guards from jail door to scaffold "allowed no person to come between them and the prisoner" nor did anybody try. But by 1863 Currier & Ives used the apocryphal encounter in a popular lithograph; then, as the John Brown legend grew, in another more elaborate one in 1870. Eventually an artist named Hovenden did a stagy oil painting that froze for all time the most widely accepted notion of John Brown—the bearded prophet with bayonets behind him, impressive as Moses, benign as Longfellow, kissing the Negro baby.

His last words on the scaffold were game: "Be quick!" But the escorting jailer, who liked the old man, "did not think his bearing on the scaffold was conspicuous for its heroism—yet not cowardly" either. Watson's and Oliver's bullet-torn bodies had been tumbled into a shallow double grave without ceremony. Their father's body went home to the Adirondacks to lie moldering where he wished it to, by the great black rock. Within eighteen months came the miraculous accident showing that Old Brown's strange luck had returned, albeit posthumously, and that Providence can use high spirits for solemn ends.

The Second Massachusetts Infantry, toughening up by repairing fortifications on an island in Boston Harbor, contained many ardent amateur singers—and a large, genial Scot named John Brown. Among the outfit's favorite songs was a Methodist hymn, "Say, Brothers, Won't You Meet Us?" with a rousing tune well adapted to throwing back the head and bellowing. Informal travesties of the lyric came into being; so did amusement at the battalion's popular John Brown having the same name as the hero of Harpers Ferry. Standing jokes arose: "Where's John Brown?"; reply: "Why, the way I got it, John Brown's dead!" with the live John Brown standing by and laughing as chuckleheadedly as anybody. Soon some improviser swinging a pick or driving a tent peg was singing to the old tune: "John Brown's body lies a-moldering in the grave . . . but his soul goes marching on!" This doubling of the verbal rhythm was irresistible. The Second Massachusetts took it up with a roar, John Brown no doubt singing as loud as anybody. After their return to the mainland it went through the Federal forces like a camp disease. And since outside the ranks of the Second Massachusetts the best known John Brown was the old Kansas jayhawker, he now rode into the world's songbook on the shoulders of a genial young man he had never heard of.[19] Being sung about is the perfect way to become a folk hero: Roland, Robin Hood, Jesse James . . . Anyway, the grandest of war songs justified Oliver Wendell Holmes in wittily writing that during the Civil War

"All through the conflict, up and down,
Marched Uncle Tom and Old John Brown—
    One ghost, one form ideal.
And which was false and which was true,
And which was mightier of the two,
The wisest sybil never knew,
    For both alike were real."

Or alike unreal—derivative fictions, literary creations.

"Let us speak plain; there is more force in names
Than most men dream of . . ."
—WILLIAM LLOYD GARRISON

Old Brown's homemade "Declaration of Independence by the Representatives of the Slave Population of the United States of America" was undated but probably of very late

composition. Its form borrows now and then from the prototype of 1776 but the tone is quite another matter.

"The history of Slavery in the United States is a history of
injustice and cruelties inflicted upon the Slave in every conceivable way, and in barbarity not surpassed by the most
savage Tribes . . . the embodiment of all that is Evil . . .
Our President and other Leeches . . . have kept us [i.e.,
the slaves] in total darkness . . . have protected base men,
Pirates (engaged in a most Inhuman traffic: The Foreign;
and Domestic, Slave Trade.) by mock trials, from punishment, for unprovoked murders which they have committed
upon us, and free Citizens of the States . . . have abdicated
government among us, by declaring us out of their protection, and waging a worse than cruel war upon us continually
. . . Our Servants, or Law Makers; are totally unworthy the
name of Half Civilized Men . . . This is a slight though
brief recital of some of the enormous atrocities, of these Idle,
haughty, tyrannical, Arrogant Land Monopolists; slave hold-
ers are lords and masters, From which Good Lord Deliver us
. . . When any set of Usurpers, Tribe, or community, fail to
protect the right, but furnish protection & encouragement
to the Villian by bestowing a Bounty or Premium, upon the
vile Thief, Robber, Libertine, Pirate; & Woman killing
Slave Holder; as a reward for their deeds of rascality and
Barbarism . . . They have transended their own limits . . .
Their Laws are no Laws, they themselves are no more than
a Band of Base Piratical Rulers . . ." and so on and so forth,
all *sic*.

This incoherence must be, as previously noted, sympto-
matic of Old Brown's deepening mental trouble. The hatred
of slaveowners is unmistakable. But the extravagance of
epithet, sick as it sounds, all this ranting about "war . . .
pirates . . . usurpers . . . thieves . . . libertines . . . murders . . ." cannot be laid at the old man's door. This was,
instead, the idiom in which Garrison's *Liberator* had reared
the Brown clan. They had learned to exult in seeing the

grave social crimes of slavery denounced by the names that
society applies to the most shameful felonies. It is a familiar
trick. Borrow onus from one reprehended set of references
and load it on another where it can apply at most only as
overstrained metaphor: Wage slave . . . Christ killer . . .
class war . . . mongrelization . . . Cossacks . . . After a
while endless repetitions tempt many to forget it is all
metaphorical. Eventually such usages are so familiar that
many participants in group movements never question their
literal force, automatically reacting to a Jew as if he had
personally been a member of the mob that chose Barabbas.
In view of such rearing and his own emotional bent, it could
hardly occur to Old Brown that to call a man like Colonel
Lee (or Huckleberry Finn's gentle Rev. Silas Phelps) murderer, libertine and pirate because he owned slaves was as
absurd as it was inflammatory. It was Old Brown's misfortune—or maybe good fortune, since it gained him fame—
that his mental illness fated him to carry out the literal
implications of militant Abolitionists' group jargon.

Here is part of the explanation of his—and the Six's—
readiness for treason. They were all soaked in this sort of
thing from wordy Abolitionist parsons: "Either slavery is
absolutely right or absolutely wrong; either sanctioned of
God, and just by human law, or forbidden of God, and im-
piously unlawful. Either slaves are the most sacred of all
property, or the most diabolical of all robbery. If slaveholding is impious, a government grounded on it, protecting it,
making laws in its behalf, is an exasperation of villainy infinitely monstrous." Or from another pulpit: "Slavery knows
no peace. Its sullen aim is the peace of the vessel captured
in the Malayan seas, when resistance has ceased, when the
pirate knife presses against the throat of every prostrate
man, and the women cower from a fate worse than death. Its
tranquil state is a worse war than the worst insurrection."
Along the leading edge of Abolitionism words and spirit had
long been that extreme. Consider George Bourne, English

hack writer who came to America when John Brown was in his teens, turned preacher-journalist, supplied some of the most influential early Abolitionist propaganda and became one of the three members of the founding committee of the American Antislavery Society in 1833. His *A Picture of Slavery*, published the next year, ramblingly sets forth the intransigent kind of Abolitionism destined to prevail. Old Brown and the Six unquestionably read it either whole or in excerpts in Abolitionist periodicals. Its doctrines—unoriginal but pungently restated—were:

"Every African introduced into this country was kidnapped . . . A white person in the southern states, who is not a man-thief, is despised . . . Slavery and cruelty cannot be disjoined, consequently every slaveholder must be inhuman . . ." Bourne's favorite tenet was that the slaveowner's lust for Negro women, which he could not so readily indulge if slavery ceased, was a principal prop of "the peculiar institution." But he recognized other sins. "What citizen, with a sane mind, can possibly suppose, that the righteous Arbiter of Providence much longer will permit a horde of oppressors, haughty, presumptuous, 'past all feeling, without natural affection, implacable, unmerciful,' profligate, unrighteous, turbulent, religious persecutors, cruel, impious in principle, and filled with all practical ungodliness, to doom two million of our fellow immortals . . . to every contrivance of misery and vice here, and to hell hereafter; only to gratify their atrocious hardheartedness and lusts, and to glut their insatiate thirst for despotism and blood . . . The only effectual and Christian method . . . is . . . instantly, universally, and altogether, to 'proclaim liberty to the captives, to loose the bands of wickedness . . . to break the heavy yoke, and to let the oppressed go free.' Amen!"

The annals of slavery in Dixie do record monstrous slaveowners to whom such multiplex vituperation might actually apply. Others showed in less lurid ways the degenerative effects on master of treating people like trained animals.

CULMINATING PHASE OF THE ARTISTIC GLORIFICATION OF
JOHN BROWN

"Last Moments of John Brown" by Thomas Hovenden, incorporating
the synthetic legend created by James Redpath, John Greenleaf Whittier, *et al.*, that, on the way to the gallows, Brown kissed a Negro baby.
Metropolitan Museum of Art, New York.

CAPE COAST CASTLE

Above: as it appeared when it was principal British slaving-trading post on the Gold Coast. Note the governor's boat in foreground. *Below*: a group of present-day Ghanaians from a boys' camp sightseeing at the Castle. *Department of Social Welfare, Ghana.*

But most of the above abjectly fails to fit any but a handful
from among the few thousand Dixie slaveowners who owned
large numbers of slaves, hence were likeliest to turn into
such walking museums of iniquity—a situation utterly lacking in the neighborhood of Harpers Ferry. Remember that
people like Old Brown, accustomed to take the Bible literally, tended to apply the same approach to other writings on
the Lord's side. Again assuming that he read Bourne—he
certainly read much equally rabid stuff—it is a wonder God
waited twenty-five years to command him to strike the slaveowner, any and all slaveowners, on their own grounds and
"let the oppressed go free."

Whence came the absolute assurance of such Abolitionist
leaders that slaveholding was a putrescent mortal sin as well
as an indecent mistake? Why did they hate slaveholders as if
they were insults to be resented as well as sinners to be pitied
and maybe persuaded into more righteous ways? Why these
condescending plans for organizing forcibly freed Negroes?
this fuzzily focused, inadequate diagram of the national cancer? this delusion that the mass of American slaves needed
only a touch of opportunity to rise in hordes? What lay behind Old Brown's—and the Six's—mistrust of and contempt
for their own domestic government, particularly Federal?
True, the Six were mostly the kind of egocentric moths usually found fluttering round such emotionally lopsided stars
as Old Brown. But what created Higher-Law Abolitionism
as perfect fuel for the old man's hard, hatelike flame? and
what particular data, in addition to general temperament,
had so well prepared the Six to exult in his pragmatic application?

The answer to these and many corollary questions begins
—or at least began for me—on an evil, charming little island under the western hump of Africa.

2 *Sunny fountains*

"Africa . . . that far-off mystic land of gold, and gems, and spices, and waving palms, and wondrous flowers, and miraculous fertility . . ."
                                                    —Uncle Tom's Cabin

One of Old Brown's favorite hymns, maybe second only to "Blow ye the trumpets, blow!" was Bishop Heber's famous apostrophe to missionaries: "From Greenland's icy mountains / To India's coral strand / Where Afric's sunny fountains / Roll down their golden sand . . ."

Europeans often set up their African trading posts on islands for easy defense against both Negroes and rival whites. Goree, the first such site that I ever visited, is one of the most eligible. Heavy masonry still fortifies its cliffy seaward end, loops down along the slopes and points up natural salients of rock. Landward the island tails down pollywog fashion into sandy flats with a crescent beach handy for small craft. Such posts usually relied on rainwater cisterns or water precariously boated over from the mainland. Goree has a small fresh-water spring for emergencies and, though far from shore in terms of smoothbore, black-powder artillery, is still well sheltered within the hooked finger of Cape Verd, where

Negro Africa juts farthest westward. Eastward, then southward stretch 2500 miles of "Guinea Coast"—now "West
Africa"—the turbulent fatherland of the slaves in whose
tragic cause Old Brown would hang.

Goree has a right to its flavor of age. The Plymouth Colony was not yet founded, Shakespeare was barely dead
when the Dutch bought it from a local "king," named it after
a Dutch island and, in the usual course of Guinea dealings,
befouled it with the physical and moral effluvia of slavery.
It achieved notoriety. Round 1800 the Negro district of
Bristol, R.I.—a port with a lively past—was known as "Goree." St. Louis, Bance, Lagos were other Guinea Coast islands thus polluted by Dutch, English, French, Danish, German, Portuguese or Spanish skippers and traders in the
polyglot and predatory scramble after West African wares—
among which man became the liveliest item.

Nowadays it feels as if much of the evil had leached and
crumbled out of this faded, orderly scrap of land looking out
to sea with its head on its paws. Late one afternoon we met
its children coming home from school. They were mostly fair,
round, small-boned French children, lacking the pastiness of
their cousins in metropolitan France, but some were plump
little Negroes. All were singing and prancing in sprightly
clumps over the sand-soft road. On the landward beach were
more children splattering in the water, watched over by
their young parents. Round the corner a shady hospital for
convalescents profits from the airy quiet of the wicked old
island. Goree has silent-footed sand alleys; stucco walls of
tan and orange-pink; glassless iron fanlights; trees gracing
little squares into which the alleys wander and wait like
small streams forming pools. A drum-shaped stone fort
pierced for many guns to command the roadstead is now the
local penitentiary. The Negro prisoners doing chores here
and there in blue shirts with "P" on the back are rather in-
nocent-appearing figures. And over there beyond the great
bight of anchorage the French, long dominant hereabouts,

have docked, paved and dredged the mainland into the large, harsh port of Dakar.

Only a few details recall a day when things were different, when Goree kept changing hands among Dutch, English and French in fighting that was sometimes bloody and always utterly crass in purpose. The strategic importance of the place was of the same order as that of Quebec, Cape Town, the Falkland Islands. Its slave "barracoon" [1] on the western shore is long since gone. So is the bastioned fort that once sprawled over the site of the present village. But in its day Goree afforded stocks of up to 700 "good choice slaves." They show you the surviving *maison des esclaves*—a crumbling little place with a "welcoming-arms" stair set in an orange-pink courtyard with a queer air of being a slum in Bermuda. Between the arms a corridor leads to long, narrow cells right and left, then to a stone sallyport and the dark, seal-sleek boulders of the beach.

Here the boats landed slaves fresh-purchased from the mainland. The cells are now obviously used as latrines. The stench was as bad or worse when they were crammed with Negroes awaiting the next ship out for Martinique, Guadeloupe or St. Domingue.[2] Yet in the liveliest times of the Guinea trade a young French botanist committed to the humane-idealistic cult of his day passed months on Goree and thought it "very agreeable . . . cool and temperate air almost the year round . . . a safe and delightful residence." It was rather like recommending Alcatraz for its view. A generation later Mungo Park, doughty martyr to African exploration, visited the place when it was in British hands and recorded nothing at all about the contrast between the bright island and its noisome function. Both witnesses were perspicuous. They merely took for granted the sights and smells attendant on the Guinea trade, slaving included, as our great-grandparents took the sights and smells attendant on horse transport.

"Africa is . . . a museum of diseases and frustration."
—JOYCE CARY

The world that eddies up round those who half-close their eyes on Goree was a far cry from ours. In 1696, for instance, the adjacent roadstead saw some curious proceedings:

A French squadron had recaptured the place from the English, found a barracoon full of slaves and sent them in two ships to the West Indies to be turned into prize money. One ship presumably made a good voyage. The involuntary cargo of the other happened to include a clique of Negro sorceresses led by a woman of magical powers formidable even in spell-ridden West Africa. By supernatural sabotage she cast on the vessel a curse so powerful that, in spite of fair winds and seamanship, it took seven weeks to make two days' normal headway. In view of the long voyage still ahead, the slaves were put on short allowance of food and water, and the usual result ensued: They began to sicken, die and be thrown overboard to the sharks.

Some of those dying ascribed their ills not to malnutrition or confinement but to the chief sorceress who, out of general dislike of the voyage and all it implied, had threatened to "eat their hearts." Autopsy of one victim showed heart and liver dried up and empty, so the captain had the lady seized up and flogged. She paid small heed to the lash; then the ship's surgeon himself took a rope's end to her. In view of this indignity, she told him, she would have the pleasure of eating his heart too. A few days later he was dead, heart and liver dried up and empty. The captain, reflecting that hanging her might only mean more difficulty if her weird sisters, of whose identity he was uncertain, sought to avenge her, tried soft words and deferential negotiations.

To prove her powers the lady cast a spell on some melons which, opened next morning, were mere husks as empty as the surgeon's liver. The captain quickly concluded a treaty: She would lift the spell if the ship put back and set her and her cronies ashore free near Goree.

This was done. The ship renewed water and stores and sailed on what proved to be a prosperous voyage. A formal account of this triumph of black art was endorsed as deserving credence by the officers of the ship, those of the Goree garrison and their English opposite numbers who had been prisoners in the enchanted vessel throughout. An astute missionary-friar named Labat claimed to have seen this document a few years later on Martinique. Observe that the sorceress had presumably first murdered numbers of her own Negro fellow exiles merely because their deaths would annoy the whites; then, once the captain was beaten, used her victory to free only herself and witchy colleagues, leaving the rest, men, women and children, to unknown terror overseas. She obviously had little sense of racial or even regional solidarity. Her concerns stopped at her own immediate circle of professional loyalties. True or not—this tale has implausible details, including melons keeping for seven weeks—it means that much. The Negroes and whites who told and retold it until it took this shape naturally assumed that all West Africa held life very cheap, and expected no Guinea Negroes to commiserate with their countrymen being shipped to the back of beyond, never to return.

The vicinity of Goree furnished a signal example three years later. In 1699 the locally dominant French traders were irked to find the Damel (prevalent chief) of the local petty kingdom secretly trading with a British ship, the *William & Jane* of 250 tons, twenty guns—a substantial threat to French interests. The Damel's stock of slaves was insufficient to cover the goods he wanted from the ship, and for some reason he preferred not to raid his neighbors for prisoners, the usual expedient in such cases. Instead he let it be known that he planned to land a siege force on Goree and needed the services of the "free fishermen"—then and now furnishing the free-lance canoe transport essential to West African trade. As soon as enough had answered his call, he seized and turned them over to the *William & Jane* as slaves in payment against his order.

Before the ship could land his goods, however, to his great fury the French surprised and took her, confiscating goods, boatmen and all as penalty for infringement of their monopoly. It was known that the boatmen were victims of treachery but their new captors scrupled not to send them off to the West Indies regardless. Whites seldom took much account of how their Negro customers had come by slaves offered in trade. Pity for the boatmen is largely wasted. They willingly hired out to move canoeloads of slaves to ships taking black ivory to the same terrifying exile that now faced them. The French "general" (head trader) engineering this unsavory arrangement was soon seized by the Damel, still smarting from his loss, and released only after twelve days' confinement and a heavy ransom in trade goods. On the Guinea Coast it was black cheat white and *vice versa,* dog-eat-dog and the devil take the hindmost.

"There is no vice, no kind of rascality . . . of which Europe has not given the Negroes an example."

—ABBÉ GRÉGOIRE

The old "slave castles"—fortified European trading posts—crowd the "Gold Coast" shoreline much farther eastward along the bulge of Guinea. Some are kept up as police stations or post offices. Over the sallyport of the one at Shama, where the Portuguese first secured Gold Coast gold, a dainty blue-and-white sign says in tones unmistakably British: "You may telephone from here." From the seaward bastion of the one at Sekondi a scarlet lighthouse guides shipping into Takoradi, the raucous modern port across the bay. These relics of the old days are now decorous, clean as an old bone. But their combined histories would make a lurid picture of what once went on throughout this septically scandalous region.

Largest, eldest and queen of them all is Elmina. The Wars of the Roses had yet to begin, Istanbul was still a Christian capital when the Portuguese founded these lofty walls on hewn stone fetched from home. Columbus touched here in Portuguese vessels long before he saw the New World.[3] A French observer of the late 1600's said that, after the conquering Dutch had remodeled Elmina, it looked "as if . . . made for the dwelling of a king [rather] than a place for trade in Guinea." Sixty years ago it housed a king. After having finally subdued the Ashanti, mightiest warriors of the region, the British imprisoned the Asantehene, their emperor chieftain, for some months in that southeastern corner turret. Thirty years later they brought him back from exile for reinstatement in his former dignity if not power. But his insulted ghost, says the police orderly who uses the room as a laundry, still walks Elmina's battlements to the discomfiture of the garrison of police recruits. They may be specially sensitive to a royal Ashanti ghost because they come largely from the Northern Territories, the far-inland area that the Ashanti used to raid for slaves to sell, or torture and kill to the greater glory of their ancestors. Down below in the great hall of Elmina they show a slotted booth whence local chiefs watched unseen, hence unreproached, as slaver captains bought local Negroes. Or so one is told. So it may have been, though shamefacedness on such points may not have been strong among the detribalized people of the town that grew up round the castle of São Jorge del Mina.

Second largest of these old focal points of brutality is within view a few miles eastward—Cape Coast Castle,[4] center of British slaving. In 1694 rivalry between the two nations had a lewdly catastrophic effect on the branch British post competing with the Dutch at Sekondi. The British "factor" (branch manager) was an emotional youngster named Johnson fresh from training at Cape Coast. While there learning how to swindle Negroes without getting swindled oneself, he had taken a fancy to an eleven-year-old mulatto girl, offspring of a local Negro woman named Taguba and one or another white soldier of the garrison. Johnson had arranged with Taguba to take the girl to wife "as they take wives in Guiny" but was shifted to Sekondi before she attained "age fit for matrimonial functions." So he took her along to "ripen under his own eye," wrote Phillips, the Welsh slaver captain to whom we owe details of this ferocious farce.

The girl had also caught the eye of the hardheaded Dutch "governor" at Elmina, a certain Vanhukeline. As Johnson's *protégée* became "man's meat and a pretty girl," Vanhukeline bribed Taguba to visit her daughter at Sekondi and carry out certain orders. One morning mother and daughter strolled out of Johnson's quarters toward the rival Dutch post, where a fast-paddling crew from Elmina had just landed their canoe. In no time it was again at sea carrying mother and daughter to Vanhukeline, who "soon cracked that nut which Mr. Johnson had so long been preparing for his own tooth." Dining at Elmina, Phillips saw the girl "brought in to dance before us, very fine, bearing the title of Madame Vanhukeline"—in token that she was favorite concubine and probably well enough treated while she lasted. News of this sent Johnson to bed, prostrated by sheer chagrin. His vexation was not prolonged. The British post was weak—"a fort which wants another to defend it," said a local expert—ill manned and worse maintained. No doubt using gossip of the affair to undermine whatever prestige the young fellow enjoyed at Sekondi—West Africans have a great sense of ridicule—Vanhukeline persuaded the tough local Negroes to surprise the place, kill Johnson and make off with the stock of trade goods.

Still to the eastward of Cape Coast, as finial to modern Ghana's sprawling capital of Accra, stands Christiansborg, the old Danish chief post—a Walt Disney dream castle set on surf-besieged rocks. The vast, silent, hospital-white "captiveries" in the hollow of its walls give no hint of the squalor they once housed. Respectability gnawed deep here while this was Government House, residence of British colonial governors with aides-de-camp telephoning invitations to lunch with H.E. No doubt it persists now that the occupant is Dr. Kwame Nkrumah, first prime minister of the new nation of Ghana.

That change was deliberate, irreversible and dignified. The last time Europeans lost control it was none of those things. In 1693, Christiansborg, weakened by deaths among its garrison, was surprised and captured by Assameni, a local Negro chief whose retainers had infiltrated under pretense of normal trade. The Danish "general," having done what he could with his single sword, jumped out of a window and ran for sanctuary to Fort James, the competing British post a couple of miles westward.[5] Left in possession, Assameni took his pick of the Danes' abandoned clothes and, thus elegantly garbed, began to drive a lively trade with their goods, welcoming Frisian and other interlopers then defying the Dutch West India company's nominal monopoly. Over Christiansborg he flew a white flag emblazoned with a black man waving a sword. He often genteelly entertained visiting ships' captains. Phillips, finding the dishes "pretty well dressed, considering the swinish manner 'tis the custom of the negroes to eat," sniffily recalled that his host had once been cook at a British trading fort.[6] The Danes finally paid heavy ransom to regain what was left of their fort and stock-in-trade. The ships handling the reoccupation were left so shorthanded that, on the homeward voyage, they fell ready prey to pirates.

These assorted outrageous doings occurred within a few years and a few hundred miles of one another. But this decade 1690-1700 was no gamier than others in Guinea history. Human beings of whatever skin color have seldom shown to less advantage than in West Africa between 1440 and the lingering death of the slave trade four centuries later. Superstition, treachery, cold murder, institutionalized sadism, buy-and-sell lust, systematic swindling, kidnaping and sottishness prevailed among both whites and Negroes, whose entangled lives and sordid deaths had all the charm of a witches' sabbath in slow motion. Some such degradation is inevitable where the usually scaly specimen of Westerner comes in economic contact with nonliterate peoples. No doubt early Phoenician traders to Iberia created parallel cultural nuisances ashore. West Africa, however, was probably something specially rank, making even the Bay of Islands in the great days of whaling seem straitlaced and scrupulous. One reason might be the special qualities of the local Negro cultures. A rash mind might refer it to the special sluggish dreariness of West Africa generally, one of the most interesting regions of the world, but the approach must be clinical, altruistic or crassly economic. Few in their right minds have ever willingly gone there for anything but hope of gain or sense of duty.

"Africa, big, sad, terrible land . . ."   —W. B. WEEDEN

That same French botanist who liked Goree found another charming memory at a Negro settlement up the Senegal River: "a perfect image of pure nature; an agreeable solitude bounded on every side by a charming landscape; the rural situation of cottages in the midst of trees; the ease and indolence of the negroes reclined under the shade of their spreading foliage; the simplicity of their dress and manners; the whole revived in my mind, the idea of our first parents, and I seemed to contemplate the world in its primeval state." This typical bit of eighteenth-century confectionery, describing firsthand as an innocent Eden the country whence slave traders tore the miserable Negroes, was quoted again and again, all in good faith, by Anthony Benezet, the Philadelphia Quaker who struck some of the most telling early blows against slavery. From it he concluded: "There is scarce a country in the whole world . . . better calculated for affording the necessary comforts of life to its inhabitants with less solicitude and toil . . . And . . . not withstanding the long converse of any of its inhabitants with (often) the worst of the Europeans, they still retain a great deal of innocent simplicity . . . they might have lived happy if not disturbed by Europeans." From the same and other accounts the great John Wesley, who was soon to swing the weight of Methodism against slavery, learned that "Guinea in general is far from a horrid, dreary, barren country . . . [instead] one of the most fruitful, as well as the most pleasant . . . in the world." [7]

This paradisaical West Africa full of sweet-tempered primitives was a cardinal article of faith with early partisans of the Negro slave, whose tone the preceptors of Old Brown and the Six inherited. Wesley and Benezet failed to allow for the way travelers of and before their day—and ours— could look squarely at a given place or people and describe not what they saw but what they were already disposed to see. Raleigh praising Guiana, John Smith recommending the site of Jamestown, Bougainville's surgeon celebrating a Tahiti that never existed—all gave pervasively false impressions as much by generalized ecstasy of tone as by self-deceiving lies. Had Benezet, who well deserved his name for

Quakerish virtues, truth-telling included, ever visited the slave traders' Africa, would much of what he saw so have resembled an aquatint of the Golden Age?

It must be said first that he would not have seen the Africa of Hemingway or Izak Dinesen or Alan Paton or Evelyn Waugh or Rider Haggard or Percival C. Wren, or yet of the comic cartoonist's boiled missionary—in short, any of the African locations that Hollywood prefers. Instead turn to Joyce Cary's Nigerian novels, which are essentially more informative than the run of anthropologists' monographs. "Africa" is a term as meaninglessly broad as "America." There are ten or a dozen Africas. That of which Benezet wrote so inaccurately is as different socially and physically from the connotations of "casbah" or "bwana" as from those of "kayak" or "potlatch." People were annoyed when, returning from West Africa a few years ago, I pled ignorance of *apartheid* and the Mau-Mau. They suspected me of disingenuous excuses when I pointed out that a man fresh from Oregon would be in no position to describe the latest desegregation developments in the Deep South.

The West Africa that concerns us was long one of the least accessible segments—an out-back-of-beyond stimulated only faintly by the great cultures of Egypt, Carthage, Roman Africa and her Moslem successor states. This region, alias "Guinea," [8] is marginal both figuratively and literally, extending down along and below the receding chin of the Dark Continent to about where the collar button would be. Its Negroes, with only dugout canoes for salt-water craft, were hemmed in on the Atlantic side by the surf-angry ocean, which they used for only coastwise work. Unfortunately for them, the advent of the magnetic compass and of ships able to beat to windward made this same salt water a highway for exploring and predatory Europeans. A few hundred miles upcountry from the ocean the too-dry desert forms a roughly parallel barrier. In between lies what the desert Moslems called "The Land of the Blacks," the Negro

Country, sometimes "only a narrow ribbon, edged on the one side by the sand sea of the Sahara and on the other by the salt sea . . ."

Near the desert it shows dryish, tree-studded "parklands." As water becomes more available, forests gradually take over, building up to big jungle. Major rivers—the Senegal, the Gambia, the Volta, the Niger—cross parklands and jungle down to the sea. Some were navigable well upcountry for the whites' small early ships and shallow-draft auxiliaries. But most are clogged at or near their mouths by the sand that oceanic surf piles up alongshore, or barred to navigation by rapids or falls within a few miles. The sightless, vine-smothered, lush big timber—"rain forest"—harbored elephants, leopards, gorillas (in certain areas), chimpanzees, crocodiles, deer, snakes (some dangerous), myriads of deplorable insects and some of the most nightmarish parasites known to tropical medicine. Most, such as the virus of yellow fever, are invisible. Some are not—for instance, the Guinea worm, a lead-pencil-size horror that wanders at will under the skin but prefers the ankle to stick itself out of when propagating.

All these beasts and microorganisms are more or less still there. But thanks partly to the partnership of man and fire the desert continually encroaches on the parklands, which in turn gnaw irregularly into the forest. When whites first encountered him the West African was already spoiling his environment as assiduously if not as rapidly as the same sort of land management would spoil Hayti in later times. Nonliterates in New Guinea or Central America as well as West African Negroes rely on such "slash-and-burn" methods, otherwise known as "shifting cultivation." It fells and burns trees so the ashes will sweeten the soil of the former forest floor, crops the clearing until fertility falls off sharply, then fells and burns another patch while the first gradually restores wild vegetation. If proper reforestation occurs, well and good. But fire often ruins the original humus, thin at best in tropical forests; or the trees fail to re-establish themselves in competition with thriftier shrubs and coarse grasses. In any case heavy seasonal rains have too much opportunity to leach nutrients out of the soil, leaving what the British West Indies vividly call "ruinate." [9]

Gorer describes "the almost physical relief [given by] a slight break in the appalling flatness and monotony of the West African landscape . . ." Nor is this new: Mungo Park described the Gambia region 175 years ago as "an immense level, generally covered with woods [presenting] a tiresome and gloomy uniformity to the eye." The mountain cluster of Sierra Leone rises from the sea with the grandeur of a classic West Indian island. But few other such welcome bumps vary the hundreds on hundreds of miles of sandbank, lagoon and brushy foreshore scattered with frowzy palms that, from seaward, look like frayed-out golf tees. Close at hand the effect is like a bankrupt real estate development in Florida. The many paths and few roads afford no vistas because harsh thickets line them right and left. The local sustenance crops—millet, corn, cassava—need or anyway get little weeding, so even gardens resemble neglected vacant lots in late summer. Villages are huddles of mud-and-wattle hovels, the elegant ones roofed with corrugated iron, the rest with thatch. Cary was frank about the typical upcountry town: "a pioneer settlement five or six hundred years old . . . without charm even of antiquity. Its squalor and its stinks are all new . . . An English child . . . with eyes that still see what is in front of them, would be terrified by the dirt, the stinks, the great sores on naked bodies, the twisted limbs, the babies with their enormous swollen stomachs and their hernias; the whole place, flattened upon the earth like the scab of a wound, would strike it as something between a prison and a hospital. But to Celia . . . it seems like the house of the unspoilt primitive, the simple dwelling-place of unsophisticated virtue."

Tribal migrations from upcountry were still going on

when the first Europeans arrived. The coast-dwelling Ne, groes were almost nomadic, readily shifting their flimsy settlements. There was no masonry, indeed building stone was seldom handy, so West Africa has few pre-white ruins of whatever her past glories may have been. The eye comes to welcome the pseudo-Gothic Anglican church in Freetown, the verandaed cafés of Abidjan, the multistoried trading-company headquarters in Accra, the misguidedly eccentric new government buildings there—because, much as all re-semble the worse aspects of Southern California, they do better express man's position relative to his environment. Even the old "slave castles" seem pleasant sights in spite of their noisome pasts.

This fecklessness in building and farming is supposed to betoken congenital West African indolence and improvi-dence of long standing. Three hundred years ago a French-man called the Senegalese "leud and lazy to excess" and re-marked that though the country back of Cape Coast was so fertile that it yielded cereals at 100/1, "yet so slothful are [the Fetu natives] that if they have but one bad year, they are in danger of starving." This was noticed much earlier: In 1542 a Portuguese reported that "In Guiné there is a great famine on the coast, worse than last year, so that men perish." Modern medicine can refer such slackness to chronic infestation with malaria, hookworm and sometimes a mild yellow fever, and to the relative lack of protein in the easy-come-easy-go West African diet. This makes sense as far as it goes but other considerations also entered, such as agricultural lag from earlier traditions of migratory hunting. And the exceptions to the old rule of lazy frowsiness were striking. Early Europeans admired the intensive planta-tion farming of the well-organized kingdom of Benin, where Negro grandees got much efficient work out of their gangs of Negro slaves. Yet these were the very regions upcountry from the Bight of Benin so disease-ridden that the old song asserted "Four come out for forty go in."

Impressive Negro states usually developed away from salt water. The seacoast was for refugees elbowed thither by tougher people closer to the North African sources of enterprise. Lady Lugard spoke of "the great migration southward of all that was least valuable in the Negro belt . . ." A Negro sociologist contrasted most of the Liberian seacoast peoples with "the finer Negroes of the interior." Some of this contempt may reflect the deepening influence of Islam[10] bringing the Mohammedan's usual disdain for the heathen to the regions where the parklands meet the desert. Actually, given the same history and traditions, the Seacoasters might have been as bright and rugged as the Upcountries who despised and sometimes bullied them.

It looked for a while as if the advent of white men's things might rescue the coast-dwelling underdogs. Their location gave them first access to the whites' gunpowder and firearms, alcohol, hardware and textiles—all items adding to prestige, power or both. In many South Pacific islands such an advantage enabled peoples settled where whites first landed to turn the tables on peoples previously dominant. West African Seacoasters had no such luck. For a century or two the Upcountries let them play middlemen between the trading posts and the inland sources of gold, ivory and slaves. But as trade expanded and the Seacoasters waxed fat, the Upcountries decided to deal directly and, when the Seacoasters demurred, applied force. Sometimes they merely blocked the trade trails, sometimes they marched down to the sea with fire and sword to the dismay of white traders already sufficiently plagued by the boisterous Seacoasters. Thus seacoast Whydah changed from "a den of water thieves and pirates" into "a prosperous ivory mart and slave port" eventually taken over by ruthless upcountry Dahomey. Strong intervention by well-rooted whites was all that kept the Fanti and other Gold Coast peoples from similar subjection to the Ashanti. These Fanti and other seacoast cousins of the Ashanti were themselves fre-

quent and formidable nuisances to Dutch and British gar-
risons. But their liveliest efforts could not compare to the
energy with which the Ashanti came muscling in. The upper-class Ashanti's military and social contempt for the Seacoasters still plagues local politics because the government of
the newly independent "Ghana" is composed mostly of Seacoasters.

"I speake of Affrica, and Golden joyes . . ."
—King Henry V, *Part II, V, iii*

"Ghana," self-conscious name for what was the Gold Coast,
sounds flat when its origin is known. Hunger for the cultural
self-respect that the world long denied him has understandably led the Negro to wishful notions of West Africa's past
glories. For parallels consider the Nazis' Wagnerian notions
of ancient Germany, or certain aspects of Irish nationalism.
Some Negro leaders in both Africa and America working
with scanty data have overplayed existing hints that long ago
certain West African polities arrived at wealth and maybe
culture superior to what Europe then knew. The focus is
sharpest on the empire of Ghana (or Ghanata), covering an
area between desert and forest as large as the Iberian pen-
insula. Its capital city is now identified some 300 miles south-
southwest of Timbuctoo, but little is left of its greatness.
Arab travelers highly admired this double city, one town for
Moslems, one for Negroes and the Negro despots who succeeded its founding dynasty of whites of uncertain origin.[11]
They celebrated the learning of its Moslem clergy and the
power of its pagan Negro priests' spells; the majesty of the
Negro king, before whom men prostrated themselves and

poured dust on their heads, a usage still surviving in some
Negro cultures; his immense metallic wealth—his watch-
dogs wore collars of gold and silver bells, his horse's hitch-
ing weight was a gold nugget weighing thirty pounds.

Whatever else Ghana was like, Moslem raiders smashed it.
Its successor states ruled even wider lands, and at least one
sounds even richer: When the Moslem emperor of Mali (or
Melle) visited Egypt on pilgrimage to Mecca, his retinue
numbered 60,000; the 500 men marching before him each
carried a stick of gold weighing sixty-two ounces. His
traveling purse consisted of twelve tons of gold on 300
camels. His largesse and purchases, saturating Egypt with
gold as he passed through, wrought havoc in the price
structure. His European contemporaries—say, Philippe le
Bel or Edward III—could hardly have seen so much gold
in several lifetimes. No doubt the plutocratic glory of old
Ghana would have astonished her contemporary Charle-
magne, whose loosely organized and tenuous empire was not
much larger and had much less flashy economic potential.
But major civilization is another matter. Bovill's caution
about Mali holds good of all these shadowy Sudanese regimes—that posterity is "unhappily very ill informed about
them."

What is known certainly makes it plumage-borrowing to
call the former Gold Coast "Ghana." The peoples of this
new nation—Fanti, Ashanti and so forth—are largely those
sturdy-made, broad-nosed local variants of the "Forest
Negro" [12] that, under the name of "Coromanti," the British
West Indian planters so valued for slaves. Some time or
other, possibly well within historic times, they migrated
from north or east into their present forest-cum-seacoast
holdings. But their forebears cannot have been the basic
peoples of Ghana, Mali, Songhai and so on, who must have
been cousins of the tall, straight-nosed, blue-gowned and
readily Moslemizing Mandingoes from upcountry back of
the northernmost segment of Guinea. These rich empires

threaded on the Niger River were well above the limits of modern Ghana, bordering on the actual desert whence came the germs of their skills and customs.[13] Ghana, Mali, Songhai were border-zone growths stimulated by contact with Arabs and Berbers carrying shreds and tags of the old Egyptian-Punic-Graeco-Roman world. By way of the thirsty caravan routes old Ghana looked northward for markets and, said Lady Lugard, "all its finest civilization. The south represented to it only barbarism and obscurity."

No doubt certain techniques and attitudes filtered south-ward from Ghana through parklands and forest to the Sea-coasters, teaching them iron smelting and smithery; the idea of a standard medium of exchange; their Mediter-ranean-style passion for haggling. From the north certainly came their awe of the supernatural power in peace and war of bits of paper marked with Arabic script that they could not read. A great West African's war shirt was sewn as thick with such papers, each in a separate case of wood or leather, as Goering's tunic was with medals. Some people along the lower edges of the old empires may have spread other Ghana ways of doing as they pushed southward and westward to conquer and mingle with the resident Negroes. But to call the newly free Gold Coast "Ghana" is as un-suitable—and as eloquent of emotional uncertainty—as if the United States were called "Hellas" because some of our present population's forebears and many of our ideas and institutions originated among the states of ancient Greece. The four new French African states recently joined in the loose "Federation of Mali" [14] have a far better case for their choice of name, since they actually do include much of the old Mali empire.

Shadowy as it was, Ghana may nevertheless have left its mark. "Guinea" may be a Portuguese corruption of the name[15] gradually misapplied to the whole West African coastal area. Among Europeans, particularly the British, it came early to connote "gold." English coins minted from unusually

pure gold from the Guinea trade were marked with an elephant to identify them as commanding a premium of a shilling in the pound over coins of lower fineness. Hence the
"guinea" of twenty-one shillings that still assuages the pain
felt by fashionable British shops and august British professional men when mentioning prices or fees.

This association of Ghana/Guinea/gold is notable because the gold-mindedness of the old Negro empires was
what gave West Africa its fatal and not too well-deserved
early reputation as a sort of overheated Klondike. It seeped
into Europe by way of North Africa, the peoples of which
alone had access to the Upper Niger until Europeans opened
up the Guinea Coast. Far from salt water, upcountry West
Africans are chronically salt-hungry: ". . . after they saw
our salt," wrote Jobson of the Negroes up the Gambia, "no
other thing was esteemed among them." The Sahara has
deposits of rock salt, slabs of which go southward by caravan.
In return the Negroes of Ghana, Jenne, Timbuctoo or whatever city then dominated the trade gave gold washed from the
alluvial deposits of the headwaters of the Senegal and
Volta Rivers. Medieval traders knew that much of the gold
circulating in the Mediterranean area had come, through
however many greedy hands of whatever colors, from the
hot countries southward across the great desert—the lands
about which Othello told so many threadbare lies.

Eventually all this meant whites infiltrating Guinea and
exiling Guinea Negroes to the New World. Scholars hold
that the Portuguese explorations farther and farther along
the Atlantic coast of Africa from the 1440's on were intended primarily to relieve the chronic, severe shortage of
monetary metals in late medieval Europe,[16] hoping, says
Plumb, to "cut out the Sahara and the Arab trader" and make
"direct contact with the mines" of Negroland. Sure enough,
once they rounded the great bulge to the point where the
natives' skins turned from toasted to charred, they found a
profitable trickle of upcountry gold offered in trade. Gold

hunger is plain in the obliging fictions that the natives spun for Jobson about a "Country above" (*i.e.,* farther up the Gambia) that "doth abound" with gold so that the houses of its "great Towne" were "covered only with gold . . ." Significantly Jobson rejoiced to learn that certain tawny people trading for gold at another town were "Moores of Barbary, the discovery of whose trade and traffic was the ground of our being so high in the river." [17]

This same European gold hunger procured Spaniards the same sort of lies, or wishful misunderstandings, in the West Indies, and moved them to annihilate the local Arawak Indians of Hispaniola by forced labor in mines of precious metals. The transatlantic trade in Guinea Negroes was created largely to supply replacements for these charming but fragile aborigines. The very name "Gold Coast" shows the chief concern of the Portuguese and their successors. So does "Rio de Oro," name of an obscure Spanish colony above French Guinea. Products traded by the Negroes of the Senegal, Gambia and Niger areas included ivory, kola nuts, honey, grain, cotton, "Hides, skins of Wild Beasts, Ostrich Feathers, Ambergrease," and gum arabic.[18] But Jobson's good Negro friend told him that the Moors' first demand was always for gold. Even in 1838 a well-meaning British Emancipationist who had never visited Africa told his countrymen that, in the Gold Coast, "the entire soil yields gold dust . . ."

Note that early lists of Guinea wares often omitted slaves. After they begin to be mentioned, the emphasis long remains on gold, ivory and the spicy local "Malaguetta" pepper[19] that seasons West African "country chop." Portuguese, Dutch, English, French eventually learned that slaves were the best way to make a Guinea voyage pay. But it would certainly have been news to John Brown and the Six that the promotion of the Negro to be miserable principal West African export came gradually and late—no savage rush of white kidnapers into a defenseless paradise but a gradual expansion overseas of an economic relationship already well established northward by land. It had come into being originally because West African Negroes considered most people to be property, their own or somebody else's, and negotiable on the same basis as gold, ivory or a promissory note.

Another of the eighteenth-century voyagers on whom Benezet and Wesley relied wrote: "The discerning Natives account it their greatest Unhappiness that they were ever visited by Europeans. They say, that we Christians introduc'd the Traffick of Slaves, and that before our coming, they liv'd in Peace." This was disingenuous of "the discerning Natives." For foul as they were, the intruding whites did not invent Negro slavery or the export of slaves from Guinea. The salt-greedy Negroes of the parklands had already learned to trade ivory and slaves as well as gold to the desert nomads. The ivory came from the elephants of the forest, the slaves were usually war captives spared for their value as field labor or trading wares by the free Negroes of Ghana or Mali. They were generally from Forest Negro peoples known to be expert archers and strongly suspected, maybe unjustly, of man-eating. The attitude of the Moslem parklanders toward such "slave labor raided from the pagan belt to the south" has been called "almost identical with that of the Spaniards toward the natives of the new world. They were idolatrous and had no rights." In any case pagan Guinea thought nothing of one Negro's enslaving another. There were mitigations: Children of slave mothers by free fathers were free. Traditions of favoring local-born slaves over war captives varied with time and place. Selling a slave away from his birthplace might be thought poor taste but, just as in the matter of Dixie's scruples against separating slave families, greed or hard times often carried the day.[20]

Hapless Negroes thus traded to the desert men for salt, sword blades or ivory—500 years ago a good Barbary horse cost fifteen male Negroes—were marched across the Sahara, maybe with a tusk of ivory on the shoulder, and sold in North Africa for work on the land or overseas to the Moslem two-thirds of the Mediterranean area. A few filtered into Christian Europe. Late medieval painters depicting the Three Kings, of whom legend made one black, knew well the everted lips and mashed nose of the true Forest Negro. The Dutch St. Nicholas who puts gifts in children's shoes has a Negro attendant named Black Piet.[21] Central African slaves were sold across the Red Sea or the Gulf of Arabia into the Middle East and India, routes that still supply the backward Arab nations. Long before whites lent the slave trade their talent for crass brutality the desert caravan routes were marked by the bones of Negroes dying en route. A nasty business: New-captured men and boys were often castrated because, if they survived—and ten per cent survival made it pay—they fetched premium prices as eunuchs to guard harems. In order to make sure market value was unimpaired, adolescent or preadolescent girls might be subjected to crude plastic operations making defloration impossible without further surgery.

All this was a going concern and its values had well permeated Guinea when the Portuguese came knocking at West Africa's back door. Not all Europeans took to slavery at once. Gold-minded Jobson's Negro friend "showed unto mee, certaine young blacke women . . . which hee told me were slaves, brought for me to buy, I made answer, We were a people, who did not deale in any such commodities, neither did we buy or sell one another, or any that had our shape." The first Negroes whom the French and the English took away were trained not as laborers or servants but as interpreter-supercargoes to facilitate barter next voyage. Whites learned readily, however. The early Portuguese bought slaves from the Slave Coast and sold them for gold to Gold Coast Negroes who used them to pack European trade goods upcountry. Here were white middlemen between slave-selling and slave-buying Negroes. In general slaveowning Sea-coasters lacking enough gold, beeswax, gum or ivory to pay for muskets, rotgut brandy,[22] silks, bar iron and gold-laced coats naturally followed the course of their inland cousins dealing with desert men: They offered slaves to make up the difference. As gold grew scarcer and gum and wax harder to come by—and as the New World took to slave-grown tobacco and sugar—slaves came to overshadow other wares. Besides, as a Negro scholar has pointed out, a slave was "a commodity that would walk to market," [23] and, as a Guinea Negro said when urged to collect ivory instead of slaves, "It is easier to catch a man than an elephant." Obviously the West African comes out of this unsavory business no better than anybody else—but no worse either. Horrors like slavery are seldom the fault of specific individuals or groups. They just happen at great cost to human decency and self-respect. As militant Abolitionism culminated in Old Brown, it had forgotten all about that. Like a child at a melodrama it wanted to concentrate on the white man as villain to hate.

"There is no unity in Africa today; there was still less in the eighteenth century."   —JAMES G. LEYBURN

Abolitionists generalized glibly about "the Guinea Negro": docile, patient, affectionate, religiously gifted, thick-lipped, broad-nosed, coal-black, strong but engagingly indolent yet hair-trigger-apt to mutiny with hellish energy. Efforts to pack human variety into too detailed a formula are usually ill advised. No such thing as this "Guinea Negro" was ever consistently distributed along the coast from the Senegal River to the Gaboon. True, though they varied among themselves, most of these Guinea peoples still less resembled Egyptians, Abyssinians, Hottentots and the jumbled-up Bantu peoples of Africa south of the collar button. But the factors and captains who shipped "black ivory" and the planters who bought it distinguished closely on an ethno-geographical basis.

Physically this made some sense. Guinea Negroes came out of Africa both tall and lean and hammered down and husky; with noses hooked as well as flat—a sound witness saw "Grecian" profiles among upper-class Ashanti women; with color ranging from rich brown to practically black. But these differences might appear among individuals from the same village. One reason was the continual stirring together of various human stocks that, whether pushing or being pushed, migrated into Guinea over the centuries. In following their traditional callings Mandingo and Hausa traders, Fula stock drovers, Kru boatmen, Gold Coast mercenary warriors sowed alien genes broadcast. Special anomalies of hair texture and skin color came of Europeans' solacing themselves with Negro women—many white factors kept several concubines at a time—siring a steadily growing stratum of mulattoes spreading Caucasoid genes among adjacent Negroes. Negro retainers accompanying traders in business travels from Cape Coast, say, to Whydah, or from Sherbro to the Senegal area often found they liked the new locality and settled down to stay—and breed.

White connoisseurs of slaves assumed that the special psychological traits discernible in this or that Guinea people were innate, like the herding instinct in collies. Modern science doubts this. Even in the late 1700's Bryan Edwards, M.P., an astute West Indian planter, held that, however native Africans differed in behavior when first exported, they soon sank to lying, thieving and a common "distrustful and cowardly disposition . . . I am afraid that cowardice and dissimulation have been the properties of slavery in all ages." Yet the differences originally noted, not all of which disappeared in all individuals, may have been real enough. In modern terms this means that the peoples of Guinea varied as much culturally as they did physically.

Edwards called the Mandingo ill suited to hard labor and given to thievery. Frenchmen with equal claims to expertness thought him "fittest for household service . . . very handy and intelligent . . ." Edwards found the best all-round disposition in the Papaws (Seacoasters from what is now French Dahomey) but he also liked the Bantu-mingled Congo type: "slender, sightly . . . naturally mild and docile," clever mechanics and very honest. Eboes he rated "lowest and most wretched because of the constitutional despondency of mind" that often moved them to suicide.[24] His favorites, generally most in demand in the British West Indies, were the Coromanti[25] (Gold Coasters) to whom he attributed "firmness both of mind and body . . . activity, courage, stubbornness . . . elevation of soul . . . [enabling] them to meet death . . . with fortitude or indifference," and high industry if rightly handled. A Barbados planter called them "the best and most faithful of our slaves . . . all born heroes . . . never a rascal or a coward of that nation . . . not a man of them but will stand to be cut in pieces without a sigh or groan, grateful and obedient to a kind master, but implacably revengeful when ill treated. My father . . . would say, No man deserved a Corromante that would not treat him like a Friend rather than a Slave."

These were the "stout, stubborn" people who so ruthlessly seized Christiansborg and, if they came to dislike the British factor at Anamabo, shipped him back to Cape Coast. The same qualities that made planters value them enabled their "Maroon" descendants to hold out for generations in Jamaica against the redcoats. Their stay-at-home cousins in modern "Ghana" show the same ferocious energy. In Accra I met a minor dignitary's funeral procession with the mourners dancing, brandishing weapons, drumming and shouting, men and women sweating and grimacing for all the world like a mob on the way to storm a West African bastille. It may be no accident that the Gold Coast was the first West African colony to arrive at independence.

"Woe! to the man in Africa who cannot stand perpetual uproar."
                                                —MARY KINGSLEY

Vigorous bodies and dispositions do not imply all other virtues. The few and scanty accounts tell little of what the local gentry were like when the Portuguese first investigated the Gold Coasters. Several good sources from the end of the 1600's make them sound distinctly dissolute. Some of this eager rowdiness may have come of two centuries of combining the worst of their own and the worst of European ways— the result usual when cultures first blend along the edges. But much of it may have been home grown.

They were, for instance, confirmed tosspots. Most afternoons the local "king"—West African "royalty" will be gone into later—sat on his official stool in the village market place among likemindedly convivial elders, commoners and women, all determinedly getting drunk as Davy's sow on palm wine.[26] For conspicuous waste the king guzzled so greedily that wine dropped from his beard to the ground. The accompanying conversation ran to "nothing but lewdness . . . in the presence of the women who . . . far from being out of countenance . . . outdo the men in that filthy discourse." Here was no people unused to alcohol corrupted by exotic firewater. Guinea had always known both palm wine and beer, seems spontaneously to have developed group carousals, and had a venerable tradition of obscenity calculated to make a hyena blush. The infiltration of Islam, which forbids alcohol, failed to discourage pot-tossing. White men's bringing spirits merely meant that West Africans able to afford them got drunker sooner. The Senegalese, says an old witness, "drink brandy as if it were water"; one snatched up the first bottle he saw in a ship's cabin and swallowed a mouthful of ink before he perceived his mistake. Gaboon men coming on board to barter ivory might swill down the whole value of a fine tusk in brandy before quitting the ship.

West African smells are less formidable now than they must have been in the old days when—take this as keynote—canoes on protracted voyages alongshore carried a decaying goat as figurehead. West Africans have always known how to make soap; in fact, they exported their palm-oil-and-wood-ash soap to Portugal in the 1400's and are assiduous washers of person and clothes. But their standards of municipal sanitation were not fastidious. An early Dutch visitor objected feelingly to the Gold Coasters' go-as-you-please habit of "easing their bodies round their houses, and all over their towns." He probably also deplored the Gaboon girls' habit of smearing themselves with rancid elephant fat as cosmetic. In many places fish were thought hardly edible until after prolonged decomposition on the roof; no doubt this began as drying for preservation, then changed to deliberate corruption for flavor, as with Chinese aged eggs or our outrageous cheeses. These details reinforce tales of how, on warm nights with a good land breeze, the effluvia of Gold Coast towns could distress the crew of a ship lying some miles offshore. Remember too that to modern nostrils the European cities of 1700 would also have seemed pretty rank. When a man of that day avers that a place stank, be triply sure it did.

This may imply more than simple disagreement with European notions of which strong organic odors are disgusting. That the Senegalese "never think [elephant meat] good . . . till it breeds maggots" has a nutritional aspect: West African diet is chronically low in high-grade proteins, so the

Guinea Negro did well to develop first toleration and then a
liking for carrion. Otherwise, with climate so warm and re-
frigeration unknown, rare and valuable nutrients would
often have been wasted. As it was he usually got most of the
good out of fish or game before letting the local vultures, indispensable and obscene, compete with children and dogs
for the rejected scraps.

Table manners might match the menu too well for Europeans. At Rufisco, the principal native shore settlement near
Goree, a French head trader was entertained one evening at
dinner by "a black lady of a good presence and very jovial
temper, widow to a Portuguese of note . . . [in] a very
warm cabin or hut, in the midst of which there hung a large
stinking piece of raw beef . . . a slave brought in a wooden
platter full of dirty water to wash our hands in, without any
towel to dry them. Every man made use of his clout . . .
and I of my handkerchief . . . a large wooden platter, brim-
full of Couscous [a sticky tapioca porridge], and another
with stinking boil'd beef . . . The lady then went about
tearing the meat into abundance of small bits, with both her
hands, and threw it into the Couscous dish, stirring it about
with one hand. Then every one of the guests . . . took a bit
of the meat and some Couscous, and rolling it together into
a ball in his right hand, toss'd it as far into his mouth as he
could; then licked his fingers, and shook his hand over the
dish, to save what had happened to stick to it . . . Dinner
being over the same dirty water, which had served to wash
before, was brought in again . . . and some washed their
mouths with it . . . This disagreeable filthy way of eating
is universal among all the nations inhabiting the western and
southern parts of Africa." I have seen Kru boys, of whom
more later, rummaging ship's garbage, though they were
well fed with local staples of rice and palm-oil gravy . . .
Daily the ship's cook filled Number Ten cans with everything unusably left over from the officers' table: meat,
pastries, fish, salads mixed higgledy-piggledy and sold it to

the Kru at a shilling a can. Yet these same apparently un-squeamish men never let a day pass without a fresh-water bath using pink carbolic soap.

In most places in Guinea the European could be fairly sure that what he was asked to eat had had four legs, scales or feathers. West Africa knew cannibalism, particularly up the Niger and Congo Rivers and among the timorous Ivory Coasters whom Barbot set down as "a hideous people to be-hold, and stink very much." ". . . happy, honest, extremely conscientious," says Gorer of an upcountry Ivory Coast people, "and cannibals . . . not for any particular reason: human flesh is just part of their diet . . ." But ingestion of man meat, where it occurred, usually had more a magical than a gastronomical significance. The Mende of Sierra Leone might kill and nibble but the main purpose was to secure human fat to lubricate secret society rites. The Adom warrior of the Gold Coast might suck blood from his enemy's wounds but only to acquire extra valor and heightened pres-tige.[27]

West African dancing was, however, everything expected of aboriginal goings-on. "It is their continuall custome," wrote Jobson of the peoples up the Gambia, "every night after . . . they have filled their bellies, they retire to this Court of Guard, making fires both in the middle of the house, and in the open yard, about which they do con-tinue drumming, hooping, singing, and makeing a heath-enish noyse, most commonly until the day beginnes to breake . . ." Both sexes, women particularly, Barbot said, "were inclined to sing till they die, and dance into the grave . . . if amidst their hardest toils . . . do they but hear any one sing, or play on their musical instruments, they will fall a dancing." The sexes "meet and fall back again, leaping, beating their feet on the ground, bowing their heads to each other and snapping their fingers . . . moving now very slowly, and then very fast . . . running against each other, breast to breast, and knocking bellies together very indecently

. . . uttering some dirty mysterious words." After seeing Senegalese dancing an early Frenchman wrote: "That these gestures are very immodest is obvious; but the other movements, which are hardly perceived, must be much more so." No doubt, no doubt. A Guinea village launched on its frequent if not nightly wingding was no place for the delicate, and the uproar was such that Jobson concluded that such occasions were partly intended "to feare and keepe away . . . ravening beasts from about their dwellings."

The heady local beer probably had much to do with it, the local passion for percussion instruments even more. Here or there West Africa had horns, tinkling strings, simple woodwinds of ivory. But drumming was what stirred them to ecstasy. After that West African has "died singing and danced into his grave" a veteran Guinea drummer working his pinkish palms on a taut piece of leather can make him rise right up again. Mary Kingsley called the African drum an instrument incomparable "for getting at the inner soul of humanity," able to "talk as well as the human tongue . . . can make you want to dance or fight for no private reason . . . be you black or white." African drummers, reared among people fond of noise for its own sake, specially loving rhythmic noise as cats love catnip, were then and now *virtuosi* unmatched for endurance as well as skill. The percussive patterns grow subtler instead of simpler as nerves and muscles should, but apparently do not, grow fatigued.

Anklets of bells or belts of nutshells clashing as the dancers moved might supplement the drums, or "they set a boy to rattle on a piece of hollow iron," probably the sort of crude gong still found in the Haytian *houmfort* (voodoo shrine). I first encountered such a boy on the long, dusty, oven-hot and fire-bright main shopping street of Monrovia, capital of Liberia, on a Saturday morning, when the normal clamor of haggling, punctuated with irregular and inexplicable crashes, thumps and rumbles, bewilders the outsider as much as it delights the participants. All through it this particular morning, whichever end of the street one visited, apparently gaining volume with distance, came a steady, heartbeat-timed clank . . . clank . . . clank . . . as emphatic and relentless as a toothache. Search finally showed the source to be a long-legged black youth in felt hat and cotton T-shirt squatting on his hams in the sun, in his right hand a steel spike, in his left an empty quart bottle dangled by the neck between forefinger and thumb. He was glassy-eyed with pure enjoyment, cataleptically motionless save for the steady swing of the wrist bringing the spike clank . . . clank . . . clank against the bottle. He kept it up for forty minutes by my watch without varying the rhythm the millionth of a second, and was at it when I left, still as regularly emphatic as a cricket. To my inappropriately educated nerves it was torture. For my Liberian fellow shoppers, conditioned to the charm of the thing, it doubtless added to the joys of Saturday in town as moonlight enhanced the delights of an old-time hayride.

Even when not dancing, the Quaqua loaded themselves with metal bracelets because they liked the clashing sounds resulting from ordinary movement. This was just as well; they wore little else. Farther eastward Whydah young folks went stark naked till marriage in order that, said a sardonic slaver, "both sides may see how they like their tackle before they go to work." After marriage the women rigged out in an ostentatious number of bright cloths "set in so loose a manner before, that if the wind blows a little fresh, what modesty requires to cover, is often exposed to view." Then, as now, no doubt, the typical beauty of Guinea's women (as whites see them) was their amazingly graceful carriage come of carrying headloads. Details of the figure are not equally successful. A quasi-masculine scrawniness may make it hard to tell men from women at a short distance. Married women's breasts are usually grotesquely elongated. An English interloper of 1555 reported with dismay that some Gold Coast women had breasts long enough to "lay the same upon the ground and lie down by them . . . very foul and long, hanging downe low like the udder of a goate . . ." This distortion, Ligon noted in Barbados in the 1650's, made slave women stripped to the waist and bent over at hand weeding look as if they had six legs. Since it is associated with maternity—woman's most honorable aspect—this pendulous breast is still encouraged by hand stretching in French Africa today. The original cause is said variously to have been the down-dragging pressure of the saronglike cloth in the back of which baby rides, or the custom of pounding rice in tree-trunk mortars with heavy poles as pestles.

Guinea's matter-of-fact polygyny did not encourage white-style decorum. Local marriages were no more romantic than those of European royalty. Basic to all was compensation of the bride's family for loss of her services; the usefulness of numerous wives as field hands and huckstresses; pride in siring many offspring; and certain special, though not peculiarly African, ideas about sexual intercourse. Loss of virginity before marriage was little regarded. Indeed many Gold Coast bridegrooms thought previous defloration "a labor saved." Overstrict primitive hygiene making it shameful to lie with a wife between awareness of conception and weaning the child obviously furthered polygyny. But a multiplicity of wives, each with a separate hut in husband's "compound," did not completely slake concupiscence. Besides, where so many adult men had so many wives apiece from a limited supply, their juniors, presumably at their randiest time of life, had few or perhaps none for some years. Hence certain noninnocent West African customs showing once again that convention can never straitjacket the erotic impulse.

A wife's fidelity was important in theory and enforced by whipping, sale into slavery, killing—depending on local tradition and husband's temper. Possessive jealousy as we know it may often have been present. But other, unfamiliar factors are hinted at in the Ashanti notion that the child belongs to its father's "totemic class" [28] even though local biological theory denied "blood" relationship between child and father. Hence to permit one's wife to lie with men outside the totemic class risks birth of an outsider into the totem, with untold damage to the delicate adjustment between its members and important nonhuman powers crucial to personal well being. Whatever these esoteric values, however, they seldom applied to white men. The same Kru boatman who beat his wife half to death for sleeping with another Negro would urge her to accommodate any white deckhand knowing his way around well enough to ask husband's leave.

As between Negroes the adulterer was also penalized. Few West Coast peoples killed him but the aggrieved husband could seize his person to force compensation, often heavy. This clear analogue to the horned Englishman's suit for *crim. con.* fits well with the West African habit of feeling in economic terms. Along 2500 miles of coast from Sierra Leone to Loanda a man with many wives might order all but his favorites to seduce poor young men and make sure to be discovered in the act, for that gave the husband the right to seize the man and, in default of damages, sell him into slavery.[29] Sai Cudjoe, a great Ashanti ruler, maintained an attractive and zealously promiscuous wife for the sole purpose of playing succubus to overpowerful chieftains with an eye to their gold hoards or even their lives. Relative wealth and social standing went hand in hand in Guinea as crassly as anywhere, so the penalties, seldom fixed, to some extent reflected the transgressor's prestige. A detected amour that cost a little man on the Gold Coast five pounds worth of trade goods would extract £100 worth from a big man. Relative social standing also affected the seriousness of the offense. Thus King Peter, magnate of the Sesters region (in modern Liberia) beheaded a commoner found entangled with one of his wives; whereas a big man similarly detected with an unimportant man's wife paid only a small indemnity. Burton believed that the death penalty mandatory for wives of the

King of Dahomey who turned up inexplicably pregnant came not so much of their immorality as of the *lèse majesté* implied.

All this—the high risks involved in adultery, the enforced celibacy of pregnant and nursing women, the early age at which girls were usually married, hence lost to casual fornication—inevitably led to pretty crass prostitution as a West African institution. The young men of a Gold Coast village might secure leave from local elders to club together, buy a woman slave and set her up as the local whore. Her availability was formally advertised by her simulating intercourse in the market place with a small boy, after which she accommodated all comers at fixed fees. In return her owners allowed her subsistence.[30] Several such professionals might compete in larger communities. At Whydah "a vast number" of prostitutes plied their supine trade in little huts clustered along the main roads. In Benin, where adultery was taken quite seriously, widows automatically became property of the king and were usually assigned to whoring, paying the crown a cut so heavy that they often resorted to such sidelines as brewing and poultry raising to make ends meet.

It seems strange to the Western mind that wealthy Benin women might bequeath handsome women slaves to the public as endowed prostitutes, a benevolence which, said Bosman leeringly, "these tender-hearted gentlewomen take for a great work of mercy and charity as some people in Europe do when buying masses for the souls in purgatory." English traders at Axim embroiled with the natives usually brought them to terms by imprisoning the town prostitutes. It was futile to seize the town elders—nobody cared about them. But being deprived of the girls soon brought the whole village round to plead for their release lest the young fellows, deprived of their usual fun, debauch all the married women. Senegalese women prostituted themselves to whites at fees so low that Barbot suspected them of not only a special hankering after Europeans but also a generally "hot and lascivious disposition." But things were also free and easy along the Grain Coast where initiation of girls into the women's secret society usually involved excision of the clitoris to reduce erotic enjoyment,[31] a procedure strikingly artificial among people reputedly so spontaneous in sexual matters.

Stranger still was the dog-in-the-manger polygyny of the kings of the great southern kingdoms. The King of Dahomey, for instance, had thousands of formally wedded wives. His officers kept sending in from the provinces more and more likely girls whom he usually accepted, maybe slept with once or twice and filed away in lifelong seclusion along with their predecessors. Attempts to escape or to insult the royal prerogative by adultery meant death. The more fortunate, because less attractive, made up the famous local corps of "Amazon" women soldiers who at least had the occasional excitement of raiding miserable border villages for slaves. The rest, usually allowed to walk out only to fetch water, did so behind harbingers shouting to the public to clear the road and look away, for it was a serious offense to meet them, however inadvertently. They must have made a fine show in their "rich Waist-Cloaths, called Arse-Clouts . . . with three or four large Strings of Coral about their Necks, and their Leaders sometimes in Crimson, sometimes in Green, and sometimes in Blue Velvet Cloaths with silver-gilt Staffs in their Hands." But it amounted, as Barbot said of similar customs in Whydah, to "perpetual widowhood"; or, as others pointed out, to the unbroken celibacy of European nuns. No wonder that Dahomeyan women thought it a calamity to be chosen as a royal bride. This practical equation of "cloister" and matrimony is ironical. Even more so was the large harem, of several hundred wives, of Tauga, Dahomeyan viceroy of Whydah—an acknowledged eunuch.

Confusions between West African and Western values were never clearer than in a suggestion from an English trader implausibly named Bulfinch Lamb, captured by the King of Dahomey and kept as a sort of honored rarity, like a

platypus in a zoo. Lamb was aware that the King's good will
was his sole stay and that his only chance of redemption was
to persuade the wilful monarch that to release him would produce more good things than the amusement of retaining
him: "If there is any cast-off Whore," this contemporary of
Lemuel Gulliver wrote to his employees in the fort at Whydah, "either White or Mulattoe, that can be persuaded to
come to this Country, either to be [the King's] wife or else
practice her old Trade; I should gain his Majesty's Heart entirely by it, and he would believe any Thing I say . . .
When I came here first, the Portuguese had a Mulattoe
Whore, who his Majesty used with Abundance of Good Manners, continually giving her Presents. He gave her two
Women, and a Girl to wait on her, but she dying of the
Small Pox, he wants mightily more to come, and says that
no white Body shall ever want any Thing he can purchase . . ." If Rodgers and Hammerstein want something to
follow up the success of *The King and I* . . .

Yet most West African women were not Orientally exiled
from life. Dahomeyan ladies of the royal clan, married or
not, philandered with impunity and relish. The able female
head chief of the Agoma people of the Gold Coast never married but always kept one or another vigorous young man
slave as bedfellow. Married women had their own property
and handled their own affairs, which checked efforts to tyran-
nize them. And for all their isolation, the Dahomeyan Amazons had the satisfaction of being better drilled and pluckier
than the men in the rather faint-hearted quasi-feudal levies
that made up the bulk of the King's forces. Many of his wives,
including many of those in-name-only, functioned as living
bookkeeping machines. Dahomey could not write and knew
only the simplest mathematics, but it had the female memory. Each responsible official in this complex polity confided
his data on population, agriculture, taxation or whatnot to
his "mother"—a lady of the royal harem assigned to remember all such data about this commodity or that activity for

regular checking against his future reports. Heaven help him if he could not account for every last one of the 197 goats registered in her memory. Like many nonliterates, West Africans were prodigies of memory and mental calculation. Their unschooled descendants still are. A Sierra Leone trading firm may extend thousands of pounds' credit to a woman trader who keeps her books in her head and cannot sign her own name.

Most of the prosperity that early traders so admired in the kingdoms of the Bights came of women's busy hands, feet and heads. They cultivated, harvested and cooked the lush crops that fed Benin and Whydah so sleek; tended the children; spun, dyed and wove the cotton of the famous "Benin cloths" highly valued by Guinea peoples to the north; and were, said Barbot, "jolly" about it to boot. They were also the family merchants, thronging from ten miles about on foot to market "dogs, roasted apes, monkies, and rats; parrots, chickens, yams, malaguetta in stalks, dried lizards, palm-oil . . ." These markets were and are today as much social as economic institutions. A West African woman on the road to town in Sierra Leone or Liberia—or modern Hayti—will refuse a good town price for her headload of fruit or chickens because accepting it would remove the excuse for walking six miles more to her weekly orgy of personal contacts and sweaty tumult.

In West Africa such "mammy traders" are a truly regional institution. Others would be iron working; plurality of wives; the powerful secret societies, one for each sex, that afford supernatural sanctions for local customary law; and heavy commitment to magic ranging from innocent and sometimes helpful love charms and "bush medicine" for the ailing into sorcery of the blackest kind relying much on poison as well as psychosomatics.

". . . morbid psychology and primitive religion—which are pretty much the same thing."   —JOYCE CARY

Plurality of gods was also universal—and West African religion bulked large in all that culminated in Old Brown and the Six. The slave trader tried to excuse his ruffianisms by saying that at least he took the Negroes out of heathen darkness into touch with Christianity. Abolitionists deplored slaveowners' sinfulness in deliberately leaving their slaves sunk in obscene heathenry and refusing them their chance of salvation through Christian teaching. In some ways this was bad judgment in any case: West Indian versions of West African religion were usually the unifying force in the great slave rebellions that gave Abolitionism its illusions about Dixie's slaves . . .

The western world is still deep in a fad of African religion, particularly as transplanted to Hayti, that would outrage Old Brown and friends. Their world was far from the mental habits requisite to the comparative anatomy of religions—to seeing, for instance, that the main difference between Haytian voodoo (or its West African originals) and the early Judaism from which Christianity descends is the Jew's insistence on immediate relation to a single God. Guinea had a vague notion of a super-god-creator of all things, but he was like the admiral in the flagship, so august that he delegated everything to subordinates. These specialized aides handling mundane affairs—rather like the Jews' archangels with wider functions—were groups or castes of slightly less august gods with various spheres and duties. Their functions, names, groupings, numbers varied widely from culture to culture. But by and large Mary Kingsley's statement is sound: The West African thought himself subject to the will, often capricious, of "gods from whom he never expected pity, presided over by a god that does not care."

A situation so precarious naturally emphasizes propitiation, whether the object is the ancient Jews' single Admiral also commanding the vessel to the terror of the crew, or the ancient Greeks' pantheon of diversified specialist gods. Regularly and in special emergencies Greek, Jew and Yoruban all sought to curry favor by performing human or animal sacrifices, libations, dances, songs—anything calculated to mollify or cajole Yahweh, Apollo or Shango, god of thunder. By adoring with one hand and bribing with the other—though he does not think of these separately—the prudent man assures Shango of his sedulous and admiring loyalty, much as if the god were a specially powerful and impulsive West African king. The rewards expected from such truckling are at least a certain security, at most special luck in women, health and wealth. To receive these does not call for elaborate thanks, however, for "what good was done to the [suppliant] was a mere boughten thing that he has paid for. No confession of sin because [he] does not hold he lives in a state of sin but that it is a thing he can commit now and again if he is fool enough. Sin to him not being what it is to us, a vile treason against a loving Father, but a very ill-advised act against powerful, nasty-tempered spirits."

Given the premises, this makes *quid-pro-quo* with a nip of cause and effect. Its emphasis on self may transmute into the good of the community—rain on the parson, drip on the clerk. The aura of healthy prosperity created by these practices round priest or "king" influences those about him. This is familiar in many nonliterate and some literate societies. Traces of it persist in Western religions. It may extend into individual devotees' cults of tutelary deities—Poseidon here, Erzulie there, St. Soandso elsewhere. Next come arcane rites and antics to bring on ecstatic possession by Dionysus, say, or Damballa, exempting the subject from cause-and-effect reality. Only for the ancient Greek adherent of Orpheus or the modern Haytian adept in voodoo the alienation is temporary, like a Saturday night drunk—self-limiting or broken by the presiding priests as though hypnotic.

This sort of thing has uses. From time to time most people need temporary release from the cause-and-effect strait jacket. The lure of gambling, some theorists say, consists of its returning the gamester blowing on the dice and invoking Lady Luck to the prerational world of Guinea and other not too remote cultures where the capricious god favors the fortunately obsequious worshiper. "Possession" by the god is taken as outward and visible sign of such favor. It assures the devotee of a special supernal patron looking after him in the dark, confused world where things happen with callous disregard of one's needs, interests and vanities; where illness, accident and crop failures due to the malice of inadvertently neglected ancestors or the essential spirits of this or that animal or vegetable are already causing enough trouble. Haytian peasants and many modern West Africans still lack the germ theory of disease and the theory of probabilities as tools to think these things out with. Their propitiatory cults are the best they could do toward an understandable universe.

In 1859 pious Yankees thought of all this as remote devil worship reeking of orgies and human sacrifice.[32] It could never have occurred to them to see parallels between Iphigenia and the ram in the bushes. They would have been outraged to see African heathen images apotheosized;[33] and thunderstruck to be told that the keys to Guinea's religions lay in the austerities of the Pentateuch and the reputedly whiterobed, flower-decked and aseptically stately world of ancient Greece. This was dull of them. But at least it spared them the artsy-craftsy, quasi-schizoid absurdities of their more acute—or anyway better schooled—descendants.

So much talk about the despots of Dahomey and Benin may
have disguised the wide variation of Guinea government in·
size as well as form. West African monarchy ranged from
sheer figureheading to despotism tempered by graft and rebellion. Here and there its place was taken by councils of
mutually mistrustful, high-prestige elders hoping to keep
the unruly commonalty in hand—like a tiny republican
Rome lacking writing in which to codify its precedents and
laws. But some single figure usually embodied some degree
of power with at least symbolic significance and to him Europeans applied the term "king."

This encouraged damaging misconceptions. True, some
Guinea despots were kings right enough, come of royal clans
and succeeding by descent though not by primogeniture.
Dahomey knew no intermediate degree of subordination between king and slave . . . "all acknowledging the right of
the sovereign to dispose of their persons and property at
pleasure." In token of this universal servile status, no Dahomeyan could wear sandals without the King's special permission; or sit on a chair or whitewash the inside of his
house. Through aggressive conquest this dynasty controlled
a large and well-centralized territory in which direct fiat
was modified by only the weight of custom and the inadvisa-
bility of goading the royal ministers into rebellion.[34] Oftener, however, the "king" was a petty local headman drawing power partly from ancestry, partly from ability or—
much the same thing among the superstitious—from a name
for preternatural good fortune, "mana" in anthropological
jargon. His people's lands might not extend beyond the ra-
dius of a leisurely day's walk, as along the Gold Coast or in

early Dahomey, where "kingdoms were not unlike those in England, when they numbered 16 of E. Saxons, 14 of E. Angles, and 17 in Kent; and kings are like those of Ireland in the days of St. Patrick, when 200 were killed in one battle." Frequent clashes among these little units tended to end in Dahomey-style domination of one by all the others. Guinea's institutions were neither idyllically static nor indeed, in many respects, long established when the whites came.

Exploring Europeans tempted complications in both America and Africa by calling petty headmen "kings" and dealing with them as if their powers resembled those of European royalty of the day. Sometimes such a "king" or "queen"—women chiefs were not unknown in Guinea—was captured in a predatory scuffle and sold into exile in the New World when unable to raise an exorbitant ransom. So whites in Demerara or Virginia sometimes heard from slaves that "My grandfather always say back yonder in Africa his daddy was a king." This carried the same weight as mentioning Mayflower ancestors, there being enough technically valid instances to flavor the whole tradition. For an early instance consider the Negro woman slave belonging to Samuel Maverick, the Massachusetts pioneer, who came early one morning to the bedroom window of a house guest "and in her own Countrey language and tune sung very loud and shrill . . . she . . . would willingly have expressed her grief in English, but I apprehended it by her countenance and deportment . . . I . . . resolved to entreat [Maverick] on her behalf for that I understood before she had been a Queen in her own Countrey, and observed a very dutiful garb used toward her by another Negro who was her maid. Mr. Maverick was desirous to have a breed of Negroes, and therefore seeing she would not yield by persuasion to company with a Negro young man he had in his house, he commanded him will'd she, nill'd she, to go to bed to her, but she kickt him out again. This she took in high disdain beyond her slavery, and this was the cause of her grief."

Such misuse of "queen" or "king" [35] need flaw neither one's sense of the misery of the lady's position nor the dignity of many a West African monarch leader. An early English interloper in the Gold Coast found little to condescend to in "the Captaine of the Towne . . . a grave man; and he came with his dart in his hand, and sixe tall men after him, every one with his dart and target, and their darts were all of yron, faire and sharpe, and there came another after them which carried the Captaines stoole; we saluted him and put off our caps, and bowed ourselves, and hee like one that thought well of himselfe, did not move his cap, nor scant bowed his body, and sate him down very solemnly upon his stoole; but all his men put off their caps to us and bowed down themselves." A Frenchman trading up the Senegal in the late 1600's portrayed a local chief as "a well-looking old man of about sixty; his Beard and Hair grey, his Face thin and wrinkled, his Eyes lively, his Voice agreeable; and had a certain Air of Quality that showed his Birth." The Dahomeyan king who so loved the mulatto whore nevertheless had "something in his countenance very taking, and withal majestick . . . the most extraordinary man of his Colour," wrote astute Captain Snelgrave, "that I ever conversed with . . . nothing in him that appeared barbarous except the sacrificing of his Enemies . . ."

Dahomeyan royal power is now badly shrunken but in the Gold Coast a few years ago I saw something of the impressiveness of the Asantehene, traditionally the most formidable West African monarch and focus of the still pungent prestige of the Ashanti. His bloody-minded but able people, a scourge to others and a glory to themselves, had a vigor in organization and commerce that inspired respect in the dullest whites. Ashanti *mana* lived in the Golden Stool,[36] a gold-encrusted seat on which none ever sat but which was produced for high honors on great occasions. When the pretentious armies of predatory Dahomey clashed with the Ashanti between their two growing spheres of influence Dahomey reeled back and never tried again. Of all Guinea fighters, white soldiers of the nineteenth century took the Ashanti much the most seriously. With spears, swords and obsolete muskets—plus a habit of charging home as often as necessary —these doughty upcountrymen occasionally bested Queen Victoria's redcoats and maintained a fierce independence up to sixty years ago. In fact, had the whites let local natural pressures take their course, the Ashanti Union might well have mastered all of what is now "Ghana" and fused its as yet ill-unified peoples into a national whole healthier than Ghana can hope to be within some generations.

My wife and I were visiting the ancient capital of these people, Kumasi. We had been told that we were to witness the proceedings of the Asanteman Council, periodical assembly of the principal leaders of the Ashanti Union. Outside the council house we saw the arrival of these Ashanti grandees, each under an immense ceremonial umbrella blazing with gold and bright colors which the bearers gaily jiggled up and down in token of their lords' importance. But we got no further briefing before being ushered abruptly into a small room where a man was sitting at a European-style writing table. We were not even instructed to bow as we shook hands, but the look of him was ample demand for deference. He was lean and long-made, his features half-aquiline, his hair close-cropped, his skin the color of dark rum—barring pigmentation, he looked like an emphatically carved and more highly stylized version of the famous portrait bust of Julius Caesar. His dress was a silk robe of parrot-bright but deeply rich colors worn toga style in the Gold Coast—and old Roman—way with one arm and shoulder bare. Long, strong toes showed through open sandals clotty with bosses and chains of gold. Round one sinewy ankle was a golden bracelet, at its narrowest as thick as my thumb.

Every few minutes came another Negro caller similarly if not quite so richly togaed to stand by the desk and tell his tale in the native tongue of which, of course, we understood

no word. Each was listened to intently, studied with great concentration, perhaps briefly questioned—and then the crisp
decision and instructions. I once saw a great general consulting on the field of battle who did not give half this effect of
authority and acumen. Presently entered a tiny woman so
unobtrusively dressed that I recall nothing she wore, only
that it was ample and dark colored. As she shook hands with
us we were somehow made aware that this was our man's
mother. She perched on a European chair and contemplated
us benevolently while we contemplated her son wonder-
ingly. As we saw his handling of his successive subordinates,
obviously men of power and substance themselves, and noticed details of his gorgeous rig, I wondered the more just
how high an Ashanti dignitary he might be, asking myself—
as in the old joke about the deck steward and the captain—if
this were what some deputy or aide wore, what would the
Asantehene wear? The answer was evident: This *was* the
Asantehene, son of the exile who haunts the battlements of
Elmina, and the tiny old woman was the queen mother,
widely influential as such and entitled to choose her son's
successor from among the numerous eligible princes of the
blood.

Presently he rose, said courteously, "Now I go to open the
Council—wait small," [37] and left the room. Ten minutes later
we were escorted to the great room where the Council were
already seated behind little tables in a horseshoe of about the
area of a basketball court. Most of the sixty or seventy members showed the same striking contrast of dark brown bare
shoulder with the brilliant toga. We were taken round inside
the horseshoe to shake hands with each, then again with the
Asantehene presiding at the apex—and then were sat down
on a couple of flimsy ballroom-type chairs out in the empty
space, about where the basketball center circle would be.
Only it was not quite empty. On a stool just within the left-
hand rank of members sat a dwarfish little fellow, rather
light colored, leaning his hands on the hilt of a vicious-look-

ing short sword much the worse for wear, and wearing a cap made of a skinned-out leopard's head, whiskers and teeth intact. He stared at me as intently as the queen mother had but with no effect of benevolence or anything else, just a cold scrutiny ruling out any possibility of any future change of expression. The Asantehene began to make a speech. After perhaps a minute of it the little man with the leopard cap uttered an explosive yelp, loud and sharp as a bursting light bulb. He did it without either changing expression or taking his eyes off me; it felt exactly as if aimed at me personally. When he did it again, and then again, I began to suspect that it had nothing to do with me but was only a sort of ritual applause, a formalized "Hear, hear!" But even so it made me so nervous that I was actually pleased when the Asantehene stopped speaking and I was given to understand that I was expected to reply to what he had been so incomprehensibly saying. It was a genuine relief to break the spell by blathering through polite and lengthy windinesses for translation to the Council.

The little man gave me none of his strange applause. Just who he was I never learned, though it was suggested that he was part-keeper of the Asantehene's soul and, in a previous age, might have looked to being lingeringly killed when the great man died. Anyway he was a surviving item of the splendors of Ashanti's great days—when no trading fort dared withhold the annual "book" of site rent; when the coastal peoples traded upcountry only on Ashanti sufferance; when the generals of Ashanti armies took victory so much for granted that they sat at headquarters ostentatiously playing games and barely turned their heads to hear reports that all was going as it should on the firing line. Some 140 years ago Bowdich, first Briton to visit Kumasi, described the apogee of Ashanti power in what has become a classic of Africana. Here are the head warriors got up to perform welcoming dances and fire off salutes as the white men arrive:

"The dress of the captains was a war cap, with gilded rams

projecting in front, the sides extended beyond all proportion by immense plumes of eagle feathers, and fastened under the chin with bands of cowries [the small shells that were currency in parts of Guinea]. Their vest was of red cloth, covered with [charms] of gold and silver . . . which flapped against their bodies as they moved, intermixed with small brass bells, the horns and tails of animals, shells and knives; long leopards' tails hung down their backs . . . They wore loose cotton trowsers, with immense boots of a dull red leather, coming half way up the thigh, and fastened by small chains to their . . . waist belt; these were also ornamented with bells, horses tails, nails, strings of amulets, and innumerable shreds of leather; a small quiver of poisoned arrows hung from their right wrist, and they held a long iron chain between their teeth . . . A small spear was in their left hands, covered with red cloth and silk tassels; their black countenances heightened the effect of this attire, and completed a figure scarcely human . . ."

All poor and simple compared to the display when the white deputation finally reached the presence of the Asantehene in "an area of nearly a mile in circumference and crowded with magnificence and novelty . . . The sun was reflected, with a glare scarcely more supportable than the heat, from the massy gold ornaments which glistened in every direction . . . the horns flourished their defiances, with the beating of innumerable drums and metal instruments, and then yielded for a while to the soft breathings of their long flutes . . . and a pleasing instrument, like a bagpipe without the drone, was happily blended. At least a hundred umbrellas . . . which could shelter thirty persons, were sprung up and down by the bearers . . . being made of scarlet, yellow, and the most shewy cloths and silks, and crowned on the top with crescents, pelicans, elephants, barrels, and arms and swords of gold . . . from the fronts of some the proboscis and small teeth of elephants projected, and a few were roofed with leopard skins, and crowned with various animals naturally stuffed . . . The [high officers] wore Ashantee cloths of extravagant price from the costly foreign silks which had been unravelled to weave them . . . of an incredible size and weight, and thrown over the shoulder exactly like the Roman toga . . . a band of gold and beads encircled the knee, from which several strings of the same depended; small circles of gold like guineas, rings and casts of animals, were strung round their ancles [*sic*] . . . and rude lumps of rock gold, hung from their left wrists, which were so heavily laden as to be supported from the head of one of their handsomest boys. Gold and silver pipes and canes dazzled the eye in every direction. Wolves and rams heads as large as life, cast in gold, were suspended from their gold handled swords . . . the blades were . . . rusted in blood . . . The large drums supported on the head of one man, and beaten by two others, were braced around with the thigh bones of their enemies and ornamented with their skulls . . . immediately behind their chairs (which were of a black wood, almost covered by inlays of ivory and gold embossment) stood their handsomest youths, with corselets of leopard skin covered with gold cockle shells, and stuck full of small knives, sheathed in gold and silver, and the handles of blue agate . . ."

For the Ashanti, as their Golden Stool implied, were as gold greedy as any Spanish *conquistador* or English freebooter. They loved the stuff because it meant ready command of firearms and gunpowder for the wars that fascinated them, but also, miserlike, for its own massy gleaming, ductile brilliance, else they would have left it in nuggets or dust and not worked it up into these lavish ornaments. As for gunpowder, that also obsessed them, perhaps because its imperative power and noisiness expressed things that felt particularly prestige making.[38] At great festivals their kings and nobles vied with one another in firing from the shoulder ever heavier charges of powder. To reduce the obvious risks they tightly bound the barrels of their blunderbusses and "long Danish muskets" with successive layers of strong twine. Even so the abused weapons often burst and sent the successful contender off to premature glory with most of his face and right arm missing. Through the din and dust and ostentation, however, shines the beauty of small knives sheathed in gold and silver, with handles of blue agate, and the style and quality of Ashanti courage and leadership. Bowdich wrote of the great Sai Tootoo, ancestor of the man who so impressed my wife and me:

"[His] manners are a happy mixture of dignity and affability, they engage rather than encourage. He speaks well . . . but his superior talent is marked in the shrewd questions by which he fathoms a design or a narrative. He excels in courtesy, is wisely inquisitive, and candid in his comparisons." He was also fortunate in entertaining a reporter who could thus wind up his account of the reception. After all the heat and hullabaloo: "It was a beautiful starlit night, and the torches which preceded [Sai Tootoo] displayed the splendor of his regalia with a chastened lustre, and made the human trophies of his soldiers more awfully imposing. The skulls of three Bandacaboceers [chief vassals], who had been his most obstinate enemies, adorned the largest drum; the vessels in which the boys dipped their torches were of gold. He stopped to enquire our names a second time, and to wish us good night; his address was mild and deliberate: he was followed by his aunts, sisters, and others of his family,[39] with rows of fine gold chains around their necks . . ."

Feeling the cool, damp upland air after sunset, one almost says "Good night, sweet prince," in spite of the skulls.

There is old West Africa, best foot forward but far from a natural and primitive innocence, and any predatory white man bursting in did well to keep his priming fresh and his guard up. Its dignities were those of gumption and conscious responsibility, not of innate human excellence. And some of its ways, particularly the bloody-mindedness of the larger polities, such as Ashanti, Dahomey, Benin, were deplorable.

The original owners of the skulls and thighbones that ornamented Ashanti drums may have had the luck to die in battle. Otherwise they came from prisoners decapitated to celebrate Ashanti power and glory or rather, as the Ashanti actually thought of it, to uphold the prestige of Ashanti grandees in Deadland, for these killings had a logical basis in notions not uncommon elsewhere: One way or another dying meant transfer to another world pretty much like this one, where importance implied wealth and slaves and important people expected service and deference. So, at the death of a great man or woman, and at periodical festivals thereafter, the Ashanti killed batches of prisoners of war or local slaves with rites insuring that they became servants of dead and gone great Ashanti in Deadland. This was not just sentiment—unless the ancestors were thus assured that their well being and prestige were properly kept in living men's minds and deferentially safeguarded, they would visit both the king personally and his people generally with untold calamities. To make sure that communications were kept up —like telephoning one's aging parents every evening—the Asantehene killed a slave every day but Wednesday, his taboo day. The King of Dahomey killed a man to take the news to Deadland whenever he did even so trivial a thing as "inventing a new drum, being visited by a white man, or even removing from one palace to another." Such notions probably did as much as the slave trade to foment West African wars, for, when the death of a great man or the eve of a great feast found a powerful nation short of human supplies for sacrifice, they naturally raided the nearest unfriendly neighbors to make up the deficit.

Sir Richard Burton, a shrewd if sulky observer, decided that the King of Dahomey whom he met did not enjoy "tortures and death, or . . . the sight of blood," that his killing 500 people of both sexes[40] as proper retinue for a deceased predecessor was merely family duty. Such gestures were irksomely expensive when the going price of slaves was high—suppose a rancher obliged to slaughter a hundred steers twice a year to please his ancestors—a point that shows how seriously these ideas were taken. But expense was the only regretted aspect. The victims were aliens, who didn't matter, or misfits better off the community's hands.

Few human institutions are consistent, however. This one skips and stutters as much as any. Nobody troubled to ask how the ancestors liked retinues of enemies and jail bait. And these kings and their peoples exulted in blood, skulls and cruelty more than the assumed needs of Deadland can explain. Some of it was fairly well rationalized. The knife run through the victim's cheeks and tongue kept him from audibly cursing the King by name, which would have been a great magical calamity. It was the filial duty of the King's small son to take a sword and saw through the neck of a living victim, no matter how long his childish arms took over the task. But consider the human jawbones mingled among the skulls in Ashanti *décor:* The Ashanti warrior often wrenched off a prisoner's lower jaw as trophy, leaving the poor devil in unrelieved agony and thirst for the hours or days between capture and execution. This is more ingenious than medieval tortures, practically up to the Nazi standard, and quite pointless except as sadism. Not his ancestors' but his own glory was on the mind of the King of Dahomey who, ornamenting his palace wall with regularly spaced human skulls, ran short 127 skulls and ordered a corresponding number of prisoners killed. I prefer not to know what inhuman twist underlay the manner in which a dead King of Benin came by his proper Deadland household, as Barbot described it:

". . . the custom is to dig a very large pit . . . wide at the bottom and very narrow above. They let down the royal corps, and then [the King's] most beloved domesticks, of both sexes, earnestly beg to be allowed . . . to wait and attend on their master in the other life; but this honour is granted only to the best qualified . . . those the deceased king seemed to be most fond of, which often occasions great murmurings and dissensions . . . The persons allowed the preference . . . being let down into the pit, they shut up the mouth with a large stone in the presence of a multitude of people, waiting there day and night. The next morning, they remove the stone, and some proper officers ask those persons who were put in the day before whether they have found the king. If they answer, the pit is again shut up, and open'd a-new the day following, to put the same question; which is answered by such as are still living . . . who also name such of their companions as are already dead . . . this strange fantastical ceremony sometimes lasts five or six days . . . till they being all dead with hunger and cold, no answer is returned. When that is made publick, the people spend all their rhetorick in the praises and encomiums of those . . . who have been so happily distinguished from all others, as to wait for ever on their deceased prince." But, unless most observers belied it, Benin was the cruelest kingdom of them all.

Apropos of burial, one wonders why the early accounts of Guinea fail to account for what the Dahomeyans, for instance, did with such accumulations of human carcasses. The heads were piled up like cannon balls and left to molder and stink in conspicuous locations. The bodies? Maybe cast aside somewhere for the vultures and hyenas; the Ashanti seem to have had a sort of ceremonial disposal ground on the outskirts of town. White visitors aware of the usual West African neglect of such problems admired the well-designed inside privies of old Kumasi. In their accounts the place sounds in many ways more attractive and better managed than it is today after sixty years of stumbling toward European ways of doing. But when the wind lay in the wrong quarter, Kumasi nevertheless stank—of human carrion.

3 *The middle passage*

"*That execrable sum of all villainies, commonly called the Slave Trade . . .*"   —JOHN WESLEY

"Every African introduced into this country was kidnapped," wrote George Bourne, the father of hyperbolic slavery-hating in America, as quoted on p. 50. He elaborated and bore down harder and harder: ". . . he who claims a colored child as his property . . . is equally a man-thief with the negro-stealer on the Gold Coast . . . [and] the Virginians, Carolinians and Georgians with their confederated man-stealing pirates." The oftener and more hotly that was said —and Abolitionism came to say it seventy times seven, always with greater fervor—the more confident the tone and the likelier people with Old Brown's temperament were to forget that, as practical description of actual slaveholding, it was hyperbole, inflammatory rhetoric spun out in a fashion and for purposes already described. It was not even true that every African shipped from Guinea was kidnaped. The Trade was bad enough, thoroughly hideous, and the best one can say for it is that it sent many of its white participants to well-deserved dirty deaths. But its wickednesses were not altogether those that Abolitionists preferred them to be in order that slavery be presented as suited their intellectual tastes—as a white monster/black victim tableau, a righteousness-vs.-slaveholding melodrama.

Richard Baxter, the great Puritan divine, began it three centuries ago when he preached that "To go as a pirate and catch up poor negroes . . . that never forfeited life and liberty and to make them slaves and sell them is one of the worst kinds of thievery in the world." He was not attacking slavery as such, only one of the reputed abuses of the Trade. But his misconception of how the Trade usually worked was later compounded by millions with wider opportunity to learn better. John Wesley assured Methodists a hundred years later that "Captains of ships . . . have invited negroes to go on board, and then carried them away. But far more have been procured by force. The Christians, landing upon their coasts, seized . . . men, women, and children, and transported them to America." Wesley had been in Dixie and should have known better. The error has permeated consideration of slavery down to our own time. A veteran Abolitionist's biography of Garrison told the 1870's how under the American flag "the shores of Africa were invaded by American man-hunters employed by New England capital to pillage, murder, burn and kidnap at their will." The latest edition of Trevelyan's great history of England describes the Trade as "carried on by British skippers crimping [i.e., shanghaiing] negroes along the African coast . . ."

The misapprehension is important because it betrays failure to grasp the place of the Trade in the world that developed it, hence misunderstanding of the morals of slaveholding. Something like what Baxter and Wesley described did go on among the Moslem slavers infesting Central Africa. They often led their own slaving raids and personally depopulated villages for their stock-in-trade. But it is safe to say that ninety-nine in a hundred of the poor devils of Negroes shipped in the transatlantic Trade were already slaves, some born so, some become so legally, some forcibly made so—kidnaped, if you like—before they were turned over to white men. Not five in a hundred can ever have laid eyes on a white man until, as property of and in custody of Negroes, they reached the seaside trading posts. The first Negro slaves fetched direct from Guinea by whites were those given to Portuguese in 1441 as ransom for certain Moorish (i.e., Moslem) and non-Negro freemen kidnaped on a previous voyage of exploration. And since slavery was well established along the Guinea Coast when the whites first saw it, kidnaping of free Negroes remained most exceptional even when, as time passed, whites came to buy thousands a year.

Scruples had nothing to do with it. The Christianity of the day accepted slavery. The Portuguese had formal leave from Pope Nicholas II "to attack, subdue and reduce to perpetual slavery the Saracens, Pagans, and other enemies of Christ southward from Capes Bojador and Non, including all the coast of Guinea." The real reason for eschewing violence was that early firearms were unreliable and the Negro's spears, bows and short swords were not critically inferior to whites' similar weapons—hence kidnaping could be hazardous. John Hawkins, who had the sordid distinction of being the first transatlantic British slaver, found the Negroes giving him as good as he got at least once. Somewhat earlier Spaniards trading above the Gambia River and mistaken by the local chief for Portuguese (hence at least nominal friends) had kidnaped him and 140 of his people. King Ferdinand forced the kidnapers to repatriate this "King"; and it is a pleasure to record that, on getting home, he adroitly ensnared some of his Spanish escort and held *them* hostage against the return of his brother and others of high local rank still held in Spain. The commoners involved were left to rot in slavery, of course. The first New England slaver to visit Guinea joined with an Englishman to raid a village for captives in 1644. They were beaten off with heavy loss and, on reaching home, had trouble with the Bay Colony authorities, who deplored such enterprise—particularly when conducted on Sunday.

Even after superior weapons raised the odds on success, raiding remained bad for business. The Guinea trade went best when the Negro trader on the other side of the bargain was confident of his own safety. After several kidnap raids into the country back of Cape Mesurado—site of the present capital of Liberia—the natives developed the inconvenient habit of taking to the woods whenever a ship was sighted. It is difficult and dangerous to deal with people whom you must flush out of the thickets before opening negotiations, hoping all the while that they live up to their reputations for not using poisoned arrows. The Ivory Coast Quaqua of the same period were fantastically timid about boarding ships to trade ivory because ". . . Europeans . . . have basely carried away or kidnap'd several of them." Wyndham points out also that "kidnapping [by a European] aroused the keenest resentment, for it defrauded the local chief of his dues, and the native traders of their opportunities." The Guinea Negro's position was that there was nothing wrong with kidnaping free people into slavery, particularly from outside your own group; but such enterprise was the rightful monopoly of West Africans themselves. Hence the slaver captain's unwritten rule was: "No raiding. No kidnaping," unless, now and then, in alliance with natives. Rash or inexperienced slavers who broke the rule were bitterly assailed by their competitors, who knew that such greediness would make trouble ashore for the just and the unjust alike.

None of this is exculpatory. The white man was often accessory before and usually after the fact of forcible enslavement, hence morally guilty. But he almost always left the actual violence to West African Negro or mulatto principals. That is, the particular hideousness that most inflamed Abolitionism against the Trade was also the rarest.

"It is very much to be wondered at, why Europeans in general, and Englishmen in particular, persevere in sending their fellow-creatures to the African coast . . . they might as well bury them at once at home, and it is pleasanter far to die there." —RICHARD AND JOHN LANDER

The lure of gold and ivory, the discovery of America, the fragility of West Indian natives, the rise of tobacco and sugar— all these combined might have created the transatlantic slave trade in any case. But the very winds of heaven and currents of the sea also helped to foster this malignant growth.

The sailing ships used by the discoverers of Guinea and the New World could beat up against contrary winds. But the process was arduous and tedious, so they tended to follow favorable winds wherever that was at all possible. This often meant going far out of the direct way. When steam took to sea, self-powered vessels from London, Bordeaux or Rotterdam to the West Indies could steer a great-circle course going nowhere near Africa. But before steam arrived, vessels making this voyage were well advised practically to double the distance by sailing a huge clockwise loop taking advantage of currents of air and water: southward as wind offered to the latitude of Gibraltar, then down the African coast with the help of a convenient current to the latitude of Cape Verde; then striking westward across the Atlantic with the northeast trade winds that prevail most of the year. Then, having discharged her cargo at Barbados or Guadeloupe or Curaçao, the ship beat her way northward out of the Caribbean as best she could close-hauled against the northeast trade, often with substantial help from the Gulf Stream, and hoped to ride homeward on the westerlies of the North Atlantic.

Now this course outward bound took such a vessel within a few scores or hundreds of miles of early exploited sources of slaves up the Senegal and Gambia Rivers. Another convenient current running eastward under the chin of Africa helped a ship go on as far as Benin. She could then drop below the equator, feel for the westward equatorial current and the southeast trade winds and, given some luck in the doldrums,[1] make a good voyage to the West Indies. It all fitted devilishly well into the export of West Africans to the Caribbean and North America, and concentrated the higher risks of unfavorable winds in the legs of the voyage in which cargo—European manufactures outbound,[2] coffee, rum and sugar homeward bound—was least perishable. The Africa-to-America leg—the deservedly notorious slave-carrying Middle Passage—took three weeks at least, seventeen or so at most; seven to eight weeks was reasonable expectation. That is a long time under slave-ship conditions, and losses were often sickeningly high. But they would have averaged far higher if the steady trade wind on port or starboard quarter had not made so many voyages relatively short.

This may not, however, have been altogether to the slaves' advantage in the long run. Had voyages been longer and losses higher, the average cost of slaves landed in the West Indies would have been higher to match. Increased value might have secured better treatment for the survivors and their descendants, in hopes of their living longer and supplying their own replacements and to spare; whereas, when replacements were pretty cheaply available, slaves were rather expendable tools than breeding stock. These are cold-blooded considerations, but then slavery was cold-blooded. That remained true though, like other businesses, it saw shifts of method and personnel.

The old descriptions of the Guinea Trade hint that, as slaves bulked larger in it, the quality of its captains and

shore factors did not improve. The most responsible and intelligent writings by English, Dutch or French participants
cluster well before the mid-eighteenth century. In the late
1600's we read of a Dutch skipper with some two hundred
slaves of his cargo still surviving but "the great sickness and
mortality" among them "together with their stink and nasti-
ness so fretted [him] that he swore . . . if he liv'd to come
to Holland again," he would rather sail before the mast at
twenty guilders a month than command a slaver at £100.
When sorely needing a berth, a rugged youngster like John
Paul (Jones) might ship as mate of a slaver—but keep quiet
about it later. ". . . the surgeons in the Guinea trade,"
wrote one of them, "are generally driven to engage in so
disagreeable an employ by the confined state of their
finances." In the day when Liverpool decorated her new
Merchants Exchange with carvings of Negroes and elephants
as symbols of her prosperity, the most respectable participants in the Trade—the owners and agents in Liverpool,
Flushing and Nantes, Kingston, Cap Français, Newport and
Charleston—were obviously, says McInnes, "not the monsters in human flesh which their enemies declared them to
be but ordinary, every-day brokers . . . never oppressed by
the misery which they helped to promote, because their calling was considered . . . essential to the life of the communities in which they dwelt." But the officers of their ships
were too frequently like Captain Barry of the slaver brig
Friendship of Bristol, who got drunk at dinner on board the
slaver *Queen Elizabeth,* off the Gallinas River one evening,
insulted his host and fellow guest, threatened to thrash them
both, then returned to his ship "and in a Piratical Manner
fir'd a shot at the *Queen Elizabeth,* which had like to have
carried away her Fore Stay . . ." The deputy town clerk of
Liverpool cannot have overstated much when he told Thomas
Clarkson in 1786 that he knew of only one slaver captain
"who did not deserve long ago to be hanged."

For seamen too a berth in a slaver was last resort, so the

hands before the mast were the sweepings of the seaports. In 1789 a Royal Navy captain told a Parliamentary inquiry that, though he used all possible care in impressing the best thirty men out of a slaver with a crew of seventy, his admiral reprimanded him "for introducing such wretches to communicate disorder to the fleet." Another had combed over some twenty slavers and found only "two men . . . fit for service" and they "such inhuman fellows, though good seamen, that he was obliged to dismiss them"—and this at a time when the King's need for sailors was critically acute. Brutalized as merchant seamen were then and for generations to come, one can understand their reluctance to ship in slavers along with such nature's noblemen. They were also deterred by West Africa's well-deserved reputation as a killer. Malaria, yellow fever and odd enteric infections made Sierra Leone specifically "The White Man's Grave" but the name could always have applied to the whole Guinea Coast. Of 140 men sailing thither in 1551 in the *Primrose* and *Lion* there "came home to Plimmouth scarce forty, and of them many died." In a Dutchman trading to Benin in the 1690's five of the hands and the cabin boy superstitiously rolled dice to determine which would survive the voyage. The boy rolled highest. When the ship left the Bights, he alone of the six was still alive.

The standing danger from the cargo further daunted seamen. Early slave ships made up their slave quotas by huckstering along the Guinea Coast wherever Negroes might be had in numbers worth putting in for, or anchoring off some relatively secure bit of sandbar and sending boats up and down with trade goods to swap for slaves. A dozen here, nineteen there, a hundred from King Jimmy up a gloomy, mosquito-plagued creek, a hundred more from his rival, King Jocko, a day's run farther eastward—the old gentleman wore little but a wool cap and a ragged silver-laced jacket—then off for the New World. Such gradual accumulation often took a long time. As competition sharpened, it took even longer. Each added day brought more illness among the hands, particularly the boat's crews, and the gradual ruin of whatever morale they had sailed with. And as the cargo acquired numbers, with the ship still temptingly close to shore and fewer and fewer whites healthy enough to mount guard, risk of mutiny among the slaves grew daily higher.

In 1776 the slaver *Thomas,* Captain Peleg Clarke, was rolling to her anchors off Accra with only the surgeon, boatswain and three seamen as shipkeepers. Her 160 slaves, let out of irons to wash, mutinied and gave the crew a very bad time till brought under. In the meantime thirty-two of the Coromanti among them, the cream of the cargo, had jumped overboard and got free ashore. ". . . had the women assisted them," the surgeon told the owner, "in all probability your property here at this time would have been but small." Such a rising, staged when few whites were on board, forced the six shipkeepers of the Yankee slaver *Perfect* to abandon ship on the Gold Coast in 1759. The Negroes then ran her ashore and plundered and burned her in spite of being fired into by another slaver standing by. In view of this sort of thing certain Rhode Island owners advised their captains not "to lay a long time on the Coast to piddle with blacks . . ." They knew how a New London slaver sloop with only two seamen left alive and two more borrowed from shore to keep watch had been hijacked by canoeloads of watchful natives, the whites killed and the vessel stripped. Collaboration between the cargo and free Negroes ashore at New Calabar did much the same to the shorthanded *Nancy* of Liverpool in 1769.

*". . . such Traders as would freely sell their own Fathers,
their Elder Brothers, and even the Wives of their bosoms
if they could black their faces and get anything for them."*
—WILLIAM BYRD

To reduce trading hazards the Portuguese early set up the
trading-fort company—the model for such later enterprises
as the East India and Hudson's Bay Companies. Organized as
a monopoly under royal charter, Europeans would thus lease[3]
a well-adapted site, such as Goree, and fortify it strongly
enough to overawe the natives. The "factor" of such a post
or "factory"—remember young Johnson of Sekondi—invited
local chiefs and other traders to offer slaves and other local
produce; accumulated slaves in the "captiveries" of the fort
or in barracoons of poles and thatch built under protection
of its walls; and, on arrival of a company ship or an independent one duly authorized to trade, unloaded the fresh
supply of trade goods that she brought, "slaved" her as
quickly as possible with the specified number of each sex and
age group, and sent her on her way with a minimum of expensive and dangerous delay. He was also supposed to
discourage "interloping" (i.e., unaccredited) vessels by bullying, bribing or cajoling local chiefs into refusing to deal
with anybody but the company. This was the theory. On its
first trial at Elmina the local "king" grew sulkily obstructive
because the Portuguese claimed such wide privileges from
the vague terms of their agreement. The powerful kings of
the Slave Coast had the gumption to refuse consent to any
"fort" stronger than a mud-walled warehouse barracoon.

The company-fort system worked best in the hands of the
Dutch, who, having won their own freedom from Spain early
in the 1600's, took zealously to depriving Negroes of theirs.

In the process they drove the Portuguese off the Gold Coast and took over Elmina and its satellite posts. As the Trade matured, however, theory and actuality agreed less and less. No seagoing nation was inclined to observe other nations' monopolies. Many "interlopers" came, coolly buying a-few-slaves-here-and-a-few-there in spite of the company forts. Dutch, English and French had thus plagued the early Portuguese. The English thus plagued the Dutch and French in their self-asserted spheres of influence, and *vice versa*. Sometimes ships of Nations A and B made temporary common cause to thwart the vigilance of Nation C.

Such operators got the benefit of the forts' cannon and soldiers without having to pay for them, and further damaged the great companies by skimming the cream off local stocks of slaves before the company could bid; bringing superior trade goods to give the chiefs hifalutin ideas; warning them how flagrantly the company was cheating them (which it probably was) and how weak it had become (which might also be true). Interlopers might even attack Negroes loyal to their pledges to the monopoly. This began early: When the "king" of Shama told some sixteenth-century English "that there was no gold to be had, nor so much as a hen to be bought, and all by reason of the accord which he had made with the Portugalls," they came ashore in force and burned his village down. The king's scruples may have been strengthened by awareness that, had he allowed interloping trade, the "Portugalls" were just as likely to burn the village as punishment. He was (in principle anyway) damned if he did and damned if he didn't.

Maintenance of adequate stocks of slaves was hampered not only by interloping competition but also by smallpox or "the flucks"—as one slaver spelled the old term for dysentery[4]—which could infest stone dungeons as well as the holds of ships. In 1570, after more than a century of consolidation in Guinea, the Portuguese still experienced a vigorous Negro siege of Elmina and a treacherous Negro capture of their smaller post at Accra. A Gold Coast chief known as "John Conny"[5] seized control of a trading fort that the Dutch had just bought from competitors and so lethally resisted efforts to dispossess him that "a little Path from the Outside Gate to the Inner Apartments . . . was paved with Dutchmen's Sculls, slain in his Engagements with them: He had a large Dutchman's Scull tipp'd with Silver, which he us'd as a Punch Bowl." The British and Dutch at Anamabo dared do little effective against the local Fanti's dealings with interlopers because the 8000-odd Fanti fighting men could at will cut off the garrison's outside food supplies without coming within cannon shot of the walls. And violence might not pay even when the odds looked good: Because the "king" of Bonny capriciously refused trading privileges to three Liverpool slavers, two of the ships were taken up the creek leading to town to bombard him into better manners. Under small-arms fire from shore one ship had to be abandoned to the Negroes' triumphant looting. White dignitaries could not count on avoiding insult as well as injury: The local viceroy of Whydah suspected that the "governors" of the local English, French and Portuguese forts planned to complain of his highhandedness to the King of Dahomey, so he had them waylaid as they started upcountry and imprisoned for several days in his stable among the horses.

None of the great monopoly companies prospered consistently. Their economic woes were due to interlopers, often including their own countrymen, and to the cynical rascalities of those manning their shore stations. The least of their sins was use of company quarters and ships for trading on their own account far in excess of what their contracts allowed. Nor were the companies' ethics unimpeachable: They competed hotly for the "Asiento"—the monopoly of the Trade to the Spanish New World colonies—not for direct profit from Negro selling but because certain privileges that went with it opened the way for highly profitable wholesale smuggling. Their shore personnel were of dismally low quality. Spanish and Portuguese in West Africa in the 1600's were notoriously "banished men or fugitives, for committing most heinous crimes and incestuous acts . . ." A French observer of the late 1600's described "the generality of those who look for such employments" as "necessitous persons, who cannot live at home." The tone can hardly have been higher among the Dutch, Danes, Swedes, Brandenburgers,[6] Italians, Brazilians, Yankees and Cubans who sought these squalid opportunities.

Seamen signing on a slaver ran only a few months' special risk while she was being "slaved." Landsmen enlisting with the monopoly companies as supervisors, armed guards or clerks had to face years in festering West Africa, so those whom shiftlessness, hope of adventure, despair or ignorance induced to do so were probably even lower than slaver seamen. They usually found themselves worse off than gossip had foretold. The climate was muggy beyond the conception of those reared in Europe: ". . . during six months it rains, thunders, and is so intolerably hot, especially in June or July," wrote Bardot of Sierra Leone, "that men must of necessity keep close within their huts and cabbins . . . to be free from the malignity of the rain-water . . . a melancholy and miserable life." The Portuguese on St. Thomas Island, where westbound slavers often wooded and watered, enjoyed a "climate . . . so very malignant, that few or none . . . would come to live here but such as are forc'd to flee, or are banished their country for some villainies." When the place was in Dutch hands, the Trade called it "the Dutch graveyard."[7]

Even in good weather company employees were largely cooped up in the forts or close to them. Local chiefs frowned on wandering whites who might spy out the land for direct trade with upcountry sources of slaves. Within the walls the routine had the ghastly monotony of a sailing ship in a calm. Relief consisted of an occasional brawl with the natives or the arrival of a company vessel bringing more human scum to replace those recently buried in the post cemetery conspicuous from the battlements. Of thirty "soldiers" (i.e., the quasi-military Royal African Company guards) landed healthy at Cape Coast in 1694 half had died within two months, and nobody thought it unusual. In 1825 a detachment of 108 British soldiers stationed in Gambia lost 87 men in four months. Such mortality persisted until the relatively recent discovery of the microorganisms causing malaria, yellow fever and the other diseases responsible. As late as 1855 the chaplain of USS *Jamestown* learned that, of ten Dutch traders with whom he had dined at Elmina, nine were dead by the next time the ship called in on her antislave-trade patrol. Local gossip said that only one in fifteen such ever lived to enjoy the life pension *after only twelve years* that baited this death trap.

Prospects so grim would have told on even self-respecting men. Consider how soddenly groups of degenerate failures would take to the half-blood whores in the village round the fort, and to a style of drinking that took aback even the rough-and-ready slaver captains. Barbot attributed much of the fantastic mortality among British traders to their passion for brandy punch. His own relatively good health during years on the Coast came, he believed, of staying out of moonlight, covering up well in bed, and always wearing a hare skin, fur side in, on the belly night and day, though it was confessedly "very troublesome and occasioned much sweating."

The topmost echelon had some amenities beyond women and drink, though they neglected neither. The "general's" smartly painted boat for fishing or visiting was manned by uniformed Negroes. Such a "general" readily accepted the Negro grandee's principle that a great man seldom walked but was carried in a hammock; it was believed besides that walking any distance under a West African sun would kill a European.[8] As gold and slaves poured into Accra in amounts that dulled rivalry, the head traders developed a miniature social world, dining back and forth and swapping business gossip.[9] Their rich clothes—velvets, silks, feathered hats, much gold and silver lace—had the pretext that "the Blacks, as well as other nations, show most respect to those who are best dress'd." Being carried ashore through the surf by slaves dripping with sweat and palm oil—the indispensable West African cosmetic—smeared up their finery with stains "scarce ever to be got out." Let this rancidly symbolize the sordid glory of command at Goree or Elmina or Anamabo.

Besides their own jailbait countrymen the companies also employed "gromettoes"—Negroes and mulattoes who stood guard, cleaned quarters, ran errands, rowed company boats, sometimes rose to posts of minor authority or learned trades ancillary to the collecting of slaves and provisioning of ships. They were bricklayers, cooks, sawyers, carpenters, laborers (of both sexes), drummers, coopers, washerwomen . . . Whether company-owned or free wage earners, they scrupled not to aid and abet the enslavements of other Negroes—in fact, had few scruples about anything. Getting the upper hand of the German "director" at Fredericksburg on the Gold Coast, his gromettoes terrorized him for months and finally tortured and drowned him out of spite. Whites going ashore from ships lying off posts with specially heavy surf avoided squabbles with the crews of canoes ferrying them back and forth, for these allegedly cowed and exploited savages often evened scores with a trader whom they disliked by upsetting the canoe and making sure that he got drowned in the flurry.

The gromettoes' lack of race solidarity shows that, like American Indians, the New Zealand Maori and many other tribally splintered-up people, the West Africans never learned to close ranks. This has always greatly helped the white man to take over. Gold Coast chiefs hired out fighting men to whites embroiled with rival tribes much as petty German princes rented out regiments in the eighteenth century. The Fanti also emigrated, like the medieval Scots and

Swiss, to fight in the wars of the Slave Coast. The Kru tribes-
men of the eastern Grain Coast epitomized this fatal callousness to other West Africans. European freighters still ship
them at Freetown or Monrovia to go south and back as steve-
dores and supplementary deckhands.[10] I remember their handling modern electrical loading gear with high finesse and
living on the forward well deck in a huge brown canvas tee-
pee. What British explorers said of them 120 years ago still
stands: "constitutionally brave and easily kept in order . . .
the life and soul of the trade on the coast." Mary Kingsley
called them "the backbone of white effort in West Africa."

Their independent-mindedness has often embroiled them
with the brittle government of Liberia, the hive whence
swarmed the colonies of Kru now located from Sierra Leone
to the Bights. It is notable—and sadly significant—that they
could not be enslaved. Their stocky, agile bodies and clever,
adjustable minds made slavers' mouths water. But those who
seized them for sale in America seldom tried it twice. Slavery
was all very well for non-Kru Negroes whom they fed,
flogged, guarded and, as coastal deck crews in slavers, helped
to exile. But slavery for Kru men themselves was unthink-
able. They preferred to commit suicide or die of sheer chagrin or remain recalcitrant to a degree ruining all commercial value. In the ship their own headman agent in charge of
each contingent could flog them as mercilessly as he saw fit.
But let a white man lay a rope's end on a Kru and he jumped
overboard.

By now the various elements of the Trade may be in
better perspective. Its high stench need not mask the relative
responsibilities of its several participants. Had all West Africans resisted buy-and-sell slavery for themselves as sturdily as
did the Kru, the United States would never have had a Negro problem—and old Brown would have had to express his
fist-clenching, thin-lipped impulses in some other kind of
self-righteous violence. Callous Europeans seeking slaves for
profit would soon have concluded about all Negroes what

early ones did about the Kru—that to keep on trying to break wildcats to harness doesn't pay. Negro resistance might have worked specially well because, in spite of fantastic profits from individual voyages, the Trade as a whole operated on narrow margins. Only a little less co-operation from King Jimmy and King Jocko; only rather fewer slaves delivered in somewhat poorer shape; only a much heavier risk of mutiny at sea, meaning still higher insurance premiums—and the Trade would have died of galloping insolvency in 1700.

Men of West African descent have fought and died valiantly for their freedom in Jamaica, Hayti, Surinam and the American South. Nobody can doubt the potential ability of West Africa eventually to have discouraged the European slaver—if only its people had seen fit consistently to go all out at the best time—early, when intruding whites were few and relatively feeble and their advantage in weapons slightest. Had bitter resistance to landing parties been invariable, had captives always snarlingly refused to work and preferred suicide to brutalizing, whites would have either given Guinea a wide berth or else confined trade to gold, ivory, the invisible export of prostitution and presently the palm nuts and palm oil that helped put the Trade's nose out of joint in the nineteenth century. It is a great pity for themselves—and incidentally for others guiltier than they—that so many West Africans took slavery as much for granted as drumming.

"I know of no method of getting money, not even that of robbery . . . upon the highway, which has a more direct tendency to efface the moral sense, to rob the heart of every gentle and human disposition [than the slave trade] . . ."
—JOHN NEWTON

Contrary to the usual notion the Trade was never monolithic. Gold, ivory, dyewoods and, for a while, Malaguetta pepper were its minor props. Most slaver captains reported "wood and teeth" (i.e., ivory) in homeward-bound cargo. This variety of items gave both sides ample opportunities for swindling as they juggled gold, gum and slaves against a wide range of things from Holland, France or England, including offbeat requests from some "king" or other for a sedan chair or a coat of mail or "a little English Dog and a pair of Shoe-buckles."

The European goods included the traditional trumpery for trade with "savages": beads of glass, coral and pinchbeck, cheap mirrors and cheap razors; gaudy secondhand clothes aping the greasy finery of the European "general"; brass and copper rings. But the bulk of the lading, even the close stools and chamber pots early in demand, had practical uses: textiles, for instance, of silk for grandees, of wool [11] for lesser folk. As Europe's industrial revolution came on, linen and cotton fabrics edged in, some sleazy but gay, some as gay and fine as the colorful East Indian madras that Negro women here and there preferred for "headties"—indeed still do in Sierra Leone. Hardware was important: bulk iron in bars; various kinds and sizes of knives; brass pans, copper and iron kettles, hooks, hoes, needles . . . There was first wine, then brandy, rum, gin, all of ghastly quality but soon absorbed into local folkways: Libations of rum accompanied libations of slaves' blood in honoring the ancestors. But the West African also wanted shirts; caps and hats for utility as well as laced cocked hats and beaver top hats for show· thread; combs, since, clean as he usually was, he was always plagued with head lice; and most of all firearms and powder to make them go bang.

In a pinch he could improvise shot good enough for the close ranges he preferred. The Yorubans cast iron balls of more or less musketball diameter. Liberian tribes near the present Bomi Hills iron mines shaped bullets from the heavy red ore. The Ashanti might stuff pebbles or bits of metal scrap into their blunderbusses. But West Africa could not make the gunpowder that specially delighted it.[12] For, aside from its usefulness in securing meat (elephant, buffalo, deer, crocodile, monkey, etc.) and things to barter for white men's goods (ivory, man) its glorious noisiness would have recommended gunpowder anyway, as it did for the Chinese who invented it. Dahomeyan royalty acquired twenty-odd cannon by purchase or capture but never mounted them for use as artillery. They could go boom in prestige salutes well enough lying on the ground touchhole up.

Illiterate Guinea wanted paper for half-literate Moslem visitors to write charms on; horse tails for ceremonial fly whisks; umbrellas as tokens of prestige, a notion from medieval Egypt; clay tobacco pipes; wheeled carriages, not for travel—there were no fit roads—but to lend swank to ceremonial processions in town; horses, not to draw the carriages —gangs of men did that—but for swank again. To the annoyance of Liverpool owners making up cargoes, the same item that People A snatched at merely bored People B only sixty miles to windward.[13] Currencies too were regional. Like sourdoughs, Gold Coasters paid for rum and quoted slave prices in Troy ounces of gold dust or nuggets. Senegal-way prices went in bars of "voyage-iron." [14] Among the Oil Rivers it was copper bars. Early Portuguese trade metals were worked up into "manilloes"—horseshoe-shaped bracelets so popular for ornament, then prestige, that they became currency and remained so in some parts of Nigeria until a generation ago. In the north and along the Slave Coast, strings of cowrie shells[15]—cognate of the American Indian's wampum—had been currency ever since they had penetrated Guinea from East Africa. At two thousand to the dollar they were a cumbersome medium of exchange. But, as a Briton exploring the Niger noted, they did defy counterfeiting.

That was about the only trustworthy item. Trade brandy cut heavily with water was doctored with soap to produce a false "bead" that the Negro thought betokened high proof. A prosperous Rhode Island owner of slavers in peace and privateers in war instructed his slaver captains always to "Worter yr rum as much as possible and sell as much by the short measure as you can." [16] False heads reduced the net contents of kegs of Trade gunpowder. When too many of a batch of muskets bought by French West Indians from the Dutch burst on being fired, the explanation was that they had been made for the West African trade. In the 1780's Britons opposing regulation of the Trade dwelt on the potential hardship to several thousand people engaged in making firearms for West Africa, admitting that no other market would accept such weapons which "killed more from the butt than from the muzzle."

The thing worked both ways: There were honest West Africans. Barbot found some of the Negro traders of Benin refreshingly honest. Now and again some slaver captain described some "king" as a man to tie to. Before Dahomey took over, Snelgrave said, the Negro traders of Whydah were "so civilized . . . it was a pleasure to deal with them." But before the whites came Guinea Negroes had been sharpened against Arab trading traditions and many of them had little to learn from Europe. Gold Coasters were just as ingenious about working bits of brass in among their gold nuggets as the trader was about switching to dishonest weights when valuing them. In the Niger Delta, said a much later witness, natives "often take as much trouble to put . . . foreign matter [into produce offered in trade] as to get more legitimate raw material." The Negro slave trader was likely to substitute sick or superannuated for robust slaves between sale and delivery. In fact, the ugly practice of branding slaves with private marks was developed to discourage this trick. And no doubt home-grown trickiness was stimulated by the spectacle of the whites' flagrant inability to refrain from swindling one another. Slaver captains agreeing to fix prices "commonly undermine, betray and outbid one another . . . they would deceive their fathers . . . if they could," wrote Phillips. Managers of neighboring trading posts might agree not to harbor white deserters from other services. But men able to shoulder muskets were scarce, and within a year a third of the Dutch garrison would be enlisted with the Danes, the English would be welcoming Dutchmen again, and so on. Such Europeans had small reason to complain when, having paid Tribe A £900 to attack Tribe B, for having dealt with the competition, the A's took another £900 from the competition to stay home peacefully after all.

> "I must own, to the shame of my own countrymen, that I was first kidnapped and betrayed by some of my own countrymen . . . but if there were no buyers, there would be no sellers."   —OTTOBAH CUGOANO

The regional names on the old maps, some still in use, reflected the variety of the Guinea Trade: The "Grain Coast" was specially rich in Malaguetta pepper, otherwise "grains of Paradise." The Ivory and Gold Coasts to eastward explain themselves. Beyond the great but so far largely useless Volta

River was the dreary, lagoon-smothered "Slave Coast" studded with centers of slave exportation: Popo, Badagry, Whydah, Porto Novo, then the Oil Rivers—meaning the Niger Delta, thus called for the slowly expanding trade in palm oil that eventually proved a sounder export than men. But the whole expanse up to the Senegal River could just as well have been called the Slave Coast. All its segments traded in slaves as well as local specialties.

A Guinea Negro could become enslaved and exported in half a dozen ways. Maybe the best was to be born of slave parents—hence no drastic change of status when sold—and disposed of because of famine, a constant threat in most of the West Africa that Abolitionism depicted as a land spontaneously flowing with milk and honey. The seller might actually be one's own father unwilling to see both himself and progeny starve when the price of one would tide the other over; presumably the new owner could feed his property, else he would not buy. A similar matter-of-factness underlay the many cases in which slavery came of debt. West Africa knew debt in most of its refinements—necessitous borrowers, mortgaged assets and interest rates high enough for a Brooklyn loan shark. Where people were property, it was natural to "pawn" a child as security to be reared by the creditor and, if payment failed, retained as a slave or maybe sold in liquidation. Misbehavior too created debt, as in fine for theft or indemnity to a husband when caught in that West African badger game. Edwards found among his imported Jamaica slaves a man sold at the age of fifteen to pay for an elder brother's adultery. One's children might be used to settle gambling debts. This seems scandalously unfair to us but it follows from the sweeping West African principle that "every person is a member of some family, and all the other members of the family are responsible to him and he to them . . . it leaves no person uncared for . . . no unemployed starving poor . . . all forms of property are subject to the same law, land, women, china basons, canoes, slaves, it matters not what, there is the law."

So far a certain order but not much farther: James Stephen, relentlessly logical antislaveryite, pointed out that "The hypothesis, that the crimes of Africa solely or chiefly supplied our demand for slaves, was . . . liable to one small objection. How happened it that the crimes of that continent always bore an exact proportion to the price of sugar . . . that when West India credit was good, and planting speculations rife, the Liverpool merchant . . . foresaw a great crop of felonies in Africa, and doubled his tonnage accordingly?" Barbot had a tale of a Senegalese who, unaware that his son knew enough trade French to get his drift, offered to sell the boy to French slavers. Talking fast, son turned the tables and sold the old gentleman on his own account for a good price in trade goods and started home with them. In a sequel that Aesop might have invented in a ferocious mood, Negro slavers seized the enterprising youth on the way, appropriated the goods, haled him back to the trading post and sold him in turn—to the same trader, one hopes; his father and he in the same coffle would have made an edifying study. This sets the tone: Kidnaping of Negroes by Negroes, sometimes slightly disguised, sometimes overt, was a principal source of the slaver's cargo.

The individual slaver among villages like those of the Grain and Ivory Coasts could readily snap up a child keeping birds out of a grain field or a young woman heedlessly returning alone from the water hole. Solitary grown men were not safe when slave prices were high. The next step was the petty slave-raiding "war." A "king" owing the trader an awkward debt for a gold-laced coat and four kegs of brandy might muster his village to attack the traditional enemy village upstream; or, in extreme need, raid an outlying settlement of his own people who had been sulky about taxes. Prosperous persons thus captured might ransom themselves. The lower orders, owning little worth having, were tied in couples or strings of a dozen and marched off to the seashore.[17]

Initiative might come the other way: The slaver captain, finding stocks low in the barracoons, advanced trade goods to able Negro traders prepared to go upcountry and set local "kings" to raiding to secure the merchandise—with due commission to the go-between, of course. Unless his reputation were high, he left with the captain a pledge of fair dealing—maybe a gold collar, maybe one of his sons. If he failed to return with enough slaves to cover the advanced goods, the son was enslaved to help make up the difference.[18] Captain Hume of the slaver *Diana* once augmented his cargo with thirty-four such "pawns" whose "relatives did not choose to redeem them." If a Negro middleman who had left security made off with goods thus advanced, the slaver captain was entitled to seize people from his home village to the value involved and, if proper settlement were not made in time, to sail away with the hostages as legitimately acquired slaves. A "pawn" boy held by Captain Peleg Clarke as pledge for future delivery of a woman slave managed to escape, so Clarke "panyar"-ed (i.e., seized, a term used for both kidnaping and more or less legal seizures) a woman from shore on sailing day. She might not be related to the delinquent boy's family. But they, understanding Clarke's rights in the matter, would adjust the loss with her family on some *quid pro quo* basis.

A slave dealer's free Negro go-between called Gray stole a jacket from Captain Cousins of the *Edward* slaver and was held on board against compensation for the theft. Gray's family said he was "a Scandal to his Country and they would not give a Slave of four feet high for him," so off he went for sale in Maryland. Such gratifying cases of the biter bit, the slaver enslaved, were not uncommon. Consider Henry Demane, son of a Negro slaver of Sierra Leone, who was kidnaped, sold into slavery in the West Indies, taken to England, sold for return to the West Indies, rescued by writ of *habeas corpus* at the instance of antislaveryites when the West Indies-bound ship was actually under way, sent as free emigrant to the free Negro colony set up by benevolent Britons in Sierra Leone—and promptly renewed his family connections and became "a great . . . *dealer in slaves*." Yet he had so acute a sense of the miseries of slavery that, he confessed after his rescue, he had definitely planned to commit suicide by diving overboard as soon as his irons were taken off.

The raid-your-neighbor technique became a sort of seasonal industry. The Ashanti's slave-catching forays into what is now the Northern Territories of "Ghana" were not unlike an annual roundup of cattle or a salmon run in the American Northwest. Yearly the King of Dahomey mustered his "Amazons" and male soldiers, alerted his ablest "caboceers" [19] (ministers and regional viceroys) and attacked neighboring tribes likely to furnish plenty of fresh captives. Home again, he reserved enough to slaughter for his ancestors' prestige and sent the rest downcountry for sale to Whydah middlemen or, after Dahomey took Whydah over, directly to the whites.

Abolitionists thought of all this as a matter of predatory whites "prevailing upon [Negroes] to make war . . . and . . . sell their prisoners," as Wesley described it: "Till then they seldom had any wars; but were in general quiet and peaceable. But the white men first taught them drunkenness and avarice, and then hired them to sell one another. Nay, by this means, even their kings are induced to sell their own subjects." The reader already knows that is inaccurate. Nobody had to train the Guinea Negro "king" in avarice, drunkenness or aggressiveness that promised prestige. And actually, said John Newton, slaver captain turned Abolitionist, in such areas as the Slave Coast direct incitement to slave raiding was unnecessary; the mere landing of trade goods usually set raids going. Hearing that well-meaning Europeans accused him of waging war to secure slaves for sale, a Dahomeyan king protested that this took things by the wrong end: It was his civic as well as moral duty to secure slaves for sacrifice. Were his motives in slave catching primarily economic, he would hardly kill scores and hundreds of perfectly salable items. And without the proceeds of the surplus whom he did sell, how could he supply himself, people and ancestors with such necessities as alcohol and gunpowder and the largesse of textiles, hardware and cowries expected as reward of loyalty? In any case it would be dangerous to leave alien, probably seditious captives alive. It was either ship them overseas for what they would fetch or kill them as pointless precaution.[20] This circuitous argument showing signs of European casuistry went far to confuse the basic issues.

Large or small slave raids plagued most of West Africa after 1700 and spread well upcountry.[21] Mungo Park's account of his journey with a slave coffle from the Upper Niger to the Coast caused antislaveryites and some recent historians to exaggerate how far the transatlantic Trade pushed its septic tentacles.[22] John Newton wrote confidently of frequent 1000 mile journeys and assumed incessant predatory wars in the heart of the continent whence slaves were sold from hand to hand along an intermittent death march from Lake Chad, say, to Jamaica and St. Domingue. This was not all fiction. Now and again slaves from Central Africa did reach West Africa presumably because of temporary blocks in normal trade to the Middle East. The average coffle marching any major distance, with water scarce, only the whip plentiful, left many a corpse behind. But this was a strong reason why really long-distance slaving, though existent, was exceptional. Deaths reduced profits. No buyer would look at the feeble, bony survivors until after costly feeding-up. Since the Negro slaver did not know how to move slaves without heavy breakage, he usually tried to minimize such risks. It is a good guess that nine out of ten Negroes in transatlantic slave ships were born within 400 miles of salt water.

Exported slaves, and Negro slavers too, often believed that they were taken to the New World to be eaten. Such a yarn nastily insisted on by the Cuban Negro slave cook of the schooner *Amistad* precipitated the famous mutiny of which more later. This belief never deterred the Guinea Negro slave dealer. On arrival of a ship to be slaved he was just as eager to exact his "dash"—present from the captain preliminary to doing business, actually a sort of fixed advance commission, a standing economic nuisance and irritation underlying the renown of minor Guinea chiefs as beggars from whom "the boldest . . . in Europe" might learn impudence. It could be costly when there was much power to be thus propitiated. Toward the 1780's a ship arranging to "slave" in ports controlled by Dahomey or Eyeo had to pay some £350 worth of presents to various ranks of shore officials from the local viceroy down—a rough equivalent of the "cumshaw" exacted in Chinese ports of the same time.

This crass monosyllable "dash" survives in modern West Africa as both noun and verb meaning "present," "tip," "bribe." One "dashes" a "boy"—who may be a great-grandfather—for carrying luggage. "Dash me!" from a child is not a Victorian Nice-Nellyism but a begging request. The word is of Portuguese origin along with "fetish" (amulet, totem, pretty much any object of animistic reverence), "palaver" (once meaning talk, now extended to imply trouble, since tribal investigations of trouble always involve much talk), and "pickin" (child, a cognate of Dixie's "picaninny"). But most of this "Black English," as it was once known, has English roots with mangled meanings and pronunciations. It lacks both the descriptive vigor of the Beach-la-Mar of the South Pacific (also English-based) and the wider if still inadequate vocabulary of Haytian Creole (derived from French).[23] As principal means of intertribal communication it sadly handicaps the peoples of modern Sierra Leone, Nigeria, "Ghana" and so on. At first it is amusing to learn that "mammy palaver" (remember Tondeleyo?) means "woman trouble"; "small chop one time" means "Bring the cocktail hors d'oeuvres at once"; but amusement dwindles as one sees how scrawny it is beyond the simplest abuse, chaffering, housekeeping and sexual congress—which activities, of course, created it.

Besides "dash" the white trader also allowed for heavy loss from theft, lively everywhere but most marked along the Slave Coast. The Whydah porters who shifted goods inland from the beach on their heads were "the greatest and most cunning thieves . . . far exceeding our European pickpockets . . . tho' they be never so closely watched and attended all the way, which is good three leagues, these villains will find a way . . . taken in the fact, they are so bold as to tell us, we cannot think they would work so hard for such small salaries as we commonly allow them if they had not the liberty of pilfering our goods." They levied toll on cowries sewn in sacks headed up in wooden casks. They cut holes in the thatched roofs of warehouses and lifted things out with crooked sticks . . . The King's outstanding son and probable successor got his cut from such thievings while his royal father smilingly warned traders they had better look sharp lest his people steal them blind.

Neither party relaxed wariness throughout the process of turning rum, iron and textiles into people. The ship's surgeon—or if he were already dead, an experienced mate—lined up the proffered slaves, stripped both sexes and did all the peering, poking and sniffing necessary to weed out those unmarketable by reason of disease, ruptures, too many missing teeth—a rite which was rather an indignity even in free-and-easy Africa. There was worse to come, however, in the slave ship, where neither privacy, modesty nor comfort could be had at all. Slaves were usually embarked stark naked because their Negro former owners would not throw into the deal the rags they had managed to retain. It was the captain's or his owner's affair whether a yard of cloth apiece were issued as they came up the side. Each had already been marked on shoulder or buttock with a small lettered brand heated to searing point. Oil applied to the site before the hot metal touched it was said somewhat to alleviate the pain.

Imaginative apologists have maintained that those who ran the old licit Trade were not as bad as Abolitionists painted them. On the average they probably were not. Few human beings are up to being as bad as what Abolitionists said about all those engaged in slaving in any given year between 1441 and 1808. But they had to have strong stomachs!

"... never can so much misery be found condensed into so small a space as in a slave-ship during the middle passage."   —WILLIAM WILBERFORCE

The slaver's ideal assortment was mostly male, with few below the age of sixteen or above thirty-five. Henry Laurens, the great South Carolina patriot, was still dealing in slaves among other things when describing "a most butiful [sic] cargo" just in from the Bights, "chiefly young people from 15 to 20." But some children to fill the chinks and a few middle-aged people robust enough to pass the surgeon were usually bought. Breakage began at once. Canoes ferrying slaves to the ships often capsized and drowned their lading, who were tied two and two. Whether in suicidal despair or in low-grade hope of somehow reaching shore before the surf, or the sharks, got him, a slave would sometimes throw himself over the ship's side before getting hustled below. Sharks knew the association between ships and man meat. "Those voracious animals," wrote a daunted visitor to Whydah, "often follow the Canoes, through the Breakers, quite ashore, in Hopes of Prey. And whenever the Dead are committed to the Sea, which happens almost every Day, while Ships are in the Roads, the Sharkes give such due Attendance that the Corps [*sic*] can no sooner touch the Water than it is immediately torn in Pieces and devour'd before our Faces." Seamen believed that sharks dogged ships all the way to the West Indies. At any rate some of these fin-bearing buzzards were always alert in the wake, though maybe not the same ones that had gathered for such grisly good reason in the shadow of the ship as she lay "slaving" at Commenda or Great Popo.

Friends of the Trade argued that Negroes shipped to America were better off than those rejected and staying ashore. The Negro or mulatto slave dealer was harsh about unsalable human trash. Merchandise thrown back on his hands might well get drowned or decapitated to save its keep. Exile in a slaver was a squalid nightmare shot through with terror of the unknown and the possibility of being eaten. But, though the victim did not as yet know it, it at least meant an odds-on chance of surviving to walk untrammeled again, to sleep with women again in the clay-and-wattle shacks of the West Indies. It was a pity that at the time of sailing, probably throughout the voyage, the slaves were too ignorant and confused to have any such hopes. Few could have visited a ship before or had much other preparation for what awaited them.

Those gazing numbly at the sawn planking, the intricacies of shrouds and running rigging,[24] the captain's dog, which they probably could not recognize as kin to his long-necked, close-haired cousins ashore, observed one detail that would also have looked strange to white seamen unfamiliar with the Trade—the temporary barricade of inch plank built thwartships aft loopholed for musketry and usually mounting swivel guns[25] to defend the quarterdeck against mutinous slaves. This ominous structure came to be as much part of a slaver during the Middle Passage as the stench that betrayed her business to vessels passing to leeward. Even in the earlier, easier—and riskier—days the afterguard thought it advisable to keep a chest of muskets ready loaded on the quarter-deck and to haul round a couple of carriage guns to command the ship's waist night and day.

But new slaves had little time to stare. They were quickly stowed below in a fashion deservedly notorious. Three feet of headroom—allowing the average Negro to sit upright—often dwindled to two-foot-six between the deck and the temporary plank "platform" making the second tier flooring for slaves to lie on. Such methods enabled slavers to pack amazing numbers of people into vessels few of which were longer than an American Pullman car. In 1667 a Catholic missionary crossing from Angola to Brazil in a Portuguese slaver reported 680 slaves on board, the men unable to lie down all at once, "the children in the steerage pressed together like herrings in a barrel, which caused an intolerable heat and stench." A century or so later the *Nancy* of Liverpool, Captain Nelson, whose owners officially rated her capacity at 500 slaves, landed 610 in Jamaica; allowing for normal mortality *en route* she must have shipped over 650.

In the 1750's 2½ slaves per ton of ship was thought adequate. By 1783 the hard-driving slaver owners of Liverpool were shipping 3.2 slaves per ton.[26] It was considered a drastic reform when Britain, in 1788, set a maximum of 1½ slaves per ton—that is, sleeping space of six feet by sixteen inches per adult male. Nor were such regulations well enforced. West Africa and the West Indies were far from Westminster. The captain of a slaver rated at 300 Negroes often loaded 350 on the grimly well-founded assumption that the survivors would not exceed the legal limit; whereas to ship only 300 might bring her into port with room for forty or fifty slaves unprofitably empty.

In view of the smells and indecencies involved, the art of managing a vessel thus freighted cannot be called delicate.

But even with good luck in weather and disease it required skill and experience. These were the maturing techniques as veteran mates taught them to Phillips on the slaving voyage that so disgusted him:

". . . they are fed twice a day, at 10 in the morning, and 4 in the evening . . . the time they are aptest to mutiny, being all upon deck; therefore . . . what of our men are not employ'd in distributing their victuals . . . stand to their arms, and some with lighted matches at the great guns that yaun upon them loaded with [small shot] till they have done and gone down to their kennels . . . Their chief diet is called dabbadab, being *Indian* corn ground as small as oatmeal . . . boil'd well in a large copper furnace, till 'tis as thick as a pudding; about a peckfull . . . is allow'd to ten men, with a little salt, malagetta, and palm oil, to relish . . . Three days a week . . . horse beans boil'd for their dinner and supper . . . these beans the negroes extremely love and desire, beating their breast, eating them, and crying Pram! Pram! which is, Very good! . . . indeed the best diet for them, having a binding quality and consequently good to prevent the flux . . . The men are all fed upon the main deck and forecastle, that we may have them all under command of our arms from the quarter-deck . . . the women eat upon the quarter-deck . . . boys and girls upon the poop . . . they will readily run there in good order of themselves . . . when they have eaten their victuals clean up (which we force them to for to thrive the better) they are order'd down between decks, and every one as he passes has a pint of water to drink . . . When they have occasion to ease nature they are permitted by the sentinels to come up and go to conveniences . . . on each side of the ship, each of which will contain a dozen of them at once . . . we have some 30 or 40 gold coast negroes . . . procur'd us there by our factors, to make guardians and overseers of the *Whidaw* negroes, and sleep among them to keep them from quarrelling . . . as well as to give us notice, if they can discover

. . . any plotting among them, which trust they will discharge with great diligence . . . when we constitute [such a] guardian, we give him a cat of nine tails as badge of his office, which he is not a little proud of, and will exercise with great authority. We often at sea in the evenings would let the slaves come up into the sun to air themselves and make them jump and dance for an hour or two to our bagpipes, harp and fiddle, by which exercise to preserve them in health . . ."

Here was something for Breughel to paint: the tubby ship solemnly heaving in the mid-Atlantic swell; the declining sun darkening the water and gilding the rigging; piper and fiddler on the break of the poop pumping out some old come-all-ye from Cork or Greenock; the main deck thick with next-to-naked Negroes already matching their native caperings and writhings to these alien rhythms. And all the while the gunner leaning on the breech of a big cannon with a lighted slow match just in case.

For obvious reasons temporary bulkheads belowdecks separated the sexes. Ships shorthanded or with specially cautious captains might keep the men in irons all or most of the time, their shackles attached to chains running the length of the platforms and fastened to ring bolts. They were sometimes brought on deck attached to this chain and made to dance in irons for health's sake, no matter how raw the heavy metal had chafed their ankles. The obvious hazard implied in the "conveniences" of Phillips' ship was reduced when Liverpool slavers began to supply large metal cans to be used belowdecks and regularly emptied. But in rough weather, when the hatches were battened down, the cans, none too many anyway, could not be emptied, and seasickness was added to the dysentery usually more or less present . . . An efficient slaver went to much trouble in the name of hygiene as understood in that day. The women were given beads to string as occupational therapy. Both sexes could have pipes and tobacco on request or maybe once a day.[27] Daily, weather permitting, the planking of the Negro quarters was scraped, washed down and swabbed with vinegar. Some ships enforced daily bathing in salt water and, in cold or wet weather, served out "drams" of rum or brandy. But all this was ideal procedure. Weather, greed, disease, dishonesty, sadism, lust and human cussedness saw to it that many a slaver's transatlantic voyage was the hideous thing that Abolitionists assumed it must be.

Phillips' *Hannibal* had a decent captain and her charterers—the Royal African Company—were more scrupulous than their interloping competitors could afford to be. Yet she reeked of trouble: At St. Thomas the crew smuggled on board enough raw rum seriously to threaten ship's discipline. Their ringleader, the ship's trumpeter, had to be kept in irons on the poop for two months. Smallpox, a frequent hazard in slavers, infected 100-odd Negroes and killed twelve. The "white flux"—slavers were horribly familiar with this now unidentifiable enteric disease—swept cargo and crew. After an unusually prolonged Middle Passage the ship made Barbados with fourteen crew dead and only 380 slaves alive of 700-odd shipped. The owners' loss from freights unpaid on dead slaves was £3360, then a fortune. The Company's loss was higher still. No urban scavengers collecting night soil, Phillips said, "endure so much noisome slavery as those who carry negroes." In view of what it must have been like in the *Hannibal* with every other tight-packed slave suffering from uncontrollable diarrhea, he had reason to call the cargo "a parcel of creatures nastier than swine." But this neglected one detail—it was the idea of the shipowners, not of the creatures, to stow them thus to begin with.

Epidemics were likeliest to strike, of course, when weather forced battening down of hatches. Lesser shipboard ailments like scurvy went almost unnoticed under such circumstances. Let the cargo go unbathed and unsunned for a while and they were eaten alive by lice, which often meant typhus.

Shore inspection failed to ward off many diseases because an apparently healthy Negro might carry in him strains of microorganisms to which he himself was immune but to which his shipmates were murderously susceptible. Any of the loathsome West African skin diseases brought latent on board was sure to infect many others; victims surviving the voyage came ashore half-flayed from uncontrollable scratching. Eye infections, sometimes blinding, might run through cargo and crew.[28]

"Criminal rapaciousness" was what Bryan Edwards, ablest apologist for West Indian slavery, called the practice of stuffing 500-odd slaves into ships of 200 tons with mortality averaging 15 per cent during the voyage and 4 per cent more in harbor before the slaves were landed. Given infectious diseases and so many susceptibles, hygiene was almost as futile as pre-inspection. Seventeenth century Dutchmen boasted that their slavers were "for the most part clean and neat" while those of the English and French were "foul and stinking." [29] But not long previously a well-kept Dutchman had made the West Indies with 45 per cent of her cargo dead and thrown to the sharks. Take it the other way: Voyages without loss were practically unknown until the last two decades of the licit trade, when some British owners and captains observed new and strict regulations to the letter. The *Pilgrim* of Bristol, for instance, sounds like a seagoing sanitarium lying at St. Vincent's in 1791 with her 370 Eboes "in the best possible order" in quarters "six feet in height between decks without shelves or double tier . . . as clean as a Dutch cabinet," and only eight dead during the voyage.

Leave to ship a few Negroes for their own profit was often part of the captain's and surgeon's bargains with the owners.[30] Abuse of the privilege was a minor cause of overcrowding. Owners complained that all slaves dying at sea were sure to be theirs, not the captain's. To encourage care of the cargo the officers might get a bonus based on average price received for the slaves on landing, which presumably reflected their condition at the end of the voyage. In one appalling case the mate of a slaver deliberately starved to death a slave badly emaciated from illness to avoid selling him ashore at a price so low that it would seriously affect the average, hence lower the officers' bonus.

Erotic morals in slave ships might be as low as the commercial morals of the Trade. The hands were supposed to stay away from the slave women, not for decorum but to prevent quarrels. In well-disciplined ships the rule was observed. Captain John Newton sought to reduce his own lust after slave women by much reading in his Bible during the Middle Passage and keeping on a meatless diet with only cold water to drink. But "On board some ships, the common sailors are allowed to have intercourse with such of the black women whose consent they can procure . . . officers are permitted to indulge their passions among them at pleasure . . ." The ladies can hardly have been very dainty bedfellows. But seamen who had valued the favors of the slippery, rancid Gaboon girls were not choosy. In fact, "some of them have been known to take the inconstancy of their paramours so much to heart, as to leap overboard and drown themselves."

> "Now, a Yankee ship in the Congo River . . .
> Oh, who d'ye think was the captain of her?
> Old Bally Gardner, way from Bangor . . ."
>   "Blow, Boys, Blow" in Doerflinger,
>   Shantymen and Shantyboys

When Mungo Park returned to the Gambia trading posts with the news that the Niger flowed eastward, his best available homeward transportation was the *Charlestown*, Captain

Charles Harris, an American ship with 130 slaves bound for Charleston, S.C., where Park hoped to find shipping for England. Leaks and foul weather forced her into Antigua, which suited Park even better. He saw "no wanton acts of cruelty practiced by either the master or the seamen . . . but the method of confining and securing Negroes in the American slave ships (owing chiefly to the weakness of their crews) is abundantly more rigid and severe than in British vessels." [31]

From her name this was a Yankee out of Massachusetts, ancestral home of John Brown and most of the Six. Legend has it that, besides tolerating slavery itself longer than did the British and French, we Americans—particularly New Englanders—were specially active in transplanting Negroes to their and our own eventual great sorrow. In our historical folklore the psalm-singing Yankee skipper taking Medford rum to Africa to swap for slaves for the Georgia rice swamps ranks with the Salem witch hunter and the New Haven blue laws as symbol of Puritanism at its unworthiest. The creature existed right enough, for all his piety exploiting black ivory as readily as any sinner sailing out of Glasgow, Nantes or Flushing. Like his Liverpool rival he was as clever at privateering in wartime as at slaving in peacetime. But the traditional picture needs correction. His home port was oftener Newport or Bristol than Boston or Salem, as the legend prefers. And his vessels, averaging only forty tons, were too small to have carried the bulk of the black flood that swelled westward after the 1650's. When slaving was "the first wheel of commerce"[32] in Rhode Island, the tonnage of the whole Yankee slaving fleet was little more than a third of that of Liverpool alone. Many Negroes imported into the mainland colonies came in larger British bottoms either direct from Guinea to Norfolk, Charleston or Savannah or in those that had already landed most of their slaves in Barbados or Jamaica.[33]

So what distinguished the Yankee in the Trade was his reputation for treating slaves in transit even worse than did the average French, Dutch, British or Danish slaver. This came of defects both marine and mental. He had got into the Trade by taking staves (for wine casks) and salt fish to Madeira and the Canaries—islands temptingly close to Guinea—in small, easily handled craft of his own building readily converted into slavers for the homeward voyage. He continued to use such vessels after learning that New England rum could compete with brandy in the Trade. He never developed the national-monopoly trading companies that used large double-manned vessels in which 600-700 slaves could be allowed on deck in good weather. The Liverpool owners whose penurious competition took the Trade away from London and Bristol skimped on wages and perquisites, not manpower; whereas Yankee slaving was a piecemeal matter of sloops or schooners manned by only a captain, a mate, maybe a surgeon, carpenter, cook, cabin boy and four or five foremast hands. To have raised the ratio of guards to Negroes nearer to European standards would have caused Rhode Island owners acute pain by requiring so many more junks of salt beef and pints of dried peas consumed during the voyage and so much heavier wage bill due to seamen surviving to see Point Judith again. As Park saw, sheer regard to their own safety forced so shorthanded a ship's company to keep the Negroes belowdecks most of the time, whatever the weather.[34]

Such callousness is better understood, though not condoned, when one knows that things were then almost as bad for Europeans—free emigrants, convicts, indentured servants, soldiers—making the transatlantic passage westward. Three slaves to two tons of ship imposed by Britain in 1788 was the same ratio as that for British soldiers in transports forty years later. In fact, a fairly impartial observer noted in the early 1800's that, thanks (he thought) to their being stowed naked and on vegetable diet, the average cargo of slaves came ashore in the West Indies in better shape than the average unit of troops. Civilian emigrants of the mid-

1700's were theoretically better off at one adult per ton-and-a-half of ship, or a "bedplace" six feet square for every four adults. But children nearly grown counted as only half-adults, small children as nothing; so 300 emigrant "freights" [35] might mean more than 400 "souls" crammed on board. The ships' provisions—"rusty" salt beef or pork—sound worse than the slaves' dabbadab and horse beans. Famished passengers sometimes caught, cooked and ate the rats with which such vessels abounded.[36] Even at best their diet guaranteed scurvy in some measure. Mortality up to one-third was pretty much expected when the passage was at all prolonged. Consider too that, whereas slaver captains and surgeons usually received small bonuses per slave landed, deaths at sea were profitable to emigrant ships, for emigrants paid fares in advance and no longer consumed provisions once their dead bodies had slid overside.

All salutary to remember; but the inhumane standards of that age merely explain, do not excuse the slaver. He had no scruples about treating innocent people exactly as European governments treated felons—subjecting them to a loathsome voyage of involuntary exile. In fact, he reduced to absurdity the sentimentalist's proverb: "Comprendre tout, c'est pardonner tout."

". . . the fury with which the slave-trader defends every inch of his bloody deck and his howling auction-platform."
—RALPH WALDO EMERSON

The luckless Negroes packed belowside in slave ships ran other than hygienic hazards. Mishap to the ship might, for instance, see them abandoned to gradual or sudden death.

When the Dutch slaver *St. Jan* broke her back on a reef southeast of Curaçao in 1659, her officers and crew rowed away, leaving the slaves to whatever rescue commercial salvage might include. In 1738 a Rhode Island sloop "with a great many Negroes on board" was fired by lightning; Captain Caleb Godfrey and his crew tumbled into the longboat and got safely home. Nobody ever knew whether the Negroes burned, drowned or were mercifully blown up.

Other slaves died violently during mutiny at sea that sometimes succeeded. In 1729 the *Clare* galley, Captain Murrell, was thirty miles on her way in the Middle Passage when the "Negroes rose and making themselves Master of the Gunpowder and Firearms, the Captain and Ship's crew took to their Long Boat, and got shore [*sic*] near Cape Coast Castle. The Negroes run the Ship on Shore within a few Leagues of the said Castle and made their Escape." Next year the *Little George* of Rhode Island, Captain Scott, was three hundred miles at sea from Sierra Leone with ninety-six slaves, including thirty-five men, when some of them got their irons off, broke through a bulkhead, killed the watch (no doubt drunk, asleep or both) and imprisoned the surviving whites belowside.

There ensued a strange siege warfare conducted on a craft about the size of a PT-boat. The whites knocked over several of the mutineers with musket fire and used ingenious grenades of gunpowder and empty bottles but enemy numbers were too great for escape to be possible. Rendered desperate by a diet of raw rice and water, the whites managed to convince the mutineers that unless terms were made, they really would sink the ship. The final agreement bound the whites to keep their hands off the seacocks and fire away from the magazine while the slaves sailed the ship back to the Coast and escaped ashore, leaving her to the imprisoned crew. More by luck than seamanship she was worked over the bar of the Sierra Leone River and run aground on the northern side of the estuary. After making sure the Negroes had gone, the ship's company crept on deck out of what must soon have become durance pretty vile. They decided the ship could not be refloated, abandoned her and took woebegone refuge in a Montserrat brig lying across the estuary at the pirate-slaver settlement already polluting the site where Freetown now stands.

In 1753 the officers of the *Narborough* slaver of Bristol allowed some of the cargo on deck to help work the ship. The Negroes got hold of firearms, killed all the crew except a few spared to steer, evaded pursuit by a sister slaver and, so far as anybody ever heard, got back safe to the Coast. The odds against such success were high, however. The usual story was short. In the *Rainbow* of Liverpool in 1756: "The Negroes rose on us after we left . . . killed my linguister [i.e., interpreter-go-between] . . . [we] secured them without further loss." But it could be lively while it lasted. In 1754 a handful of slaves brought on deck in a slaver sloop three hundred miles from land brained the captain and took over the cabin with all the firearms. The mate rushed up and locked the cabin door from outside. The rebels found a chest of ready-loaded muskets and fired them all through the door in succession but hit nobody, merely blew the door to bits. While they fumbled to reload, the officers rushed the cabin and overpowered them. In a matter of minutes things were normal again—except for the ruined door, the dead captain and the slave ringleader who, wise man, broke away and jumped overside. Slavers advising novices that kindness never paid probably made much of what happened to the captain of the *Ferrers* galley of London with three hundred war captives fresh from the Grain Coast upcountry. He made a fatherly point of himself seasoning their "chop" and, when they were airing on deck, visited them with inadequate escort to show good will. One suppertime late in the afternoon the slaves on the forecastle beat out his benevolent brains with "the little Tubs out of which they eat their boiled Rice" and rushed the quarterdeck barricade. A blast from a carriage gun loaded with small shot took care of that—but expensively. Between the gun and numerous cases of jumping overboard the owner lost eight valuable slaves.

Successful mutiny too might bring harsh automatic penalties. Few Negroes fresh from Guinea were seamen, none were navigators. Once the ship was seized, the likeliest alternatives were gradual starvation, breaking up on a reef, foundering in a storm. A Newport schooner once fell on such a horror in progress: a slaver drifting miles from anywhere with nobody on board but fifteen slaves surviving of a hundred in the original cargo. It is stupid to risk death to capture a vessel that you can't handle. But life in the Guinea bush followed by the stultifying brutalities and privations of a slaver did not make for cleverness. Besides, most West Africans had the sad little belief that death in exile meant return of their souls to Africa or an exact facsimile,[37] which made death, quick or eventual, not unwelcome. This may account for numerous attempts at mutiny that otherwise look irrational. Maybe the same notion was what often moved new-shipped slaves to refuse to eat. Standard countermeasures included hot coals held blisteringly near the lips. "I am naturally compassionate," wrote Bardot, "yet have I been necessitated sometimes to cause the teeth of these wretches to be broken, because they would not open their mouths . . . and thus have forced some sustenance into their throats." Liverpool slavers carried a special tool, a sort of reverse pincers, to force open stubborn jaws. "Compassionate" men doing such things probably felt about them as humane ranchers do about castrating calves.

In fairness to slavers it should also be pointed out that—back to mutiny—it takes courage to charge outnumbered into a room full of powder smoke and desperate enemies even if one is fairly sure of having counted correctly the number of muskets going off. "Though cowards are cruel," said James Stephen, who knew seamen in the Trade firsthand, "I am sorry to say that every cruel man is not a coward." Scum, rascals or brutes as most of them were, they were usually brave as lions. This explains their success in combining slaving and privateering. Because pirates were rife on the Guinea Coast and slave ships occasionally needed to bombard a "king" into resuming trade, the slaver usually mounted more guns than the regular merchantman. In the wars that covered two-fifths of the eighteenth century and much of the globe both England and France put these slavers' armaments to national use—and private profit—by commissioning them as privateers or giving them "letters of marque and reprisal." Either status allowed preying on enemy vessels without its amounting to piracy. Many a Liverpool Guineaman came into Bridgetown or Kingston with her usual quota of slaves and a French ship with a prize crew on board meekly following to be condemned and sold for the benefit of her conquerors. The same *vice versa* came into Martinique.

Even against ships of superior force these slaver privateers were awkward customers. In 1798 the *King William* slaver of Liverpool, Captain Bent, "having on board only fifteen effective hands able to stand to their quarters," got away from a Frenchman of sixteen guns, after taking hits from 602 projectiles in two-and-a-half hours of running fight. The *Amelia and Eleanor*[38] slaver, Captain Spears, fought off a Frenchman of eighteen guns and made Barbados after all with bowsprit and foremast shot away, several holes below the waterline and two ports smashed into a single ragged gap.

During such actions the Negroes in the stinking darkness belowdecks must have gone half-mad with terror as the solid shot smashed at the ship's timbers and she quivered and heeled to her own broadsides. Sometimes a shot penetrated far enough to kill some slaves. Nor were they always allowed the relative if terrifying safety of staying below. Here is an eloquent detail: In view of the many instances of slave mutiny at sea when home was already hopelessly far away, and of slaves' assumed readiness to rise against their captors, there is something remarkable about the occasional decision of a hard-pressed captain to risk arming the sturdiest slaves among the cargo to fight alongside the white crew. Certain Gold Coasters thus released helped gallantly to repulse French boarding parties from the *Knight* slaver, Captain Boates, in the Seven Years' War. Captain Noble of the *Brooke* slaver armed "fifty of our stoutest slaves, who fought with exceeding great spirit" beating off a Yankee in the Caribbean in 1777. On no such occasion were the slaves reluctant to surrender musket and cutlass when the action was over. The *Brooke* case is specially striking because these fifty armed slaves may well have outnumbered the whole white ship's company;[39] she had already made Barbados, so they knew land was near; death and wounds had cut the whites' effective numbers; all were under the relaxation following on an exacting fight; the Yankee licking her wounds in the offing was in no shape to interfere . . . yet opportunity was not seized.

For that matter sizable forces of British West Indian slaves were armed, drilled and did good service in interisland fighting in the eighteenth century and, on command, surrendered their arms dutifully. Old Brown and the Six should have known and pondered such anomalies before so confidently assuming that, given weapons and half a chance, Dixie's slaves would rise for freedom.

"The Slave Trade is the great cause of the depopulation and degradation of Africa."
—SIR THOMAS FOWELL BUXTON

Abolitionism taught that slaving had meant the ruin of the areas exploited; that for centuries it had reduced population, turned lands once covered with smiling agriculture or at least bucolic charm into haunts of snakes and leopards and nests of internecine war. Soon the West African would go the way of the Red Indian . . . That chief of sinners, the predatory white man, had not only brutally kidnaped millions of nature's noblemen but also spoiled their idyllic native land for the terrified huddle of their kin lucky enough to have been left behind.

How many persons the Trade cost Guinea first and last cannot be estimated reliably. Nobody now—to say nothing of partisans on either side then—knows how many were landed alive in the New World. A recent respectable guess is that between fifteen and twenty million got there, meaning maybe eighteen to twenty-four million shipped. It sounds a lot. But it covers several hundred years. The yearly average is something like 60,000—less than one per cent of the total population of West Africa at any time up to 1800. Make a ghastly large allowance for deaths between home and shipside—from the wars or raids that enslaved many of the stock-in-trade, from fatigue and starvation in the coffle, from disease in the barracoon and drowning in the surf—suppose two Negroes dead for every one sailing, a ratio higher than modern authorities suggest. The resulting average drain of 180,000 a year was rather less than average Italian emigration to the United States in the decade 1900-

1910[40]—during which nobody suggested that Italy was being "depopulated."

"Even when the slave trade was at its height," says Fage, a modern analyst of these issues, "[the Gold and Slave Coasts, both conspicuous sources of slaves] were remarkable for the density of their populations and for their elaborate political organization . . . We still cannot say with any certainty that, had there been no slave trade, the population of West Africa today [say 40,000,000] would have been larger, or very much larger, or even that it would have been of a higher physical standard." In much exposed areas, of course, population-loss referrable to the Trade might run maybe 2-3 per cent a year. Local ability to recoup this probably came of two special advantages: Slavers preferred males, so the loss was lighter among potential mothers of whose fecundity Guinea customs could make optimum use. And directly or indirectly whites were bringing from the New World new food plants that raise the local potential of nourishment. Even today the West African standard of feeding is pitifully low, and sky-rocketing populations press heavily on available nutrients. But it would all have been far worse by now if West Africans had not early and well taken to such New World exotics as Indian corn, cassava and sweet potatoes.

By supplying these crops—plus writing and eventually steel, concrete, the internal-combustion motor, preventive medicine and in the long run, no doubt, atomic power— whites may have done West Africa more long-range good than slaving and hard liquor ever did harm. A far-sighted Negro statesman of 1450, as cynical about deals as most Guinea leaders were, might well have welcomed such a swap—25,000,000 human beings not particularly needed at home in exchange for the eventual technical tools to make West Africa what she may be in the year 2450. But this un-edifying thought is no excuse for slavers. More scrupulous traders—and there always were a few who thought slaving untouchable—would have made their profits and brought Guinea much the same indirect benefits without subjecting so many poor black souls to the moral and physical horrors of the Middle Passage.

4 _U.S.S._ Frustration

"In vain has nature given to Africa noble rivers, man is the only merchandise they carry."
—SIR THOMAS FOWELL BUXTON

The story of the schooner _Amistad_ did much to mislead Abolitionists about slaves' attitude toward slavery. In mid-1839 this Spanish colonial vessel was bound down the Cuban coast from Havana with some fresh-landed Africans—mostly Mende, a vigorous people of the Sierra Leone upcountry active in slave catching and selling. Three days out they rose under a chief's son named Cinquez, killed the captain and took over. Two seamen escaped in an open boat. The mutineers spared their owners, Pedro Montez and Jose Ruiz, on condition that they navigate the ship back to Sierra Leone.

So far it resembled things that had often happened before. But, though the Cubans steered more or less eastward when the slaves could observe the sun or stars, they worked northward, even westward, whenever obscured nights allowed, hoping to fall in with the northeasterly trend of the American coast. Their risky game worked. After sixty-three days the zigzagging *Amistad* made Montauk Point, got into Long Island Sound, staggered about alarming coasters and shore people, and was finally taken in charge by a surveying brig, USS *Washington*. The commander of the brig turned the schooner over to shore authorities but claimed salvage on the value of both ship and slaves. The Cubans claimed free restitution of both. Abolitionist friends of the cargo claimed freedom for the slaves because they had been landed in Connecticut, where slavery was illegal.

The ensuing litigation ended most gratifyingly in the return of the Negroes to Sierra Leone. It was substantial justice. The slave trade was illegal under Spanish law effective in Cuba; hence these obviously African slaves had been smuggled into Cuba; hence they could not legally belong to the claimants. But the case was hard fought and took a long time during which the press spread details all over the nation. Abolitionists made out Montez and Ruiz as the impudent ruffians they certainly were but also got in many foolish hints that the mutineers were nature's noblemen, a species not readily found in any chance group from any race or culture. But then Abolitionism had to have all its blacks white and all its slave-holding whites black. Cinquez' portrait was painted, his followers' stories were told at great length through inadequate interpreters. An eminent phrenologist[1] examined and described them as "young and unoffending men and children . . . converted into mere 'property' by Christians."

Here was the bitter old assumption that whites were the original enslavers; and the sister error that any normal group of slaves, afloat or ashore, was always on the verge of mutiny. Antislavery Americans had long hoped this was true. Now the *Amistad* case added apparent confirmation spiced with the always stimulating tang of melodrama. It was just what Abolitionism expected of innocent primitives gallantly seeking to regain the spontaneous freedoms of their gorgeous forest paradise. At one point a Federal judge's opinion sounded like something out of an antislavery romance: Cinquez, wrote Justice Judson, "shall not sigh for Africa in vain. Bloody as may be [his] hands, he shall yet embrace his kindred." Through the mist of hero-worship he still sounds like a clearheaded, plucky credit to a good Mende rearing and a very useful man to have on one's side in case of trouble.

The actual significance of the *Amistad*'s cargo, however, lay in its being contraband, unlike those described so far. The ship was up to her lee rail in slave bootlegging, which had been an international ulcer ever since Britain and the United States had barred the slave trade from their ships and ports in 1808. Like the bootlegging of the 1920's this sordid industry owed its existence to well-meaning outlawry of something previously taken as normal. By making prohibition look silly the rumrunner inadvertently encouraged repeal. The bootleg slaver's zealous abuse of opportunity moved no nation to readmit the Trade because outlawry was proving impractical. Instead his success furthered the abolition of domestic slavery in those residual markets—Cuba, Brazil, to a minor degree the States—that he supplied. The slaver had once been able to esteem himself a useful member of society carrying out a necessary function that might trouble the squeamish but did not rule out self-respect. But 1808 had seen the Trade internationally proclaimed too foul for further countenance. By persisting in it regardless, the illicit slaver kept the fire of indignation hot under the influential Britons who had first got the Trade outlawed and then got the British West Indian slaves freed in the 1830's. And the fires of British reform usually send fat sparks flying across to set lively blazes in the States. At such secondary fires Old Brown's backers heated their romantic self-righteousness red-hot.

The British kept their men and ships pretty well out of slave smuggling. So did the Dutch. The French record was cleaner than the American. The Portuguese and Spanish clearly showed that their antislaving laws were the perfunctory result of Britain's bribing or bullying them into conforming. But in the year of the *Amistad* the Americans could look for relief from national shame only to the callous opportunism of Brazil and the colonial Spanish in Cuba—and to the Guinea "kings" who protested shrilly when European nations sought to wipe out their main sources of revenue and prestige.

British and American outlawry of the Trade came in the middle of the intensive privateering of the Napoleonic wars. Then after Waterloo, Latin-American revolutionary governments commissioned many privateers under even looser controls. For centuries "privateer" and "slaver" had been almost synonymous. Particularly in Caribbean and Latin-American contexts "pirate" was a ready third. It was mere realism when, in 1820, the States made slave trading equivalent to piracy, thus invoking the death penalty. As the shape of the post-1815 Trade emerged from the fogs of war and the maneuvering of diplomacy, Atlantic ports both sides of the water in both hemispheres contained plenty of tough old salts with few scruples and long experience in taking large risks for high stakes.

The same circumstances furnished the right ships for slave smuggling—speedy, slick-handling, raking-sparred former privateers: "some of the most beautiful and . . . fastest ships that ever cruised deep water under sail," wrote the late Fletcher Pratt. ". . . flimsily built but they were not expected to last long, and lightness meant more speed . . . beyond anything the Royal Navy possessed or had seen. They could sift through a blockade like smoke, eat right into the wind's eye, and outrun anything." Since short voyages meant lower ratio of slave loss, speed had always been a point. It was more so when slavers were outlaws liable to seizure by men-of-war on antislaving patrol. Early slave smuggling saw famous American privateers from the War of 1812—the *Commodore Perry,* the *Commodore McDonogh,* the *Argus,* the *Criterion*—back at sea in the black ivory trade. True to their aggressive traditions they were like as not to fight when inescapably involved with patrolling men-of-war. But their successors, just as beautifully built but nothing like so heavily armed, the rakish "Baltimore clipper" schooners, brigantines and brigs, trusted to chicanery and speed without often burning powder.

Opponents of outlawing the Trade argued early that it made illicit slaving inevitable, and that delays while await-ing opportunity to land "hot" cargoes would increase the slaves' hardships.[2] Modern apologists for the Trade—there have actually been some—contend that its bad name came not so much from pre-1808 horrors as from far worse over-crowding occasioned by the "sharp" lines and higher risks necessary to illicit slavers. The point has little merit. True, the stench and squalor belowdecks in post-1808 slavers were appalling, as nauseated naval officers frequently testified.

Extreme instances were much publicized: Here were seventy-odd Negroes stacked like cordwood in a decked boat of ten tons; slaves illicitly stowed in a Spanish ship were never once allowed on deck from West Africa to Cadiz to Havana . . . But such stowage had long been common in the Indian Ocean slave trade, and the general transatlantic ratio of slaves-per-ton was no higher in 1850 than in 1750.[3] The famous slave smuggler *Wanderer,* of which more later, was about as large as the *Brooks* of Liverpool, cited as typical slaver by British antislaveryites in the 1780's; yet the Liver-pool Guineaman carried substantially larger numbers of slaves than the *Wanderer* ever did.[4] "The old slave traders," says a recent authority, "had nothing to learn in the art of packing," and the sharp-built smuggler's speed might often shorten the slaves' ordeal. Nevertheless accurate reports of how illicit slavers crammed the Negroes were horrible enough from any absolute point of view and greatly en-couraged antislavery sentiment right up to the Civil War.

Sentiment building up to Harpers Ferry was further inflamed by widespread belief that Dixie was a principal customer of the slave smuggler. This was unjust. There had always been some leakage, of course. While Florida was Spanish alien Negroes were run through the swamps into Georgia. Salt-water gangsters like the Lafittes filtered slaves in via the Gulf of Mexico. Others operated a Guinea-style slave depot on Amelia Island at the northwest corner of Florida until Federal forces wiped it out. But no such early development became permanent. In 1859, in fact, two slaves fresh-smuggled from Africa were shown as curiosities at the South Carolina State Fair—good proof that such Negroes were rarities.

As the 1860's neared, however, Abolitionists' suspicions became acute because certain Southern leaders openly advocated reopening the licit Trade. They founded an "African Labor Supply Association" and encouraged local pro-Trade organizations like the "Congo Club" of Port Gibson, Miss. Their avowed purpose was to consolidate Southern feeling against Abolitionism by increasing supply and lowering cost of slaves to where every Southern white man could afford at least one—for, as "the peculiar institution" had worked out, slaveholders were embarrassingly in the minority in their own region. Thus encouraged, loud hotheads began to run in conspicuous cargoes of bootlegged slaves—how many cannot be known, of course. Stephen A. Douglas saw some hundreds at Vicksburg and Natchez and guessed that 15,000 had been imported in 1859. This implied thirty or forty largish ships landing full cargoes—which may well be high. Yet Southern big talk really had begotten a miniature boom in slave smuggling further stimulated by the disgraceful lightness of penalties imposed on slavers caught. Whatever the precise facts, the South defiantly played up successful landings, which further agitated Yankees already convinced that most slaveowners were Simon Legrees. The North took it that Dixie was set on legal or, if necessary, illegal retraction of one of the two great steps that the United States had managed to take against slavery.[5]

The high visibility of smuggled "salt-water niggers," as their American-born cousins called them, would have caused talk anyway. On an Alabama River steamboat in 1861 an English reporter saw a Negro slave with teeth filed to points and initiation scars on his chest, obviously a born African; his owner had taught him to claim to be Carolina-born, for the slaves of the Carolina rice swamps were reputed to be most like African savages. The same was alleged of a batch of fresh-landed Africans passing through Atlanta.

A most notorious smuggling success was that of the aforesaid yacht *Wanderer* under the colors of the New York Yacht Club. "To hear [James G. Baylis, her builder] tell it," said an old-timer, ". . . you'd think she could fly instead of sailing." She was sold when still new to one W. G. Corrie, fronting for a syndicate of unscrupulous Southerners but elected to the Club as owner of one of the finest vessels in the squadron. In her as supercargo he shipped "Captain" Egbert Farnum, a veteran of William Walker's malodorous filibusterings in Nicaragua; tanks for 12,000 gallons of water; and clearance papers for a pleasure cruise to Trinidad. Actually she crossed the Atlantic, picked up 400-odd "prime" Congo slaves and landed them on one of the Sea Islands of Georgia.

Most of the Negroes were probably disposed of there. But a river steamer sneaked 150 of them up the Savannah at night under the guns of a Federal fort in which (says legend, doubtless well founded) C. A. L. Lamar, chief of the syndicate, had arranged a timely party to distract the attention of the garrison. "Pitchfork Ben" Tillman once boasted that his folks bought thirty of these raw Africans. The end of the caper shows the Buchanan administration's cold neglect of anti-Trade laws and bore out Lamar's assurance to a Spanish operator interested in an illicit slaving scheme: "the authorities will take no pains to look after anything of the kind, yet, if it is brought to their attention, they will be bound to notice and prosecute . . . One thing is certain. Nothing can be done in the way of conviction . . ." Though the *Wanderer* was brought to the attention of Uncle Sam, the two owners arrested were freed on inadequate bond and disappeared. She was seized and sold at auction, but to a front for Lamar at merely nominal value. The heaviest penalty that anybody incurred was the expulsion of Corrie from the New York Yacht Club.[6]   Within a few months Lamar[7] refitted the *Wanderer* under a Captain Martin ostensibly to carry coolies from China to the West Indies. Her real purpose was known only to owner and skipper. Officers and hands seem to have signed on anticipating a legitimate voyage. But one day Martin suddenly got all available supplies quickly on board and, as night fell, put to sea—without clearance papers or charts, in such a hurry that some of the crew's chests were left ashore and two boatmen bringing the supercargo on board were carried off willy-nilly. A display of Martin's pistols quelled protests. Under persuasion of rum and the same pistols all hands presently signed fresh articles for a voyage to Africa for what Martin called "blackbirds." [8] Lamar complained for the record that Martin had "stolen" his ship and "undoubtedly gone to Africa for a cargo of negroes . . ." All very clever but Martin made a grave error: He failed to reconcile his ship's company to the voyage. Between the Azores and the Cape Verdes the ship met a French vessel which he boarded to buy provisions. The moment he was up the Frenchman's side, the *Wanderer's* first mate cracked on sail, took the ship back across the Atlantic and turned her over to Federal authorities. Condemned as a slaver, she became a revenue cutter out of Pensacola, then was sold into the Honduras coconut trade and met her death on a Caribbean reef. The fate of smart Captain Martin is unknown.

The very last ship to smuggle Africans into the States was

probably Captain William Foster's fast schooner *Clotilda* of Mobile, chartered in 1860 by certain local steamboat men who had made a heavy bet they could get away with a slaving venture. With a crew of Northern seamen she sailed for West Africa ostensibly to trade rum, dry goods, salt beef and flour for palm oil and other local produce. Twice she easily outran inquisitive Portuguese naval patrols. The U. S. Consul in the Cape Verdes was tactfully slack about asking questions. At Whydah, still a slaving center, Foster bought 130 slaves for $16,000 worth of merchandise but got to sea with only 116 because two men-of-war hove in sight while he was loading and he had to run for it. Entering the Gulf of Mexico, he altered the ship's rig to disguise her as a sluggish coaster. A steamboat took the Negroes up the Alabama River for disposal; the beautiful *Clotilda* was scuttled and burned; her backers presumably collected their bets and a profit on the cargo; and the crew were sent back North to scatter, so any tales told out of school would be difficult to confirm.[9] As some of the Negroes were being marched inland from the steamboat for sale, a traveling circus came along. The slaves were hustled into the woods for concealment, squatted with their backs to the road. The circus had an elephant which, maybe smelling these nearby but invisible strangers, flung up its trunk and trumpeted—at which utterly familiar sound the poor black exiles wailed and wept, shouting in their own language: "Elephant! Home! Home!"

They all came of the same upcountry people and stood out the rest of their days among the Alabama-born Negroes who, they thought, were disgracefully dirty by West African standards. After freedom some of them bought land and set up a West African-style village with its own leaders and discipline, flogging conspicuously included.

". . . and many an eye has danced to see
    That banner in the sky!"
                                —HOLMES, Old Ironsides

The *Wanderer* and *Clotilda* had a savor of amateurism, smuggling slaves as much for proslavery propaganda as for profit; whereas the backers of other illicit slavers were as professional as brothel keepers, often Latin-Americans with Norto-Americano fronts. In 1859, for instance, the estate of John McDonogh, New Orleans philanthropist, was obliged to free forty-odd Negroes and send them to the West African free Negro colony of Liberia. The annual Liberian emigrant ship from Baltimore would not leave for months. The owners of the *Rebecca,* a 500-ton Baltimore clipper registered out of New Orleans, offered her for charter to transport the Negroes directly and comfortably at a very low cost. So it was arranged. The *Rebecca* shipped as doctor a young medical student named Howe, eager for an adventure, and sailed with the emigrants, their bulky outfits of tools and supplies, two Spanish passengers Congo-bound and a cargo of trade goods belonging to them.

As Dr. Howe told it thirty years later the adventure part began very soon: The mate informed him that the ship was a slaver running Negroes into Cuba against both Spanish and American law; the Spanish "passengers" were her actual owners and the Liberian errand was only a blind to secure clearance; and the doctor could count on handsome rewards for keeping his mouth shut. Anguished protests finally secured him permission to quit the ship at the mouth of the Congo River to pick up a British mail steamer home. Nearing Liberia the *Rebecca* was overhauled by HMS *Viper* on antislaving patrol. Her commander, obviously alerted about the *Rebecca*'s character, was highly annoyed to find her on so openly innocent a mission that he dared not detain her. Once the emigrants were landed, the Spaniards took over command and signed the ship's company—except Howe, he implied—to new articles at wages highly eloquent of how extremely well slave smuggling paid: captain and mate $5000 each for the voyage; second mate $3500; carpenter $3000; seamen $1500 each.[10] After certain delays the ship entered the Congo, the destination specified in her papers, to feel things out and, if possible, get "slaved."

Most inopportunely here was HMS *Tigris* prowling up, also well alerted and setting her longboat to keep round-the-clock watch on the *Rebecca*. Then came a Portuguese cruiser—even less welcome, for Portugal had recently acquired a nasty habit of sending slavers to her notoriously brutal penal colonies. HMS *Vixen* and USS *Vincennes,* a ship noted for speed, were rumored to be in the vicinity—altogether too much patrol vessel thereabouts. The *Rebecca*'s captain let the hovering *Tigris* know that trade was miserably slow and he was going home disconsolate—dropped the *Rebecca* downriver unslaved and put to sea on an ostentatiously northwest course.

Once well over the horizon, the ship was brought to, stripped of all identifying marks, painted black for disguise and sailed back to land well south of the Congo for a prearranged quick "slaving" and getaway. She shipped almost 1200 Negroes, two-thirds males, some children included—no great overcrowding as practice went, and no unusual mortality resulted. As the last were coming on board the *Vixen* hove in view and stood in eagerly for the kill. For her this was a pretty sight: a large notorious slaver likely to bring her captors £2-3000 in prize money and maybe £5000 head money.[11] Warning shots were ignored, so the *Vixen* opened fire in good earnest at long range. But the *Rebecca* got smartly under way, got to sea unscathed and—Baltimore-built, she could do fourteen knots to windward—

readily shook off pursuit. The homeward voyage was un-
eventful. The Negroes were landed on a small island off
Cuba for the great, quasi-official black market for slaves, the
ship was scuttled and burned and that was that; only young
Howe never did explain why he failed to quit her when she
reached the Congo.

This reticence does not impugn his veracity on most
points. This voyage epitomized slave smuggling as it flourished in the year of Harpers Ferry: The big, fast American-
built ship. A few venal Yankees in the crew but mostly skim-
mings from all over: Turks, Scots, Greeks, Danes, Italians,
Spaniards—"the matured villainy of the world," said a U. S.
Navy commander of the period. United States registry
masking actual Latin-American ownership. Much hide-and-
seek with antislaving patrol ships. Cuba as market . . . The
non-typical detail is the *Rebecca*'s fitting out in New Orleans. Occasionally illicit slavers did hail from there, or Boston, Portland, Salem or Philadelphia. But more and more
New York City came to dominate this racket, furnishing
ships, navigators and trade goods—and, as time passed, putting ever larger minority capital into it well hidden under
layers of subterfuge, the profits duly winging back into the
tills of respectable merchants with offices on William
Street.[12] In the twenty months ending August, 1860, a good
hundred slavers were known to have sailed from New York
harbor.

Such wholesale effrontery becomes more credible when
one knows of cases like that of the *Mary Ann.* In 1848 this
American ship sailed on an ostensibly legal voyage to West
Africa in the growing palm-oil trade. Apparently her crew
were unaware that anything else was in the wind. On her arrival off the Gallinas, a notorious slaving area, however, her
real mission grew obvious. The mates and crew, who wanted
no part of it, left the captain ashore and took the ship on
down the Coast in search of a U. S. Navy antislaving cruiser
to turn her over to. Finding no such thing in the period

allowed by the ship's stores, they took her home, surrendered her to Federal authorities—and as reward for having behaved so scrupulously well, found themselves facing charges of mutiny. The courts held leniently that they had had "probable cause for the arrest" of the ship and let them off with no heavier penalty than forfeit of their wages for both outward and homeward voyages—a remarkable example of getting things by the wrong end and of how Federal shore functionaries usually enforced antislaving statutes with the hand of putty in the velvet glove. Ships caught red-handed might be condemned and sold but, as in the *Wanderer* case, the buyer would be a front for the original owner and, for all the law's big talk of piracy and hanging, the ship's company probably never saw the inside of a jail longer than was needed to raise lowish bail promptly forfeited.

This laxity even smirched the U.S. Navy. It is clear in the foregoing tales that, whereas the Royal Navy was always popping up at awkward seasons, Uncle Sam's antislaving patrols were scarce off West Africa. This was less the U. S. Navy's than the politicians' fault. But in any case it allowed the Stars and Stripes to become the handiest of all the slave-smuggler's bag of tricks. The reasons for the politicians' gingerliness were either discreditable or wrongheaded. Because the insurgent American colonies had feared increasing numbers of alien Negroes—and because many of the founding fathers personally deplored slavery—the Constitution of 1787 specifically opened the way to Federal exclusion of the overseas slave trade from American ports and ships in 1808. In 1807 the indicated law passed. No more acknowledged slavers cleared from Newport or Charleston; only now and again a Yankee ship was taken into Halifax by a British cruiser and condemned as a disguised slaver. In 1807 Britain had passed parallel legislation in order to cut off the supply of African Negroes to the British West Indies. No more acknowledged slavers cleared from Liverpool or Bristol, and the Royal Navy saw to it that few British ships ever got into illicit slaving. But half a dozen other national merchant marines remained unaffected by British or American laws. If Britain wished slaving banished from the high seas—the avowed purpose of many supporting the legislation of 1808 —she had to force or persuade all those other powers to suppress slave trading after her example. Otherwise slavers under non-British flags would continue to pour Negroes into the non-British West Indies and Latin America, where slavery still flourished, and also effect some smuggling into the United States and the British West Indies.

So, in tidying up after Waterloo, Britain attacked the Trade with two weapons: pressure on all nations to prohibit it; and, for enforcement, treaties of "reciprocal search-and-seizure." That is, the Dutch, say, agreed that thenceforth Royal Navy vessels could stop and examine Dutch vessels on suspicion of slaving and, if evidence warranted, seize them for condemnation before courts representing both flags. Dutch men-of-war could do the same to British ships but actually, the Royal Navy being far larger than any other after 1815, and Britain being the only great power consistently severe toward slavers, a system of such treaties actually turned antislaving patrol over to the British.

As the Baltic and Latin-American states fell in line, slavers could no longer hide behind their flags. France long resisted such agreement and the French flag, in licit as well as illicit use, covered much slaving out of Nantes, La Rochelle and heaven knows where else. In 1831, however, Louis Philippe's new-born government accepted reciprocal search. The slavers shifted to Spanish registry. When Spain allowed Britain to bribe her into nominal compliance, they went to Portuguese registry. For a while Portugal managed to retain international countenance for the lively slave trade south of the equator between Angola and Brazil. But between 1839 and 1845 high-handed if high-minded British action against slavers under both the Portuguese and the new Brazilian flags brought into the British antislaving system all sizable maritime powers—except the United States.

Had Uncle Sam signed up, the slavers would have had nowhere to turn. But Uncle Sam held out—and the Stars and Stripes remained the last refuge of slaver scoundrels until the Civil War broke out. Like the converted privateers and their unsavory crews, this stiff-neckedness was a relic of the Napoleonic wars. In coping with Boney Britain had ruthlessly abused the belligerent's right of search, which became the outstanding cause of the foolish little War of 1812. American skippers bitterly resented Britain's Orders in Council[13] enforcing on neutrals British notions of permissible cargoes, and Royal Navy captains inspecting Yankee vessels for contraband had a nasty habit of impressing seamen on the grounds—valid sometimes but not always—that they were renegade British subjects. Memories of it all long survived the war and doomed any proposals to let the Royal Navy inspect American vessels for the slave smuggling that most Americans, North or South, deplored. Once, in 1824, reciprocal right of search, modified to suit American sensitivity, seemed possible. Britain had agreed to follow the American lead in declaring the Trade piracy; to send seized slavers into American ports for adjudication in American courts; and to forbid her naval commanders to remove a man from a searched ship under any circumstances. It was the fairest treaty ever drawn up. But certain rabble-rousing politicians eager to succeed Monroe as president made such effective appeals to mistrust of Britain that the Senate insisted on amendments unacceptable to the long-patient British.

It was a great day for slavers. Cuba was demanding ever more Negroes to be worked to death on sugar plantations. Though Spain presently abolished the Trade and agreed to reciprocal search, the pace of importation hardly slackened as *Rebecca*-style smuggling flourished. In too many ports U.S. consuls failed to ask searching questions as to the actual ownership of vessels claiming a right to fly the American flag. Cuban authorities looked the other way in return for so much graft per slave illicitly landed. The commissioners of the Spanish-British court set up at Havana to adjudicate slave ships brought in by British antislaving patrols used to draw straws for the cases. It was taken for granted that any ship the Spaniard drew, however strong the evidence, would be released. The Queen of Spain had a financial interest in slavers violating her own laws.

The swift clipper built for slaving might be taken to Havana by American crews and sold to Cuban smugglers, maybe on a profit-sharing basis; or retain American registry and sail for West Africa also carrying Spanish supercargoes, spare Spanish crew and bogus Spanish papers. If challenged by a British man-of-war on the outward voyage, she ran up American colors and was usually left unsearched, since Royal Navy officers were personally liable for damages if they guessed wrong and stopped American ships that they could not quite prove were slavers. Arrived on the Coast, she got "slaved," the Spaniards took over, the Americans in turn became passengers, and she made the homeward voyage as a Spaniard though still likely to hoist the Stars and Stripes to discourage Britons. The game developed curious ramifications,[14] but throughout the slaver sheltered pretty confidently under Old Glory. He risked only mistaking a U. S. Navy cruiser for a Briton—unlikely since Uncle Sam had few ships off West Africa—or encountering a British commander so confident that he would risk going behind the American flag to investigate.

The results of such chance-taking could be extremely gratifying. In 1839 the Baltimore-built but Havana-owned slaver *Catharine,* nearing West Africa, was chased by HMS *Dolphin.* Unable to shake her pursuer after two hours, she hoisted American colors. The commander of the *Dolphin,* for some reason sure of the character of the chase, stuck to her and opened fire. Hove to and searched, she proved to have on board cooking arrangements for 300 persons; planks marked and numbered for a half deck for slaves to lie on; 570 wooden spoons and 175 pairs of handcuffs. In the American captain's pocket were written hints how to convince boarding officers that his Spanish and Portuguese shipmates were passengers and his handful of American seamen his entire crew. He was keeping one log in English, one in Spanish to match his two sets of papers and flags. Ingenious but futile—a prize crew of *Dolphin*'s took the *Catharine* into New York and a Federal court condemned her. But this was exceptional. The usual thing was the freeing of the American slaver brig *Tigris,* sent home for condemnation by HMS *Water Witch,* because, said the court, the British prize crew had no standing in the matter, "being incapacitated by a wrongful exercise of the right of search."

The most edifying exception was the hard luck of Captain Sylvanus Gordon of Portland, Maine, in 1860. Chased by a man-of-war steamer off West Africa, he apparently assumed she was British, so he ran up the Stars and Stripes. The stranger was actually USS *Mohican,* which poured on more coal and soon had a boat's crew of Gordon's countrymen on board his ship. "Found her to be the ship Erie of New York," says the faded entry in the *Mohican*'s log, "without papers or any person claiming to be captain, and with 893 slaves on board, having a mixed crew of Spaniards, Americans and Frenchmen." Gordon had evidently followed the slave-smuggler's known practice of throwing the ship's papers overboard at the last minute to confuse the issue of jurisdiction. His officers swore that one Manuel had been in charge. But several seamen testified that Gordon had given the orders as the *Erie* got to sea after "slaving" . . . Eventually his wrong guess as to the nationality of that man-of-war steamer made him the first Yankee skipper ever hanged for slaving. It was high time. The statute equating piracy and slaving had been in force forty-one years and violated daily.[15]

As the American flag lent slavers protection so long and well, the outside world naturally assumed that this suited Uncle Sam. The involvement of Stateside shipbuilders and the growing amount of American capital behind Cuban slave-grown sugar lent the assumption weight even before New York's slaving boom of the 1850's. Uncle Sam's case had logic: He maintained that, in the old rural phrase, every nation should skin its own skunks; that only its own men-of-war should examine and seize its slave-smuggling ships, thus discouraging fraudulent use of its flag without giving other nations undue privileges. Had all navies been as large as the Royal Navy, had all governments been equally hot against slaving, this might have made sense. But what with piracy to combat in the West Indies and growing concerns in the Pacific the U. S. Navy could never, even with all the will in the world, have kept British-scale strength on the West African station. The only possible way to stop slavers' abuse of the Stars and Stripes was to allow the British the right of search—and Washington would never hear of that.

Year in and year out the Royal Navy struggled gamely against the advantages that American stubbornness gave to slavers. Prize and head money for the crews of vessels taking slavers stimulated zeal. But they also gave rise to charges of venality: British patrols, it was alleged, stood callously by while ships "slaved" so that, when overhauled at sea, they would be prizes worth taking. This was inevitable when the actual presence of slaves on board was needed to prove a ship a slaver. The remedy was the "equipment clause"—a provision in British treaties with other maritime nations permitting seizure of ships carrying most of the things that slavers usually needed, whether or not slaves were actually found at the time of search. Critical data included implausibly copious stocks of rice, beans or other known slave staples; too much water or too many casks clean enough to stow it; extra-large hatchways fitted with gratings for ventilating slave decks; stocks of chains, leg irons . . . Such common-sense evidence was sometimes admitted even in American courts:[16] remember the *Catherine*'s over-ample cooking facilities and stocks of spoons and handcuffs.

Slavers sometimes tried to pass as whalers or palm-oil traders. Either mission explained large numbers of casks or staves to make them—one of the telltale items—and represented the big cooking coppers as whaler's trypots for rendering blubber. But all-round pretense was difficult. Once this principle of circumstantial evidence was widely accepted, the fast-stepping, overmanned, polyglot ship unable to give a good account of herself was in far hotter water than before. After 1840, in fact, the "equipment clause" bit so deep that wary slavers ceased to ship slave irons—worst telltale of all. Instead they trussed up the Negroes in a much crueler fashion—with rope yarns prepared from cordage by the crew during the outward passage.

Wariest of all was Captain Cyrus Libby of Maine, master of the brig *Porpoise,* which made three slaving voyages as nominal property of Brazilians but showed American colors and American papers, captain and crew whenever it suited her game. On her last voyage she had no slave on board— merely pimped for the American-built *Kentucky,* which actually loaded the slaves at Inhambane on the East African coast.[17] That is, the *Porpoise* fetched thither a Brazilian supercargo, a spare Brazilian crew and trade goods to swap for slaves. At the rendezvous the goods were landed and the Brazilians changed places with the American crew who had sailed the *Kentucky* out. The two ships then went home in company, the *Kentucky* under Brazilian colors with papers and crew to match—and a full cargo of slaves—the *Porpoise* playing all-American but prepared to hoist a provocative flag and ostensibly try to run for it to decoy any patrol ship away from the actual slave carrier. USS *Raritan* seized her while cutting such capers in 1855. And in spite of all Captain Libby's 'cuteness, the judge condemned her exactly as if she had had on board every kind of equipment known to slaving.

British and American naval officers usually got on well as their paths crossed on the West African station. Their common distaste for the abuse of American colors suggested "joint cruising"—hunting in couples, HMS *Towser* co-operating with USS *Jonathan*. This was poison for slavers. Show American colors and *Jonathan* pounced. Show any other flag conceivable in West African waters and *Towser* fired the "Heave to!" gun. Show no colors and both ships treated you as presumed pirate without any national registry. In 1840 Lieutenant Paine of USS *Grampus* signed a joint-cruising agreement with the Royal Navy base at Sierra Leone, and officers who knew West Africa besought the U. S. Navy Department to authorize and recommend joint cruising in standing orders to its antislaving squadron. In view of the mutual respect between *Towser* and *Jonathan,* the two services might well have eliminated slaving in five years if given their heads. But Washington apparently felt either that dignity forbade acting as junior partner to John Bull or that a scheme so obviously hostile to slavery was an affront to Southern constituents. In any case joint cruising was frowned on—another great day for slavers.

Now and again, and much to his credit, some American commander dabbled in collaboration with the Royal Navy without bringing down on himself rebuke from on high. Thus in 1845 USS *Truxtun,* Commander Bruce, sent two cutters and twenty-seven men to help boats from HMS *Ardent,* Commander Russell, harry the slaving nests up the River Pongo. While the two ships waited the *Truxtun* made no objection as the *Ardent* fired at an American brigantine to bring her to for search; in fact, the formal search was carried out by both commanders arm in arm. Then out of the river came the American slaver schooner *Spitfire* as prize to the *Truxtun's* cutters and the Spanish slaver brig *Dos Hermanos* as prize to the *Ardent's* boats—both caught red-handed, or perhaps black-handed is better. The *Ardent,* a steamer, towed the prizes and *Truxtun* in a string to

Sierra Leone. A prize crew took the *Spitfire* to the States.[18] All efficient and internationally cozy—a tantalizing example of how much fear of God could have been thrown into slavers if only Uncle Sam had seen fit to honor his commitments.

Some hope of better things had come in 1842 when Daniel Webster and Lord Ashburton sat down to settle matters in issue between Britain and the States. The Webster-Ashburton Treaty failed to mention joint cruising, but did bind the States as well as Britain to keep on the West African station a patrol squadron mounting at least eighty guns. This sounded good but several details were wrong: It should have stipulated number of men-of-war, not of guns. A slaver knuckled under to an eight-gun sloop as readily as to a forty-four-gun frigate. Ten such sloops or small schooners could cover five times as much coast as the two frigates that would meet the gun requirement. The U. S. West African Squadron usually wasted much tonnage in heavy frigates, and never exceeded seven vessels. And number of vessels *actually on patrol* should also have been stipulated. The U.S. ships based on Porto Praya in the Cape Verdes, 2000-odd miles of uncertain sailing from the slaving nests in the Bights; 800-odd from the minor nuisance area of the Gallinas. Under an unusually brisk commander USS *Truxtun* cruised her station only 181 days as opposed to 152 in port and 135 to and fro. USS *Mohican,* under a most energetic commodore, had 118 days in port to 157 on station. The Royal Navy got much more use out of ships based on either Sierra Leone, next door to the Gallinas, or Fernando Po, right in the heart of the Bights.

But the worst of it was, to put it bluntly, Uncle Sam's bad faith. His West African Squadron often slipped below the eighty-gun total.[19] The growing unwillingness of Southern politicians to see any aspect of slavery slowed down encouraged the Navy Department to drag its feet. Ships went home before their relief, sailing tardily from Brooklyn or Charlestown, had arrived. When steam took to sea, the Royal Navy learned and proclaimed that steamers, able to overhaul the fastest clippers in uncertain airs or calms, were highly useful in antislaving work. But it was fifteen years before the U. S. Navy sent steamers after slavers. Its ships off West Africa were ordered primarily to support the American-founded Negro colony of Liberia and protect American trade, with slaver-hunting secondary. In 1860 Commodore Inman, USN, reported drily that "the African Squadron, under my command, has performed its whole duty . . . in the face of positive discouragement from the Department." A disgusted young officer operating under a less dynamic commodore called this duty "sending a squadron of gallant ships to chase shadows in a deadly climate."

American policy sometimes looked like positive sabotage of British antislaving effort. In 1841 Lewis Cass, eminent American politician then minister to France, openly plumed himself on having persuaded the French not to renew reciprocal right of search, instead to adopt the feckless American system of policing slavers under one's own flag exclusively.[20] The French West African Squadron, larger than the American but capturing fewer slavers, thus became principally a chaperone for French commerce and a needless flaw in the system that Britain had so doggedly constructed.

Flag wavers like Cass chose to ignore what all concerned knew or could have known: that all the while Uncle Sam resisted British examination of ships under American colors, his own men-of-war were stopping and examining ships of other nations, Britain included, whenever they saw fit. A few days before joining in the Pongo raid, USS *Truxtun* had boarded two English vessels, the second under the ruse of showing British colors.[21] Just before capturing the *Erie,* USS *Mohican* had boarded a Portuguese brig, a Hamburg barque and a British brig. The logs of USS *United States* and *Boxer* in 1846 show such boardings of British, French, Genoese, Swedish and Italian ships. Uncle Sam merely changed the subject when British diplomats mentioned such matters. Soulsby, an expert in this field, well says: "Rather than consent to the slightest diminution of its rights . . . the United States elected to maintain the full freedom of the seas. The policy would have been happier in a nation whose flag was not abused to cover traffic which it had denounced as piracy . . . Doctrinaire ideals may be upheld at too great a cost; and the trans-atlantic slave trade, which vigorous combined action would have exterminated in a few years, was prolonged far into the nineteenth century."

"*The unweary, unostentatious and inglorious crusade of England against slavery may probably be regarded as among the three or four perfectly virtuous pages in the history of nations.*"
                                                    —W. H. LECKY

While the French coolly withdrew co-operation and the States played seadog-in-the-manger, His and presently Her Majesty's schooners, sloops, brigs, corvettes and frigates stubbornly maintained good faith afloat.

The indicated tints are not all rosy. The Admiralty was not as consistently zealous in the good cause as were the imaginative politicians, such as Palmerston and Russell, who insisted that HMS *Towser* stay on antislaving patrol. Between 1808 and the 1830's the "Preventive Squadron" off West Africa was hampered by vacillations from on high, ships unsuited to the work and inability to apply the equipment clause to Spanish and Portuguese vessels; and up to 1861 by the demands of the Crimean War and home attacks on the Squadron as ineffective and on its personnel as venal and irresponsible. Some of its officers and ratings did not feel strongly about slaving one way or the other, and few could like the West African station for its own sake. But the operation was sound at bottom. Whatever the private sentiments of Commander Brass and Able Seaman Binnacle, they almost always carried out their orders with a will. In 1822 HMS *Snapper* set an early record by capturing twenty-eight slavers in three months. Twenty-five years later HMS *Prometheus* nabbed forty within a month. And many commanders showed great dash and ingenuity in hacking away at slaving's hydra-heads—often at considerable risk to their own pockets as well as persons.

The flavor of these unsung Hornblowers comes out well in a grim farce—with a sour ending—staged before equipment clauses existed by Commander Meredith of HMS *Pelorus*. Watching a slaver at New Calabar, he duly gave chase when she sailed. She dodged back before he could close with her, and hastily sent her cargo ashore. Since he could seize her only if she actually contained slaves, he could only resume watch. Some days later she loaded again, sailed again, was pursued—and again turned back and got unloaded in time. Several more repetitions of this—by then the bewildered slaves must have been well trained in rapid disembarking—and Meredith lost patience, ordered his own men to herd the slaves back on board and then formally seized and sent ship and Negroes to Sierra Leone for adjudication. There the fun ended. The mixed court handling such cases declared the ship illegally seized and allowed damages that cost Meredith £1800—six and a half years' worth of his basic pay. Three years later the commander of HMS *Fair Rosamond* forced the owner of an empty slaver to transfer slaves into her from a consort to qualify her for seizure. This variation got him repudiation from the courts, a reprimand from his superiors and similarly heavy damages to pay.

Or consider Commander Denman of HMS *Wanderer*, who reasoned that slaving would suffer in the branches if one cut its roots—the West African slaving depots stocked with Negroes for the ships and trade goods for the "kings." In 1840 he tried the theory out in the notorious Gallinas region—seized the traders' warehouses and barracoons and offered the local "king" the whole lot of trade goods in exchange for consenting to Denman's burning the depots and taking the slaves away to freedom. I have conveyed little of the essential West Africa if anybody doubts the offer was accepted. There must have been high times as the sun-dried thatch of the barracoons blazed and crackled and the king and his henchmen went to work on the gin and gun-powder.

The approach was pellucidly unselfish. Capture of slaves ashore did not secure the *Wanderer*'s the head money paid for those taken at sea. Both Foreign and Colonial Officers endorsed it; the Admiralty commended the example to all commanders. If "kings" would always be so shortsighted—and doubtless most of them would—this clean-out-the-nests technique bade fair to smother the Trade at its source. In 1842 a Commander Matson applied it to the active slaving depots south of the equator, obtained consent of the chiefs on much the same terms, burned five barracoons and bagged 1100 slaves. That was too much for the Liverpool merchants who, though no longer slavers, still sold textiles, pottery, hardware and squareface to the polyglot ruffians of the Trade. There was outcry in Parliament about the slave-traders' sufferings, and court proceedings in their behalf against Denman the innovator. He was luckier than Mere-dith—that after-the-fact approval from his superiors was held to relieve him of personal responsibility. But due to a flaw in the wording of a crucial legal opinion it was six years before barracoon burning could be resumed to destroy the eight new ones that had sprung up in the Gallinas.

Denman's *Wanderer* was a famously fast ten-gun sloop of a new class built after 1840 specially to harass slavers. Another, HMS *Fantome*, ran down "the fastest brigantine out of Havana" after a twenty-four-hour chase. Even more famous for sailing qualities were certain slavers taken into the Royal Navy as antislaving cruisers after capture and condemnation—particularly HMS *Black Joke* and *Fair Rosamond*.[22] They were used as "tenders" to a slow, heavy frigate, returning regularly to report and take on fresh supplies much as with "mother ships" and flotillas of submarines. Before they were broken up—the *Black Joke* was beyond repair by 1832 but *Fair Rosamond* lasted until 1838— they had seen hard fighting as well as nippy sailing. Armed with only one carronade (a short-barreled gun for short-range smashing power) and a long eighteen-pounder amidships, the *Black Joke* beat a fourteen-gun slaver in an eighty-minute engagement—one of the few occasions when a slaver showed fight against a man-of-war.[23] Two such former slavers actually got back into slaving, being sold by the Royal Navy after a couple of years service as tenders, bought in by enterprising West African Portuguese and used again in their old profession. To prevent that sort of thing the British presently instituted a policy of burning or breaking up any slaver prizes likely to be useful in the Trade if bought in by fronts for slavers.

The advent of man-of-war steamers not only made slaving more hazardous[24] but also reduced mortality among the cargoes seized. The time that a prize crew required to work a captured slave ship all the way to Sierra Leone against prevailing winds was often longer than was normally expected in the Middle Passage. The fact of capture did not increase the ship's supply of food, water or cubic feet per Negro, so this probably meant more dead slaves, no matter how humane the prize crew. A prize of *Fair Rosamond*'s, for instance, lost half her slaves *en route* to Sierra Leone. In another case 110 died in a six weeks' voyage, in another 120 in eleven weeks. Sir Charles Hotham set average mortality during post-capture voyages at 9 per cent as opposed to 5 per cent in the Middle Passage. In 1828 HMS *North Star,* Captain Arabia, captured the slaver *Veloz*[25] in mid-Atlantic with 517 slaves obviously bound for an illegal destination. She had to be let go because her water supply, though adequate for making the West Indies, would never have kept her cargo alive to Sierra Leone. Had the *North Star* been a steamer she could have towed her prize into Sierra Leone in a reasonable time in defiance of wind and currents, saving many lives, much head money—twice as high for slaves landed alive—and making sure that help was at hand if the prize crew had trouble on board.

That too was a consistent hazard. Prize crews—say, a midshipman and eight or nine bluejackets—were necessarily outnumbered by their slaver prisoners, and further hampered by the presence of several hundred Negroes just as likely to mutiny as before the ship changed command. These black upcountry victims of cupidity saw little to choose among seagoing white men and to them the long beat to Sierra Leone was just another unexplained calamity. It speaks well for the prize crews that they usually made port uneventfully. In a grim exception of 1845 fourteen of the captive crew of the seized slaver *Felicidade* rose on their ten captors and killed them all. The ship was retaken and a British court convicted the killers of murder but an appeal set them free on the grounds that the original seizure had been technically illegal. Even in the hundreds of cases where all went well, there was the nagging toil and discomfort of working to windward shorthanded, the stench from belowside daily richer, the corpses hauled out from among the half-alive daily more numerous—and at the end of it all the humid slatternliness of Sierra Leone.

In spite of impressions then current, West African duty was not necessarily lethal. Ships staying well offshore—as the U.S. Navy usually did, the Royal Navy often—were inadvertently out of range of the local mosquitoes, hence of yellow fever[26] and malaria. But ships watering and wooding at the British bases at Sierra Leone or Fernando Po (a high island in the bend of the Bights) had serious trouble. The commandant at Fernando Po, it was said, permanently divided his force into two details: one to make coffins, the

other to dig graves. A zealous commander sending boats'
crews to cut out a slaver or burn a barracoon risked having
half of them down with Yellow Jack within a few days of
their return.

After 1840 minor miseries were added to these major
risks by "inshore blockade" tactics developed by Denman
and others. These anchored Preventive Squadron vessels
close inshore within signal of one another off notorious
slaving depots, thereby increasing the chances of seizing in-
bound slavers under the equipment clause and reducing outbound slavers' chances of slipping out to sea late in the day
when the land breeze was making and the cruiser could not
get within range before dark. The system was the despair
of the slave-raiding "king" and the illicit trader—but also
miserable for the man-of-war's crew. Preventive Squadron
vessels were usually small—hardly the size of a modern seagoing tug—and ungodly things to live in when rolling
scuppers under in the great Atlantic swell under the fiercest
of suns. Nothing to look at but the sway of the topgallant
masts against the sky and the dismal West African shore; the
whole fabric of the vessel creaking and groaning day and
night; all the ship's daily business a half-seasick bore; the
daily issue of rum the one event . . . These men earned the
monetary rewards that, in spite of its drawbacks, kept this station popular among the ratings.

In spite of skilful abuse of the American flag "inshore
blockade" almost stifled the Trade to Cuba out of the Gallinas and the River Pongo and kept the Angola traffic within
bounds, if not decent ones. Thanks largely to the Royal
Navy, within a generation of Waterloo export slaving was
largely dead along 1500 miles of coast between the Senegal
and the Volta. The British governor of the Gold Coast
could report that no slave had been shipped from a local
beach since 1830. This was implicitly confirmed by the
Ashanti's bitter protests. They felt about British outlawry of
the Trade much as Brazil would if the United States were

to declare coffee contraband.[27] As King George persisted in ignoring their demands that he reopen the Trade, their resentment expressed itself in fierce resistance to British blandishments throughout the nineteenth century. Things seldom come of single causes, of course. The rise of palm oil somewhat distracted the less shiftless local traders and the more stable "kings" from dealing in human flesh. Britain furthered this through local treaties pledging king Jocko to renounce slaving in consideration of widened opportunities for legitimate commerce—usually negotiated by those able gentlemen, the commanders of Royal Navy vessels.

Throughout their performance was very able, stubbornly decent and often hearteningly gallant. We have concentrated on the West African cruising ground but good work was also done off Brazil and in West Indian waters. In 1849 HM Steam-frigate *Rifleman,* cruising off Brazil, chased a slaver whose crew beached and abandoned her with her cargo of slaves still on board—and a fair chance she would break up in the surf. Heavy seas were breaking clean over her. Commander Crofton worked his ship in close enough to rig a hawser with the aid of which three officers and a re-enforced boat's crew, up to the waist in surging salt water, passed 127 slaves to safety on board the *Rifleman.* Before the rescuers would eat or change their clothes, they personally revived, clothed and fed the naked, half-dead Negroes. Only the most abject cynic could suggest that they did so after such ghastly risk because these scrawny blacks meant five quid apiece alive and only half that dead.

The officers and men of any U.S. Navy ship of 1840 could and no doubt would have shown equal gallantry and humanity. But USS *Jonathan* seldom had the opportunity. Whenever encountering an American man-of-war, the *Rifleman* would have been well justified—the whole Royal Navy would have been justified—in making the signal: "Where were you, brave Crillon?"

Such a situation could not be hushed up. In the 1830's the

refusal of the Federal Post Office to protect antislavery propaganda in the mails had disgusted many non-rabid anti-slaveryites as well as the zealots. Federal failure decently to prosecute slavers had the same effect. The Fugitive Slave Law of 1850 had a great share in persuading the North that the allegedly well knit "slave power" had taken over the Federal government as both weapon and shield. But the most flagrant detail, because most deliberate, after 1842 was this cynical disregard of the Navy's plain duty down in print in a treaty. The bad taste it left in the national mouth put special bite in the mingled exasperation, contempt and self-righteousness with which such as John Brown and the Six had come to view their own national government. It was not a good excuse for treason, but for people like that it was a highly welcome pretext.

5   *The curse of cane*

". . . Where every prospect pleases,
And only man is vile."

John Brown was altogether American. So were the Six and so were most Abolitionist leaders. Yet the terms in which they deplored slavery were flawed by attitudes and data unsuited to Stateside situations. Their cause was achingly good. The more one knows of Dixie's slavery, the clearer its heinousness becomes. But this slavery was not what Abolitionism based its case on. It had patterned itself too closely on the victorious British campaign against the specific hideousnesses of slavery in the West Indies in an imitation extending through diagnosis and prognosis, ideas and emotions, organization and tactics. Thus it happened that the assumptions moving that handful of men to attack Harpers Ferry belonged—so far as they touched reality at all—not in the Shenandoah Valley of 1859 but in the Jamaica, Surinam or St. Domingue of 1780. It would have been strange if their skewed filibuster had not been ill conceived.

This is an old story. We Americans may never get shut of

our colonial-mindedness. Midwestern plutocrats have ridden
to hounds over snake fences. Yankee universities have set
up undergraduate "houses" intended to bloom into Oxford-
style colleges. Manhattan finishing schools have infected
their pupils with a pseudo-British manner of speech that
makes them sound like decayed actresses. Liberals have
borrowed Fabianistic attitudes better suited to Leeds than
to Pittsburgh, and cultivated Americans have recently discussed the subtleties of British caste dialects as raptly as if
they had cut their U-teeth on them. Before that it was mass
obsession with The Coronation . . . But hands across the
sea has seldom been worse advised than on that drizzly fall
Monday in 1859. True, other, stronger forces underlay
John Brown's foray. But to understand requires awareness
of what had previously occurred in the West Indies. In
what follows, by the way, the bulk of evidence unfavorable
to slavery comes from people reconciled to or anyway not
indignant about it.

"... the Planters choose [slaves] as they do Horses in a
Market; the strongest, youthfullest, and most beautiful
yield the greatest prices ... most of them are as neer
Beastes as may be, setting their souls aside."
—RICHARD LIGON

Slavery was, after all, slavery, and racism was racism. Many
symptoms of these combined ailments were the same in the
West Indies as on the North American mainland. Dixie
and the Islands both developed laws to protect the slaves
from the sporadic tantrums or sadistic tastes of their
owners—and both honored them largely in the breach.
South Carolina's slave code of 1740, prototype of many Dixie

codes, was very like that of Barbados; but the exigencies of slave management might well have worked out such parallels without a model to follow. Both Dixie and the Islands used written passes to control slaves' movements— and in both instances the system was so ill policed that nobody had a good word for it, not even the slaves whom it restricted less than was intended. The small, sluggish, slovenly towns of both areas reflected the poor cohesion and economic backwateriness of these societies split along racial lines. Owners in both areas were too much impressed by the toadying loyalty of the house slaves close to them, and by their own notion that Negroes in general were happy, capering, grinning automata content with the lives of draft animals.

But such clinical resemblances should not blur the meaningful contrasts between the Islands and Dixie. Even the slave English of one differed from the other's. The Negroes of both came largely from the same West African stocks and heard much the same versions of English from early owners and overseers, most of them from identical strata of British society. Yet a man adept in the Negro speech of Georgia or Lowland Arkansas needs weeks or months to get the hang of what he hears from day-labor Negroes in Montserrat or Jamaica, which a Royal Navy purser described in 1722 as "a kind of Gypsey Gibberish, that runs smoothest in swearing." Consider how far the pronunciation of calypso lyrics is from the speech of either Miss Watson's Jim or Winston Churchill. The speech of West Indian whites varies to correspond. The difference is less marked now than it was one hundred fifty years ago, when the wife of a governor of Jamaica found local white ladies confusing their pronouns and slurring and slacking in the fashion of their slave servants; but the end effect is still most unlike that of the same process among the white ladies of Alabama.[1]

One difference between the two areas is so marked that it must somehow have entered into the contrasts. Both began with tobacco and eventually shifted to other dominant export crops: Dixie to short-staple cotton but the West Indies earlier and even more fatefully to sugar. Long-staple cotton, certain spices, coffee and other odd tropical crops gained footing and still persist here and there. But sugar was the economic disease that swept the arc of the Islands end to end, always leaving festering problems that defy solution even today. The Dutch brought sugar cane from Brazil to Barbados three centuries ago. Thence it infested St. Kitts and Jamaica; flared high for the French in St. Domingue; singed the Spaniards' Puerto Rico and then swept Cuba in the ruthless nineteenth-century boom that sent so many Baltimore clippers on evil African voyages. Each such conquest of these and lesser places called for more Negroes to plant, fertilize, cultivate and refine for a world with a rapidly growing number of people able to afford a sweet tooth. By the end of the 1600's these sugar-committed Islands were the main props of the Trade. The mainland British colonies' demand for Negroes—satisfied by the cargoes of small slavers supplemented by "refuse" unsalable in the Islands —could never have made slaving the key industry it was in Benezet's time, when France and Britain took their West Indian holdings more seriously than they did any mainland possessions. Britain once considered equating acquisition of the small but rich sugar island of Martinique with return of all Canada to France.[2] Her struggling mainland colonies were, on the other hand, little more than tolerated for minor reasons—for instance, as sources of the salt fish and meat, spars, lumber and draft animals that enabled West Indian slaves to grow cane.

Slaves surviving the Middle Passage to make Barbados or St. Domingue in the mid-1750's did not find their ordeals finished.[3] In the interval required to sell them they went on dying of shipboard diseases. Shore agents might expedite disposal by auctioning off the feeblest and smallest for what they would bring and selling the better specimens "at scramble"—taking purchasers' money at so much per head, then turning all purchasers loose at once among the slaves to grab a corresponding number. Or they might be landed and fattened up for eventual sale piecemeal to choosy owners while the ship carried the culls on to Jamaica or perhaps to Savannah or New Orleans. Then came "seasoning" to local diseases and climate, which carried off still more while being fed up to working strength and trained to West Indian-style tasks. Some owners allowed a "seasoning" mortality of one third. Special precautions reduced but never eliminated this risk. So, just as the slaver captain allowed 10-20 per cent breakage in buying a cargo, the planter expected to pay for maybe four new-landed Negroes in order to secure the eventual services of three.

West Indian demand for black ivory remained heavy because even the surviving "seasoned" slaves never quite bred their own replacements. It was occasion for comment when a sugar "estate" kept up its labor force without "having recourse to African recruits." The data are startling: In fifty years (1712-1762) Barbados imported 150,000 Negroes; her Negro population rose by only 28,000.[4] In the late 1700's the annual population deficit of all the British West Indies was set at 2½ per cent; for Dutch Guiana, where working conditions were rather worse than usual, at 5 per cent. One obvious cause of this consistent shortcoming was scarcity of women among the imports, which, in the great eighteenth-century days of sugar, usually ran three or four men to one woman.[5] Miscarriages too were plentiful: the reasons might be heavy field work too close to term; or overstrain from taking heavy headloads of produce to town for sale for cash income; or maybe being kicked in the belly by an impulsive overseer. Infant mortality was ungodly high, particularly from "jaw-fall" (lockjaw), probably due to slave midwives tying up umbilical cords with hands polluted by the horse and cow manure with which "cane pieces" were fertilized.[6] But the chief trouble seems to have been infrequent conception. On a Jamaican estate supporting more women than men—an unusual situation—seventy-seven women of breeding age bore only eighteen children in three years. "Monk" Lewis, the London intellectual who left a rueful account of his visit to his Jamaica properties, complained that, of 150 women on his "Cornwall" estate in 1817, only eight were in the family way:[7] "I really believe," he wrote, "that the negresses can produce children at pleasure; and where they are barren, it is just as hens will frequently not lay eggs on shipboard, because they do not like their situation."

That is lightly stated but need not be taken so. Such low fecundity cannot have come of ascetic chastity—a virtue incompatible with West Indian slave ways. After all, until the eve of Emancipation men outnumbered women and planters did little to modify the polygyny tempered by semi-promiscuity prevalent among their imported Africans.[8] Virginity and anything like stable marital fidelity were probably even rarer on West Indian estates than on Dixie plantations, since nominal conversion to Christianity and its hampering notions was rare on most of the Islands. Now consider that, as is now widely accepted, a conjugal couple are likelier to achieve conception "when they like their situation"; and that the model Martin estate on Antigua, renowned for a labor force growing without outside purchase, showed "a large troop of healthy Negroes [under] . . . a kind and beneficent Master . . . Well fed, well supported, they appear the subjects of a good Prince . . . The effect of this kindness is a daily increase of riches by the slaves born to him on his own plantation." In 1775 the place had fifty-two "wenches" pregnant; local opinion was probably right—good treatment had something to do with this high fecundity. Several other particularly humane British West Indian estates and at least one in Cuba in 1860 are recorded as showing the same eloquent coincidence.

Now the Negroes of Virginia and the Carolinas came of

much the same ethnic stocks as did their Island cousins. Mainland climate must have been less favorable to transplanted Africans. Yet mainland slaves were more than reproducing themselves early. In 1749 the governor of North Carolina reported that though import duties and war had stopped importation of Africans for nine years, "our number of negroes is [not] diminished, but on the contrary increased . . . negroes bred from our own stock, will continually recruit and keep it up, if not enable us to supply the sugar Colonies with a small number." Colonial Virginia sought earnestly in the mid-1700's to curb the Trade out of fear of piling imported Africans on top of heavy local natural increase. By 1830 Dixie's slave population, with only very minor help from Africans smuggled in since 1808,[9] was rising 23 per cent each decade in spite of shocking infant mortality. The British Islands, cut off from legal slave imports the same year, steadily lost population until the Negroes were fully emancipated in the late 1830's; whereas Hayti, in 1810 half-depopulated by revolutionary disasters, vividly showed the demographic effects of freedom by regaining its pre-revolutionary population level by 1830.

Consider too that Dixie's early ability to more than replace slave losses meant less dependence on the Trade; hence lower ratio of Africans to "Creole"[10] slaves; hence less likelihood of slave rebellion; hence, other things being equal, milder discipline. Colonel William Byrd, who owned slaves but disliked slavery, was not trying to whitewash his native Virginia, merely slightly overstating observable fact when writing in 1736 that, though slaveowners had often to be "severe . . . We have nothing like the Inhumanity that is practiced in the Islands, and God forbid that we ever should." Theodore Weld, American antislaveryism's ablest propagandist, admitted that specially hideous "inflictions and privations" were heaped on the slave in the West Indies. Dr. DuBois, no man to give Dixie an even relatively good word, considered West Indian slavery "far different from that which the late Civil War abolished." Mainland slavery was sickeningly wrong and too often demoralized master as well as brutalized the slave. But it differed in degree, maybe even in kind, from its cousin institution in the Caribbean on which British antislaveryites based the doctrines and attitudes that their American emulators so eagerly imported.

> "... the Dunghille wharone England doth cast its
> rubidg ..."
> —WHISTLER in PITMAN, Development, 5

The West Indies committed hideousness against a lovely backdrop. The South Seas can show little more beautiful than the finest Caribbean Islands: Jamaica, Hayti, Dominica, the free-standing volcanic cone islands along the Leeward chain, all far handsomer than the slaves' dismal ancestral lands. But scenery can hardly have compensated the bought-and-sold Negro for the harshness of the Whites already settled in the Islands wherever they had got the better of the local Indians.

As John Smith learned to his cost at Jamestown, emigrants to the New World were often a poor lot whether British, French, Dutch, Spanish or Portuguese in origin. Average quality nevertheless varied somewhat according to destination: New England got the best of it. Her settlers' motives for emigrating—a desperate scheme in terms of the time— were heavily if not invariably religious. Farther down the Atlantic seaboard many other immigrants were religious or political refugees exiled in arbitrary groups, hence showing wide variations in self-respect and ability. Even below the

Chesapeake, where slavery would so damagingly persist, rag, tag and bobtail were heavily diluted by French Huguenots and British Quakers direct from Europe and by Scots-Irish and Rhineland Germans pushing southward along the Appalachian valleys. The West Indies got the fewest such promising people and the heaviest dose of the feckless and the reckless.

On this opinion is near-unanimous: "Rodgs and hors and such like peopel are those which are generally Broght here," wrote an early visitor to Barbados, the first major British island settled.[11] "A rodg in England will hardly make a cheater here; a Baud brought ouer puts on a demuor comportment; a whore if hansume makes a wife for some rich planter." Early Barbados was likened by Burn to "a combination of a mining camp and a penal settlement." The *Cambridge History of the British Empire* describes the British founding fathers of Jamaica as "soldiers ejected from their regiments and vagrants swept up from the streets," and calls "the . . . Caribbean colonies . . . the dumping-ground for the riffraff of the parent country." Pares attributes the second round of colony founding—in St. Domingue by buccaneers spreading from Tortuga to the main island, in the Virgins and the Neutral Islands by similar elements seeking lawless freedoms—to settlers too noisome or aggressive for the older and maybe staider colonies. This is impressive. A man too gamy for early Curaçao or St. Kitts was gamy indeed.

Certain descendants of the exiles whom Britain poured into Barbados as "servants"—sold for involuntary labor as penalty for crime or in order to pay the passage out—survive there as the "red legs," a local caste of whites looked down on by all other strata of local society, white or black. They are pitiable now but Burn, a modern historian, sensibly remarks of their emigrant forebears that "only by confusing suffering with virtue, is it possible to idealize these wretched men"—mostly lost souls, their own worst enemies, almost tempting the mistreatment generously afforded them by more fortunate whites already settled on the ground. In the 1650's a Barbadian deplored the white servants' "very hard labour, ill lodging and . . . their dyet very slight . . . no bone meat at all unlesse and [sic] Oxe dyed . . . I have seen an Overseer beat a Servant with a Cane about the head till the blood has followed, for a fault that is not worth the speaking of; and yet he must have patience or worse will follow . . . such cruelty . . . I did not think one Christian would have done to another."

As Negro slaves began to replace this white labor, black men and white often worked side by side and, as came of the same situation in early Dixie, heartily hated one another. To the West Indian mind sugar required large acreage and Negro labor: the latter because of the convenient notion that, in spite of known examples to the contrary, the full tropical sun was lethal to whites while endurable for Negroes; the former for the sounder reason that the equipment used to refine exportable sugar was uneconomic unless it had a great deal of cane to process. Hence sugar gradually squeezed out the tobacco farmer, who could get along with a smaller holding.[12] He often emigrated again, a few of him to the Carolinas, many more to get in on the ground floor of sugar in newly developing islands like Jamaica, taking up acreage, acquiring a growing force of Negroes and, with luck, rising to riches and arrogance. Or he might turn buccaneer to acquire capital and, unable to keep gold from slipping through his fingers, stay in that sordid trade until taken off by syphilis, hot lead, cold steel, alcohol in the blood stream or salt water in the lungs. In its day Jamaica was quite a port of missing men, a thing clear in its persisting place names: Starvegut Bay, Trouble Hill, Fatality, Frightful Vale, Hard Bargain, Cutlass Bay, Boozy Ridge, Bloody Bay, Rat Trap, Louzy Bay, Running Gut, Maggotty Cove . . . they make the old American West sound like a real estate subdivision laid out by one's maiden aunt.

There is a tale about the son of Sir Thomas Warner, founder of British St. Kitts, that confirms the flavor. He "went with an expedition to suppress the Caribs [the tough kind of West Indian aborigines], who were headed by his half-brother, his father's son by a Carib woman . . . he was received in a friendly manner by his relative. In the middle of the repast, upon a signal given, the Caribs were . . . all massacred . . ." and one accepted reason for "this act of atrocity" was that "the murderer was ashamed of his Indian relation." Had Sir Henry Morgan not died in bed, his career would be the ideal early West Indies' strive-and-succeed story. Welsh as his name, come of respectable people, young Morgan may have been kidnaped and sold in early Barbados as an "indentured servant." By the age of thirty, having presumably worked out his time, he was far, far from Barbados and high among the buccaneers of Tortuga, who, though the flavor of their catch-as-catch-can colony was basically French, included seagoing gangsters from all Western nations. He had his advanced training under a renowned Dutch buccaneer commodore operating under commission from the British governor of Jamaica, an enterprising gentleman who encouraged thousands of dangerous rascals to make their headquarters at Port Royal, then coming to be known as "the wickedest city in the world."

Presently Morgan succeeded the Dutchman as leader of a piratical squadron and became confidant and partner of the governor. Under British commission he commanded fleets of buccaneering craft that captured and sacked Maracaibo and Panama. These feats against the Spaniards, not to be looked into too closely because helpful to Britain at the time, secured him knighthood, interim service as Lieutenant-Governor of Jamaica, and title to promising lands in the island, where he spent his last days in prospering retirement: "lean, sallow-colored," wrote an acquaintance, "his eyes a little yellowish, and belly a little jutting out . . . much given to drinking and sitting up late." Pirate fanciers consider him by no means the lowest of his kind. He certainly had both courage and military-naval skill. They buried him at Port Royal, where he had been cock of the walk. When the great earthquake of 1692 half-destroyed the town and let the sea into the graveyard, there must have been hissing noises as the water penetrated his grave.

Now this was the most eminent West Indian of the seventeenth century. The eighteenth produced few more of such note: Napoleon's Josephine, conspicuous only for her marriage; Toussaint L'Ouverture, reared a slave; Alexander Hamilton, still a minor when he left St. Croix—a showing strangely meager for an area then the focus of world attention, the cockpit of world wars from Cromwell to Napoleon, the wealthiest speculation in the world. During the same 1700's the Dixie colonies, also committed to slavery, were rearing and training the majority of the great lawmakers and administrators who altered world history by bringing the United States into being: Washington, Henry, Jefferson, Madison, Mason, Wythe, Marshall, Jackson, Laurens, Harrison were all born in British mainland colonies south of Mason's & Dixon's Line. Historians try many explanations why, though subject to most of the same strains, the British West Indian colonies did not seek to join their North American sisters in rebellion in 1775. But one of them is always lack of adequate local leadership.

Maybe this dearth of silk purses shows it is unwise to heap so high a proportion of sow's ears in one place. With that either party in the heredity-vs.-environment debate can agree. The low social standards and maybe lower-than-average intelligence of the early West Indian whites persisted in their descendants—as the environmentalist would expect of a semi-isolated group of such origin. Or, as the eugenist would expect, genetic influences may have caused relatively low intelligence and sense of responsibility to persist. In either case the result would be a society unlikely to show much decency in handling the abominable problems implied in slavery.[18]

Comparisons are unfavorable to the Islands throughout. The Church of England obviously thought the West Indies either hopeless or pointless. Even on paper—and many of the livings were never filled—Jamaica had only forty-two clergymen for the whole great island. Of the newer colonies Trinidad had none at all, Dominica one, St. Vincent one. The twenty-four parishes of the four older Windward colonies had only sixteen parsons among them in the 1780's. While the pre-1776 mainland colonies founded eight colleges, three of them in Dixie, the wealthier West Indies set up only one— Codrington College in Barbados, which never came to much.[14] Observe the West Indian whites' failure to become West Indies-minded. Those of their forebears to whom exile had meant bullying, short rations and frustration naturally hated both the Islands and the luckier or tougher whites whom exile enriched. The successful were bent on amassing wealth and going "home" (i.e., to England)[15] to spend it.

As "all West Indians with the slightest pretension to quality" pursued this ambition, the mother country saw many vulgar *arrivistes* "fresh landed and full of cash," as a playwright of the day wrote. Their cash meant rich pick-- ings for toadies and tradesmen; bought their way into Parliament in rivalry with their betters; financed such pretentious follies as Beckford's Fonthill Abbey. Their ostentation and impulsive insolence annoyed London and Bath just as the same qualities in the "cotton snobs" of the 1850's annoyed Saratoga Springs. They seldom returned to St. Kitts or Jamaica to see how their property—animal, mineral, vegetable or human—was faring. Their sole concern was annual profit or, in poor years, advances against future profit. Their sons and grandsons, often born of English wives and polished in English schools, seldom even considered such a trip and understood little of the sweat, whip leather, dust and smells that transmuted an outsize grass into golden sovereigns. No doubt some of them had decent impulses, but they were not exercised in behalf of slaves thousands of seasick miles away.[16]

The absentee's West Indian holdings were handled by a local white "attorney"—a man hoping to make his pile by milking several properties simultaneously managed. "Creaming" might fit better—it was estimated in 1797 that these gentry and their lawyer jackals skimmed four shillings off every pound paid for Jamaica exports. On each estate the attorney put a resident white "overseer" whose subalterns, usually white, called "bookkeepers," [17] supervised the Negro slave "drivers" who were directly over the field hands. The white managerial caste were "wretched alike in their vices, their pleasures and their lack of training"; "needy adventurers, without either principle, religion, or morality." They were out from Britain, particularly Scotland, to learn the ropes, struggle to become attorneys, snap up estates mismanaged until foreclosed on, restore them to profitable shape—and in the most successful cases return "home" as a new and no prettier generation of absentees.

Modern scholars agree with observers of that day that this absenteeism was the curse of the Islands. The morbid effects were double: the owner did not personally observe his land and Negroes. And public life suffered from the absence of those with the largest stake in intelligent colonial government. Governors of the elder islands unable to find local talent fit to sit as legislators and advisors had to make do with councils and assemblies of "professional men of low caliber, little education, mean abilities, and small proprietary interest." This is a particularly sharp contrast: While the Byrds, Henry Laurens and George Washington were gaining experience in colonial legislatures, their West Indian opposite numbers were strutting about London leaving the Islands in charge of third-rate understrappers.

In ruinous side effect the ratio of whites to slaves in the

Islands steadily declined as sugar took hold. In 1628 Barbados had 1400 whites and *no* Negroes. Forty years later it was 20,000/40,000. By 1809 it was 15,000/69,000. In 1800 all West Indian whites numbered only 65,000 to 465,000 slaves and maybe 10,000 "free colored." "Deficiency laws" fining estates that failed to keep a certain proportion of whites to blacks were futile; the fines, regularly paid, became a sort of backhanded tax counted into colonial budgets. All this contrasted scandalously with the way natural increase as well as immigration was raising the mainland colonies' numbers into the millions.

Antigua's renown as a humane sugar island was confidently ascribed to its high ratio of planters resident on their own estates. The Dixie of John Brown's day held that, other things being equal, slaves were well treated in proportion as the owner was on the place. And the typical Dixie slaveowner of the 1850's was no absentee. He had probably never seen a town larger than the raw, new state capital or been over a hundred miles from home. His ten or a dozen slaves dwelt within easy call on his three-mule cotton farm, and master often worked out in the sun in the same field with them, sometimes even at the same task—a thing unheard of in the Islands. Nor did the white-column stratum of a few thousand large plantation owners show many absentee expatriates. Most of them whether aristocrats of several generations standing or "cotton-snob" newcomers lived on their plantations at least part of the year, hence had some opportunity, sometimes well used, to foster humaneness as well as production-per-slave. It was about Jamaica, not Dixie, that leftist Lord Olivier wrote: "Capitalist exploitation, absenteeism and slavery created in concert the most perverting complex of human iniquities that any modern civilization has yet exhibited." A tall order but probably—at least until Communism and Nazism came to flower—a true bill.

Another Dixie axiom, endorsed by Jefferson Davis among

others, was: The larger the plantation, the worse off the slave.[18] And what Davis would have called a large place— say 1500 acres and 100 slaves—the West Indies in their heyday would have rated small. Zachary Bailey, Bryan Edwards' patron, had three contiguous Jamaica estates totaling 5000 acres and working 1100 slaves. The largest I know of in Dixie was John Acklen's cotton operation in Louisiana: 20,000 acres organized in six plantations all together working 700 slaves; whereas a single-unit show place in Jamaica, Spring Garden estate, had 3000 acres and 600 slaves. Consider too that the social values developed on these huge installations were not modified, as in Dixie, by the presence of thousands on thousands of small cotton or tobacco operations or single white families owning a few slaves with whom personal relations were usually less harsh than in the size-committed Islands. If Davis—a successful and humane large plantation owner himself—knew what he was talking about, the West Indian economy, combining large scale[19] with much absenteeism, was the worst possible for forced black labor.

Visitors sometimes found tolerable qualities among resident West Indian proprietors and the upper layer of the attorney-factor-lawyer class. Father Labat of the French Jacobin order, who knew Louis XIV's Paris, saw taste as well as opulence in Barbadian country mansions and silverware so fine that he advised his countrymen to raid the place at the first opportunity. A Scottish gentlewoman who knew good society was charmed by the nonabsentees' establishments in relatively happy Antigua. But to mention such exceptions need not distort the emphasis. The opulent West Indian of the great period preferred to concentrate his architectural spendings in Britain. The old prints of West Indian "great houses"—local equivalent of Dixie's "big house"—show mostly undistinguished, roomy but crude dwellings usually set on stilts for coolness and freedom from vermin; nobody minded if dogs and chickens spent the heat of the day underneath. Few had the elegance of "Sam Lord's Castle" on Barbados or the imposing scale of Rose Hall in Jamaica, the atypical specimens that the tourist sees. Bryan Edwards ironically contrasted "the general plenty . . . of

Creolean Patience.

"Mimbo
"Here Missee
"tell Quashebah to tell Prue to tell Dido
    "to tell Sue to come and pick up
    "my Needle.
"Yes Missee
"Quashebah is gone to Market
    "Missee and wont be back dis
    "tree hour
"What am I to wait three hours for my needle?
    "tell Prue to tell Dido to tell Sue to come.
    "and pick up my Needle"
Yes Missee
Sue is scratching my Massah's Legs
    and cant come for dis two hour.
Oh dear me! one must have the Patience
    of Job to live in this world with any
    comfort, here I must wait two hours
    for my Needle — Oh dear me!'

West Indian luxury among the planter caste as conceived by a London artist in 1808—the year the slave trade was outlawed. Institute of Jamaica.

the [uppermost whites'] tables . . . and the meanness of
their houses . . . a splendid sideboard loaded with plate,
and the choicest wines, a table covered with the finest dam-
ask . . . in a hovel not superior to an English barn." The
slave butler might wear shoes but his assistants were always barefoot and like as not half-naked. Housekeeping was
as slovenly or worse than that of the contemporary Dixie
household.

Labat, who talks like a sound amateur cook and in any
event was French, also admired the Barbadian dinners he
ate while mentally weighing up his hosts' silver platters
and beakers. Many others agreed—how nice at last to have
something cordial to say of the West Indian white!—that
the topmost stratum ate variously and well. The astringent
"Lady of Quality" likened Sunday dinner on Antigua to a
Lord Mayor's Feast; she specially relished the delicate local
fishes and exhilarating sauces based on red pepper and lime
juice. "Monk" Lewis reveled in subtly prepared turtle, wild-
fowl, turkey, fruits (including pineapple, then the Briton's
symbol of gastronomic luxury), barbecued pork, pepperpot
. . . Another British visitor wrote gloatingly: "I would back
the Sambo [*i.e.*, one-fourth white] . . . *chef de la cuisine* of
the governor [of Jamaica], against a synod of French cooks
for serving up a dinner of turtle and calipever, mountain
mullets, ringtailed pigeons, black crabs, and wild guinea-fowl
. . ."—which, given even fair cooking, does sound toothsome.
The butter, sent out heavily salted from Ireland, was always
rancid, but who would miss butter at a dinner like that?

The drinking was less civilized. During the West Indies'
"flush times" inordinate guzzling was the fashion "at home,"
so West Indians able to afford to ape gentlemen guzzled too
—the French on wines from home, the British on Madeira
rather than claret or port because West Indies-bound ships
could pick up supplementary ladings of wine at Madeira
on the outward voyage. (This also accounts for the quantities
of Madeira drunk in the mainland colonies.) In both

areas whites with slimmer purses could still drink themselves blind on local spirits: on the mainland peach brandy or whisky, rum in the Islands. "Killdevil" was Barbados' early name for the spirits distilled from fermented molasses, by-product of sugar refining. The successor name of "rumbullion" (derivation unknown) was soon shortened to "rum." In Jamaica in 1722 it cost about a shilling a *gallon*—the same as a gallon of whisky in western Pennsylvania in the 1780's. The French called it "tafia," [20] and Father Labat found it frightening: "The savages [i.e., the surviving Caribs], the Negroes, the lower orders of the whites drink nothing else. Their intemperance . . . is indescribable; they ask only that this tipple be strong, tough and cheap; never mind that it's harsh and unpalatable." As the less reckless learned to age it, it ramified into the excellent rums from half a dozen islands that now dominate the world market and supplied so much of the Dutch courage that heartened seamen in the naval actions of the 1800's. But in the Islands more palatable rums meant merely that the well-to-do, already drinking much heavy wine, drank still more in the shape of rum punch exploiting the pungency of West Indian limes and the sting of West Indian sugar without much resort to the diluent powers of West Indian water.

The domestic arrangements of well-to-do West Indian whites resembled those of New Orleans rather than Dixie's in general. Quasipermanent *liaison* with a colored mistress, slave or free, usually mulatto to quadroon, was pretty much taken for granted. "In our town," wrote a Royal Navy surgeon turned parson and settled ashore in the 1780's at Basse-Terre, St. Kitts, "first commerce with the other sex, at an unripe age, is an article of trade for their mothers and elder sisters; nay, it is not an uncommon thing for the mistresses, chaste matrons, to hire them out, and take an account of their gains; or, if they be free, they hire their services and their persons, to some one of the numerous bands of bachelors." "Housekeeper" was one euphemism for the relationship. One such told Lewis: "I am Mr. Such-a-one's *Love!*" and otherwise called him her "husband." She might even act as lady of the house except for presiding at table. Much modesty and fidelity were required of her. Among lower whites this arrangement gave place to exploitation of slave women to whom a white man's favor meant prestige and special privileges. Lady Nugent was disgusted by the way "white men of all descriptions, married or single, live in a state of licentiousness with their female slaves," and sought in vain to persuade the young fellows on Nugent's staff to abstain from this sordid custom of the country.

These are not far from the terms of a Dixie town and of many a large plantation. But in the Islands offspring of either formal or casual miscegenation might have a different destiny. By common consent West Indian mulatto or lighter slaves were usually exempt from field work, instead trained for house servants or special crafts. Darker fellow slaves might call a mulatto housemaid "Miss." If pretty, she stood a good chance of having quadroon children begotten on her.[21] The likelier of the latter might be formally freed by owners, also bequeathing them property as implicit acknowledgment of paternity. Thus the Islands developed a three- or maybe four-ply society: At top the few resident landowners and their outstanding parasites. Next minor whites also often begetting and sometimes freeing mixed-race offspring. Then "people of color"—half-, quarter-, eighth-Negro, many free, some well off economically, all specially privileged in view of their lighter skins, seeking to emulate the whites, despising the blacks with great animus, reputedly specially harsh to the slaves whom they did not scruple to own when possible.[22] And at the bottom darker crosses and full Negroes doing the hardest or dirtiest work and hating "people of color" heartily. Dixie showed the same trends but they remained tenuous except—again this special resemblance—in sugar-ridden, West Indies-flavored Louisiana. The British Islands allowed the presumption that fifteenth-sixteenths "white blood" qualified one for the "white" caste; whereas Dixie moved steadily toward the position that any degree of known "Negro blood" still meant "nigger."

These West Indian caste systems—particularly that of St. Domingue—were closely involved in the historical events that persuaded Old Brown and the Six that Negro slaves were always potential rebels. The mixed-blood/Negro cleavage is still the curse of Hayti. In the British Islands it has gradually weakened, not yet disappeared but likely to go on dwindling. Neither situation is any credit to the sordid white man taking the local line of least resistance.

Generalizations are risky, occasional exceptions always pop up. Yet it can be maintained that these upper-crust West Indian whites must have averaged a cut or two below those in charge of Dixie's slaves. Lady Nugent summed them up as outstandingly grasping, almost innocently money-minded —as fitted those still hoping to make and take a fortune "home"—but about most other things ". . . indolent and inactive . . . almost entirely under the domination of their mulatto favourites. In the lower orders . . . the same, with the addition of conceit and tyranny, considering the negroes as formed merely to administer to their ease, and to be subject to their caprice . . . [I] have much difficulty to persuade [the lower orders] . . . that the blacks are human beings, or have souls." Loyalists from Savannah, Charleston and elsewhere who migrated to the West Indies after the American Revolution are always assumed to have raised local moral and social tone; and though few of them can have been saints or heroes, no doubt they did so, that local tone being what it was. Nobody ever said the same of the several waves of French planters fleeing St. Domingue in the early 1800's as murderous convulsions showed them to have been impossibly bad stewards of their own interests —maybe even worse than their Jamaican hosts.

Consider too that, whereas Dixie produced a dozen Abo-

litionists who had been slaveowners, mostly from the
higher strata, all reared in slave states, the West Indies produced not one such.

> "[West Indian slaves] had little cause to lament their
> removal from the wild woods of an opposite shore; and
> could as little desire to change their present lot for the
> high-rated freedom of European paupers . . ."
>
> —DR. GEORGE PINCKARD

Sugar came so to dominate many of the West Indian islands
that they imported practically all their slaves' food. It is
still near the truth today that, as Dr. Eric Williams has
written, the West Indian "produces what he does not eat
and eats what he does not produce." The staples of slavery
times were about like the seaman's rations of the day: in
the British islands salt fish (from New England and Canada); salt beef and salt pork (from Ireland); cereals from
various sources. Reliance on supply so distant was risky.
During the Seven Years' War the French planters of block-
aded Martinique had to kill the oxen that turned the sugar
mills; even so, many slaves died of starvation. When the
American Revolution stifled trade from North America to the
Islands, thousands of slaves were thus lost. Islands with room
still to spare, such as Jamaica and St. Vincent, insouciantly
reduced this risk by making the slaves grow most of their
own food in their spare time, root-hog-or-die, on "provision
grounds" allotted them in poor or hilly areas. Such fresh
diet was healthier in some ways. But Jamaican slaves died
off as fast as or faster than those in islands where full
rations were issued, maybe because working the provision
grounds heightened the general strain.

Neither system would have suited the capable Dixie plantation owner. His long standing ideal, whether his acres were many or few, was to raise the slave's basic diet of pork and corn or rice on the place, and also allow him free time to eke out the basic ration by fishing and raising odd vegetables and poultry on his own.[23] Policy as to clothing also differed. No matter how warm the climate—and in summer the Gulf Coast and the Sea Islands are hotter than most of the West Indies—Dixie slaves' work clothes, however shabby and tattered, usually answered the minimum that Western modesty required. Men might strip to the waist in the field but trousers were almost invariable.[24] Women in the hoe gang might kilt their skirts high for freedom and coolness but they seldom worked barebosomed, African style; whereas the West Indies sometimes allowed even women house servants to do so. In Antigua, the "Lady of Quality" found, women slaves "are hardly prevailed on to wear a petticoat." In Jamaica a generation earlier: "The Negro Women go many of them quite naked . . . don't know what shame is . . . are surprised at an European's bashfulness, who perhaps turns his Head aside at the Sight. Their Masters give them a kind of Petticoat, but they don't care to wear it." We no longer regard nakedness as indecent in itself. But this indifference to exposure was well below the standard of most of the West Africa whence these Negroes came. It must have betokened a coarse contempt of master for slave, a feeling that decency was pointless among half-animals bought stinking and naked off shipboard.

These naked backs often showed the scars of flogging. True, barbaric punishments characterized the times in which the West Indies most flourished. The wheel and the stake still competed with ax and gallows. The lash was the basis of discipline in all Western armed forces halfway through the 1800's. Dixie had both standardized brutalities and sporadic atrocities eagerly collected by Abolitionists.

From close acquaintance with all Dixie was ever accused of, however, I must judge the mainland's general level of brutality not so bad as that of the Islands. The occasional atrocity of Dixie might be more or less standard practice in the West Indies. Round 1700 the penalty for a third running away in Martinique was hamstringing—which crippled the man for life and spoiled most of his value as a slave. Sir Hans Sloan, who had no special reason to exaggerate, listed as accepted West Indian punishments for crimes slightly less grave than mutiny "Gelding, or chopping off half the Foot with an Axe . . . sometimes merited by the Blacks, who are a very perverse Generation of People." We shall presently see that the Islands applied torture much more freely to slave rebels than Dixie did under the same provocation. It is symbolically right that whereas the Dixie "driver" carried only one whip, sometimes none, on even relatively humane Antigua he carried two, one long, one short.

Say that the differences between a typical Jamaican sugar estate of 1790 and a typical large Alabaman cotton plantation of 1850 were on the order of those between a really rough old-time chain gang and an old-fashioned penitentiary with a not-too-bright warden authorized to flog at discretion. Neither situation has much to recommend it to prisoners. But given a choice, all would unquestionably prefer the second. Yet the Abolitionist propaganda that shaped the emotions of Old Brown and the Six was based on the first.

6 *The Spartacus complex*

"GLENDOWER: *I can call Spirits from the vastie Deepe.*
"HOTSPUR: *Why so can I, or so can any man;*
But will they come when you doe call for
them?" —Henry IV, *Part One: III, 1*

West Africans are adept poisoners. In one of their judicial
ordeals the accused drinks a poison that kills the guilty but
merely makes the innocent vomit. Their slave descendants
in the New World retained much of such lore, and the West
Indian slave occasionally poisoned master; whereas Dixie's
slaves used poison almost exclusively on other Negroes. Obviously no exact data are possible. But contemporary accounts show the West Indian white convinced that poison
was a genuine risk. His opposite number in Dixie hardly
thought of it.

The strongest hint, however, that West Indian slaves had
it worse lies in the sharpest contrast of all: the higher inci-
dence and often larger scale of slave mutinies in the Islands.
Jamaica alone saw serious trouble every decade or less, a
record unmatched by any Dixie state. This difference went
largely unnoticed by Abolitionists and slaveowners alike—
hence a false view of potential slave rising underlay both the
Six's ability to take Old Brown seriously and Dixie's hysteri-

cal reaction to his raid. The old man was as much deceived as anybody. In holding forth on how best to kindle the assumed latent insurgency of Dixie's slaves he might refer to the rare serious revolts in the histories of Virginia and the Carolinas. But what most haunted him, what he pretended to have studied exhaustively, was the case of Spartacus, who led the great slave rising against Rome; and the mutiny-gashed past of the West Indies culminating in the noisome horrors of St. Domingue. And neither he nor anybody else thought of asking how much these lurid episodes had to do with eventualities in Dixie.

The slave rebel was an inevitable but distinctly exceptional product of the Trade. Sometimes, as we have seen, he led a shipboard rising. In the new country specially bad treatment or his own specially hot temper might make him run away, and he was by no means always recaptured. By the early 1500's the Portuguese island of St. Thomas off the Slave Coast had shaped up as a sort of prototype of the West Indian sugar colonies soon to develop across the Atlantic: Sudden wealth, imported Negro slaves, white masters in large wooden plantation houses with mulatto concubines, much drink—and up in the hills clusters of runaways difficult to dislodge and, by their persistence, imperiling the discipline of slaves still under the yoke. The Spaniards of Panama and Hispaniola (Columbus' name for the great island now split between Santo Domingo and Hayti) had early trouble with Negro slaves joining the local Indians. In spite of terrain ill adapted to hiding out, small Barbados had such problems. On St. Vincent a batch of Negro slaves escaped ashore from a wrecked slaver, took firm root, eventually subdued the local Indians—tough Caribs, not the mild Arawak —and mixed with them to become "black Caribs" who doughtily resisted both French and British. Something similar produced the "Sambo" segment of the Mosquito Indians of Honduras. So far Dixie showed cognates: the small, tenuous colonies of runaways in the Great Dismal and Belle Isle swamps; the Seminoles of Florida fusing fugitive Negroes and shattered Indians into a plucky new people. But Dixie saw nothing like the scale and stamina of the Negro tribes in the upcountry of Dutch Surinam and British Jamaica.

Fresh-landed slaves early evaded the Dutch in driblets, took to the steamy Guiana bush and created permanent runaway colonies far up the sluggish rivers. Eventually government learned to let them alone instead of sending arduous punitive expeditions into such country against wily resistance. For two centuries now these stubborn mutineers have largely managed their own affairs in quasi-African style. Jamaica, however, provided the case best known to British antislaveryites, hence to their American pupils and eventually to Old Brown: In the mid-1650's the Spaniards' sluggish cattle-raising colony on Jamaica was overrun by a large British force of rag-tag-and-bobtail. The Spaniards held out in the hills for some years, then abandoned the island—and the Negro slaves who had taken to the bush with them. These accidentally freed Negroes had learned guerrilla fighting, valued the confusedly jagged interior as good country to hide out in, and knew that surrender would mean re-enslavement by some of the scaliest Britons who ever went soldiering. They chose freedom, however rugged, took women from the remains of the local Arawak Indians, and stayed in the hills as germ of Jamaica's thenceforth celebrated "Maroons."

The term is said to derive from the Spanish *cimarron,* meaning "wild, unruly" with suggestions of roughing it in a wilderness. If so, it well suited the growing gangs of black marauders who, loosely organized under one Juan de Bolas, continued to harass the British even though the Spaniards were long since gone. Methodically they massacred any whites settling near Maroon "towns." During the next eighty years forty-four successive acts of amnesty sought to tempt them to join Jamaican society as free Negroes. Each brought numbers of them into camp but there was always a large recalcitrant fraction maintaining a force in being. As Jamaica turned from piracy to sugar and heavy slave buying, Coromanti runaways fresh from Africa and full of new hate for whites trickled upcountry to join and make them even more formidable.

Their principal settlements were hidden in the least accessible mountain areas, particularly the droughty "Cockpit Country" of western Jamaica—a limestone region of funnel-shaped basins drained by sinkholes and separated by sharp ridges—curiously beautiful but a soldier's nightmare.[1] There were hundreds, some said a thousand or so, of Maroon fighting men. Their women and children raised corn and yams; the men hunted wild hogs for subsistence and also for dried pork to trade clandestinely with plantation slaves and town shopkeepers for firearms, gunpowder, lead, rum and a few other indispensables, and raided plantations for supplementary provender and sometimes comely slave girls to add to their polygynous households. They spoke a modification of Gold Coast tongues and their village chiefs, styled "captain" or "colonel" for white-style prestige, often had African-flavored names: Quaco, Cudjo, Cuffee.

For decades government could hardly check them. By building connecting blockhouses at strategic points and importing from Honduras part-Negro "Mosquito Indians" who were just as clever bush fighters as the Maroons, it scored a half-success in the 1730's. The harassed outlaws, though still on their feet and fighting, agreed to call it quits on condition that their freedom and title to adequate lands be acknowledged; their leaders recognized; and their trade with whites legitimized. For a bounty of three pounds a head they also agreed to return instead of absorb runaway slaves. Finding it irksome to drive captured runaways to the white settlements, they beheaded them and brought in merely the heads when applying for bounty. This rendered valuable slaves useless, so government arranged to pay a few pennies per mile traveled in delivering runaways alive, and the practice ceased. The Maroons also turned out as auxiliaries against slave risings, sometimes doing good service, sometimes not. On the occasions when they proved reluctant, the reason was not race solidarity but resentment because government had let payments of head money fall in arrears. As relations with the whites stabilized, Maroon "towns" became resorts for local dignitaries enjoying great hunting and drinking parties including feasts of wild boar, land crab and pigeon; sham battles; and use of local women in a sort of bush Saturnalia lasting for days.

This era of good feeling lasted, with some frictions, until the 1790's, when white and Negro revolutionaries trickled over from revolt-shattered St. Domingue to make Jamaican Negroes restless and fill Jamaican whites with dread lest their Negroes follow this nearby violent example. The specific spark that exploded the Maroons was the tactlessness of Montego Bay magistrates who had two Maroon hog thieves flogged by a slave "driver" in the presence of other slaves. This insult to Maroon pride in freedom sent the culprits' village, Trelawny Town, on the warpath at a time when war with France was straining every British resource. Again the soldiers found a Maroon uprising almost hopeless to suppress. The outlaws merely holed up in difficult country, sent out raiding parties and made the redcoats dance clumsily to a Maroon tune. As last resort the British brought from Cuba numbers of huge, savage dogs trained to track and seize runaways—a measure denounced by the humane-minded but crucially effective. The dogs terrified the Maroons as soldiers never had and, after a prolonged siege of their inmost holding, with all outgoing paths blocked and water ever scarcer, they accepted an offer of amnesty for those turning themselves in by a certain day.

It took too long, however, to muster the various bands. When they finally marched in, the set day had passed. Over the protest of the indignant general who had secured the victory, a harsh governor took this pretext to exile 600-odd Trelawny Maroons to Nova Scotia.[2] There, though nominally free, they were set to forced labor building a part of the citadel of Halifax, still called "the Maroon bastion." They continued to present problems after being settled on the land. They persisted in polygyny, for instance, which scandalized the local whites, and grumbled against the cold climate and the bad faith that had subjected them to it. Finally England bundled them off to strengthen Sierra Leone, the new West African colony for the rehabilitation of indigent free Negroes resident in Britain. For Maroons with Mende or Temne ancestry this was nearly full circle, and at least complaints that the climate was not warm enough ceased. The newcomers did bolster up the sweltering, struggling little settlement; their name and reputation linger there today. But the place was a slovenly stepchild with little future, and the shabbiness with which the Maroons were treated is dismally like what we Americans did to the sturdiest Indians.

Their eventual decline and fatal lack of race solidarity were ignored by antislavery zealots hoping that slave rebellion was always imminent in Dixie. Such doctrinaires observed only the striking fact that these doughty Negroes had held out for five or six generations against persistent attack. Given moderate help from friendly whites, it was assumed, Dixie's Negroes might do the same indefinitely. In any case repeated escapades of the sort, even though good for only a year or two each, would alarm Dixie into abandoning slavery. Oceans of misapprehension flowed from these optimists' failure to reflect that the Maroons' success had never slowed down Jamaican slavery; and that Dixie's Negroes, products of other circumstances, were not the toughened guerrillas stiffened by vigorous and war-minded West Africans whence came the Maroons' special edge.

Such confusions affected even Southerners: In 1736 Colonel Byrd spoke of "at least 10,000 Men of these descendants of Ham fit to bear Arms . . . in case there should arise a Man of desperate courage among us . . . he might with

more advantage than Cataline kindle a Servile War . . .
dreadfully mischievous before any opposition could be
formed . . . We have mountains in Virginia . . . to which
[mutinous slaves] may retire as safely, and do as much mischief as they do in Jamaica." Byrd certainly knew that only
seven years earlier his fellow Virginians had contradicted
this by wiping out the only such rebel colony ever reaching
any size in the Old Dominion. But the bare notion of extensive trouble, so appalling to Dixie, seems also to have fascinated many of her leaders, as the notion of hellfire fascinates
sinners at a revival. Maybe Old Brown had somewhere
stumbled on some guilt-laden Southerner who talked like
Byrd, and so derived from slaveholders themselves the shaky
cornerstone of his scheme to ruin slavery by creating a hill
colony of insurgent slaves.

"*Here's to the next insurrection of the Negroes in the
West Indies!*"   —DR. SAMUEL JOHNSON

Maroon-style colonies had no revolutionary purpose.
Whether in St. Thomas, Surinam or Jamaica, slaves taking
to the bush hoped only to disengage themselves from slavery.
Once they personally were free of it, it could persist for all
of them. It might even be useful as source of bold recruits
and pilfered supplies. Mass risings of plantation slaves, however, meant crops and buildings burned, discipline temporarily shattered and high likelihood of islandwide trouble.
The numerous West Africans among slaves involved might
include men skilled in command back on the Gold or Slave
Coasts and capable of coherent plans. The chiefs of the large
Jamaican conspiracy of 1760, for instance, avowedly aimed

at "entire extirpation of the white inhabitants; the enslaving of all such Negroes as might refuse to join them; and the partition of the island into small principalities in the African mode . . . distributed among their leaders . . ." Such confessions were probably secured under torture but they are likely valid all the same. Little in the above fails to fit what the St. Domingue slaves actually did when their day came. The Maroons did most to suppress this outbreak, killing or forcing to suicide some 400 insurgent slaves. Sixty-odd whites too died before it was over. Most of the rebels were, as was logical, African-born. A sorcerer renowned for skill in Obeah —the British West Indian magic religion of largely African origin—had distributed among them powders conferring invulnerability to gunshot and taught that Tackey, a principal leader, could catch bullets in his bare hands and throw them back at the enemy. This signal talent did not save Tackey from being shot dead by Maroons who ate his entrails and heart and sent his head to be stuck on a pole set up on the road to Spanish Town.

These revolutionary risings usually included such magic to reassure the fainthearted; failure to see slavery as an evil in itself; sound secret organization among the slaves of several adjacent estates; and sporadic distant outbreaks as rumor spread. West Indian whites held with reason that a heavy proportion of African-born slaves heightened risk of insurrection; and that it was higher still when too many Africans of common origin—Eboes, say, or Mende or the high-charged Coromanti—were clumped together in one island. Serious trouble could nevertheless occur without such factors. Antigua's slave plot of 1736 included mostly specialist slaves, most of them locally born, hence unaffected by the personal outrage of having been snatched out of Africa to the terrifying far end of the world. Thus Tomboy, one of their two "generals," was a mason working on his own and paying his owner for the privilege, even allowed to take apprentices. His comrades were coachmen, coopers, carpenters, fiddlers, fishermen, footmen—none getting the brunt of toil under the whip in sun-broiled cane pieces. Their tasks enabled them to move about with unusual freedom. Egged on by a redoubtable Obeah man, they laid their heads together to take full advantage of this privilege—and who's to blame them?

They were put down with a severity proportionate to the violence of their plans. Thirty-six minor participants were sold off the island but the bulk of those identified died for their rashness. Seventy-seven were burned alive; five "broken on the wheel"—that is, bound on a horizontal cart wheel to die slowly of exposure, a sort of sluggish crucifixion with arms and legs broken and allowed to dangle over the rim; six gibbeted alive in chains to die even more slowly. And Antigua was noted for humaneness! Dixie never saw official brutality on such a scale in that or any other century.

Even after outlawry of the Trade jogged the British West Indies into treating slaves a little better, serious revolts occurred. Conversation about antislaveryism picked up by house servants and spread among field hands set off outbreaks in the early 1800's. Newly developing Trinidad had a mutiny of fresh-from-Africa Negroes landed from an illicit slaver and drafted into a Negro regiment willy-nilly. An African-born "Eboe king" connived with a Negro from St. Domingue and an Obeah man in western Jamaica in 1814 to organize hundreds of slaves, mostly African-born. A clever overseer got wind of the scheme at the last minute. Sentenced to hang, the Eboe burned out the door of his cell and escaped, only to be tracked down and fetched back for the gallows by a "captain" of Maroons. He died promising Jamaican whites that his followers would bloodily avenge him. These slave rebels were tough. Two of Tackey's men hanged in chains[3] on Kingston parade lived over a week and to the end showed only "hardened indifference and brutal insensibility." Plato, a Jamaican runaway who set up as an independent Maroon in the 1770's, warned the court sentencing him to be

burned that his death would bring on a terrific storm, and
told the jailer who bound him to the stake that he might as
well lie down and die, an Obeah curse was on him. A most
destructive storm followed the execution, and the jailer,
understandably impressed, died of sheer apprehension.

Such black wildcats may have been commonest among
Coromanti. But the leader of that Trinidad mutiny was a
Slave Coaster; so was the "Eboe king"; Cinquez of the
Amistad was a Mende. No West African people had a monop-
oly on white-hating, magic-inspired, bloody-minded bravery.
Consider that the most cataclysmic slave rising that the West
Indies ever saw occurred in St. Domingue, where French
planters had preferred Congo and Slave Coast Negroes.

The French West Indies were both typical and special.
Those colonies remaining pretty consistently in French hands
as European powers snatched islands back and forth—Martinique, Guadeloupe, the western fourth of Hispaniola known
in its French colonial phase as St. Domingue, eventually to
become Hayti—developed rather like the British and Dutch
sugar colonies. But, being latest to take up sugar, hence
exploiting still unexhausted soil, toward the end of the 1700's
St. Domingue became the world's outstanding sugar pro-
ducer. Unfortunately it was also outstanding for the virulence
of local race and caste hatreds. True, its estate owners—the
grands blancs—though normally "home" and money-minded,
did not go absentee quite as often as did those of Barbados
and Jamaica—a salutary thing. But it also had a nastily thick
stratum of *petits blancs*—white overseers, shopkeepers, parasites of shipping, many emigrating under indenture or from
jail deliveries—bitterly resenting *grands blancs;* and a third
stratum of mixed-blood *gens de couleur,* mostly free since it
was customary to manumit the children of whites by Negro
women as they matured. Sometimes the father set his mixed-
blood child up well in life, and some of them owned prosperous sugar or coffee estates. This group of freedmen
(*affranchis*) also included socially as well as technically a

number of full or anyway distinctly dark Negroes who had bought or otherwise secured freedom.

Of whatever shade, the *affranchis* hated the *grands blancs* because of the humiliating civil and social restrictions heaped on them by a culture that drew a Dixie-style color line[4] much more rigid than that of the British West Indies. The full-black field Negroes, the overwhelming majority of the population, hated the *affranchis* because they were the zealous if resentful backbone of the militia patrols—and because they gave themselves airs over their black cousins. Field Negroes also despised the *petits blancs* as what Jamaican slaves called "walkfoot buckra"—unable to afford riding horses and other luxuries proper to white prestige. The *affranchis* jeered at the *petits blancs* on the same grounds, and contemptuously loathed the Negro slaves. The *grands blancs* naturally despised all lower strata. The thing had a horrible symmetry—each group bitter against all others— and an unique animus. Many sugar islands developed such strata and bad blood to match. But for some reason—maybe because both *petits* and *grands blancs* included a high ratio of women,[5] maybe just because of the Frenchman's genius for hating other Frenchmen—the divisive emotions ran shrillest in St. Domingue.

The slaves' circumstances differed little from those in Surinam or Jamaica.[6] Louis XIV's *Code Noir* was decently intended but seldom strictly enforced. The "marrons" in the hills were never wholly brought under, but never quite got utterly out of control. Firm handling kept sporadic plantation mutinies from spreading, and then shootings, floggings, burnings, breakings-on-the-wheel and hangings-in-chains stamped any red embers into a hardly perceptible smolder. Between rapid expansion of cane acreage and annual population loss of 3 per cent, however, the ratio of African-born to "Creole" slaves was ominously high—about 2/1—and many of them came from the markedly related cultures of the Slave Coast. Resulting similarities of language and custom kept most *marrons* and plantation slaves closer than most West Indian Negroes to West African magic and propitiatory religions. Just beneath their dead-panned surfaces ran the strong, secret current of *voudun*—the "voodoo" dear to the tourist—a cult blending West African pantheons with half-witted borrowings from Catholic hagiology.[7] Its drum-smitten, god-ridden mysteries were clandestinely familiar to many *affranchis* and by no means a matter of indifference to the *blancs,* many of whom regarded the cult as uncomfortably dangerous to have about, like a naked wire that might carry a heavy charge. The judgment was sound. Voodoo proved disastrously superior to Obeah as supernal cohesive force of slave risings.

The dogmas and decrees of the French Revolution set off fulminating reactions among these layered corrosives. Alternately fumbling, granting, denying and hurrying the application of *liberté, égalité, fraternité* and the Rights of Man to the colony, the mother country made sure that each faction would do its best to disembowel all the others. By trying to turn the home crisis to special advantage the *grands* and *petits blancs* and *affranchis* brought on St. Domingue a mass of miseries the sequelae of which still plague Hayti—as the eventual new Negro nation named itself from the aboriginal term for western Hispaniola. An English anti-Jacobin foe of slavery judged the *petits blancs* to have been the worst villains, but choice among the candidates is hard. In any case "in their struggle . . . they at length dropped a match into the immense powder magazine on which they lived," wrote Henry Adams. Regional risings of *affranchis* here and there were followed by an explosion of the Negroes in the North, the largest sugar area, in a great conspiracy cemented by the exaltation of voodoo and here and there supported by the *marrons.* Irresistible slave mobs looted, burned, killed, tortured, raped in exactly the bestial fashion and on the mass scale that West Indian whites had always dreaded.

Then came battle royal among many snarling factions.

Colonists clinging to the old order, mostly *grands blancs;* colonists betting on the new Republic, mostly *petits blancs;* French troops fresh from home under command of hot-eyed doctrinaires; Spanish troops gnawing at the colony from the rear; British troops from Jamaica taking over at the instance of *grand blanc* refugees; the opportunistic *marrons;* the *affranchis;* the Negroes. The last two groups, allied singly off and on with most of the others as fortune changed, finally remained the only two combatants in the ring.

Grands blancs lucky enough to survive had fled to New Orleans, Jamaica and American ports mostly in Dixie. Those venturing back when things looked better met renewed massacre. The *petits blancs* also fled or disappeared by grisly attrition as both Negroes and *affranchis* settled old scores with them. After long holding coastal vantage points and considerably damaging the other factions, the English sailed away because the Negroes were too tenacious and local diseases too deadly. The remains of the Republican French had already gone. The *marrons* blended with the Negroes. As First Consul, Napoleon sent 20,000 men and LeClerc, a first-class general, to restore the colonial government and slavery. Success looked near, though fighting and disease heavily thinned the ranks. Toussaint L'Ouverture, the Negroes' brave and subtle leader, was treacherously captured and sent to France to die. But soon enough yellow fever killed LeClerc and it grew clear that merely to keep the lid on the Negroes and the *affranchis* would bleed France of men and money ill to be spared. In 1803 a new European war put further adventures in St. Domingue out of the question.

After twelve years of ineffable chaos Hayti was *de facto* free[8]—unencumbered but ominously prone to fission, the Negroes dominating the northerly parts, the *affranchis* the southerly. Toussaint had revived the plantation system and something close to slavery, with colored or Negro masters working Negro labor tied to the soil, though nominally paid a quarter share of the produce; he even considered buying African slaves. After the capture of Toussaint his ablest Negro aides, Dessalines (later Emperor Jacques I) and Christophe (later King Henry I), fought the *affranchis* and also revived virtual slavery. Christophe's grandiose organization of northern Hayti, based on West Africans imported as slaves and trained as an *élite* police, was strikingly like that of an upcountry Slave Coast kingdom. In the end, however, the fragility inherent in personal regimes relegated all Hayti to the more liberal if stagnant conditions that the *affranchis* had created in their segment of the country—small peasant holdings and feckless, ignorant freedom for all.

It was both calamity and ominous symbol that neglect during these struggles ruined most of the irrigation works on which much of Hayti's sugar acreage depended. The tremendous bloody explosion of the Haytian revolution, the greatest effort that the Negro slave ever made in his own behalf, left his country ruined—ruined still to this day. The key dam of the Artibonite Valley system, collapsed in 1800, was rebuilt only a few years ago with outside money and at international, not Haytian, instance. The peasant bulk of the population are handcuffed by primitive farming of tiny plots of degenerating soil; cut off from the world by a stultifying local *patois*; preyed on by political buzzards; committed to ever more children per mouthful; even more voodoo-ridden than when, 150 years ago, their own leaders sought to curb the cult as too handy for underground plotters. Worst of all, the hatred between the Negro peasant and the *élite*—the tiny minority, cultural heirs of the *affranchis,* who scorn work with their hands, monopolize what education is available and cling with a sterile colonial-mindedness to metropolitan French culture—is still viciously strong.

*"What though [slave-rebellion] baptize the South in blood?
What though smoking towns and desolated plantations
should robe her in a pall black as the midnight of despair?"*
—THE REV. MR. PARKER PILLSBURY

Most Abolitionists contended that Negroes freed under favorable circumstances could handle their own affairs. This happened to be true, but it left open the question what circumstances might be sufficiently favorable. As first example of self-freed slaves attempting self-government, Hayti might have been a heartening case in point. Hope that Anglophile King Henry I's taut ship of a kingdom would stay creditably afloat caused many well-meaning British antislaveryites to ignore or dishonestly apologize for his sickening brutalities. But between his suicide (1820) and the Civil War, Hayti's failure to stabilize herself gradually grew so glaring that fewer and fewer Stateside antislaveryites,[9] however careless about fact, could respect the new nation. The immense impact of Hayti on them came rather from the blood-lustful assaults of Negroes and *affranchis* on the whites. These were taken to mean that a slave economy necessarily seethed with readiness to conspire and rebel; that such risings stood a good chance of success; and that they inevitably meant looting, arson, torture, death and rape after the Haytian example. The last had some validity; the rest of it even less than is usual in conclusions drawn from too few instances. But together they made up a magnificent propagandist's bogeyman: "Divest yourself of slavery at once," Abolitionists told Dixie, "or any day Magnolia Hall will be burned, your sons' throats cut and your wife and daughter raped before bloody black hands disembowel them."

Certain antislavery leaders came to dwell on this with

regrettable morbidity. In 1831, when Abolitionism had only begun its shift toward hysteria, the militant Rev. Samuel J. May assured the public that Dixie's slaves were "already writhing in their shackles. They will, one day throw them off with vindictive violence, if we do not loose them." Twenty-five years before Old Brown struck at Harpers Ferry, George Bourne wrote that, in view of how slaveowners treated women slaves, "How can [white] women expect to escape if the Lord . . . permit our southern states to be convulsed with a resolute struggle . . . of the slaves to be free. What pleas could they offer to a colored ruffian against his atrocious assault?" [10] Garrison, the most extravagant American antislaveryite, vowed that only his scruples against violence—which he made up for by the pathological violence of his language—kept him from putting himself "at the head of a black army at the South [to] scatter devastation and death on every side." He never doubted that such a black army would gather on summons. He felt only abstract revulsion from the bestial horror that he assumed would follow, slaves massacring whites and then, with cumulative viciousness, whites massacring slaves as numbers and outside help began to tell. Extreme Abolitionists, including Old Brown and the Six, never doubted their right to make up Americans' minds for them and impose the wager of servile war on the 99.9 per cent of the nation, Negro slaves included, whom they had not consulted. Listen to James Redpath, the Scottish flame breather, Old Brown's self-elected press agent, when the oracular-rhetorical fit was really on him:

"I regard property in man as robbery in man . . . let [the robbers] be smitten down . . . with bloodshed and violence . . . Rather than consent to the infringement of the most insignificant or seemingly unimportant of human rights, let races be swept from the face of the earth—let nations be dismembered—let dynasties be dethroned—let laws and governments, religions and reputations be cast out . . . in an insurrection, if all the slaves in the United States—men,

women and helpless babes—were to fall on the field or become the victims of [white] vengeance . . . if only one man
survived to relate how his race heroically fell, and to enjoy
the freedom they had won, the liberty of that solitary negro
. . . would be cheaply purchased by the universal slaughter
of his people and their oppressors." Most unfortunately the
story of St. Domingue-Hayti inspired that sort of thing
among irresponsible whites.

The "dreadful scenes of carnage and desolation" occurring in that luckless island moved Bryan Edwards, who
visited the place during the British occupation, to exhort his
fellow West Indian proprietors to stop making excuses for
the Trade and adopt local measures gradually to abolish it.
This was about the only constructive conclusion drawn; it
came to nothing. The contemporary American reaction, particularly in Dixie, was all the sharper for the flood of *grand
blanc* refugees into the ports of the Chesapeake. Their very
presence was alarming enough. Their accounts of atrocities
gruesome to begin with lost little in the telling and sickeningly confirmed Dixie's nightmares as all too possible. Tide-
water Virginia was not St. Domingue's Plaine du Nord, nor
were Dixie's slaves the prevalently African victims of West
Indian crassness. But throughout the troubles of the next
sixty years Dixie always distinguished herself in misjudging
realities.

Steps were taken to bar importation from the West Indies
of slaves who, it was assumed, would gossip inflammatorily
about Negro rebellions and liberty-minded French soldiers
and politicians in St. Domingue. Though well advised, such
measures could not keep the news from the mainland slaves'
grapevine telegraph. A few years later, when Virginia barely
escaped a serious local rising, the rebellious slaves' leader included among whites not to be harmed white trash and
Quakers—and Frenchmen, presumably because of the
French Jacobins' support of the St. Domingue Negroes. Any
Frenchmen then in Virginia were probably embittered

grands blancs despising both Negroes and their well-wishers. But the slaves' information, garbled and regarbled as it leaked from plantation to plantation, nevertheless left a vague feel of friendliness round "Frenchman."

This luckless conspiracy of 1800 was led by a young slave blacksmith named Gabriel, whose owner kept a tavern a few miles from Richmond. A kind previous mistress had taught him to read, and his book was the Bible. He came to identify himself with Samson and to wear his hair long in token of his destiny to rescue his race from bondage. Religious meetings of slaves gave him opportunity to organize; his deputies were his wife, his two brothers and a fellow slave who, having been at the siege of Yorktown, was thought skilled in warfare. The day before the summer Sunday chosen for striking, two slaves involved warned their master, who got word to the governor, James Monroe. Monroe acted quickly, but communications were slow in those days and a muster of the militia did not prevent the gathering of a good thousand slaves near Gabriel's owner's premises armed with clubs, some homemade cutlasses and a few firearms. On many of his free Sundays Gabriel had reconnoitered Richmond with special attention to the location of arms and ammunition. All that saved the still new and small state capital from a very bad time was a tremendous August thunderstorm the runoff from which made impassable a swamp between the rebels and the town. Unable to move quickly on his objective, Gabriel, whose tactical sense was keener than Old Brown's, wisely disbanded his force. Next day it was obvious that the whites were alerted, the jig was up. Gabriel hid out until things should cool off, eventually stowed away on a schooner dropping down the James to Norfolk—and was recognized and arrested there some six weeks after the abortive rising.

Under examination he said little except that he knew he was to die, get it over with. He and fourteen comrades hanged with him died silently stoical. Some twenty others went the same way. There must have been much supplementary private flogging, but even so the relative humaneness of hanging only thirty-odd members of this conspiracy—the most formidable that Dixie ever saw—contrasts eloquently with West Indian approaches. Some of this clemency may have reflected Jefferson's advice to Monroe: "The other states & the world at large will forever condemn us if we indulge a principle of revenge, or go one step beyond absolute necessity." But this narrow escape also left public opinion crippled with permanent scar tissue. Thenceforward for sixty years armed guards patrolled Richmond's key points against slave risings—and contributed heavily to the impression of Yankees and foreigners that insurrection was a standing heavy threat. The real state of the case was sketched accurately in the official report of the Denmark Vesey conspiracy of 1822, South Carolina's most serious experience, which grimly advised "a *certain* portion of our population, that there is nothing they are bold enough to do, that we [whites] are not powerful enough to punish."

As the state where average conditions for slaves were presumed worse than anywhere else except Louisiana, South Carolina too contrasts significantly with the West Indies. She had no Maroons nor any such tenuous runaway colony as that in the Great Dismal. As the slavery cancer took firm hold she did have sporadic, sometimes sizable slave risings, of course: In 1739 a slave named Jemmy, leading twenty-odd followers, killed two whites in charge of a depot of arms and powder and started south for Spanish Florida and freedom "[calling] out Liberty, [marching] on with Colours displayed, and two Drums beating." Their number had quadrupled by the time the militia caught up with them and killed some thirty on the spot or during pursuit; most of the rest were hanged after capture . . . A generation later "a deep laid Horrid Tragick Plan" to rebel in Beaufort County saw a few slaves killed in the first scuffle; the forty arrested got off with ear cropping and whipping. At Camden in 1816

one of Colonel Chesnut's slaves betrayed a minor plot implicating many particularly active in Negro churches. In
1829 Georgetown suppressed a fairly serious conspiracy by
multiple hangings. But except for the important Vesey case
those are the only sizable risings or rebellious conspiracies in
the historical record of South Carolina during the eighty
years before American Abolitionism became a cult and
Dixie's hatred of it an obsession.[11]

Certain details of Dixie's episodes had West Indian parallels: the religious touch, for instance. In Christian or pagan
terms—or a strange mingling of the two—the rebel leader
was likely to be a religious fanatic, often to the point of
grave mental disturbance of a paranoid flavor. Not that a
slave's impulse to rebel is *prima facie* evidence of being off
his head; but the broodingly aggressive personality trending
off into the psychopathic makes the likeliest nucleus for slave
discontent to crystallize round; think of Fletcher Christian
and HMS *Bounty*. Religion was usually supplemented by
magic, either the leader or a lieutenant consulting dark
powers and supplying spells and amulets for protection in
battle. Sometimes preachings and prayer meetings masked
conspiracy—hence the West Indian planters' harshness toward Dissenting missionaries and Dixie's regulation or prohibition of Negro religious gatherings. The leader was probably already conspicuous among his fellows as conjurer or
preacher, "driver" or craftsman in a high-prestige trade:
Toussaint was a coachman; Tomboy a mason; Gabriel a
blacksmith. And in Dixie—not the West Indies—the plot
was almost invariably betrayed by slaves trying either to
save a well-liked master or to curry favor with a stern one.

Direct influence from Hayti, when detectible, usually came
to no more than rumor-born awareness, as in the Gabriel
case, that faraway French-sponsored Negroes had risen suc-
cessfully. The one exception to this—the Vesey plot—revived the terror of the bare words "St. Domingue" all over
again in 1822. Well before the French Revolution set St.

Domingue on fire, a slaver captain named Vesey sold there a bright and personable adolescent boy whom he had called Télémaque. Eventually Télémaque was thrown back on his hands as unsound—given to epileptic fits.[12] The captain kept and trained him as a servant. In 1800 Télémaque—his name by then corrupted to "Denmark"—won a $1500 lottery prize, bought his freedom and set up as a prospering free carpenter in Charleston, S.C. In his forties and fifties he grew haughtily domineering among his fellow Negro freedmen and notoriously ill treated the several concubines, with families to match, whom he maintained in the little city.

How long he had dreamed of insurrection is not known. By 1818 he was secretly recruiting disgruntled members of the freedman-craftsman-house-slave stratum of Charleston Negroes, many of them African-born: an Eboe harness maker who had his own shop; a ship's carpenter; a preacher; a house servant of the governor's. An Angola-born blacksmith secretly made pike heads for the cause.[13] An Angola-born wizard gave each recruit a magic-soaked crab claw to keep in the mouth to ward off bullets on the great day. A Negro church covered the organizing. Sometimes recruits were assured that after the rising English ships would come and take them away to freedom in Hayti.[14] Oftener the tale was that Hayti would send a supporting fleet and army at the right time. Through the cook of a schooner in the Charleston-Hayti trade Vesey actually had been in touch with Haytians, among whom he probably had some acquaintances remaining from his life there as a slave. There was some reason to believe that his actual plan was to plunder Charleston, load the cream of his loot and the pick of his men on a seized ship and sail away to Hayti, leaving the rank-and-file to face the music of white vengeance.

However that may have been, he organized well both within and without the city, even setting up a small body of scratch cavalry. Like Gabriel he chose a Sunday, when Negroes were allowed special mobility; in summer (late June) when the steaming weather would have sent many whites away; at midnight when fewest people would be about. As zero-hour approached, however, the conspirators became aware that the city guard was being heavily reinforced by militia mustering at strategic points. Vesey saw that word had somehow got to the authorities—actually a minor member of the plot had been boastfully indiscreet to a loyal house-servant—called everything off and went into hiding. Whole-sale arrests of his followers culminated in his being captured in the house of one of his "wives." The ensuing trials, conducted with a decorum notable under the circumstances, actually acquitted several suspects. The gallows took thirty-five, including all the ringleaders except the harness maker who, having aided the law, got off with being sold out of the state. Thirty-six others were thus exiled. Under extreme strain on nerves and temper South Carolina had been about as temperate as Virginia had in dealing with Gabriel.[15]

Slave plots, like Old Brown's, always faced the plotter's dilemma: Organization wide enough for a chance of success increased the likelihood of betrayal, inadvertent, as with Vesey, or intentional; yet forces small enough for safety would be too weak to get off the ground. Dixie's most notorious revolt, during which the searing fires of St. Domingue did actually seem to threaten—Nat Turner's rising in Southampton County, Virginia, in 1831—was small and hardly organized at all. But enough slaves joined on the spur of the moment to massacre sixty-odd whites of both sexes before they were got under control.

This Nat Turner, an eccentric field hand, had likely material—a local Negro/white ratio of 3/2 in this southeastern corner of Virginia, where hard times were making rations short and masters short-tempered. But he had no special grievances to set him brooding. He rather liked his owner, who allowed him many privileges as a Negro preacher so long as he got his work done. Local-born of an African mother and a slave father who had run away and never come back, Nat considered himself a marked man from birth—or even earlier, for he could remember things that had occurred before he was born. As he matured he received messages from supernal forces and began to see visions of "white spirits and black engaged in battle, and the sun . . . darkened . . . blood flowed in streams . . . I heard a voice saying, 'Such is your luck, such you are called to see; and let it come rough or smooth, you must surely bear it.' " On another occasion "the Holy Ghost was with me, and said 'Behold me as I stand in the heavens.' " At work in the field he found "drops of blood on the corn . . . on the leaves in the woods hieroglyphic characters and numbers . . . in blood." [16] And presently he was supernaturally assured that the time was nigh when "the first should be last and the last should be first."

Cautiously he recruited four fellow slaves eager to help in "the great work laid out for me to do" planned for July 4, 1830. Certain portents postponed it until, late in August, 1831, a greenish sunrise struck Turner as orders to delay no longer. As it happened, many local white men were then away at a camp meeting across the North Carolina line. On a summer Sunday evening, armed with only a hatchet and an ax, the blood-obsessed prophet and his disciples killed his master and family, then set off killing whites as they moved, with a vague notion of gathering up weapons, mounts and slave recruits and holing up in the nearby Great Dismal swamp. The rest is sickening reading. At one farm they slaughtered a woman and ten children; at the next a man and two small boys—the wife got away but they galloped after her, fetched her back and made her lie down beside her dead husband to be shot in the head . . . Many slaves tried to protect their owners, others joined up readily. Some combined the two courses by first seeing the family safely hidden, then going with the rebels.[17] They violated no women but did waste time braining them when they might have been making for the swamp. Posses and troops soon swarmed in, broke up the blood-drunken mob of forty-odd and massacred local Negroes rather indiscriminately until militia officers halted such destruction of valuable property. Weeks later Turner was found half-starved in the woods. Tried and condemned to the gallows with a score of followers, he died as intrepidly as had Gabriel or Vesey.

This striking example of what a mental case can accomplish under favorable circumstances had important consequences: Stampp, a recent expert, says ". . . the speed with which it was crushed and the massacre that followed . . . soon . . . known to almost every slave in the South" discouraged further "attempts to win . . . freedom by fighting"; while its sudden explosiveness left Dixie's whites with "something resembling a mass trauma, from which [they] had not recovered three decades later . . . the fear of rebellion, sometimes vague, sometimes acute, was with them always." That was true of Dixie before Nat Turner struck. But he added much to the load on the minds of the Virginia legislature when, next year, it came tantalizingly close to setting up a program to rid the Old Dominion of slavery. Further, accidental coincidence of "the Southampton affair" with the first year of Garrison's inflammatory new *Liberator* convinced many Southerners that Turner's impetus came from Abolitionist instigation. The charge was groundless.[18] Turner's notions of slave freeing were much less definite than either Tackey's or Vesey's. Russel Nye has pointed out that "none of [the rebels testifying at the trial] could provide any rational explanation, at least one understandable to a white man, of why they had done what they had done." Most Abolitionists deplored white efforts to foment slave risings on the sound grounds that, since success was so unlikely, insurrection would only make the slaves' situation worse. But Dixie was determined to mistrust intruding Yankees— preachers, peddlers, itinerant quacks—and uncovered just enough instances of whites risking their necks to tamper with the slaves—say half a dozen over a hundred years[19]—to keep the possibility lively in Southern minds ever readier to see things under the bed.

All such mutterings in the nation's ears encouraged militants like Old Brown to see insurrection as really as imminent as Dixie feared. The readiness with which Southampton slaves had followed Turner without having been forewarned —what plans he had were known to his five disciples only— was taken by both Dixie and wishful Abolitionists as confirmation that most slaves were pining for an opportunity to turn on the whites like circus cats on a long-hated trainer; or like Chinese firecrackers strung in sequence and needing only a spark, any spark, to set them off. Instead Turner was a special case that probably meant nothing of the sort. Squat, dark and glowingly eloquent, he had an awesome reputation as a formidable prophet in close touch with the unseen. He both frightened and fascinated local slaves—the usual effect of the *shaman* on devotees—and they followed him where they might well have followed no other. It was sheer psychopathology that made him the American Negro's Wilhelm Tell. The conclusion from his story is not that slavery was generally ripe for rebellion; rather, that in order to raise the slaves round Harpers Ferry, Old Brown should have enlisted some conspicuous local Negro preacher with religious delusions of grandeur as marked as his own. A substantial body of slaves thus recruited and inspired would have made God's plan much clearer than it actually was about 4:00 A.M. in the firehouse that drizzly Monday.

"The pseudo-African tradition is at the centre of anti-slavery."
　　　　　　　　　　　　　　　　　—WYLIE SYPHER

The less levelheaded Abolitionists soon made a hero of Nat Turner, unctuously describing him as "a preacher . . . distinguished for his eloquence, respected by the whites, loved and venerated by the negroes"—a figure like De Lawd in *The Green Pastures* instead of the shambling megalomaniac of Southampton County. Harriet Beecher Stowe avowedly modeled on Turner the melodramatic title character of *Dred: A Tale of the Great Dismal Swamp;* his autobiographical confession was appended to this prolix and calamitously successful novel. Her Dred is no more like what is known of the actual Turner than Old Brown was like his posthumous portraits. Turner dreamed dreams and saw visions because he was a sick man misled by his disease. She linked Dred's "inspiring belief that he was the subject of . . . supernatural communications" with "a preternatural keenness and intensity" of perception and a body "so completely under . . . sympathy and community with nature . . . that he moved about [in a jungly swamp] with as much ease as a lady treads [*sic*] her Turkey carpet." His grandfather, an African wizard, taught him snake charming and fostered his natural clairvoyant gifts. Turner was short and ill made. Dred was "of magnificent stature and proportions . . . skin intensely black and polished like marble . . . neck and chest of Herculean strength . . . the muscles of a gladiator. The head . . . rose with an imperial air from the broad shoulders . . . He wore a fantastic sort of turban, apparently of an old scarlet shawl . . ."

If Old Brown had not read *Dred* he was the only Abolitionist neglecting it. For all such this apparition off a Victorian newel post probably strengthened the notion that a rising-up of Dred-type slaves against the sinful whites would be categorically "a good thing" like Newfoundland dogs rescuing children from drowning and Nicholas Nickleby thrashing Squeers. Much of this must have rubbed off on Old Brown, else he would not have harped so on Toussaint and Spartacus. It is not easy, though necessary, to grasp that Abolitionism could in the same breath warn the South of arson, rape and murder and sentimentally admire the implied Negro mob leaders brandishing axes, torches and human heads. That Abolitionists could do so hints again that they felt hatred of slaveowners as much as solicitude for slaves, and glorified the leader of the lynchers because they thought nothing too bad for the pirate being hanged. Toward this frame of mind they had much encouragement at the right, or wrong, time from a book famous in its day: the Abbé Raynal's *Philosophical and Political History of . . . the East and West Indies.*

Published in 1772 in Holland to evade Louis XV's censors, it had some twenty French editions and almost as many English—"a 'best seller' which both expressed and influenced the minds of its contemporaries," says an expert on the period. Though remaining nominally in holy orders, Raynal had made a small fortune in colonial trade and become intellectual hanger-on of anticlerical great minds. His many-volumed work describing in detail many, many places that he had never laid eyes on showed a disregard for authenticity notable even in the go-as-you-please eighteenth century.[20] But it met a contemporary need by using the colonial systems of the day as occasions for violent attacks on Catholicism, mercantilism and other handy targets. Most of these attacks are so much more cogent than Raynal's other writings that scholars ascribe them to Diderot and other intellectual princes of the Enlightenment. Among them is the first fully developed European denunciation of slavery and the Trade: "We are filled with indignation at the cruelties of our ferocious [medieval] ancestors . . . imaginary distresses draw tears from our eyes, both in the silent retirement of the closet, and especially at the theatre . . . only the fatal destiny of the Negroes . . . does not concern us. The torments of a people, to whom we owe our luxuries, can never reach our hearts." Raynal takes up and ably demolishes one by one the standard excuses for slavery. Eighty years later Southerners defending it could think of few additions to the list thus annihilated. His suggested plan for gradual emancipation is not unlike that tried by Britain in the West Indies in the 1830's. Gibbon and Franklin were only two of thousands of the educated and well meaning who read and praised this catalytic work. It may be no coincidence that the decade of its publication saw the beginning of organized antislaveryism in England. Violently Raynal apostrophized:

". . . ye nations of Europe . . . Your slaves stand in no need of either your generosity or your counsels, in order to break the sacrilegious yoke of their oppression. Nature speaks a more powerful language than philosophy or interest. Already have two colonies of fugitive Negroes been established [Surinam and the Jamaica Maroons] . . . These are so many indications of the impending storm, and the Negroes only want a chief, sufficiently courageous, to lead them on to vengeance and slaughter. Where is this great man, whom nature owes to her afflicted, oppressed, and tormented children? . . . He will undoubtedly show himself . . . lift up the sacred standard of liberty . . . the companions of his misfortune will rush on with more impetuosity than torrents . . . all their tyrants will become the victims of fire and sword. The plains of America will suck up with transport the blood which they have so long expected, and the bones of so many wretches, heaped upon one another, during the course of so many centuries, will bound for joy . . . Then will the *black code* [Louis XIV's regulations for colonial slavery] be no more; and the *white code* will be a dreadful one . . . If nature should chance to add a great soul, and a powerful understanding, to the outward form of a Negro; if some Europeans should aspire to the glory of being the avenger of nations that have been oppressed during two centuries; if even a missionary should know how to avail himself properly of the continual and progressive ascendent of opinion over the variable and transient empire of strength . . ." and there the author, whoever he actually was, breaks off breathless with delight in this butcher's vision.

There is good reason to believe that Toussaint studied Raynal's book in his slave days. Certainly when he did appear on the world stage it was as what the Abbé Grégoire, packing Raynal into a nutshell, called "the new Spartacus." Actually Toussaint was more like a gnarly little Cardinal Richelieu as clever with a weasel word as with a guerrilla ambush, cat-brave and man-dignified. But with such advance billing from French doctrinaires he could have been as bloody-handed as Hitler, as ruthless as Stalin and still have been admired by the high-minded and immortalized by Abolitionist novelists, a good Wordsworth sonnet and a dismaying piece of Whittier doggerel. Thanks to the intellectual fashion started by these passages from Raynal, thenceforth Negro rebels, whether cool, able and unscrupulously constructive like Toussaint or frenetic like Nat Turner, carried an indiscriminate savor of historical virtue—the implied blessing that goes with something demonstrably and, on the whole, gratifyingly inevitable.

A "new Spartacus" is an ideological blueprint. Of the original model little is known in detail: He was a Thracian enslaved by Rome and put to the gladiator's trade who led a body of gladiators who mutinied in southern Italy in 73 B.C. They enlisted numerous slaves and poor peasants and chewed up several large and then larger Roman armies before Crassus crippled and Pompey finished them off. This last and hottest of Rome's "servile wars" still interests the tendentious fictioneer: Arthur Koestler and Howard Fast wrote

moody novels about Spartacus with a flavor recalling the fact
that the intransigent German Socialists who formed the German Communist Party called themselves Spartacids. A "Spartacus" ballet, pretty juicy to judge from photographs, is a
conspicuous favorite in Moscow today, and as this is written
Hollywood is hard at a Spartacus movie. Old Brown probably first encountered the name in Plutarch, where Spartacus
appears as a factor in the careers of Pompey and Crassus.
This certainly accounts for his wide renown in that time,
when all literates read Plutarch and schoolboys glibly de-
bated whether Lycurgus were greater than Caesar, or Caesar
than Alexander.

Presently too the American Spartacus became burly flesh
and blood with a bull voice, a bull neck and a black goatee[21]
—Edwin Forrest, "The American Tragedian" in playbill
type as large as the printer had in stock. *The Gladiator,* a
stage version of the Spartacus legend written expressly by
Robert Montgomery Bird to give Forrest new scenery to
chew, came to rival *Virginius, King Lear* and *Metamora* in
the great man's repertory. The play is not all trash. Bird was
skilful with the archaistic blank-verse dialogue of the day,
and got a recognizable illusion of dignity into the sentimental values that had long dominated English-speaking play-
writing. Noble as one of the oaks of his native Thracian
hills, this Spartacus was a Child of Nature with certain over-
tones of the late Bernarr Macfadden. Snatched from his
bucolic hut by Roman greed, he consents to fight in the
arena only on condition that his captive wife and child be
restored to him. When he finds that his opponent is his own
brother, he rallies the gladiators to cut their way to freedom:

"Ho slaves, arise! It is your hour to kill!
Kill and spare not—for wrath and liberty!
Freedom for bondmen—freedom and revenge!"

Dr. Bird must have been as clairvoyant as Nat Turner. He
finished this script in mid-1831; Forrest scheduled it for

autumn; it may even have been in rehearsal in late August when Turner struck. Only five weeks later, when the terror of Southampton County was still at large, *The Gladiator* had its brilliantly successful first production in New York City. The skin colors differed but the analogy was inevitable. During the entire pre-Civil War era Forrest's performance of this role—and he was a great actor whether in shoddy or Shakespeare—kept slave revolt associated in the public mind with the actor's righteous, brawny validity, not with ignorant, ragged men who happened to be black killing, killing, killing in panting blood lust, raping in ecstatic hatred, deliriously devastating their own means of livelihood because enemies owned it, as in the nightmare of St. Domingue. Old Brown probably never went to a theater in his life, but the Spartacus figure—heroic, stagy, defying the lightning of oppression, bathing the slave rebel in celestial pink —was as much a part of his time and as deeply imbedded in his emotions as Lafayette or Uncle Tom.

So far so good in transmuting Nat Turner into Dred. But the Spartacus figure had to change complexion to turn into the Negro Child of Nature on whose assumed reality and virtues antislaveryism greatly depended—the picturesque and prophetic, murderous and yet innocent, ingratiating and yet haughty, African and yet un-Negro Noble Savage who came into people's minds when they heard of Toussaint or Cinquez of the *Amistad*. The French had defined the need for this Negro-noble-savage-rebel; British writers supplied him. But for once the printed word was only prelude. Cadmus and Gutenberg now yield to Thespis. Already the Negro-noble-savage-rebel, a synthesis of stage roles, of-the-stage-stagy, all rant and pinchbeck, crepe hair and burnt cork, was a stock character of the English-speaking stage along with the comic but honest sailor, the betrayed village maiden and the devil-may-care, debt-ridden young hero.

*"Ain' you got no mo' sense 'an to let white boys 'suade
you play you Affikin heathums?"*   —Penrod and Sam

West African chiefs being "kings" in European esteem, it
followed that their many sons by numerous wives were all
"princes." Hence the Trade's West Africa was as thick with
"princes" as the Russian Caucasus of 1917. In the mid-
1600's a deviant young Englishwoman known as Aphra Behn
may have visited England's new West Indian colony of Surinam and met, or heard of, an enslaved Negro "prince" taking part in a local slave rising. She returned to England
when the Dutch took over Surinam and turned author, doing well both on the stage in the Restoration's lewdest style
and as the first considerable woman fictioneer in English.[22]
Her best known story, *Oroonoko,* depicts Surinam's rebel
"prince" under this presumably African-style name. An Ed-
wardian editor called it "the first emancipation novel . . .
also the first glorification of natural man." Actually it was
only a satire of colonial society with noble-savage trim-
mings; for no "emancipation novel" could have afforded to
show such contempt for the run-of-mine Negro slave. At the
first sign of danger Oroonoko's fellow rebels beg for mercy,
forcing him, Imoinda, his lovely wife, and his one faithful
follower to yield to the vengeful whites. What this tale did
accomplish was a muzzy identification of leaders of Negro
risings with princely majesty and windily noble ideas.

The work also has a certain juiciness. Oroonoko, heir-
apparent to his father, a Coromanti king, so loves his fiancée,
Imoinda, that he swears never to take any other wives—
instant proof of how little Mrs. Behn knew of West Africa.
In a fit of senile concupiscence the king roughens the course

of true love by haling Imoinda away to his own harem and
soon, jealous of Oroonoko, sells her overseas as a slave. It is
made clear that the king is rather too old fully to consum-
mate his desires and that Imoinda, *virgo intacta* for all of
him, has conceived in consequence of the single night that
she and Oroonoko had together. Bought by a Surinam
planter, she sets all local white men languishing after her
incredible beauty but—instant proof of how little Mrs. Behn
knew of the West Indies either—is chivalrously allowed to
remain chaste.

Presently Oroonoko is kidnaped by a slaver, sold in Surinam and so reunited with Imoinda. Accorded special privileges, he kills a jaguar singlehanded and wins a drowning
match with an electric eel. He has learned European
languages from traders, hence can be monstrous polite and
eloquent in Surinam society,[23] which is as snobbish about
royalty, black or white, as heart could wish. He has the added
social advantage of "a native beauty so transcending all of
his gloomy race, that he struck an awe and reverence, even
into those that knew not his quality . . . the most famous
statuary could not form the figure of a man more admirable
. . . His face was not of that rusty black which most of his
nation are, but a perfect ebony or polished jet. His eyes . . .
very piercing; the whites of them being like snow, as were
his teeth. His nose was rising and Roman, instead of African
and flat; his mouth the finest shaped . . . far from those
great turned lips . . . so natural to the rest of the Negroes."
In short, a classical statue blacked up. These Negro noble
savages so important in the growth of antislavery feeling
usually lacked the physical traits, except skin color, associated with West African Negroes. Since the year 1500 illustrations in books about Africa and the West Indies, done by
artists who had learned to draw from classic statuary, had
insisted on showing Negroes of both sexes with the faces and
bodies of the Apollo Belvedere and the Medici Venus. The

same thing, Chinard notes, happened to the shapes of Noble Savages in other areas.

Oroonoko's mighty feats and turgid rhetoric mark him as a printed example of the standard hero of the bombastic "heroic drama" of the Restoration. Most of those strange beings died unlamented with the seventeenth century. But for a century and a half Oroonoko lived on with a vitality maybe implying a steadily growing interest in Negroes and slavery. The novel was translated into French in 1745 and became one of the most popular English fictions of the period. And not long after Mrs. Behn died a hack dramatist named Southerne greatly expanded Oroonoko's public by dramatizing the novel in alternate layers of pompous melodrama and smutty farce populating Surinam with the stock figures of Restoration comedy: the rich, licorous widow; the halfwit son; the handsome soubrette wearing breeches . . . To spare the actress playing Imoinda from having to black up, which would put off her admirers, the play makes her the Africa-born daughter of a French expatriate by his white wife. The title role is very fat, culminating in Oroonoko's killing Imoinda to save her from rape and probable torture, assisting his faithful henchman in suicide, then killing both himself and the evil governor who has broken faith with him. The divinity that doth hedge the sons of even West African kings and the chasm between them and the average bought-and-sold Negro remain clear as in the novel. A new-landed white girl exclaims "O miserable fortune!" at the sight of a lot of fresh Africans for sale; but her escort explains: "Most of them know no better; they were born so and only change their Masters. But a Prince [Oroonoko], born only to command, betray'd and sold; my Heart drops Blood for him."

With commendable candor Oroonoko does not claim freedom-on-principle as his motive for revolt. He makes no bones of his own previous participation in the Trade and defends the whites' titles to their Negroes' persons; to kill the masters, he says, is to "Murder the Innocent" because

> ". . . they did not make us slaves;
> But bought us in an honest way of Trade:
> As we have done before 'em, bought and sold
> Many a Wretch and never thought it wrong.
> They paid our price for us, and we are now
> Their Property, a Part of their Estate,
> To manage as they Please . . ."

His main reason for consenting to lead a rebellion is the thought that, no matter how well the whites treat Imoinda and him as aristocratic pets, their child will be born a slave by definition. Only later do the whites add vengeance to his motives. I incline to guess that, as slavery lost popularity toward the 1800's, these ambiguous motivations tended to drop out of the script. In any case, cleaned up by revisions made in the 1760's, it remained conspicuous on the English stage well past 1800. It was still one of the chief vehicles of the American career of Junius Brutus Booth, who played it barefoot, at about the same time that Forrest was ramping round with Spartacus. Both must have markedly affected popular ideas of slave rebel leaders.

By then the English stage had added a third to the Spartacus-Oroonoko team exploiting what G. M. Young diagnosed as "the melodramatic streak in the early Victorian temperament." Enter the hair-raising shape of *Three-Fingered Jack, the Terror of Jamaica*. Like Spartacus, he too had been a real figure far back of the stagy claptrap. In 1780 the governor of Jamaica offered £100 reward for this leader of "a very desperate gang of Negro Slaves . . . [that] hath, for many months past, committed many robberies and carried off many Negro and other Slaves . . . also committed several murders . . ." Freedom was promised the slave fetching Jack in dead or alive; his head and hand with two fingers missing—hence his nickname—would be evidence enough.

This was no legally tolerated Maroon but a runaway turned bandit, fair game for Maroons. One of them—reputedly the man who, in a previous encounter, had cut off those missing fingers—determined to take up the chase but so dreaded Jack's notoriously formidable Obeah amulet[24] that he had himself baptized and took the new name of Reeder in the belief that Obeah would be less effective against a Christian. In due course Reeder and his Maroon comrades caught up with Jack in the mountains near his hideout. Resisting desperately with a cutlass, Jack broke clear and escaped down an almost precipitous cliff. Equally plucky, Reeder went down after him singlehanded, found him still alive and fighting—the thick brush had broken his fall—and at it they went hammer and tongs. Jack had three bullets in him and was streaming blood from cutlass wounds but even so was getting the better of Reeder when the other Maroons arrived by a roundabout route, stunned him from behind with a stone and then beat his brains out. Head and arm were stored in a pail of rum to prevent rotting and duly delivered in Kingston.

Tempted by extravagant versions of this story, the hacks dramatizing it naturally made the hero an African-born, revenge-craving victim of slave-raiding white men. In one stage version, having captured his owner's virgin daughter —disguised as a boy to provide the eternal "breeches part" —he answers her plea for mercy for self and virtue with all the sonorous validity of stage thunder:

"I had a daughter once, did they spare her harmless infancy? Where is my wife? Was she spared to me? No. With blood and rapine the white men swept like a hurricane over our native village . . . How at their lordly feet we begged for mercy and found it not. Our women knelt—our infants shrieked in vain as the smeared murderers ranged from hut to hut, dragging the husband and the father from their homes to sell them into bondage . . ." Earlier he has given as his motive for murdering his owner's wife and taking to the bush the severity of the punishment he received for trying to rape her.[25] His motive was not primarily lascivious, however, according to the speech in which he urges a witch to hurry with a wax image of his owner to be melted before "a blue fire kindled with dead men's eyes":

"Hag! The gods of my fathers frown on my delay. Years have elapsed since I sacrificed the wife of the white man . . . to the memory of my beloved Olinda, whom he tore lifeless from these arms, as they dragged me from my native land . . . As Africa receded from my gaze, I swore that the first white man who purchased [my] services should feel [my] hate." His plan to ravish the daughter is part of his program to avenge himself on his owner by sacrificing "his every remaining joy to the memory of my brokenhearted wife . . ." Supposing his departed Olinda a diamond as rough as her spouse, her vengeful ghost may have found his raping of other women acceptable tribute; but the approach, making no sense in West African terms and not much in European, is notably original. In the end the Maroons and a detachment of marines rescue daughter, still intact, and kill Jack in a blood-and-thunder, cut-and-thrust finale. In one version or another *Three-Fingered Jack* was a standard favorite in the "transpontine" [26] melodrama of the first half of the 1800's, directly and indirectly persuading hundreds of thousands of Britons that white men personally raided Guinea villages for slaves and that Negroes in slavery invariably seethed with the urge to rebel.

As Britain's antislavery crusade neared its victory of the 1830's, *Three-Fingered Jack* was significantly prominent in the repertory of Ira Aldridge, "the African Roscius," a New York-reared, British-trained Negro actor. Among his other favorites were *Oroonoko* (sometimes as *The Royal Slave*) and what sounds like a dramatization of Miss Edgeworth's "The Grateful Negro," a melodramatically moral tale of slavery in Demerara. He was probably a considerable actor. His Othello could stand up to Charles Kean's Iago; he got away with occasional performances of Richard III, Macbeth and Shylock. But his career necessarily hinged on his Negro-ness. Playbills identified him as grandson of a Senegalese "king"—as he may have been—and invoked antislavery sentiment by calling him "a triumphant answer to those advocates of the slave trade, who founded their defense of that nefarious traffic on the inferiority of African intellect and feeling." As professional Negro he sang "Possum Up a Gum-Tree," capered as Sambo in a probably deplorable farce called *Laugh When You Can,* and staggered round as the drunken slave of *The Padlock.* He could also turn blacked-up Nature's Nobleman to dance the principal part in the *Cannibal Chief* ballet and play *The Savage of the Rocks, The French Pirate, or The Ethiopian Father,* and Orson the Wild Man of the medieval tale, the innocent child of Nature suckled and reared by a bear.

The effect of this varied repertory as he took it all over the three kingdoms was uniform: Because audiences always tend to identify the actor's appearance and ostensible personality with his role, Aldridge's success further committed antislaveryism to the Negro rebel as wronged Child of Nature—innocent as Spartacus, intrepidly vengeful as Three-Fingered Jack, noble as Oroonoko and handsome and charming and intelligent as Ira Aldridge, which, according to surviving portraits, was saying a good deal. He even had Oroonoko's nose, a semi-aquiline affair consistent with his reputed Foulah descent.

These were Dred's ancestors, and it was the cumulative reverberations from such claptrap that encouraged the Six to savor the enticing inevitability and poetic justice implied in Old Brown's broken-backed scheme. True, most antislaveryites had scruples against going to the theater. But they were wide open to Spartacus and Oroonoko in print and to second- and third-hand reflections of the Negro-noble-savage-rebel in the pervasive cant of the day. In net effect what many antislaveryites were trying to do was like trying to solve the American Indian problem in terms of "Hiawatha" and *The Last of the Mohicans.*

7   *A man and a brother*

". . . *the crimes of* slave-dealing *and* slave-holding *become* crying sins, *which presumptuously invite the divine retribution.*"

—GRANVILLE SHARP to BENJAMIN FRANKLIN

The stage versions of *Three-Fingered Jack* drew heavily on a pseudo-biographical *History and Adventures of Jack Mansong, the Famous Negro Robber and Terror of Jamaica,* concocted in England toward 1808 by somebody borrowing bits and pieces from Mungo Park's *Travels.*[1] The African-born Oroonoko-style hero has acquired great military renown and a lovely royal sweetheart with the Polish-looking name of Zaldwna. He is seized by a treacherous enemy and sold in Jamaica where his "bold and martial appearance [and] keen and penetrating eye" make "the overseers . . . tremble as they [smite] him" for neglect of duty. He runs away, stirs up a slave rising which the Maroons crush, then turns solitary bandit. An army officer named Orford is betrothed to Rosa, lovely daughter of a planter near Jack's territory. Meeting Orford in the bush, Jack wounds and abducts him. Rosa runs away "dressed as a sailor-boy to secure her from violence" to search for Orford. She plans to reveal her sex if Jack catches her, relying on his reputation for never harming women . . . Such balderdash would be beneath notice had it not been set down as actual fact under the august auspices of the British Committee for the Abolition of the Slave-Trade. On its last page is the propaganda moral: Jack "would have lived happy, and been an ornament to his country" had there been no "AFRICAN SLAVE TRADE!"

Below that is a silhouette of a kneeling Negro holding up chained hands, with the motto: "AM I NOT A MAN AND A BROTHER?" In Regency England this device was as well known as the lion and the unicorn. It was the seal symbol of the world's first modern-style propaganda campaign.[2] An immense zeal spurred the group of gifted anti-slaveryites whom this chapter describes into originating practically all the standard public relations techniques that promoters have applied ever since to advance causes good or bad, prohibition or "planned parenthood," Social Credit or women's suffrage. These Britons preparing the way for Madison Avenue were high-minded as well as brilliant. Yet the longer they agitated the more elaborate their methods and the less scrupulous the approach, the higher the toleration of sharp practice in the good cause. This was probably inevitable. Such moral coarsening is implicit in the indirect "educational" approach to public questions.

The late Lincoln Steffens wrote a fable about a man taking a sociable stroll with the Devil and remarking that his companion had always managed cleverly to pervert promising new things: Christianity, for instance, labor unions . . . Presently they see in the distance a man "reach up into the sunshine and grasp a piece of truth," an emergency that leaves the Devil strangely unperturbed. When the man asks what he means to do about this threat to Evil, "Why," says the Devil, "I shall tempt him to organize it."

"Slaves cannot breathe in England; if their lungs
Receive our air, that moment they are free,
They touch our country, and their shackles fall."
—WILLIAM COWPER

The impeachment of Negro slavery at the bar of Western conscience led to the risks of organization. But it began as the work of individuals thinking and feeling for themselves—certain French Protestants, English parsons and English and American Quakers—who deplored slavery out loud in the later 1600's. The rapid growth of antislaveryism in the later 1700's depended on Benezet's attacks on it widely distributed among Britons; on the effect of Montesquieu and Raynal on the literate world; for mass effect, on John Wesley's committing Methodism against slavery. And in the same decade a stubborn gnome named Granville Sharp had almost single-handed forced English law to call slavery too barbarous to be tolerated in England.

This came of West Indian brutality. Planters coming "home" often brought slave servants. Sometimes such transplanted slaves, sold to new owners for return to the Islands or otherwise moved to discontent with slavery, ran away and secured Christian baptism, which was taken to spell freedom. The master caste procured august legal opinion that neither baptism nor any other change of circumstance affected ownership of slave property. Thus reassured, planters continued to import slaves and, on occasion, sell and export them as freely as they did at home. Gradually advertisements for runaways and the high visibility of the Negro, whether as slave or as beggar turned adrift by master when disabled, led some Englishmen to offer legal help to Negroes in specially hard luck. Thus in 1765 a certain

Barbadian master living in London pistol whipped his slave
Jonathan half-blind and, finding him useless, turned him
out to starve. An eminent surgeon named Sharp treated his
hurts and, when he was well, found him a job. Two years
later Jonathan's old master met him on the street, saw
that he had regained value, seized, jailed, and sold him to a
Jamaican returning to the West Indies. Word of this came
to Granville Sharp, brother of the surgeon, who had known
and pitied Jonathan. That proved to be the best possible
thing in the interest of Jonathan and his fellow slaves.

These Sharps were a prosperous mercantile and professional family of serene eccentricity. Cultivated, musical,
pious, they formed a family orchestra which specialized in
religious selections played on the deck of a family barge as
it was gently towed along waterways near London. Granville
sang bass in family choruses; played oboe, flute or kettle-
drums; and had many solemn hobbies such as crusading
against "breeches-parts" for actresses and pursuing the
hidden meanings of the gaudy prophecies in the books of
Daniel and Revelation. He taught himself Greek and Hebrew in order better to defend his interpretations. Less able
in business than his brothers, he eventually settled into a
routine post in civil service. But once something caught
his fancy he could not be distracted or discouraged from
pursuing it. Learning that an early employer of his had
some claim to a peerage, he doggedly worked out an
elaborate body of evidence that, sure enough, got the man
acknowledged in a barony. Now with equal doggedness
and mordancy Sharp laid Jonathan's situation before the
magistrates—and got him discharged.

The West Indians countered with damage suits. Sharp
examined the precedents on which slaveowners relied, saw
reason to hope that they might be vulnerable and determined to get them overturned. He had no professional
knowledge of law, so for some years he toiled to make himself a sound amateur lawyer. Great jurists such as Sir Wil-

liam Blackstone tried to dissuade him from stirring up
trouble, but his formidably organized findings so discouraged the West Indians' counsel that they dropped their suits.
His blood up, Sharp pressed several other cases of like
tenor. In time the harassed West Indians began also to wish
the situation clarified. Chief Justice Mansfield was stiffly reluctant to rule and used every procedural loophole to avoid
the basic issue. Not until 1772—the year of Raynal's *Deux
Indes*—did Sharp's persistence prevail. Mansfield ruled—
ruat coelum, he said grimly—and West Indian hopes vanished: "Slavery," he held, ". . . is so odious that nothing
can be suffered to support it but positive law. Whatever inconveniences[3] therefore may follow . . . I cannot say that
this case [of James Somerset, Virginian slave brought to
England, run away, caught and sold for sending to Jamaica]
is allowed or approved by the law of England . . . the black
must be discharged." James Somerset thus became as famous
in the annals of antislaveryism as Dred Scott ever would be.

The ruling did not directly affect slavery in the colonies.
But it did force any Briton thinking of slavery at all to wonder why it was not just as "odious" on a major scale in
Virginia or the West Indies as on a minor scale in England. It took another sixty-six years to work out the details
but that unanswerable question necessarily doomed West
Indian slavery. Lord Mansfield's gruff opinion was first of
Britain's three widely spaced steps toward that great humane end, and made "Little Greeny" Sharp, as the family
called him, the first hero in the Valhalla of antislaveryism.

Conspicuous in Freetown, bedraggled capital of Sierra Leone in West Africa, is a large brick meeting hall not far—by no means far enough—from the local hotel. Its principal use in my time was for frequent and tumultuous dances. Toward daylight the revelers straggled into the dirt street to stand around quarreling or rejoicing—there was no telling which —for another thirty or forty minutes. By then here came the market women from the country with their head-loads of produce, conversing at several hundred yards' range by shouts and whoops and seizures of shrill laughter . . . The point is not so much that Freetown is no place for catching up on sleep as that this all too adjacent structure is named Wilberforce Hall. The name indeed belongs in Sierra Leone. William Wilberforce was one of the eminent friends of the Negro (led by Sharp) who founded the place as refuge for slaves cast adrift in England as a result of Mansfield's decision. But the contrasts between this rowdy temple of din and its gentle namesake are striking. Wilberforce was a mighty power but not noisy—a little man of great abilities but unaggressive; a doughty battler for the Lord but without venom, in fact usually charming about it. This was certainly the subtlest and probably the most original of all the extraordinary actors in Britain's antislavery drama.

He was no initiator. By the time he espoused the cause

things were already moving in both Britain and North America, slipping and halting but always soon jarred forward again by decency or spite, smugness or simple conscience, schizoid enthusiasm or foresight—by economic as well as spiritual forces. It was 1784 when he entered politics in the England of stagecoaches and rotten boroughs as precocious crony of precocious William Pitt. He was basically conservative as even a nominal Tory needed to be, but also had a hankering for causes, such as Parliamentary Reform, and a distaste for the scandal of slavery not uncommon during the liberal-flavored 1780's among gentlemen without direct West Indian connections. In his childhood his mother had been alarmed when an aunt—a sister of William Thornton, pious chief of the "Clapham Sect," of which more later —infected the boy with religious ideas. Thenceforth Mama deliberately reared him with an anxious eye to cure and prevention of relapse. At Cambridge tutors and undergraduates did their best to spoil with sloth and drink his lizard-quick mind, rickety health and generous sensibilities. Later in London Pitt and he and several other special intimates gambled pretty hard and, on occasion, drank harder. But none of it flawed the eager charm, the sweet, untrained singing voice and scapegrace talent for mimicry of the pompous that recommended him to the candlelit, smelly, elegant and wittily wordy world of George Selwyn and Boswell, Mrs. Siddons and the Duchess of Devonshire.

Just as his mother had probably come to consider him immune to godliness for life, he backslid. He took a European tour with Isaac Milner, a Cambridge scholar eminent in the "Evangelical" movement in the Church of England that had been created by Dissenting pressures on Established neglect of souls and morals. From Milner Wilberforce learned to dread the world to come, fear his own presumption and corruption and yearn for the emotional revolution that Evangelicals, unlike the easy-going, perfunctory, orthodox communicant, considered essential to the name Christian.

(It may be difficult for the modern reader to sense validity in these issues, but they were utterly valid then; current psychiatry shows some cognate approaches, though the parallel could be overdone.) As the clouds of awe and fear closed round him he consulted his Thornton kin, who sent him for spiritual help to their *protégé*, John Newton.

This phenomenon—mentioned only casually up to now —was a former slaver captain who had had a stormy youth and a curious rehabilitation. During several voyages he read the Bible and experienced mystical longings in the cabin while cargoes of slaves were stinking and sweltering and dying forward of the bulkhead. He was incumbent of a City of London parish when the Thorntons, who had put him there, confided Cousin William to him. Though well acquainted with Newton's record, I refuse to judge him even in terms of his time as I have learned them. Little as I like the cut of his holy jib, it remains true that no crudely whited sepulcher could have maintained the respect of the best of his comrades in the antislavery wars. This skilled, stern midwife brought Wilberforce through what sounds like a model conversion that greatly richened his life until he died forty-eight years later. But consider also the horror that would have come over his mother had she ever known that her son's book, *A Practical View of . . . Real Christianity,* would become the soul-searching handbook and touchstone of the very Evangelicals whom she most despised and detested.

Wilberforce still attended gay dinners as part of his human and political duty—and duly scolded himself when he enjoyed them. He went to such affairs always ready to inveigle any likely fellow guest into discussion of such "serious" topics as where-will-you-spend-eternity. It sounds like most uncomfortable behavior, yet in clinching proof of his candid charm—"a galvanic stream of vivacity, humour and warmheartedness" said a youthful witness—some of the worldliest and most highly placed people of that worldly age nevertheless went right on asking him to dine and heartily hoped he would accept. You and I can hardly believe that self-conscious soul saving and engaging urbanity can exist in the same person—especially in a Protestant. But consider that Mme. de Staël, a witness who met Wilberforce long after he became pious, rated him "the wittiest man in England."

John Wesley had strongly advised against the very tactics that British antislaveryism soon adopted;[4] he recommended reliance on persuading individual slavers and slaveowners to renounce slavery as an obvious violation of the Golden Rule. Unquestionably his view was logical, but it strikingly overestimated such people's willingness to be persuaded. Antislaveryism was tactically sound in ignoring it, instead seeking to muster both individual politicians and public opinion against slavery. British Quakers already had an antislavery committee circulating Benezet's writings and petitioning Parliament against the Trade. Now they admitted to it non-Quaker antislaveryites like Granville Sharp. All the while the "Clapham Sect" were gathering strength. Pitt and Charles Fox, pre-eminent leaders on each side of the House of Commons, joined up as gentlemen volunteers regardless of party. Their readiness to stand up and be counted made it clear that, whatever Wesley had advised, Parliament could be the most effective weapon against the ancient scandals of slavery and the Trade. In due season the game was planned out: Get Parliament to outlaw the Trade; then the West Indies, deprived of imported replacements, would have to treat their slaves better—a process likely to lead to the gradual elimination of slavery itself.

Wilberforce was obvious leader of antislaveryism in Parliament. He was already rated a great speaker in a House that included Burke, Pitt and Fox, and had a "cleverness and astuteness" in political footwork that E. M. Forster has likened to Gandhi's. Yet his commitments were vague enough for Whigs to vote with him on antislavery measures.

As disciple of John Newton he met and learned special zeal from the most forceful—and usually pious—leaders of anti-slaveryism. His new "seriousness" qualified him to speak for them in Parliament while his intimacy with Pitt, worldling leader of the Tory majority, assured him great tactical advantages. Actually it had been Pitt himself who, after due consultation with Wilberforce and others of their coterie, suggested that the young member from Yorkshire take up war on the Trade as his Parliamentary specialty. This was in 1787—the same year in which the framers of the United States Constitution half-pledged outlawry of the Trade by 1808.

While the Quaker-cum-Evangelical committee laid propaganda groundwork Pitt arranged a Privy Council inquiry into the Trade that uncovered masses of devastating data. A law limiting the number of slaves shipped per ton of vessel passed in spite of West Indians' sulky opposition. In 1789—the year of the Bastille and the Rights of Man—stooped, eager-faced little Wilberforce rose on his spindle-shanks in the House of Commons formally to open the campaign to see Britain's hands washed of slaving. What he said survives only in cutdown paraphrase but Burke, greatest British orator of his day, said it "equalled anything I have ever heard in modern times, and is not perhaps to be surpassed in the remains of Grecian eloquence." The admirable temperance of his opening struck the note that characterized his antislavery career:

"I wish exceedingly . . . to guard both myself and the House from entering into the subject [of the Trade] with any sort of passion. It is not your passion I shall appeal to. I ask only for your cool and impartial reason . . . I mean . . . to take the shame upon myself in common with the whole Parliament . . . for having suffered this horrid trade to be carried on under our authority. We are all guilty . . . I therefore deprecate every kind of reflection against the various descriptions of people who are more immediately involved in this wretched business." Orderly and deliberate, he showed that the Trade was ruinous to West Africa; not essential to the economy of the West Indies; a constant drain on the supply of British seamen; a moral scandal . . .

Pitt, Fox and Burke doughtily backed his motion but it was rejected, as everybody had assumed it would be the first time, 163 to 84. Regularly thereafter for ten years this slight, winning man of principle rose unruffled by defeat again to ask the House as decent, intelligent gentlemen to abolish or at least curb the Trade—not so much because slavers and slaveowners were fiends in human form as because it was destructive, unnecessary and wicked. Each time he ingeniously varied his content. This periodic speech ornamented by his exquisite voice was as much of an institution as, and far more entertaining than, the traditional Speech from the Throne. Defeat succeeded defeat but Wilberforce never lost his tone of courteous recapitulation. As prosecutor of the Trade, says his modern biographer, he was never "morbid . . . [took no] pleasure in dwelling on the unsavoury vices of his fellow men . . . [did not] pile up the horrors and revel in the atrocious details . . . [shocked] not [nauseated] the imaginations of his hearers." The antislavery movement would gradually shift away from this temperance and toward the irresponsible screamings that so appealed to Old Brown.

The pressures of the Napoleonic wars broke the series in 1799. Resuming it in 1805, Wilberforce was still too much of a gentleman to resort to abuse and too much of a Christian to hate evildoers because he reprehended their evil. By 1807 the friends of the Trade failed to defeat measures severely curbing it; they were obviously on their last legs. Wilberforce was cogent and charming as ever in the final debate. Pitt had died the year before but the chiefs of the new Fox-Grenville government hated it just as bitterly. Fox even asked the House to vote against the Trade as a memorial to his dead arch rival, who had sometimes risked his political life in the cause. The vote was overwhelming. That same month the United States barred the Trade from American ports and ships. On either side of the water few would have denied that, of all those sharing in the great victory, queer little Wilberforce deserved the greatest share of credit.

> "... Clarkson, the true Apostle of human redemption
> ... resembles in his person and lineaments more than one
> of the Apostles in the Cartoons of Raphael. He deserves to
> be added to the Twelve." —WILLIAM HAZLITT

Thomas Clarkson was a more familiar type—the austere, dedicated zealot taking himself as seriously as the good cause for which he tore himself to pieces. Sharp, Wilberforce and he—the prongs of the trident that killed the Trade—are a striking trio and it detracts not at all from Clarkson's work and glory that Wilberforce was central and protruded farthest.

His enlistment in antislaveryism reflected growing antislavery feeling among the highly placed. While at Cambridge preparing for the Church he hoped to win for the second time a valuable prize for a Latin essay on a set subject. The University officer setting it was a hot antislaveryite, hence the topic: "Is it allowable to enslave persons against their will?" Clarkson took this as an invitation to denounce the Trade but he knew little about it and had only a few weeks to learn in. He spoke with relatives of his in the Royal Navy who had seen North Africa but was still unhappily floundering when he noticed an advertisement of Benezet's *Historical Account of Guinea*. He hurried to London for a copy of "this precious book," as he called it, and therein found "almost all I wanted." He meant those cullings from early eighteenth-century accounts of West Africa on which Benezet so heavily relied—and a curious mixture too, gurglings about the Golden Age sandwiched between occasional bits of traders' realism. These data and, no doubt, Clarkson's own skilled Latinity won him his prize.

As he rode home from reading his essay before the prescribed University dignitaries "the subject . . . almost wholly engrossed my thoughts . . . I stopped my horse occasionally, and dismounted and walked . . . tried to persuade myself that the contents of my Essay could not be true." But he could not shake his faith in Benezet's sources: "I sat down disconsolate on the turf by the roadside . . . a thought came into my mind . . . if the contents of the Essay were true, it was time some person should see these calamities to an end. . . ."

As a beginning he translated it into English and learned, while seeking a publisher, that others—the Quakers, Sharp, Wesley *et al.*—had heard of his essay and hoped to recruit him for antislavery agitation. He was offered the assignment of collecting factual data about the Trade for use, as personal testimony from actual witnesses when possible, before Parliamentary inquiries into its iniquities. This implied his giving up his future in the Church, which had already ordained him deacon. So harebrained an interruption of his studies was bound to alienate the family connections on which the promising but needy youngster was counting. "I had . . . a thirst after worldly interest and honours," he wrote later, "and I could not extinguish it at once . . . At length I yielded, not because I saw any reasonable prospect of success [against slavery] but in obedience, I believe, to a higher Power." All this sounds priggish now. But this intense volunteer was certainly sincere in such beliefs then, when conviction of being a Divine instrument could still come to sane religious persons—and among the mentally disturbed, such as Old Brown, remain as a permanent symptom.

His essay, backed up by his own zealous person, went far toward confirming Wilberforce's interest in antislaveryism. But Wilberforce had yet publicly to commit himself when Clarkson set out as amateur investigator. He knew nothing of mercantile affairs, law or the sea. For this delicate and rather unsafe mission his equipment consisted largely of amazing persistence; ability to stay keen long after driving himself past any normal dropping point; encouragement from Sir Charles Middleton, comptroller of the Royal Navy, a recent convert to antislaveryism; and undercover help from the Quakers' connections with knowledgeable men in the slaving ports. It was a Liverpool Quaker who gave him a number of slavers' muster rolls proving with grisly finality that almost half of all seamen sailing in slavers never came home again; so much for the contention of pro-Trade admirals—among them Rodney, Nelson, Jervis—that slavers were indispensable "nurseries of seamen." [5] It was Middleton who got him leave to search all Royal Navy ships "in ordinary"—laid up with caretaker crews—for a certain nameless sailor said once to have accompanied a slaving expedition up a West African river, hence knowing firsthand whether slaves were bought or kidnaped.

All round the dockyards of the Thames estuary he boarded ship after ship; no trace of such a man. Chances were high that he had never existed, for few whites were allowed to join such parties lest they learn the secrets of the Trade inland. Clarkson went to Portsmouth and boarded all indicated ships there; no trace. The sole remaining hope was Plymouth at the far end of England. Thither he dragged himself, boarded ship after ship . . . His total had topped the 300-mark when here in the *Melampus* frigate was one Isaac Parker, the very man in question, eager to testify and, since he was a picked man who had sailed with Captain Cook, making a most impressive witness.

Taking only minor precautions to conceal his errand, Clarkson was soon notorious in Liverpool and Bristol. He got hard looks, then hard language in his Liverpool inn, then virtual ostracism, finally an attempt to crowd him off the end of a pier where people were watching an unusually boisterous run of sea. But he also got occasional undercover contact with a seaman or surgeon moved to tell what he had seen in the Trade and sometimes—but discouragingly seldom—willing to testify openly. The landlord of a seamen's public house who hated the Trade squired Clarkson through the Liverpool crimping dives whence hapless Jack-ashore, drunk and penniless, was shanghaied on board short-handed slavers. Another ally was "athletic and resolute-looking" Alexander Falconbridge, former surgeon in the Trade, who told Clarkson all he knew from four Guinea voyages[6] and acted as his informal bodyguard. When Clarkson was reproached with holding forth about slaving when he had never seen Africa, Falconbridge would boom out that *he* had seen plenty of Africa, everything his friend said was well founded, and anybody denying it had him to deal with. He also wrote an impressive antislavery pamphlet and made an excellent witness in person. But best were the dumb witnesses: the wrist manacles, ankle shackles, thumb-screws and *speculum oris*—the tool that wrenched open the mouth for forcible feeding—that Clarkson bought from Liverpool ironmongers supplying the trade.

He soon learned, however, that he had to seek witnesses elsewhere than in seaports. Whenever he heard of a man who had quit the Trade, hence might not mind talking about it, wherever he had gone, there Clarkson followed him down. He thought the luck good when an evidence-chasing tour of 7000 miles netted twenty men willing to testify. And these were no eight-cylinder miles. They meant the swaying weariness of too long on horseback, the sleepless lurchings of stagecoaches; the likelihood of a botched supper and a dirty bed over a clamorous taproom after going forty-odd miles out of the way only to learn that Captain Fletcher, retired slaver, was six weeks dead. And the horror stories that kept turning up weighed on Clarkson's fagged mind as the fatigue of travel dragged on his nerves and muscles. Weariness and tears mingled. "I do not know of any period in my life," he wrote later, "in which I suffered so much in mind and body." It was worst when those who had testified publicly brought him bitter stories of berths denied, families sold up, orders canceled as Liverpool retaliated on persons foolish enough to talk.[7]

Sometimes they reconsidered and refused to testify after all, or by the time the Committee for the Abolition of the Slave-Trade was ready to summon them, they had shipped out again to Archangel or Leghorn. Renewals of Wilberforce's motion sent this nerve-frazzled scholar on the road again to beat the bushes for fresh witnesses. In seven years he logged 35,000 miles besides keeping up a huge correspondence and writing several anti-Trade books. Then he broke down—memory gone, noises in the ears, dizzy spells, heavy sweats, stairs heaving up and down . . . Had he died then, the antislavery cause would have had a martyr personally worth a dozen Old Browns. Actually he retired on lean resources scraped together by his colleagues—a process that brought on an unhappy coolness between him and Wilberforce—and spent six years recuperating and writing a history of the battle against the Trade. By 1805 he was active again and lived to the age of eighty-six, practically blind past the seventieth birthday but still laying about him, sometimes wrongheadedly, in the Negro's interests.

Such zeal often leads to overreaching oneself and to seeing nonexistent virtues in one's own allies; witness Clarkson's early adventures in France. Friends of the Trade contended that it was futile for Britain unilaterally to quit it; other nations, France particularly, would take over the British segment of it, supply slaves to non-British slave-and-sugar colonies and probably smuggle a good many into British islands as well. This would divert the profits of slaving to others without helping Jamaica's slaves much. Necker, Louis XVI's renowned minister, had already proposed in print an international treaty outlawing the Trade. The suggestion stuck in Pitt's mind. As the French Revolution began in 1789 and the National Assembly set about remaking France nearer to the Encyclopedists' desire, Pitt and Wilberforce hoped that the new reforms might include a French renunciation of the Trade cutting the ground from under the pro-Traders in Parliament. Clarkson was sent to Paris to encourage this.

He was too fitting a choice in some ways. Those were heady times, foaming with Wordsworthian optimism, and Clarkson was only twenty-nine and very earnest. He dined with the great Necker and was promised his help. He was warmly welcomed by the *Société des Amis des Noirs*—liberal, eminent pro-Negro doctrinaires including Raynal, la Rochefoucauld, Condorcet, la Fayette, Brissot, who assured him that outlawry of the French slave trade was likely, whether written into the new constitution or left for action by the first session of the new national legislature-to-be. He soon learned, however, that France too had an unscrupulous, powerful West Indian sugar-and-slavery lobby able to fight a stiff delaying action, revolution or not. Its tactics were those of the British pro-Traders: predictions that, once France renounced slaving, sly Britain would take over the French segment of the Trade and reap the profits; after all, Parliament had strongly rejected anti-Trade measures sponsored by Pitt himself. This new and ingenious version of "Gentlemen of the Guard, fire first!" effectually braked what Wilberforce and Pitt—and the *Amis des Noirs*—sought to hasten.

For ammunition Clarkson had a large edition of a French

translation of his prize *Essay on the Impolicy of the Slave-Trade;* ditto of colored engravings depicting slaving atrocities as described by his witnesses; and ditto of a document already famous in Britain, the best known piece of antislavery propaganda except that man-and-a-brother seal: a diagram of the slave decks of a Liverpool slaver (from measurements taken by a Royal Navy captain) with her legal quota of 454 slaves laid elbow to elbow. It was justifiably pointed out that, inhuman as such cramming obviously was, ships of this size had carried upwards of 600 Negroes in the same cubage before the new regulations took effect; presumably French slavers still did so. Mirabeau, dynamo of the early Revolution, had a three-foot knockdown model of the ship made with 454 tiny black figures of appropriate shapes and sexes carved to scale, which highly educational toy he kept in his dining room to horrify visitors. He planned a major speech to explode the National Assembly into immediate outlawry of the Trade;[8] eagerly Clarkson supplied sheaves of data. Only Mirabeau never made that speech. As Clarkson's time in Paris ran out, the great man vexedly confessed that he could muster only 25 per cent of the Assembly for unilateral French action against the Trade. Only "unequivocal proof" of British determination to follow suit would produce enough additional votes for a majority. He gave Clarkson a letter to Pitt asking immediate action on this; but obviously no such assurance could be given when the Commons contained so many slaveowners and allies and the Lords so many peers suspicious of anything smacking of innovation.

That letter was all poor Clarkson had to show for six months of grueling effort; that and an entanglement with ill-chosen and ill-fated bedfellows. He had openly made much of the six mixed-blood deputies whom the *affranchis* of St. Domingue sent to demand seats in the Assembly and equal rights with whites for their constituents. They were hot anti-Trade and, maybe sincerely, spoke of a fifteen-year program of gradual emancipation of slaves. Clarkson and they also had the mutual bond of receiving the same exasperating treatment: great cordiality from the *Amis des Noirs* who, forgetting their corporate name, innocently made much of these light-skinned opportunists;[9] slanderous attack from the *grands blancs'* lobby in Paris; and the daily mild torture of official delay and equivocation. Clarkson advised patience but eventually the *affranchis* gave up in disgust and, abetted by the *Amis des Noirs,* attempted a rebellion in St. Domingue that ended in failure and the death of their leaders, including one of Clarkson's friends, by breaking-on-the-wheel.

Two years later came the Negroes' cataclysmic rising in the Plaine du Nord of St. Domingue. Two years more and the French Revolution was in its Terror phase, imputing slavering blood lust to anything even remotely connected with French doctrinaires. And Clarkson had halfway wedded the British anti-Trade cause to both the surly *affranchis* and the windy, deluded and conspicuous *Amis des Noirs.* Condorcet and Raynal had little in common with Pitt, Burke and Grenville, even with Wilberforce and the grave Quakers of the Committee. But West Indian slaveowners, said Clarkson hand-wringingly, "had the injustice to [represent the Committee], though it had existed before the French Revolution or Rights of Man were heard of, as a nest of Jacobins."

"The history of all great causes," says Coupland's biography of Wilberforce, "is full of set-backs from the left . . . It was an easy game . . . to spy out the Jacobins among the British *Amis des Noirs;* to suggest that the good, simpleminded Wilberforce was unaware of the sinister forces . . . enlisted under his banner . . ." and to exploit Clarkson's smug persistence in allowing British admirers of the *sansculottes* to lionize him for having touched the hem of Revolution's garment. Obviously the late Senator McCarthy would have been right at home in the London of the 1790's. Presently the French Jacobins, assuming that any eminent enemy

of the Trade must subscribe to all of *liberté, egalité, fraternité,* horrified Wilberforce by creating him an honorary
citizen of the French Republic: nor did it help much that the
honor was not singular but shared with Dr. Joseph Priest-
ley, the exiled "atheist"; Tom Paine, the renegade Briton
turned Jacobin; and George Washington, notorious rebel
traitor. With comic haste Wilberforce snatched at Burke's
suggestion that, as antidote, he take the lead in relief for
aristocratic refugees from the Terror. For the little member from Yorkshire was the more useful to antislaveryism
because he was as conservative as many pro-Traders. Radi-
cals of that day and later never forgave him for his mistrusting Jacobin France and supporting harsh measures
against press and people during and after the Napoleonic
wars. He was not, as charged, inhumanly numb to his countrymen's sufferings. He backed pioneering measures to limit
hours worked by child factory hands and alleviate the amazing miseries of chimney sweeps. But his bent, like that of
the rest of the "Clapham Sect," emphasized the fate of souls
in the life to come rather than carnal sufferings on earth.

> "*He depicted slavery as a comprehensive system of soul-
> murder . . . vividly portrayed the awful guilt of those
> who were plunging [the slave] into an abyss of degrada-
> tion, depriving him of knowledge, and ruining his soul by
> a systematic process . . . it was upon* the shoulders of
> Christianity [*that*] *the anti-slavery cause was carried tri-
> umphantly to the goal of emancipation.*"
>   —W. L. GARRISON on GEORGE THOMPSON

Of the "Clapham Sect" we have met Wilberforce and John
Newton. Its core was the Thornton family, Wilberforce's
kinsmen, high-minded London bankers. At one time the

House of Commons contained three Thorntons voting for Cousin William's perennial anti-Trade motion. As a bachelor he lived with Henry Thornton, best known of the three, in a beautiful Georgian house[10] on Clapham Common. Henry acquired other houses nearby and rented them to his close friends in politics, religion, business and well-doing. Equally cohesive in effect was Clapham parish church where, not at all by coincidence, the Rev. Mr. John Venn, a great man among the "Evangelical" [11] faction of the Church of England, masterfully expounded the subtleties of justification by faith.

The scoffer who labeled the "Clapham Sect" lent it a deceptive air of organization; whereas "it was not a closed sainthood . . . but the members of it shared so many interests that they hung together, and lived as near each other as they could," says E. M. Forster, great-grandnephew of the Thorntons. All were more or less devoted to undermining slavery and to societies for the Conversion of the Jews, the Suppression of Vice, the Church Missionary Society, the London Missionary Society . . . Clarkson and Sharp worked with but were personally somewhat peripheral to the Sect. Some of the Quakers active in such causes qualified through family alliance; a striking number of these people intermarried with Friends. Wilberforce, however, was always central to the Thorntons' personal world and to the Sect. So were Charles Grant and Lord Teignmouth, great figures in the East India Company; Thomas Babington, the learned country magnate who made a great antislavery warrior out of crude young Zachary Macaulay; Hannah More, the "bishop in petticoats" whose widely circulated writings[12] did more than any other single agency to create and impose "Victorianism" on Britain. The Sect made great use of a special advantage: their James Stephen had personally known the West Indies for years; so had their James Ramsay, as parson-physician and their Zachary Macaulay as a sugar-plantation manager, who had personally made a voyage in a slaver. Ramsay's regard for truth was not all it might have been, but Stephen and Macaulay[13] were glaringly scrupulous and dismayingly able to assure spokesmen for the West Indian interest that they knew whereof they spoke.

Most of the Claphamites were well-to-do or rich and lived softly while devoting much, sometimes the bulk, of their incomes to good causes. Some people scoffed at the contrast between the contemporary slums and the comforts of Clapham. Its residents were also unbecomingly prone to refuse to mind their own business about the emotional —in their view the spiritual—well-being of others. As Evangelicals they were trying to give a Methodist flavor to the Church of England, and their standards of virtue aimed so high that, though genuine, they were necessarily precarious. "Clapham Common . . . thought itself the best of all possible commons," wrote one of Stephen's brilliant sons, ". . . a less liberal expenditure of wisdom immediately after dinner would have improved it." And any trace of cant meant immediate lapse into self-travesty—the "serious paradise" of *The Newcomes* at Clapham: "As you entered the gate, gravity fell on you, and decorum wrapped you as in a garment of starch . . . The rooks in the elms cawed sermons . . ." and little Tom Newcome repeated "hymns about the punishment of little sinners . . . to his stepmother after dinner, before a great, shining mahogany table, covered with grapes, pineapples, plum cake, port wine, and Madeira, and surrounded by stout men in black . . . who patted his head with their fat hands . . ."[14] But, as Forster has made clear, the cream of these "Saints," as Parliamentary scoffers called them, were neither chronically somber nor achingly obsessed. They went in for spontaneous affection and family japes as well as for family prayers. It was vulgarization of their special style that led to the stuffiness that we think of as eminently "Victorian"—though all this, of course, was all alive before Victoria was born.

However sleek and prim they looked to the cynical, however much unregenerate worldlings like Pitt and Fox helped the antislavery cause, the Claphamites' devotion to it meant that they were taking the hazards of the needle's eye far more to heart than did most wealthy men of their day. It is important to sort out their motives. In their view the principal reason for thinking West Indian slavery evil was not so much that it whipped and bullied Negroes—though that was a crying shame too—as that it denied their souls opportunity for salvation and tempted masters to cruelty and fornication, "hardening their hearts, so that they and their offspring become alienated from God," as Benezet early wrote. As influential Britons they were, as they saw it, accessory to Britain's sponsorship of slavery. Hence they—and their Dissenting and Quaker allies holding the same views—were bound to strive to cleanse their country and themselves of the sin of thus abetting sin, lest God's patience give out and He visit Britain and Britons with condign calamities. To them this was an emergency real as a typhoid epidemic, calling for drastic chlorination of water supply, would be to a modern epidemiologist. When outlawry of the Trade finally carried in 1807, Clarkson's sigh of relief was loud.

"At this awful crisis," he wrote—and Britain was then in a bad way both in war and at home— "when . . . kingdoms are on the point of dissolution, [at least] the stain of the blood of Africa is no longer upon us . . . we have been freed . . . from a load of guilt . . . long hung like a millstone from our necks ready to sink us to perdition."

Tom Paine had already seen the imminent miseries of the American Revolution as Divine visitations on men daring to talk liberty while sending ships to enslave Negroes.[15] James Stephen adopted this sort of thing as a theory of history, asserting that "many strong coincidences . . . indicate the chastisement of kings and nations, for the impious crimes of the slave trade." Thus Louis XVI was guillotined as penalty for not suppressing the Trade when he had the power.

Louis XVIII was dethroned in 1815 as penalty for failing to back anti-Trade forces at the Congress of Vienna. Charles X was dethroned in 1830 as penalty for winking at the illicit Trade. The general political turmoil of that year was obvious indication of "Divine . . . chastisements on the nations of Europe" for French and Spanish persistence in slaving. Mark how Britain's outlawry of the Trade in 1807—when Napoleon was at his apogee—was quickly followed by the French penetration of Spain, which gave Britain a brilliantly exploited opening, and then by the fatal "infatuation of the march to Moscow." Now (1830) Stephen warned that such crimes as having allowed the Trade to revive in Mauritius would bring on Britain "the chastisements we deserve . . . the quiver of Divine vengeance is not empty . . . The same identical scourge from the just inflictions of which our penitence [of 1807] delivered us may soon be felt again." The propounder of these notions was no half-literate crank bawling from the tail of a cart on a village green but a great admiralty lawyer who believed, as did all good Evangelicals, that God's world contained no fortuitous coincidences, that instead His Providence orders all things, punitively when necessary, for His ends and to His will.

This habit of mind helps to explain how Claphamites could heartily support societies to Christianize India and give Bibles to slum dwellers while neglecting to battle against the owners of "dark Satanic mills" and for the workers' right to organize. "You perceive not their voices raised in behalf of their suffering countrymen," says a gentlemanly Barbadian white in one of Marryat's novels. "They pass the beggar in the street; they heed not the cry of starvation at home; but everywhere raise petitions for emancipation . . . the destruction of the property of others." Dixie slaveowners would soon say the same of Yankee Abolitionists concentrating on the miseries of slaves rather than on the plight of the urban unemployed in the North. Forster has agreed "with the above line of criticism. But," he goes on,

pretty much unanswerably, "I do not share the moral indignation that sometimes accompanies it. The really bad people . . . do no good anywhere and help no one at home or
abroad. There are plenty of them about . . ."

In any case the charge was usually exaggerated. These alleged hypocrites knew well that it became valid Christians
to succor the needy: Much Clapham money went into distributing soup, blankets, even shillings at times. Sir Thomas
Fowell Buxton, who succeeded Wilberforce as chief antislaveryite in Parliament in 1822, began his career in good
causes by organizing relief for the miserable poor in East
London. But this did not flaw the Evangelical belief that it
really did a hungry family in a fetid hole more long-run good
to give them a Bible than to try to re-engineer the world to
give them regular square meals. "The misery of the oppressed," Clarkson wrote, "is . . . not contagious like the
crime of their oppressor. The body, though under affliction
. . . if it even perish, what is the loss of it but worthless
dust? But when the moral springs of the mind are poisoned,
we lose the most excellent part of our natures, and the divine
image is no longer perceptible in us." Wilberforce's comrades were ill versed in our theory that to wipe out overwork
and poverty prevents violent oppression, delinquency, prostitution—behavior including much of what was then set down
as "sin." Our day has largely forgotten the theory, of which
Evangelicals were equally confident, that to save the soul is
to save all at last. Buxton explained this with a cogency that
a parson might have envied:

". . . the main purpose of our living here is to prepare for
eternity. It matters little how we fare in this world, provided
a better awaits us. Death will soon overtake both the sick and
the healthy; you and I, and all now alive, must soon quit this
world; and it is an awful thing to know that either perfect
happiness or perfect misery awaits us." So the true Christian
did well to struggle against his assumed complicity in the sin
of slaveholding—a purpose so commendable that too much

carping about the practicality of this or that antislavery measure might be almost sacrilege. Antislaveryites, wrote Elizabeth Heyrick in 1824, "have not gone the right way to work . . . apprehension of *losing all by asking too much* has driven them into the danger of losing all by having asked *too little* . . . [should have] entered the lists . . . with more of the spirit of Christian combatants and less of worldly politicians . . . remembered . . . that it was a conflict of sacred duty against sordid interests . . . in fact, an *holy war* . . . in which courage would be more available than caution; in which success was to be expected less from prudential or political expedients than from that all-controlling power which alone gives efficacy to human exertions . . ." That is, plunge in regardless and leave the details to God— which, please recall, is exactly what Old Brown did.

> "It is one of the evils attending associations and an argument against them that, by growing popular, they attract to themselves unworthy members, lose their original simplicity of purpose, become aspiring, and fall more and more under the control of popular leaders."
> —W. E. CHANNING to JAMES G. BIRNEY

The target of antislaveryism in its earlier phase was small and compact. Parliamentary Reform, though launched, was forty years from success. Most seats in the Commons were either virtually private property or filled by elections held among highly limited franchises. And Parliament alone had any legal leverage on the Trade or colonial slavery either. To take effect antislavery feeling had to soften up either the peers and M.P.'s themselves or the literate oligarchy, maybe 100,000 strong, whence came members of the two Houses,

the clergymen of the Church of England and the officers of
army and navy; or conversely, the social strata to whom went
the best openings in banking and overseas trade. Social and
political cleavages were sharp between them and the Dissenters—Methodists, Baptists, Independents, Quakers—usually
keenest on antislaveryism. A pro-Trade M.P. might well twit
the House with the likelihood that, however ably great men
like Pitt and Fox might deplore the Trade, Parliament
would vote Wilberforce's motions down indefinitely. He had
in mind not so much the fifty or so members of the actual
West Indian bloc as the more numerous squires, younger
sons and lesser peers who, though without West Indian connections, disliked meddling with property, even property in
man. The Trade could be got at only by changing the frame
of mind of either these or their successors.

For this end Wilberforce's few dozen Saints were well cast.
Barring their crotchets about such things as sin and the
Trade, they were mostly typical of the lower but acceptable
strata of the oligarchy and, being mostly Evangelicals, not
Dissenters, retained the social advantages of adherence to
the Church of England. Buxton, Wilberforce's eventual
choice of replacement, neatly combined the wealthy brewer
with the country magnate of ancient blood—tall, broad,
bluff, mad about guns, dogs and horses, unmistakably to be
taken seriously by fellow M.P.'s yet also "serious" in the
Evangelical sense. His temper is delightfully clear in his account of what he did when his coach overturned at night:
"with a most noble crash. As I was not injured, I did not
feel in the slightest . . . disturbed . . . I put on my spectacles . . . exchanged my cap for my hat . . . ascended
through the broken window and got upon the body of the
coach, where I immediately delivered a lecture to the coachman on the impropriety of swearing at any time, but especially at the moment of delivery from danger." Such an M.P.
could serve the cause extremely well. But indirection was an
even better trick. Lords and Commons alike had families,

friends, patrons or dependents, mostly numb to antislaveryism, true, but that might be changed. Devotedly the antislaveryites launched upon propaganda experiments aimed at altering Parliament's mental and emotional climate by persuading literate Britons of the heinousness of what West Indians so shrilly defended. It was a fateful step.

Let the Evangelical Countess of Southdown marry her daughter, Lady Jane Sheepshanks, to Sir Pitt Crawley, Bart.: Lady Jane's harping on the woes of the Negroes might eventually influence him against property in human beings, possibly changing his vote as a member of the House of Commons. Let Lady Jane incessantly wear the Wedgwood man-and-a-brother cameo on brooch, bracelet and ornamental hairpin. Let her give Sir Pitt on his birthday the same cameo on a shirt pin; and next year the same on the lid of an elegant snuffbox. He goes to the play in London or his own county town and the bill includes Bickerstaff's durable musical farce *The Padlock,* with Mungo, the comic Negro of the piece, stepping before the footlights with a new epilogue saying in effect, now stop laughing, being human and a slave is a sad and terrible thing. He opens his bedroom window the next morning and hears a street singer dwelling on Cowper's lugubrious *Negro's Complaint* set to music at antislaveryites' behest:

> "Forced from home and all its pleasures,
>   Afric's coast I left forlorn;
> To increase a stranger's treasures,
>   O'er the raging billows borne.
> Men from England bought and sold me,
>   Paid my price in paltry gold;
> But, though slave they have enrolled me,
>   Minds are never to be sold.
> Still in thought as free as ever,
>   What are England's rights, I ask,
> Me from my delights to sever,

Me to torture, me to task?
Fleecy locks and black complexion
    Cannot forfeit Nature's claim;
Skins may differ, but affection
    Dwells in white and black the same . . ."

It was well understood that, even though Sir Pitt resisted his wife's notions, his children were likely to acquire them. The small Crawleys might ask about and be impressively taught the meaning of that man-and-a-brother cameo. Once they could read, or be read to, there was a sizable antislavery literature aimed at children and governesses. Miss Edgeworth's and Mrs. Barbauld's renowned collections of stories for the young included antislavery sketches. Well reared boys were supposed to read—and many did—Thomas Day's *Sandford and Merton,* presenting a West Indian's son as a nasty spoiled brat and a vagrant Negro as an eloquent Noble Savage. Sir Pitt's son might never have seen a Negro, let alone a slave, but when he took his father's seat in the still unreformed House of Commons in the late 1820's, he was mortally sure that slavery was a social horror and a moral shame—as indeed it was, however soprano the terms in which he had learned to feel so. Multiply him by thousands and a change in mental climate is clearly on its irresistibly glacierlike way.

After Waterloo the West Indian slaveowners and their British creditors, up to their ears in sugar-estate mortgages, lent their enemies a hand by going more and more mulish. They held out as long as possible against "registration" of existing slaves—the only way to discourage smugglers from substantial evasion of the anti-Trade statutes. Lack of supply of fresh Africans was supposed to force owners to treat better the labor they already had. Then, as working and living conditions gradually improved, slavery would gradually wither as had the virtual slavery of medieval "villeinage." But, though conditions did lighten, the effect was not consistent

or marked enough. Early in the 1820's antislaveryites turned
to a new target: "amelioration" programs aimed at gradually preparing the slaves for eventual freedom, such as
encouragement of thrift and marriage (which implied religious education); limited working hours; the Spanish colonial system of letting the slave "buy" one day of the week,
then another and so on until he arrived at total freedom;
abolition of flogging of women and of carrying whips in the
field . . .[16] Every step of the way the West Indians and their
creditors fought every such proposal, regardless of its specific
merit, just as the Dixie redneck fights anything tending to
flaw complete school segregation.

They had long subsidized journalists to write and publish
anti-antislavery propaganda, some of it responsible, some
viciously slanderous. James Ramsay died under such fire,
and nobody gainsaid the West Indian M.P. who boasted:
"Ramsay is dead—I have killed him." They sought to gag
debate of Amelioration even in England on the pretext that
such talk might leak over to the Islands and foment risings
among slaves overhearing it. Government imposed certain
gingerly Amelioration measures on Trinidad—newest and
least developed of the "Crown Colony" islands—and instructed other colonies to try them. Local response ranged
from indolence to insolence. The governors and councils of
Crown Colony islands, which lacked elected legislatures, did
exactly nothing. The older colonies, possessing elective legislatures, notably Jamaica and Barbados, denounced Amelioration measures as the fantasies of crackbrained, hypocritical psalm singers bent on destroying the brightest jewels
in Britannia's crown—and denied Parliament's legal right
to force laws on them. Jamaica actually threatened to join
the United States, which treated slavery better. This made
notably little sense. All that kept the Jamaican economy
alive was British tariffs discriminating against the growing—
and largely free-labor—sugar culture of India.[17] Jamaica,
antislaveryites jeered, would do Britain a favor by quitting

the nest. The mother country would then have cheaper Indian sugar for her tea without needing to maintain costly military and naval forces in the Caribbean.

These West Indian diehards could have served their own interests no worse had they been Mississippi politicians staking all on the omnipotence of King Cotton. Presently they outraged devout Britons—particularly the growingly influential Dissenters—by persecuting Dissenting missionaries trying to give slaves some notion of the Seventh and Eighth Commandments. In Demerara a bungling governor had supplied occasion for a slave rising on a plantation on which a Baptist missionary named John Smith was active. After the Negroes were bloodily put down, Smith was arrested for inciting rebellion, tried by court-martial—on the curious but maybe tenable grounds that military officers would at least be fairer than a jury of planters—and sentenced to hang. The governor probably meant to commute this to something milder but Smith, ailing, well-meaning, simple-minded and almost unquestionably innocent, died in jail before His Excellency got round to it. Antislaveryites rushed to make the most of such a martyr in Parliament and before the public. Klingberg, a modern authority, says it did for British antislaveryism what Old Brown's martyrdom did for American Abolitionism.

Rising emotional pressures sharpened propaganda techniques all through the 1820's, as the aging Saints and their replacements verged nearer demanding outright slave freeing by Parliamentary fiat. The Quakers had petitioned Parliament against the Trade back in 1783, and continued to use this method. After Waterloo it was immensely expanded, and every man asked to sign a petition for Amelioration or against slavery had, in merely reading its terms, been exposed to propaganda. True, M.P.'s were as far as ever from popular election, but they were human and to varying degrees susceptible to massive pressure from public opinion. Muggleton, the "ancient and loyal borough" where Mr.

Pickwick saw a cricket match, had "presented at divers times
. . . one thousand four hundred and twenty petitions against
the continuance of negro slavery abroad, and an equal number against any interference with the factory system at
home." [18] Well before Parliament reformed itself, Buxton
thought it worth while to deliver to the House of Commons
a rolled-up petition so long and heavy that it took four men
to carry it. All the signators were women. Such intrusion of
women into public questions naturally caused headshaking,
though more in Church than in Dissenting circles, for Quakers and Methodists in particular gave females a good deal of
leeway.

Women were soon all over the movement, holding antislavery fairs and antislavery teas, circulating antislavery
tracts with the man-and-brother emblem, infiltrating the
press with antislavery verses. Professional he-poets had been
showing the way with enthusiasm ever since, early in the
1700's, Thomson's *The Seasons* had dipped a gingerly toe in
the horrors of the Trade. The purpose was admirable, the
quality of their verses usually deplorable. When touching on
slavery Cowper, Blake, Wordsworth and Southey produced
drivel. Southey heard of a sailor's bitterly repenting having
shipped in a slaver and prefaced a ballad based on it thus:
"By presenting it as a Poem, the story is made more public;
and such stories ought to be made as public as possible."
Amen; but the wretched man should not begin his tale:

> "I sail'd on board a Guineaman
> And to the slave-coast went;
> Would that the sea had swallow'd me
> When I was innocent . . ."

As the scope of antislavery propaganda widened, the proportion of such stuff steadily increased, and standards of ability
steadily fell.

Pressure for mass Emancipation of West Indian slaves al-

ways raised the question of how this had worked out in
Hayti, the only place where it had been tried on a large scale.
After 1811 this meant close attention to self-crowned King
Henry I (Christophe), that terrifying Negro version of Mus-
solini. On such a phenomenon one might not expect too
much realism from Clarkson, admirer of the *Amis des Noirs*
and Ogé's *affranchis,* who had never been near Africa or the
slave colonies and was excusably subject to the cult of the
Negro-noble-savage-rebel from which the prestige of Christophe as well as Toussaint so greatly profited. Some of the
above might also apply to Wilberforce, though he was subtler
and with no personal commitment to French fantasies. But
even Macaulay, who knew West Africa and the West Indies
so well, joined in seeing a sort of blacked-up King Alfred in
King Henry I. They eagerly abetted his childishly Anglophile efforts to transplant English culture—governesses as
well as improved agriculture—to Hayti. Their overwilling-
ness meant that they dared not really look into the mind and
methods of their dictator *protégé;* it was emotionally essential for them that a Negro nation of former slaves under a
leader who had himself been one should quickly arrive at
stable civilization as Clapham Common conceived of it.

Maybe neither Wilberforce nor Macaulay would have
judged so ill in the 1790's. But all this was after Waterloo,
when both were older and had been much longer immersed
in the cantings and temptations to juggle facts consequent
on admitting more and lesser men to the councils of antislaveryism. Christophe's suicide in 1820 ended the relationship but the delusions continued. As Hayti entered on the
long, sad slide into malnourished chaos that began in the
1820's, antislaveryite lectures continued for a generation to
assure their hearers that none of the massacres of the 1790's
had originated with the slaves but were wholly blamable on
the whites and *affranchis;* that after freedom Haytian slaves
had continued spontaneously and quietly to work the plantations; and that highly competent and trustworthy witnesses

continued to find "the peasants of Hayti as happy as any portion of the human family." On the authority of their British preceptor-models American Abolitionists simultaneously
parroted these flagrant misrepresentations. And they too got
misleadingly woven into the delusions of Old Brown and
the Six.

*". . . one's own propaganda is intoxicating even when only
half believed."*   —STIMSON BULLITT

Early in 1832 the Demerara story repeated itself in Jamaica.
Official clumsiness about a last stab at Amelioration caused
rumors that Emancipation had been granted but the governor was withholding it. These sparked a serious rebellion
with much bloodshed, several missionary chapels burned
and their Dissenting ministers exiled. The white organization instigating this arson and kidnaping had the effrontery
to use the name "Church Union" and pose as protecting the
Church of England against encroachment. As he was put
aboard the ship taking him to England, one of the ejected
missionaries, a doughty Baptist named Knibb, was told that
Parliamentary Reform had finally been effected. "Now!"
he said, "now if that's true, we'll have slavery down!" Thus
sent home full of facts and fight, he became a highly effective
antislavery spellbinder. But he had the emphasis right to
begin with. All the talk in the world could not yet have done
slavery down had not Reform more strongly sensitized Parliament to the kind of public opinion that the Knibbs could
stir up.

History between Marie Antoinette and Victoria often
meshed with antislaveryism. The Jacobins flavored the cause

with sentimentality and then with blood from the guillotine and a hundred battlefields. In 1803 union of Britain and Ireland sent to the House of Commons new Irish members outside West Indian influences. In 1805 sea victory at Trafalgar killed the threat of French invasion of England and reopened the possibility of outlawing the Trade. In 1814-15 land victory over Napoleon gave Britain the leverage for steady pressure on other powers to abandon the Trade. In 1830 France's "July Revolution" showed timid Britons of good will that success for the elements enthroning Louis Philippe—not unlike those seeking Parliamentary Reform in Britain—did not necessarily imply another Terror and another Napoleon. So in 1831 Reform—a good cause coeval with antislaveryism and popular with many of the same people—came gloriously to pass, wiping out "rotten boroughs," widening the franchise and allowing better representation to the new industrial towns, strongholds of Dissent and of Emancipation. Thus it not only swept many West Indian-minded M.P.'s out of the Commons; it also made popular support newly important to M.P.'s generally. Petitions had proved useful even when antislaveryism was going hat-in-hand to legislators dependent principally on how noble or wealthy patrons liked their votes and speeches. But now instead of merely signing their names for M.P.'s to take as seriously as they chose, many antislaveryites were in a position to tell candidates that their votes went only to men pledged to ram Emancipation down West Indian throats.

In 1830, the year before Reform, new circumstances and younger men had stiffened the Anti-Slavery Committee's demands. Amelioration-and-eventual-withering was replaced by "immediate Emancipation" as goal. "Immediate" was given a weasly meaning. The scheme was "immediately" to abolish the legal status of slavery and the slave's inequality before the law while still leaving room for long-term transitional arrangements preceding full freedom: the most widely accepted suggestion was "apprenticeship," a sort of bound-to-the-soil serfdom for a number of years with a magistrate instead of master determining punishments. This was a compromse with a rapidly growing sentiment for granting overnight freedom bolstered by, among other things, those delusions about Hayti. Language was also growing as harsh on the antislavery side as it had often been on the West Indian side. Buxton could still follow Wilberforce in mistrusting vituperation and flashiness, still assure the House that he "had not the slightest feeling of hostility toward the West Indian proprietors . . ." and would not adduce "cases of individual atrocity, though abundance of them might be brought forward." But others less finicky had come to the fore: Charles Brougham, a brilliant but opportunistic lawyer; the able, aggressive sons of James Stephen; and a new lot of Quakers most articulate of whom was a wealthy Birmingham grain dealer named Joseph Sturge.

Impatiently aware that the newly enfranchised voters were the prime target now, young George Stephen and Sturge's friends formed an "Agency Committee" for "a more vivacious propaganda than the [Anti-Slavery Committee] . . . would sanction." To blur the discrepancy between policies this new committee took offices in the same building that housed the Society, a slightly unworthy measure in which the Society saw fit to acquiesce. Then far and wide the Agency Committee flooded Britain with the man-and-a-brother figure; hired platoons of bill posters to plaster London with placards denouncing the West Indians so violently that government considered prosecution of the authors; and invented a system of paid and unpaid "agents"— roving lecturer-press agents, who spurred up local antislaveryites in county towns, arranged and addressed antislavery meetings, organized local Anti-Slavery Societies where none had existed, cajoled local editors into printing antislavery matter, organized hecklers and opposition meetings when the West Indians sent counteragents on the same circuits . . . It was all exactly what any such crusade would do today; only these were the first people who ever thought of thus co-ordinating all these propaganda devices.

Sturge and friends paid for the beginning of the campaign. Soon hat passings at meetings more or less covered agents' expenses and the paid agents' salaries of £200 a year. An outstanding unpaid agent was Charles Stuart, "the antislavery Quixote"—Jamaica-born former Indian Army officer, religious zealot, teacher, vegetarian, dressed in gaudy tartan summer and winter and attaining a new high in antislavery shrillness when calling slavery "an infraction of all righteous law . . . the bane of all true love . . . high treason against God . . . an outrage, concentrating in itself all outrages, against men." He had lived for years in Canada and the States, was close to some eminent American Abolitionists and had come to England specially to join the Agency warhawks. The outstanding paid agent was George Thompson, a character straight out of H. G. Wells. He was a precocious poor boy from Liverpool, working as soon as he could earn, converted to Methodism at the age of fifteen, a grocer's apprentice in London at sixteen. He did well speaking at self-improvement debating clubs, and gained further polish by taking lessons from a famous teacher of elocution.[19] He saw the Agency's advertisement for fast-talking recruits and applied, claiming to know little about slavery but able to qualify as a trained speaker who could show a good character; no doubt £200 a year and traveling expenses attracted him. Turned crusader in this curious way, he proved the most torrentially voluble and effective agent of them all, clever at sarcastic infighting and, during his tours of the States in later years, courageous enough as a favorite target for mobs and rotten eggs. When Emancipation passed the Lords in 1833, Brougham rose from the woolsack to say: "I . . . take the crown of this most glorious victory from every other head and place it upon George Thompson's. He has done more than any other man to achieve it."

This was unfair to several of Brougham's elders and bet-

ters. Wilberforce had just died, Clarkson and Macaulay were
still alive. Buxton had even made a crucial contribution to
Agency propaganda. At his instance Henry Whiteley, a
young man aghast at the cruelties to Negroes and persecution of Dissenters that he had seen during a few months in
Jamaica, wrote a vivid pamphlet about it all which has
been called the British parallel to *Uncle Tom's Cabin* for
rousing antislavery feeling. But Brougham was glib and in
one way he was right. Thompson's facile vituperation and
shyster's disregard of fact were the true representative of
the new-style antislaveryism that fought the final two battles
in Britain's war on slavery. It was a long way, all downhill,
from Wilberforce assuring the House that he himself felt as
guilty about the Trade as any slaver captain to Thompson
railing at Buxton for compromising with the West Indians
in order to get Emancipation under way.

The Agency agents' instructions were well drawn: To
eschew politics as such, instead to hammer away at the doctrine that "To uphold slavery is a crime before God, and the
condition must therefore immediately be abolished." But
they were also allowed to clamber down from such high
grounds and publish lists of candidates for the first post-
Reform Parliament with their stand on Emancipation—
pledged for it, set against it or still wavering—noted after
each name. Buxton had already made great play with new
figures compiled from "registration" of slaves showing that,
even with allowance for new freedmen, the actual slave population of the West Indies was still dropping by some 5000
souls a year in spite of sporadically nominal Amelioration.
Not slavery but the slaves were withering away: whereas in
certain nooks of Empire where the East India Company had
declared children of slave mothers free at birth, the Negro
population had reversed its trend and begun to increase. In
the result the first Reformed Parliament had "An Antislavery House [of Commons] returned by an Antislavery public."

Literally "immediate" slave freeing was still thought inadvisable by the more levelheaded antislaveryites. The bill gradually developed to include a seven years' "apprenticeship" with restricted hours of labor; encouragement of slaves to buy their full freedom in advance of the seven years; the whip taken away from master . . . But any colony wishing independently to try immediate Emancipation was permitted to do so. The planters' clamor about the rights of property was stilled by payment of £20,000,000 "compensation" —without which provision the Society's case would have been much weaker in Commons and probably impossible in the Lords. It was Buxton who saw the whole tortuous process through and took the responsibility for the exact nature of the bill that passed both Houses in 1833 and received the royal assent—from William IV, who, as naval-minded Duke of Clarence, had staunchly defended slavery in the Lords. Wilberforce did not actually live to see it but it was unmistakable before his death that victory within a few weeks was inevitable.

Militant Agencyites like Sturge and Stephen were furious, however; they had contended throughout that paying anything whatever to the slaveowners was immoral, since their title to their slaves had been invalid to begin with, and payment blurred the absolute injustice of slavery. Sturge, a wilful, smug man, had also convinced himself that nothing would do but literally immediate freedom. He could not stop the payment of the money—most of which went to the creditors, of course, doing the planters small direct good— but he could attack the seven-years' apprenticeship. After a good deal of sniping at it within Britain he and another Agency man sailed personally to investigate how apprenticeship was doing.

Naturally they found what they were looking for. Antigua, small, always noted for better treatment of slaves and for giving the stabilizing influence of missionaries ample opportunity, had tried immediate freedom and found it practicable. This did not mean the same would happen in Demerara but Sturge ignored colony-to-colony differences. Then in Jamaica they had the luck to find a young apprentice named James Williams, who, fallen foul of a brutal master and a sadistic magistrate, had been periodically half-killed by whip and treadmill for minor offenses or none at all. Most Jamaican masters were not that bad. Such a magistrate was almost unique in the new system. But Sturge eagerly took down Williams' tale—probably true enough as an individual case—and unblushingly published it in England as typical of the miseries everywhere concealed under "apprenticeship." Among Britons already trained to take a dim view of West Indian whites this narrative had a success like Whiteley's. Parliament, reflecting it all, abolished apprenticeship in 1837, and Buxton, always game and gentlemanly, generously congratulated Sturge on having been right.

Here was complete freedom for all slaves under the British Crown arrived at ten years before the Revolution of 1848 let France follow the example; twenty-five years before the States did so; sixty-two years after the first anti-Trade motion had been presented in Parliament; fifty-one since the Quakers had formed the committee that begot the great Anti-Slavery Society. There is no indication whether the Devil was satisfied with the side effects of the organizing necessary to this triumph. But he can hardly have been displeased with Sturge's barefaced misrepresentation of the Williams case and other data that he published on his return. This was only the final item in a long list of well-meaning fictions uttered by antislaveryites in the wishful belief that lies whiten in proportion to the righteousness of the liar's intent. Inevitably truth had suffered and cant prospered as organization shifted the intellectual and moral climate to favor antislaveryism. The momentum of organization is itself exhilarating to many—and usually a good many of those are dubious specimens, with standards and methods to match.

So the great, gaunt, unpopular cause of Sharp, Pitt, Wool-

man and Hopkins became a swaying platform on which
priggish bluestockings recited smug tales for little ones;
cheap playwrights instructed several strata of customers in
the nature and needs of the miserable West Indian slaves
diked out as Noble Negro Savages; and the side-of-the-angels
poets and fictioneers glowed with conscious virtue as they
ladled antislavery *clichés* into their wares. The parallels
come in several sets for readers to choose from according to
their leanings: *Ten Nights in a Bar-Room* or *Waiting for
Lefty; Father, Dear Father, Come Home with Me Now* or
Solidarity Forever; the rear platform displaying Civil War
generals quavering out pro-McKinley speeches in 1896, the
temperance lecturer in the Chautauqua tent of 1910, the
proletarian spellbinder in Union Square in 1930. For our
purpose, consider that American antislaveryites, understandably dazzled by their British preceptors' success between
1830 and 1837, imported the whole machine—organization, attitudes, data—in, as Madison Avenue says, a package,
at the very time when the British antislaveryites' moral
and intellectual standards were at their lowest. This really
has the air of the Devil's work.

8 *Borrowed plumage*

> *". . . it is impossible not to hate men when you think them wicked."* —BERNARDIN DE ST. PIERRE

> *". . . Our anti-slavery cause was a mere means of catching up with Europe."* —JOHN JAY CHAPMAN

Now and again British or French critics suddenly find high significance in an American writer of only mild renown, and presently his new transatlantic glory makes him more sought after at home. Don't press the analogy too far, but something like that came to the antislaveryism of Friend Anthony Benezet of Philadelphia. His attacks on the Trade and slavery were influential in converting Raynal, Wesley, Clarkson—all master cogs in early antislaveryism. Eventually repercussions from these European pioneers rumbled back to the New World thunderously exhorting Americans to go and do likewise—a thunder gladly heeded. It was British Emancipationists telling how they got on the high road to victory who inspired the founding of the American Anti-Slavery Society—at Philadelphia in 1833, only three months after Parliament passed the Emancipation bill.

The trouble with the analogy is that Benezet, though writing from America, was not exactly an American. He was

French-born of Huguenot parents who soon migrated to England as refuge from religious persecution. It was British Quakerism, not American, that he joined as a pious adolescent, and his formative years, Franco-British in flavor, were behind him when his family emigrated to Pennsylvania. He was influenced against slavery by an elderly Friend, Benjamin Lay—a pitiable figure, hunchbacked, semi-dwarfed, a crusading Quasimodo—who had followed the sea and then settled in Barbados, where his sympathy with slaves made him unpopular. Removing to Philadelphia, he found a Quaker wife—also deformed, poor woman—and scope for his talent for agitation. He eschewed all animal products whether as food or clothing; denounced tobacco, coffee, tea and alcohol, and early advocated mitigating the savage criminal laws of the day. He once faked suicide in a Quaker meeting, and once almost killed himself in good earnest by trying to emulate Christ's forty-day fast. It is understandable that he was "read out of meeting" for unbecoming turbulence. Many an Abolitionist of Old Brown's time thus piled multiple causes, some admirable, some crankish, on one another, and combined antislaveryism with behavior that was, to say the least of it, neurotic. But resist the temptation to see Friend Benjamin as precursor of the crank segment of American Abolitionism,[1] for he was no American either. English-born and reared, he was fifty-two years old when Philadelphia first saw him.

His antislavery pamphlets were published by Benjamin Franklin, first president of Pennsylvania's pioneer society for the relief of Negro freedmen—who had spent fourteen years in London first as journeyman printer, then as lobbyist for certain colonies. Tom Paine, early "American" writer against slavery as well as other things, was an Englishman thirty-seven years old on landing here. In the same period, granted, Samuel Hopkins, native American, was denouncing the Trade in Rhode Island, its North American lair, and giving Granville Sharp and others the ideas about free Ne-

gro colonies that resulted in Sierra Leone. Several great
Virginians had come to think the Trade and slavery social
cancers the sooner excised the better. But in view of the
curiously British flavor of later Abolitionism, this early,
heavy admixture of English leaders cannot be ignored.

British influence remained heavy as Abolitionism took
and changed its major shapes. Sharp corresponded zealously
with antislaveryites in both Maryland and New England. So
did Clarkson, clear into the 1840's, and Wedgwood gave him
hundreds of the man-and-a-brother cameos to send to transatlantic friends. George Bourne, dean of American "immediatist" antislaveryites, was thirty-four when he came from
England to Virginia. His frank antislavery feelings made
Virginia too hot to hold him, so he moved North, preached
here and there as a Presbyterian parson, and became the
most conspicuous antislavery writer of the day. His hysteri-
cally abusive style damagingly affected Abolitionists' thinking as well as their taste.[2] Fanny Wright, the six-foot tall
lady crank-intellectual who tried to combine good-life communities with slave emancipation in West Tennessee, in the
1820's, was Scottish-born and British-reared. We have met
Charles Stuart as an extravagant Agency lecturer in Britain
but not in his previous role as the eccentric schoolteacher in
upper New York State who channeled Theodore Weld's
zeal against sin into antislavery action and so gave Abolitionism its greatest propagandist. Arthur Tappan, nucleus of
the American Anti-Slavery Society-to-be, was in constant
touch with British antislaveryites. J. G. Birney, Alabama
slaveholder turned Abolitionist, was deeply influenced by
the British antislavery authors in his library—Clarkson, Wilberforce, Thompson, Macaulay . . . Of the most militant
New Englanders, Arnold Buffum had spent years in England
and had come to know the great antislaveryites; Maria Weston Chapman had her schooling there. During the 1830's
prolonged visits from George Thompson and Joseph Sturge

kept Abolitionism close to the least responsible British zealots . . .

It need surprise nobody that the inaugural "Declaration of Sentiments" of the American Anti-Slavery Society in 1833 contained a close imitation of British propaganda programs: much emphasis on agents sent out to organize branch societies, hold meetings to hearten local antislaveryites, circulate antislavery tracts and periodicals, enlist pulpit and press, promote boycott of slave-produced cotton, rice, etc. When Abolitionists flooded Congress with antislavery petitions in the 1830's—inadvertently enabling John Quincy Adams to identify slaveholding with political as well as personal tyranny—they had in mind how well petitions to Parliament had served Wilberforce and Buxton. When they enlisted women as effective signature gatherers—a cultural novelty of great importance—their avowed reason was that "Female [antislavery] societies probably did more for the abolition of slavery in Great Britain than did those of the other sex . . . They scattered anti-slavery tracts . . . circulated petitions . . ." Abolitionism rejected the notion of compensating slaveowners when slavery should be abolished not because the issue was at all imminent but because the Sturge-Stephen faction had denounced compensation of West Indian slaveowners. True, similar frictions might have elicited similar tactics as antislaveryism grew on each side of the water. But Abolitionism did not wait for spontaneity. Its imitativeness reminds one of the tale of the Singapore tailor who, given the customer's old patched breeches as pattern for new ones, neatly reproduced them patches and all.

Now it can make sense to borrow schemes for transplantation. Steam engines, though invented by Scots, work well in Siberia. Borrow only what suits circumstances, however, or you will be fighting off Comanches with tactics developed to besiege Petersburg. And there was a fatal difference between the relation of Parliament to West Indian slavery and that of Congress to Dixie slavery. No matter how Jamaicans and Barbadians blustered, nobody ever seriously questioned the power of Parliament to outlaw colonial slavery any time its enemies could muster enough votes in both Commons and Lords.[3] So British antislaveryites did well to flood Parliament with petitions for Amelioration and then Emancipation; to stir up antislavery emotions in their legislators' environment and, after Reform, to force candidates to stand up and be counted on the great issue. Parliament being both able and potentially willing to annihilate slavery, it followed that each Briton at home in Britain touched by that man-and-a-brother device was another tiny nail in slavery's coffin.

In the States, however, even the American Anti-Slavery Society admitted that "Congress . . . has no right to interfere with any of the slave states in relation to [slavery] . . ." Being merely Federal, the national legislature could not go beyond excluding slavery from Federal territories (largely the southern and western areas that might sometime become states) and the District of Columbia; and banning the domestic slave trade between slave states. To cause the bourgeoisie of Leeds to loathe colonial slavery was sound tactics. It was largely waste effort to urge Abolitionism on Western Reserve farmers, for Ohio had already renounced slavery and her state legislature had no power over the institution outside her own boundaries. "This difference in . . . the two countries, British critics of American slavery seldom realized," says Barnes, a trenchant modern expert, "and, with disastrous effect upon the movement in the United States, Americans frequently did not realize it either." The American Anti-Slavery Society did work hard for abolishing the slave trade and slavery in the District of Columbia; Congress abolished the first in the Compromise of 1850. It sometimes assailed the "internal slave trade." But principally it devoted itself to bootlessly "rousing the country" in the North for no better practical reason than that doing so had worked in Britain. One result was to set thousands, including Old Brown and the Six, to despising their own government for not doing things it was powerless to do.

Country rousing might have made sense had it gone nationwide and exerted pressures on the legislatures of slaveholding states. But Dixie was already so inflamed against antislaveryites and so handy with whips, tar and feathers, and jail terms against Abolitionist missionaries that their work pretty well stopped short at Mason's & Dixon's Line. Gradually she spewed forth the Southerners—mostly from North Carolina, Tennessee, Kentucky—who spoke or published against slavery. When Abolitionists mailed propaganda pamphlets and newspapers to influential Southerners, local postmasters were persuaded or forced to bar such matter from the mails, in which states-rightist impudence the government at Washington acquiesced. The childishly poor judgment of Abolitionists of Garrison's school was never clearer than in their continuing insistence that somehow inflaming the North would reform the South.

"If we express frankly and firmly our opinions," wrote David L. Child in 1834, "they will give up their slaves . . . The thing may be done with the stroke of a pen." In 1836 Garrison was still at it. "Let the public sentiment in the free states become thoroughly *abolitionized,* and slavery will speedily be crushed by its mighty pressure." This extreme fatuousness is suspicious: It may mean that the Garrisonians so relished the Pharisaical game of vituperating Dixie sinners in public that they preferred believing any absurdity to giving it up. Catherine Beecher, bluestocking elder sister of the author of *Uncle Tom's Cabin,* acidly defined the Anti-Slavery Society as an "association in one section of the country . . . to awaken public sentiment against a moral evil existing in another . . ." and expressed doubt that "to convince their fellow-citizens of the faults of *another* community will lead that community to forsake its evil practices." Lyman Beecher, her famous father, asked: "What shall we, philanthropists? . . . rail against the slave-holder, taking

*Typical Abolitionist depiction of Negro slavery in Dixie.
Note snake attacking child in background while overseer
lashes mother for attempting to leave her work to rescue it.
From Charles Ball,* Slavery in the United States, *1836.*

care, however, to keep clear of his territories?" J. Q. Adams
made the same point. Hints that Abolitionist agents were
yellow were unjustified. Under Northern mobbing they
were braver than most would have been. But they never
found a good answer to: "Why don't you go tell all this to
the slave-holders?"[4] Russel Nye has well stated the results of
their misplaced activity. They "failed to make the North
abolitionist [but] did . . . succeed in making a major portion of it anti-Southern."

Under the circumstances it would have been better had
the two sections been Chinese-walled apart, coming face to
face only in Washington. But Dixie merchants kept traveling
North. Prosperous Southerners—those most deeply committed to slavery—kept coming to Northern summer resorts.
Correspondence and the press were other sources of irritation. Though Garrison's *Liberator* spoke for only his small
personal following among antislaveryites, Southern editors
loved to quote its most violent rantings as demonstrating
Yankee fear and hatred of slaveowners. For a generation be-

fore Old Brown laid his plans, Dixie had been snarling back at what she took to be a North dominated by slander-mouthing, Pharisaical Abolitionists. As the cotton fields spread westward her surly insistence that slavery was no subject for discussion grew more stubborn, confining antislaveryism to merely sectional growth. This in turn prevented her from reading handwriting on walls much better than West Indian planters had. It had mattered little in the long run that Wilberforce & Co. had similarly exasperated the handful of slaveowning whites in London and the Islands. Parliament's attitude alone carried weight. But it mattered immensely that Abolitionism's aping of British strategy and tactics further exasperated the already oversensitive hundreds of thousands of slaveowning Dixie whites.

Abolitionism even used "immediate" in the confusing British sense, again with even more damaging results. The word attracted many Britons sentimentally heedless of what it might mean to free West Indian slaves overnight. The Islands were far away and West Indian whites, as Britons had been taught to think of them, probably deserved anything that might result. Those shying away from the risk might be reconciled by casuistic explanation that "immediate" meant a freedom half-nominal at first with a long transitional preparation for actual self-responsibility. This juggling afforded Emancipationists the best of both propaganda worlds. But the device backfired when Abolitionism imported it. The North was too Negro-conscious to ignore the possible results of overnight freedom. Abolitionists' explanations could never catch up with the nationwide impression that their ideas were just as recklessly fanatic as Dixie said they were.

W. E. Channing, most thoughtful of antislaveryites, called it "unwise . . . to choose a watch word which can be rescued from misapprehension only by labored explication." Unwise indeed, but worse followed. Abolitionists investigating the post-Emancipation West Indies wishfully followed

Sturge's rash lead, reporting that neither "apprenticeship"
nor any other decompression device was necessary; that
West Indian experience had already demonstrated that overnight Abolition was highly advisable. It would be fifty years
before any such conclusion, right or wrong, could be responsibly arrived at, but never mind, these were amateur so-
ciologists and this was what the American Anti-Slavery Society wanted to hear. Now word-twisting concessions to
common sense became unnecessary, and "Immediate Abolition!" could stand forth in all literal defiance. The new
party line shifted the focus back from community action to
the individual: Slaveholding was a sin. Sin is, by definition,
to be reprehended and at once abandoned as soon as its
sinfulness is realized. The Christian must testify from the
housetops against Southerners persisting in this sin lest God
in his wrath confound him with his Dixie fellow countrymen
and their Northern accessories. Garrison's editorial aide ably
explained that, when people objected to Immediatism as
impractical, the answer was:

". . . slaveholding being a sin, instant emancipation [is]
the right of every slave and the duty of every master. The
fact that the slaveholders were not ready at once to obey the
demands of justice and the requirements of Divine law mili-
tated not against the soundness of the doctrine . . . The
minister . . . does not cease to proclaim the duty of immediate repentance for sin because he knows that his message
will not be immediately heeded . . . He dares not encourage [his hearers] to delay repentance for a single hour,
though he knows that in all probability many of them will
do so to their dying day." Hence so many Abolitionists
sounded as if they denounced slavery and slaveholders not
so much because they felt for the slave's miseries and valued
his dignity and welfare as a human being as because to keep
quiet would risk their own chance of personal salvation.[5]
In 1959 this is hard to understand. We prefer more Good
Samaritan and less "Lord, what shall I do to be saved?" But

one is as Christian a position as the other, and which dominated in a given sincere antislaveryite was probably a matter
of temperament. Another complication was the old Puritan
doctrine that the righteous man sins against God unless he
makes every possible effort to reform erring brothers. This
all too readily turned into the notorious inability of Yankees
—and others under similar teaching—to mind their own
business. In any case fervid reprehension of others' sins leads
almost irresistibly to sinner hating. Some Abolitionists managed to avoid one or another of these emotional pitfalls. A
most fortunately endowed few may conceivably have avoided
all. But the typical specimen, it must be admitted, gave an
unbecoming amount of time to the mote in his brother's eye
and the welfare of his own soul.

Whether misunderstood or grasped with all its obfuscat-
ing refinements, the slogan "Immediate Emancipation" split
churches, confused discussion of measures to confine slavery,
encouraged talk of dissolving the Union—and was very
little help to the slaves. Not one slaveowner in a thousand
did anything to bring to pass the hopes gravely stated in the
Anti-Slavery Society's official organ in January, 1835: "The
reformation has commenced . . . When any individual slaveowner is brought to believe that slavery *is* sinful he will immediately emancipate his own slaves . . . When the people
of the several slave states are brought upon the same ground,
they will severally abolish slavery within their respective
limits . . ."

This was the simple-minded, religion-cumbered approach
that led to the incendiary antislaveryism of Old Brown and
the Six. They found it intolerable that God should hang fire
so long over Sodom.

"Abolitionists in the mass were not fanatics, but every fanatic was an Abolitionist, and a great deal more."

—REGINALD COUPLAND

Contrary to most schoolbooks, Abolitionism in America was no lithe Yankee goddess sprung full armed from the knobby forehead of William Lloyd Garrison as he ran off the first *Liberator*. She had had important forerunners in Baltimore, New York City and Philadelphia during "The Era of Good Feeling"—more than in New England, as it happened. Men as eminent and different as Noah Webster and John Randolph succeeded Franklin and the Revolutionary Virginians as conspicuous decriers of slavery. After 1800 American as well as European antislavery pamphlets and books were circulated; individual slave freeing was promoted; petitions against slavery in the District of Columbia were frequently presented. Long before any of the Six had laid eyes on a runaway slave local sympathies were steadily expanding trackage of the Underground Railroad through Pennsylvania and the Middle West—where the Northwest Ordinance had hamstrung slavery before Clarkson ever set out for Liverpool. The debates ending in the Compromise of 1820 had shown an ominous weight of antislavery feeling cogently expressed when Garrison still had six years to go on his apprenticeship to a Newburyport printer.

"Abolitionists of an earlier day," wrote Locke, specialist in this period, "had seen the truth and spoken it as boldly as any of the later generation." But "their language was usually more temperate; not from timidity or indifference, but because they believed that persuasion was more effective than provocation"—that is, they had the Wilberforce, not the Stephen-Sturge-Thompson approach. Note how dutifully the shift of American tone followed a few years behind the same shift of British tone, and that both coincided with a marked increase in the proportion of cracked-wheat cranks like Charles Stuart in the antislavery cause. Their adherence could not discredit the cause in the eyes of stabler men of good will. Many of its most loyal adherents—Channing, Charles Francis Adams, William Cullen Bryant, R. H. Dana and numerous Quakers—were as well balanced as Franklin before them. But the cranks' high visibility made antislaveryism look at once ridiculous and incendiary in the eyes of too many lesser men.

Theology was not essential to their zeal. The new strong language also had an enticing savor of flightiness and infallibility that attracted schizoid arrogance—a crucial ingredient in most crankishness though often below the pathological level. It lent antislaveryism a greater appeal to those secretly proud of possessing the higher sensitivity, greater intelligence and social courage implied by their previous espousing of such glowing causes as phrenology and vegetarianism. The religious crank often added to the above theology a deep conviction that the end of the world was nigh and his battle against others' sins had to be frantically intensified lest the great day find him and his allies unfaithful stewards. The secular crank thought or hoped or felt in his bones that the day had come when wide enough application of benevolence, logic and ingenuity could make men righteous and life beautiful by re-educating hearts, revitalizing bodies and re-engineering the stupid old institutions that had warped them. He was aghast at the callousness, cynicism and brutality of a social order allowing foul things like slavery, rum and meat to degrade and poison such fine things as human beings. He unsheathed tongue and pen with clear-eyed confidence that—given his own special schemes, of course, and him to carry them out—reason and good will would soon change all that. And no language was too strong for denouncing the reactionary who counseled going slow about slavery or scoffed at phrenology.

The religious reformer is rare these days, the secular type still rife. They often share some of the same emotions and, since their objectives frequently coincided in Old Brown's day, could pull pretty comradely on the ropes attached to the same block of stone for building the New Jerusalem or the Commonwealth of Man, depending on which one was interviewed. Indeed there were blendings as secular temperaments religiously reared expressed their yearnings in terms of sin and repentance and inchoate mystics grew ecstatic over Dr. Graham's wholewheat bread. Abolitionism included them at all levels of instability: Crude, self-vaunting liars like Redpath still quite able to cope with life; hypochondriacs like Gerrit Smith finally breaking down into a psychotic episode; the man-sized juvenile delinquents who made up the cutting edge of Old Brown's force; and a few, such as the famous Abigail Folsom,[6] whom even the hottest Abolitionists suspected of being "insane."

The crusades through which they showed their emotional strains were varied. James Russell Lowell could hardly believe his own memories when harking back: "Every possible form of intellectual and physical dyspepsia brought forth its gospel," wrote this ardent antislaveryite years afterward. "Everybody had a mission (with a capital M) to attend to everybody else's business . . . Communities were established where everything was to be common but common sense . . . All stood ready at a moment's notice to reform everything but themselves . . . This was the whistle and trailing fuse of the shell, but there was a very solid and serious kernel, full of the most deadly explosiveness." That was cataclysmically true. Abolitionism was both emotional detonator of the Civil War and least common denominator of Reform—the large word then used to cover everything from proposals for universal suffrage to spiritualism. Not even

Gerrit Smith or Garrison took up all "reforms." People in pretty good Reformist standing might draw the line at "non-resistance" (forerunner of pacifism) or hydropathy (treatment of all diseases with water, hot, cold, luke, outside and in). They were not obliged to adopt John Humphrey Noyes' extraordinary theory of sexual congress.[7] But whatever else he did or did not adhere to, practically every Reformer was antislavery, usually an avowed Abolitionist; and conversely Abolitionism derived much of its special momentum from the abnormally vivacious energies of the Reformers.[8] To this extent Reform was an asset. But it was dearly bought at the cost of public suspicion that, to judge from the company it kept, the cause of the Negro had too much in common with head-feeling, sexual promiscuity, denial of the existence of God and pants for women.

To us the causes that Reformers usually espoused seem strange bedfellows. Abolitionism, women's rights (including "dress reform," meaning the famous "Bloomer" garb), "phonography" (shorthand) and "manual labor education" (schools where students paid their way by farming, handicrafts, etc.) have the right ring. Even the "non-resistance" and "no-human-government" movements are acceptable to liberal good will if not to common sense. On both sides of the water Reformers pioneered in prison reform; universal public education; humane care of the blind, insane and feebleminded; humane societies; movements, however naïvely conceived, to rehabilitate prostitutes; and a dozen other new physical or social decencies now deeply imbedded in what we think of as civilization but novel then and gratifyingly consonant with the text about "one of the least of these my brethren." But their smug wars on rum, tobacco and Sunday mails, and their susceptibility to crude quackeries—spiritualism, phrenology, vegetarianism, etc.—set today's teeth on edge. Wishful credulity, mistrust of objective reality, self-dramatization underlie the versatility of their interests. Few of them—some of the Quakers and J. G. Birney seem to have been exceptions—got into Abolitionism simply through encountering the problem of slavery and determining to do away with the horrible thing. They were willing to force society to pay whatever reckoning of blood, starvation and individual horror might come of carrying out notions they dreamed up to assuage their own skewed consciences and impress their own flawed psyches. To slake their emotional thirsts they had to add cause to cause. They were called harsh names, not all deserved, but none who knew them ever shouted "Monomaniacs!" [9] And yet the slave would have been better off in the long run had Abolitionists been persons of one idea—or at least of one idea at a time.

The Rev. Dr. Samuel J. May, one of the worthiest Garrisonians, had a clever defense of the Reformer-antislaveryite: "We Abolitionists," he told Channing, "are what we are— babes, sucklings, obscure men, silly women, publicans, sinners, and we shall manage this [attack on slavery] just as might be expected of such persons . . . It is unbecoming of abler men who stood by and would do nothing to complain of us because we do no better." This bit of sleight of hand was true only of the Garrisonian faction of Abolitionism and not too pertinent even there. Of Garrison's early inner circle Francis Jackson, Amasa Walker, Samuel Sewall, Ellis Gray Loring, Wendell Phillips at least were highly placed socially. Most of the Six were, as we have seen, sizable figures in their own right. New York City's antislaveryites definitely gone Abolitionist included William Jay, son of the first Chief Justice of the United States, and Lewis and Arthur Tappan, eminent silk merchants with hands in a dozen pious Reforms. True, the cause did suffer in New England, as May hinted, from the half-baked capers of Garrisonians from lower social strata. But what ailed the main movement, based in New York and most active in the Western free states, was trying to use British tools on American raw materials. Not that Garrison let them alone either . . . It is time to make this man's acquaintance instead of just muttering about him. He was Old Brown's mentor in print.

"I cannot listen to any proposal for a gradual abolition of wickedness." —WILLIAM LLOYD GARRISON

"Garrison" was once synonymous with Abolitionism. Thirty years ago scholars[10] began to find impressive evidence that he needed deflation. His conspicuousness in the antislavery struggle cannot be questioned. His genius for invective and the frequency with which Dixie editors quoted him gave him high visibility. But how helpful he was is another matter. The subscribers to his famous *Liberator* were principally Northern free Negroes. His white followers were a grimly devoted Yankee splinter group in a movement larger and certainly far broader than they. He had small part in converting to antislaveryism the crucial minority of Northerners, millions of them by the time of Harpers Ferry, who had come to take aversion to slavery for granted among God-fearing folks like monogamy, teetotalism and a clean shirt on Sunday. That was the work of many others—Theodore Weld, Birney, Mrs. Stowe . . . Had Garrison actually been the key Abolitionist whom later hero-worship and Yankee parochialism invented, antislaveryism might have had as dim a future as some of his many other causes, such as "steam doctoring." As it was, his deplorable taste combined with his disproportionate notoriety seriously to damage the Negro's future.

In his eyes no height of fame could have been out of proportion. As a brash young printer-journalist in Boston he

told a Portland editor who had sneered at him as obscure:
". . . my name shall one day be known so extensively as to
render private inquiry unnecessary . . . I speak in the spirit
of prophecy, not of vainglory . . . with a strong pulse, a
flashing eye, and a glow of the heart. *The task may be yours
to write my biography.*" After dallying with conservatism he
chose as his avenue to renown the practice of maligning
things-as-they-are and the duty of scolding them into taking
the shape that he prescribed. The choice of which things to
assail was secondary to his generalized urge to flay, denounce
and dominate. R. H. Dana, a sturdy Yankee antislaveryite,
called him "a hater of everything established and traditional
. . . a fanatic by constitution." But I do not imply that his
turn to Reform was coldly deliberate. In his day and place
his talent for hating would probably have brought him
about on the Reform tack without any conscious design of
his own.

His pitiable rearing probably had little to do with this;
after all, Wendell Phillips, his ally in blackguarding the
cosmos, was a born-wealthy Brahmin. When William was a
small boy his seafaring Yankee father abandoned his over-
godly Nova Scotian mother with a brood of children and no
resources. She managed: "Only a cannon-ball could kill
Fanny Garrison," she said. When William reached the age
of thirteen she unwittingly set him on his road to fame by
apprenticing him to the printer's trade. It was for him what
it had been for Benjamin Franklin and thousands of clever
boys since—education as well as livelihood. He grew bookish, deep in Moore, Mrs. Hemans, Scott and Byron. He
acquired the old-time printer-editor's knack of composing
verse and prose directly out of his head into type and was
soon doing bits for his master's paper. At the age of twenty
"the heroic printer's lad"—Harriet Martineau's phrase—
had borrowed money, bought a paper of his own in Salem,
Mass., and begun to denounce slavery in its columns. Three
years later he was running an early "temperance"—Cause

Two—paper in Boston. Three years more and he is in Bennington, Vermont, running another paper and adding Cause Three—the "peace movement"—to his string. Then in 1829 he was invited to Baltimore to work on the *Genius of Universal Emancipation* paper of Benjamin Lundy, the Quaker saddler-printer-editor antislaveryite.

With the cause so hot in Britain and heating up sympathetically in the States, an antislavery paper was headed for trouble anyway in slaveholding and slave-exporting Maryland. But Garrison's presence hastened it. On learning that a certain ship taking slaves by sea to New Orleans from Baltimore was owned in Newburyport, his home town, he denounced the owner in the *Genius* as a "highway robber and murderer" deserving solitary confinement for life. Out of his own seethings and long soaking in recent British antislavery tracts he had already developed the polemical style that made his fame. The ship owner had him indicted for criminal libel. Convicted, Garrison went to jail for lack of $100 fine and costs.

Seven weeks later Arthur Tappan, "angel" of New York antislaveryism, paid the court and Garrison left for Boston to avoid civil actions for damages. Lundy can hardly have been displeased to see him go. The youngster's vehemence jarred the gentle Quaker, who was Abolitionism's nearest thing to a saint, and the pair disagreed over Garrison's new scorn of the "Colonization" movement,[11] in some forms of which Lundy had sunk much emotional capital. By 1839 Garrison was denouncing Lundy's schemes for settling free Negroes in Texas and accusing him of "a jealous and envious spirit . . . abusive and insulting language . . . a very irritable disposition . . ." This was almost inevitable. By 1860 Garrison had quarreled with nine out of ten persons of stature in Abolitionism outside his own special clique.

On New Year's Day, 1831, Garrison and his printer-ally, Isaac Knapp,[12] using press and type secured as pay for journeyman work, issued the first number of their momentous *Lib-*

erator. Its original subscribers were mostly free Negroes whose support Garrison had solicited for an uncompromising "immediate abolition" paper. He may not have made it altogether clear that he used "immediate" in the subtle Abolitionist sense. But the Negroes naturally liked to have slaveowners called the hard names the *Liberator* was so generous with, and had further reason to keep on supporting the paper because it reflected Garrison's soundness on the racial issue. He and his clique of followers have the distinction of being the only definable group of antislaveryites to assert the Negro's potential mental as well as biological equality with whites.[13]

While seeking backing Garrison had approached Lyman Beecher, already a muddled antislaveryite, who excused himself on the grounds that he had already "too many irons in the fire." "Then," said Garrison, always a man of too many causes himself, "you had better let all others go and attend to this one." No doubt he thought he was being tempted on a high mountain when Beecher said he had only to temper his zeal according to his elders' advice to become "the Wilberforce of America." It was an ill-aimed reference. Wilberforce would have been the last man ever to set himself up as a one-man cult of irresponsible invective:

". . . many object to the severity of my language," said the famed opening statement of the *Liberator,* "but is there not cause for severity? I *will be* as harsh as truth, and as uncompromising as justice. On [slavery] I do not wish to think, or write, or speak with moderation. No! No! Tell a man whose house is on fire to give a moderate alarm; tell him to moderately rescue his wife from the hands of the ravisher; tell the mother to gradually extricate her babe from the fire into which it has fallen! . . . I am in earnest—I will not equivocate—I will not excuse—I will not retreat a single inch— AND I WILL BE HEARD!"

He kept his word. For thirty years his profuse writings were like messages in Morse on a steam whistle, usually

clear, always screaming. Even when trying to speak softly, as
when colleagues asked him to go a little easy on a rival antislavery organization, he had to call it "cold and proud in its
spirit, defective in its organization, corrupt in its origin,
deceitful in its object . . . delusive in its action . . . a
wretched imposition . . ." Under no such pressure to let
the American Colonization Society off easily, he called this
well-meaning if wrongheaded organization "a monster of
cruelty, violence and blood." A proslavery newspaper was
necessarily edited by "rum-drinkers, lechers, pimps and
knaves." An editor accusing him of having maligned his
country in antislavery speeches made in England was "a
miserable liar and murderous hypocrite." Others mentioning George Thompson's financial pecadilloes, whatever they
were, Garrison called "the human hyenas and jackals of
America, who delight to listen to negro groans, to revel in
negro blood, and to batten upon human flesh." Once he
came to think the Union a clog on Abolitionism it became
"conceived in sin and brought forth in iniquity . . . a 'cove-
nant with death' . . . 'agreement with hell' . . . 'refuge of
lies' . . . Accursed be the American Union, as a stupen-
dous, republican imposture!"

As the paper came shriekingly to berate organized religion
for paltering with the slavery issue—which was a true bill
too—its editor found himself unfairly labeled "infidel." Actually, for all his zeal for "no-human-government," alias
"Christian anarchy," he retained an egocentric religiousness
of his own and a deep devotion to the Bible as mine of
rhetorical ammunition, as in the denunciation of the Constitution above. He had "the whole language of the Old
Testament at his tongue's end, and a text from the old
prophets [always] ready like an arrow on a bow string," said
Mrs. Stowe, an adept Bible-miner herself. This skill in Scriptural epithets, images and catchlines was like that of Old
Brown, another Bible-soaked mistruster of churches who
had also identified himself with truth.

The most appalling testimony about Garrison comes from his admirers: "Of all the heroes of ancient or modern days," wrote Higginson, closest to him of the Six, "he stands most firmly on his feet. If he knew that at his next word of truth, the whole solar system would be annihilated, his voice, in saying it, would not tremble." Possibly commendable in an archangel, not in a mortal—yet Higginson meant this as a compliment. "[Garrison] seems to have understood by instinct," said Wendell Phillips' funeral elegy of the man, ". . . that one, with God, is always a majority . . . I never saw the moment that serene, abounding faith in the rectitude of his motive, the soundness of his method, and the certainty of his success did not lift him above all possibility of being reached by any clamor about him." This was—if psychiatry does not use this term, it should—the *superiority* complex.

Chapman's panegyric of Garrison attributed his hero's "debauchery of language . . . to . . . his occupation; he was a journalist . . . [he] became a common scold—and yet not a common scold, because his inner temper was perfect." This must refer to the waxwork calm that so struck Phillips. The reference to journalism could extend into saying, as Nye does, that the newspapers of the day dripped "bad taste, vilification, and abuse" and Garrison's shriekings could "easily have been matched in . . . the partisan press." Valid as far as it goes; yet to me his abusive rhetoric seems more than the tricks of a penny-a-liner spewing invective as deliberately as a lawyer squeezing out tears for a jury. Sometimes he hinted at this attitude, true. When May expostulated with him because "some of the epithets you use . . . are not precisely applicable to the sin you denounce," he replied:

"Ah! until the term 'slaveholder' sends as deep a thrill of horror to the hearts of those who hear it . . . as the terms 'robber,' 'pirate,' 'murderer' . . . we must . . . multiply epithets . . ." But bitter animus seems to me to be there

Above: The slaver *Antonio* lying in Bonny River, West Africa—a typical sharp-built, raking brigantine for the illicit trade, designed to outrun patrol vessels. Colored lithograph by T. C. Dutton after N. M. Condy. *National Maritime Museum, Greenwich, England.*

Below: Cudjo Lewis, last survivor of slave cargo bootlegged by American schooner *Clotilda* into the United States in 1860, probably the last such enterprise. This photograph of Cudjo—now many years dead—with his great-grandchildren was taken in 1931. *Overbey Studio, Mobile.*

ABOLITIONISTS, BRITISH AND AMERICAN

Left, above: Thomas Clarkson—portrait by A. E. Chalan, R.A. Clarkson collected the minerals and artifacts pictured in the lower right-hand corner to convince influential people that West Africa was to be taken seriously. *Wilberforce House Museum, Hull, England.*

Right, above: William Wilberforce. This portrait by Richmond, engraved by J. Jenkins, best conveys the gay charm that somehow accorded with Wilberforce's religious earnestness and purposeful political strategy. *Wilberforce House Museum, Hull, England.*

Below: Left to right, Wendell Phillips, William Lloyd Garrison, George Thompson. This daguerreotype, though of unstated date, probably shows these three pillars of Garrisonian Abolitionism at the height of their most active period. *Boston Public Library.*

too, as well as propaganda strategy. Hear him: ". . . the
Union . . . is founded in unrighteousness, and cemented
with blood . . . a horrible mockery of freedom . . . mis-
shapen, incongruous, unnatural." Of "desperadoes from
the South in Congress" he wrote: "We would sooner trust the
honor of the country and the liberties of the people in the
hands of the inmates of our penitentiaries . . . We do not
acknowledge them to be within the pale of Christianity . . .
of humanity." Furious with an elder statesman for promoting the Compromise of 1850, which stiffened the fugitive
slave laws, he wrote that "HENRY CLAY—with one foot in
the grave . . . just ready to have both body and soul de-
scend into hell—as if eager to make his damnation doubly
sure, rises in the U.S. Senate and proposes . . ." never mind
what; this is obscene, the sort of self-intoxicated invective
that made Senator Bilbo notorious. It is also 100-proof
hatred; or if not, it shows an unholy passion for the stigmata
of hatred.

Southerners apparently felt that Garrison's rhetoric was
something special. By his time Abolitionism offered a large
body of propaganda writing, much of it from hands as professional as his, and some of it, particularly the later British
materials, pretty sharp-spoken. But it was usually Garrison,
not his colleagues, whom Dixie chose to quote. Thus the
principal result of his work was to further proslavery feeling.
Southerners used his writings as anti-Nazis used against Nazism the telltale threats and rantings of *Mein Kampf*. For
the fire-eating Dixie secessionist he was almost as good promotion as Old Brown would be later.

The obvious affection in his letters to his loyal wife makes
him sound like a man of good will in fair mental health. But
a few lines farther on he is too often muttering suspicions
that Soandso is conniving behind his back and Suchanone is
a secret creature of the Colonizationists. His admirable fairness in printing hot anti-antislavery and anti-Garrison material in the *Liberator* was spoiled by his innocent glee in pub-

lishing absurd praises of himself. When Lincoln was elected in 1860, the paper carried Wendell Phillips' fatuous remark that "the *slave* has chosen a President . . . Lincoln is in *place,* Garrison in *power*." His own firm's imprint was on the American edition of Miss Martineau's *Martyr Age of the United States,* which called Garrison "one of God's nobility." There is no denying his courage. His calmness probably saved him from a roughing-up when bourgeois Bostonians mobbed him for having imported Thompson to tell Americans how to handle slavery—or at least that was the Boston merchants' pretext for a gesture sure to please their Dixie customers. But sometimes the occasions for his showing courage were invented by his own delusions of persecution. When about to sail for England the first time, he was convinced—there is no evidence that there was anything substantial in it—that he was in real danger of being kidnaped for the reward for his person that certain Southern jurisdictions had offered as part of new laws against circulating Abolitionist propaganda. ". . . but I cannot know fear," he wrote home, ". . . it is impossible for danger to awe me." His return landing in New York happened to coincide with a meeting of the Anti-Slavery Society against which a mob was forming. Gratifiedly he assumed that he was the occasion of the mob. "As soon as I landed," he informed his brother-in-law, "I turned the city . . . upside down. Five thousand people turned out to see me tarred and feathered, but were disappointed." In 1867 he made the utterly unjustified claim that he had been first in "unfurling the banner of immediate and unconditional emancipation" in America.

Self-esteem underlay much of his bad effect on the anti-slavery cause. Stubbornly he insisted on the *Liberator's* promoting whatever struck his cause-minded fancy. Rashly he lent his name and publicity value—created largely by Dixie's reaction to his vehemence—to schemes lumping the cause of the slave with crackpottery. Though such sabotage was not deliberate, its root was wilfulness. No expostula-

tions—and many were made by devoted antislaveryites close
to him—could turn him from any ill-advised caper that occurred to him. At one point, in fact, he thought the "no-
human-government" movement so important that he considered dropping antislavery agitation in its favor.

We all know people like that. As a whole, however, his
personality puzzled all but abject hero-worshippers too admiring to analyze. His appearance did not match his printed
screams: middle-sized, spare and nimble, prematurely bald,
a prim air enhanced by his usually wearing spectacles, a
thing commoner now than then. Photographs show a ghost
of a smile at once stern and eager as if he were graciously
urging the universe to resolve to mend its ways, yet with a
touch of the look familiar on a discussion leader at a youth
meeting. Miss Martineau considered him "the most bewitch-
ing person I . . . had met in the United States" and wondered
at the contrast between the "harshness, the bad taste of his
writings" and the low pitch of his conversation. "There's
Garrison," wrote Lowell, "his features very/Benign for an
incendiary . . ." When his clique met at the printshop Garrison sometimes preferred to stand aside at the type case
with that strange smile on his face listening with half his
mind only while he set up something particularly blistering
for the next *Liberator*.

He "dreamed habitually, except in sickness" but "despite
his daily contemplation of the horrors of slavery," they were
very seldom the subject of his dreams. He himself thought
this singular but did not proceed to the possible explanation
that compassion for the slave was not a prime motive for his
militancy.

It is astounding that, so far as the surviving record shows,
he never lost his egocentric calm during his rhetorical on-
slaughts on slaveholders, Colonizationists, compromisers and
all others reluctant to see things his way. Apparently his
emotional and intellectual integration was so complete that,
shrill as he might be *ex cathedra*, he retained the dignity

appropriate to one born to be right all the time. Old Brown had some of this arrogance so complete that it sometimes imitates gentleness. As they set out for the Ferry he warned the boys against any but absolutely necessary bloodshed.

Clinically interesting bits sometimes appeared from under Garrison's blandly opaque shell. For what it is worth, he was a suppressed lefthander trained by raps on the knuckles to write a copperplate hand with the wrong side of his brain. He was a marked hypochondriac devoted to quack remedies. His numerous quarrels with fellow antislaveryites were always their fault and usually proof of some "mighty sectarian conspiracy against him," said Higginson regretfully; but then we already know that Garrison had classical delusions of persecution.[14] Though "dollar-honest" in the politician's phrase, his sense of honor might slip when the cause was in great need. Wishing to go to England in 1833 to get to know the great Emancipationists, he raised the necessary traveling funds from free Negroes by promising to collect British contributions to set up a school for free Negro boys. Once in England, he did little or nothing about this project but concentrated on gaining the confidence of Wilberforce, Clarkson, Buxton, *et al.* Then, needing passage money home, he borrowed it from an American free Negro who really was collecting for this purpose and eventually shuffled out of repayment in a fashion smelling strongly of sharp practice. In 1849 he wished to rescue the American Anti-Slavery Society from its stiffneckedness about doing what he advised. So his adherents chartered a steamer and offered a free trip to New York to all New England antislaveryites willing to come along as delegates and vote down anti-Garrison elements in the Society's annual convention. These 450-odd pilgrims secured him a 550 to 450 victory in the crucial ballot. His account of the matter accuses his *opponents* of unscrupulous efforts to "pack" the meeting.

For our purposes it may not matter whether he believed his own rantings or merely used abuse as a tool; whether he hated slaveowners as well as the sin of slave holding—which is my view—or merely borrowed from the Old Testament hate-rich phrases and images as missiles. Note only that these diatribes were a major part of Old Brown's antislavery conditioning and also did much to prepare such men as the Six for his gospel of righteous violence. For, however consistently Garrison personally stuck to antiviolence on principle, his words were either shrieks for action or meaningless. At their first meeting in early 1857, Old Brown and Garrison disagreed as to the bearing of Scripture on antislaveryism. Again in 1859 their paths crossed at a meeting of Garrison's New England Anti-Slavery Society; Old Brown is said to have listened to the speeches and left saying: "These men are all talk; what is needed is action—action!" And what he soon did was only what Garrison's "journalistic" rhetoric had been implicitly demanding for twenty-eight foaming, rasping, tooth-gritting years.

"Brown stood on the platform that Garrison built," said Wendell Phillips in his funeral eulogy of Garrison. "If the approaching conflict was irresistible, Garrison was at least a factor in convincing the South that it was so," wrote Nye recently. "By proslavery logic, Garrison led to John Brown." By any logic. Scream that loud and that long and somebody—regrettably unstable, no doubt—will take your screaming as orders to march. White Citizens' Councils please note.

"If abolitionism is grounds for canonization, Weld deserves sainthood more than Garrison." —J. G. RANDALL

Old Brown and Theodore Dwight Weld were so likely to meet that to prevent it must have taken a special Providence. Weld too was Connecticut-born, only three years younger, stumped against slavery in the very part of Ohio where the Browns settled, very probably knew old Owen Brown as a trustee of Oberlin, certainly knew all the eminent Abolitionists who took Old Brown for a hero . . . Yet never did the most bloody-minded Abolitionist exchange a word with the most significant Abolitionist—significant first for what he did and then for what he stopped doing.

The pair would have made a memorable picture. Old Brown with his springy grimness, juxtaposed with Weld: loose-hung, tousled and tall with a face so formidable that a small girl catching a first glimpse of him at an inn ran screaming to her elder sister and begged her to take that man away, he looked so cross. Several antislaveryites who came immensely to value him confessed that the "deep wild gloom" and "moveless severity" of his swarthy, wry-nosed, shaggy-browed countenance violently repelled them at first. Maybe the very strikingness of this ugliness in contrast to his noble voice, spontaneous eloquence and glowing good will helped to make him so effective a speaker. Yet for all his platform success, he was the most retiring of great leaders —seldom signed the antislavery books he wrote, refused to report his speaking tours for antislavery papers or to attend antislavery conventions. Specialists in these matters usually agree that Weld's relative obscurity in standard accounts of Abolitionism was a tribute to his diffident success in keeping his name and face out of the spotlight.

Here is the British *motif* again. It was the personal influence of Charles Stuart, the tartan-clad catalyst, that enlisted Weld in the antislavery wars. His previous history had been eccentric: At Andover Academy, where he paid his expenses by running a farm at the age of fourteen, he made a hobby of memory training. Overwork and eye trouble forced him to quit school, so he became a sort of lay missionary lecturing on mnemonics all up and down the United States. After three years of that he entered Hamilton College and came under the spell of Charles Grandison

Finney, the great revivalist preacher then well launched on his crusade to convince all his fellowmen of their sinfulness and their obligation to help bring on the millennium by re-forming all others. As one of Finney's "Holy Band" of ex-horters, specializing in "temperance," Weld met Stuart, long a zealous Finneyite. The two fell into a sort of non-erotic love—a flowingly articulate emotional affinity like that between a mother and a deeply beloved and loving son, supposing Freud left out of it. They decided that Weld should train for the ministry at the Oneida Institute, a new "Reform"-soaked school mingling theology and "manual labor," with Stuart paying the small tuition required. After Stuart went to England to join the Agency Emancipation-ists, his remittances to Weld were enclosed in voluminously loving God-filled letters that kept the emotional bond as close as ever.

He also bombarded his transtlantic soul mate with his own and others' antislavery propaganda of the latter-day sin-shouting sort which turned the youngster from a nominal belief in Colonization and made him pledge himself to concentrate his sin-assailing efforts on slaveholding. This pledge, says Dumond, a prime authority, combined with J. G. Birney's drift toward Abolitionism to mean that "the fate of slavery was sealed in the ensuing few years [1833-1837]." First on his own, then as official of the American Anti-Slavery Society, Weld recruited young theology stu-dents and preachers, mostly Finneyites, as British-style "agents" to apply Finney's special revivalistic tactics to antislaveryism. They swept the Midwestern states with the doctrine that slaveholding was sin and so had to be abandoned at once. Garrison's *Liberator* directly reached only a few thousand already convinced Abolitionists—includ-ing old Owen Brown's family—and a hundred-odd South-ern editors eager to quote it for their own purposes. Weld's handpicked "Seventy"—so numbered to match Christ's apostles—carried the stirring words to thousands on tens of thousands in the states where most of the Federal soldiers-to-be were then growing up or being born.

The Seventy were mobbed as often and usually more roughly than New England handled the Garrisonians. Much of this rowdyism was recruited by merchants and editors in cities having close economic relations with Dixie. The rest reflected surly reaction to the "immediate Emancipation" slogan and to the impression, largely Garrison-created, that Abolitionism was essentially subversive crankishness. Broken windows, rotten eggs by the basketful, well-aimed stones on occasion[15]—Weld was several times knocked senseless, for he traveled as far and fast and spoke as often as any of his recruits. Only once—in Troy, N.Y.—did he fail eventually to get a hearing as the neighborhood tired of turbulence and decided, after hours or days of it, to quiet down and let this burning-eyed gargoyle in cowhide boots have his say. Then he had them. For two or three hours he poured God's will on them, his great voice booming, the words rolling ever hotter and heavier off his tongue. When he finally challenged his hearers to dedicate themselves against the heaven-defying sin of slavery, they usually rose to their feet as at the Last Trump. Next day a good many still felt the same, and a considerable number would stay antislavery —or anyway anti-slaveowner—for life. Nothing remains of these speeches in print. He had neither manuscript nor notes, just stood up in the sight of God (as he knew Him) and let His truth (as he believed it to be) speak for itself.

Merely to train and organize so redoubtable a propaganda tool as the Seventy would have been a major contribution. Weld's work far exceeded that. He had a large hand in bringing to militant antislaveryism such men as Birney, spearhead of the Liberty Party that begot the Republican Party, and Ben Wade and Joshua Giddings, indispensable antislaveryites in Senate and House respectively. When he lost his voice by abusing it, never to regain full power, the mischance only diverted him into wider services. The cause needed an elaborate tract summing up rebuttal to Dixie's contention that the Bible countenanced slavery. Weld wrote it; it became a standard weapon. The Anti-Slavery Society's emissaries, Weld's adherents, investigating the results of West Indian Emancipation, returned both too sick to put their report into usable shape; Weld used their data to produce the crucial document that swung Abolitionism over to out-and-out Immediatism. A summary of the horrors of Dixie slavery was wanted. Weld, his wife and sister-in-law sifted thousands of Dixie newspapers and scores of antislavery Southerners to get authentic data for *American Slavery As It Is*, a hair-raising compilation of atrocities and barbarously phrased advertisements for runaways that remained the keystone of antislavery propaganda for the duration. It sold over 100,000 copies its first year and supplied much of the material for *Uncle Tom's Cabin*. Antislavery Congressmen needed a researcher advisor to feed them antislavery data for debates; Weld moved to Washington and assumed this function so well and earnestly that even J. Q. Adams, then at his very crustiest, came to love him personally as well as respect his gifts.

He was undeniably queer as Dick's hatband, with a habit of repairing alone to secluded spots at dusk or dawn to "cut capers"—leaping and whirling, turning somersaults and running madly with flailing arms. Since he looked strange enough in repose, anybody happening to witness one of these hygienic frenzies risked having the daylights scared out of him. He wrecked Lyman Beecher's new Lane Theological Seminary in Cincinnati by first filling it with Finneyite comrades and then taking them away in a body[16] when the faculty forbade the students to concentrate on antislavery agitation. Throughout the episode, his attitude was as headstrong as the faculty's, but he kept a civil tongue and did not thenceforth call the Lane professors hoary-headed sons of Belial venally truckling to the scarlet whore of man stealing as Garrison would have done. His Reformisms included some of the least worthy—anti-tobaccoism, vegetarianism, belief in the imminence of the Second Coming—as well as women's rights and antislaveryism. But he avoided Garrison's error of encumbering the Negro's cause by harnessing it with the others. His shrewd sense of tactics taught him that Abolitionism would go farthest when it traveled alone. And though no word mincer—no effective prosecutor can afford to be—he deplored Garrison's style as "the vibration of serpents' tongues . . . envenomed stings."

In a manner of speaking his distaste for Garrisonism got him a wife. He had vowed never to marry while slavery lived. But then he met the Grimké sisters, Sarah and Angelina. They came of slaveowning Charleston aristocracy—their father had been Chief Justice of the South Carolina Supreme Court.[17] Their mother was a severe religious zealot, at least four of whose numerous children showed strong inclinations to leave the nest. The eldest had transplanted himself to New York City and joined the tight little circle of highly placed Reformers that included the Tappans; he died while planning an investigation of slavery intended to make him an avowed Abolitionist. Under his influence sister Sarah, and presently sister Angelina, had come to live in Philadelphia, where they became Quakers restlessly seeking good works to perform, and then Abolitionists uneasy about the ambiguous position of many Philadelphia Friends toward slavery.

Angelina read the *Liberator* and wrote an adulatory letter to Garrison, who printed it; then published a pamphlet calling on her Southern sisters to oppose slavery, which made her name known all over antislaveryism. The Anti-Slavery Society invited the two to speak to women's meetings, and they accepted. Sarah, though a fair writer, never made much of a speaker. Angelina, whom Weld, as director of the Seventy, coached personally, showed platform talent and a useful willingness to describe Dixie's treatment of slaves as —on the word of a born Southerner—utterly atrocious.

Asked whether Abolitionists overdrew the horrors of slavery, she replied: "They *cannot* be exaggerated. It is impossible for imagination to go beyond the facts."

The sisters came heavily under Garrison's influence as their speaking tours took them into New England. Curiosity drew Boston men-Abolitionists to infiltrate women's meetings at which Angelina was billed. This was even more scandalous than women's circulating petitions to Parliament or Congress: an alleged lady actually so indelicate as to address "mixed audiences." Garrison came charging to the defense of his new *protégées* and soon had firmly entangled Abolitionism with the thorny new movement for women's rights. He had Sarah writing feminist articles and Angelina making speeches against male tyranny as well as slavery. A Garrisonian member of Weld's Seventy, Henry C. Wright, former hatmaker and "non-resistant" leader—a choice bound further to confound antislaveryism with crankishness—was assigned to squire the girls round their circuit of lectures.

The "mixed audience" issue did not disturb Weld. He had long since countenanced women exhorters at revivals. But he deplored Garrison's diverting the sisters' time and effort toward women's rights, thus muffling their optimum effect as real, live Southern gentlewomen witnesses to the evils of slavery. Add a personal angle: Weld's brotherly and comradely respect for the sisters now began to get out of hand. Not in the direction of angular and doleful-looking Sarah, an amateur religious fanatic given to soul searchings and visions. But Angelina was twelve years younger, blue-eyed and at least somewhat more attractive. The voluminous correspondence between Weld and the girls during their speaking tours began to focus on Angelina. Weld disliked the incessant presence near her of Wright, whom he had always suspected of eagerness for notoriety and other unbecoming traits. As manager of the Seventy he transferred Wright to Pennsylvania, far from the sisters, who protested strongly. The inevitable proceeded. Small personal touches grew more frequent in Angelina's as well as Weld's letters, shyly appearing among the pious exhortations and the pros and cons of Garrisonian tactics . . .

Weld proposed. Angelina accepted. Within a few months they were married in Philadelphia in the presence of many Reformists. Garrison and Wright had the impudence to try to persuade Angelina to jilt Weld a few days before the ceremony lest his "sabbatical notions . . . church-going" and other reprehensible conformings "bring her into bondage." But she held firm. For thus marrying outside the Society of Friends she was "read out of meeting"; so was Sarah for having attended the ceremony.[18] This mattered little since the sisters were already used to ostracism and since, except for carnalities, Weld had in effect married both. For thirty-five years until her death Sarah was their housemate, an arrangement that all parties accepted cordially as both right and practical. It has been suggested that Weld married to save the sisters from Garrisonian error. This may not be exactly what happened; but Wright's possessive presence certainly helped to precipitate matters and, once vows were exchanged, the girls dropped Garrisonism without a backward glance, thenceforth thinking Theo's thoughts and loyally upholding his gnarly hands as props of their pious world.

As idyls go, this one was bleak and watery but these innocents had no way of knowing that. They rejoiced in setting up housekeeping in a house on the Palisades at Fort Lee, whence Weld commuted by steamboat to the New York office of the Anti-Slavery Society. Angelina learned to prepare victuals in the style laid down in *The Young Housekeeper,* the married vegetarian's handbook. She duly followed its advice about cooking for several days at once and eating everything cold; this left the girls freer to do clerical chores for Weld. The first child, a boy named for Charles Stuart, almost starved after he was weaned because the book said that most people are shamefully overfed. The approach of her third greatly agitated Angelina because the probable date of birth

was close to that of one of William Miller's predictions of
the end of the world, and she was nine-tenths convinced that
God had chosen her to bring forth the new incarnation of
Christ. Her anxiety ceased when the child proved to be a
girl and the end of the world failed to occur on schedule.

Crankishness, yes; but in these people it went with a high
integrity not always present among other Abolitionists.
They did much less of the backbiting, status-anxious, one-up-
manship feuding that marred the careers of otherwise admirable men like Birney. They were most likable when, after
the Civil War, the sisters heard of two freedman students
named Grimké at Lincoln University, a Negro institution in
Pennsylvania. On investigation they proved to have a certain
right to the name, being sons of the girls' dead brother
Henry by a slave concubine. The Welds invited the boys for
a visit and thenceforth treated them exactly as if they had
been legitimate lily-white nephews in need of hospitality
and help. They were bright and did well: Francis attended
Princeton Theological Seminary and became a Presbyterian
minister and Negro leader in Washington, D. C.; Archibald
trained at Harvard Law School, practiced awhile, turned
author, rose high in Republican politics and eventually
received the Spingarn Medal of the National Association for
the Advancement of Colored People for outstanding achievement by a Negro.

The self-reliance beneath Weld's crankishness was so far
from self-righteousness—the crank's great failing—that it
could confess basic error. And what he owned up to in middle age was what most seriously ailed Old Brown, the Six
and organized Abolitionism in general. In 1840 he had
bought a small farm on the Passaic River in northeastern
New Jersey and worked it as basic subsistence for his family
and the relatives and antislavery colleagues who were always turning up to stay a day or two or a year or so. In early
1844, well settled into the place after his long counseling
duty in Washington, he refused invitations from Giddings to

come and take up that work again. Of numerous excuses that
he gave none would have been decisive a few years earlier.
Nine years later he was still there on the farm, hardly making ends meet but apparently content to be away from the
antislavery wars, though their noise was rising higher since
the publication of *Uncle Tom's Cabin*. The fact was that,
for reasons best known to his own scrupulous self, he had
hung up his sword.

One summer Sunday in 1853 there came to the farm one
Henry Blackwell, a handsome young Reformist, British-born
but American-reared, who had just persuaded Lucy Stone,
the pioneer feminist Abolitionist, to marry him—without
changing her name, of course. For Lucy's beloved it was
no shock to find Sarah and Angelina in Bloomer costume[19]
reading to a bevy of local children. Weld was gardening.
During a confidential chat Blackwell asked directly why this
antislavery Achilles had stayed in his tent all this time.
Weld, who probably liked the candid youngster, carefully
explained: "He found he himself needed reforming. He was
all wrong. *He had been laboring to destroy evil in the same
spirit as his antagonists.* He suddenly felt that fighting was
not the best way to annihilate error . . . I wish," wrote
Henry to his Lucy, "I had more time to comprehend it. Certainly I dare not criticize [a man] so noble and so earnest."

Italics mine. Somehow it had come over Weld that what
drove him so hard and secured him such fanged bedfellows
as Garrison was not so much concern for the slave as hatred
of the slaveowner. His preceptor in the art of fighting slaveholding as sin, Finney himself, had already reproached the
Seventy for slipping into "a censorious spirit" likely to carry
the country "fast into a civil war." Daniel Cady, Gerrit
Smith's uncle (and father of Elizabeth Cady Stanton, another great feminist Abolitionist) was hot antislavery but he
too had been warning his zealous nephew that he had "no
faith in driving men to Heaven [*i.e.*, to a realistic Christianity that would mean slave freeing] by applying to them every

abusive epithet . . . in the English language." If it came to
the push, Dan Cady said, "I go for slavery rather than civil
war" and waiting for "machinery worked by steam and elec-
tricity . . . yet to be invented . . . to render slave labor un-
productive."

Maybe Weld had heard such unsettling talk from fore-
sighted men whom he knew to be soundly against slavery.
He had already been showing certain signs of impending
emotional shifts. He was impressed by the way Southerners
in Washington aware he was a pillar of Abolitionism showed
him no personal antagonism. He had relaxed strict vegetarianism and taken to meat once a day. It all could have been
a perspective-altering change in biochemistry occurring, or
beginning to, as his age crossed the forty mark. Yet he became
neither a Candide of the Jersey meadows nor a burned-out
bonfire. He lectured cogently until he was ninety, and lived
to ninety-two. Soon after seeing Blackwell he was deep in a
new career teaching school in a good-life Reformist community near Perth Amboy;[20] the forbidding man from whom
the little girl ran screaming became an imaginative experi-
mental teacher. He tried to serve in the Sanitary Commission when Civil War came but lacked enough previous training. So, gingerly trying the old voice again, he went on pro-
war and pro-Republican speaking tours with marked success.
Maybe, as wartime pressure mounted, he slackened his grasp
on his new doctrine and in some degree hated such objects as
Copperheads and Nathan B. Forrest. But the old full-throttle
animus was probably lacking. And in any case for those
many years of his middle life he had been free of the thirsty,
itching, dizzyingly personal and appallingly irresponsible
luxury of hatred. And it is a great luxury. The old French
song says it's love, it's love, it's love that makes the world go
round. Maybe so; but hatred can make it spin so fast that
the machine flies apart and wrecks everything in the neighborhood.

"So wise, so young, they say, doe never live long."
—King Richard Third, III, 1

Of those of Old Brown's men who failed to report at the farmhouse base the reason for defection is clear in only one —a strange little Englishman named Richard Realf, whose abandonment of the cause has a certain maimed significance. He was very probably a mental invalid subject to what doctors vaguely call "explosive episodes." But in one of his frequent and extensive rational intervals he managed gratefully to learn the second fallacy underlying the kind of Abolitionism that brought the old man to the gallows.

Born son of a rural policeman in Sussex, he proved precocious and literary. Benevolent local gentry took him up and arranged for publication of his verses under title of *Guesses at the Beautiful.* Lord Byron's widow heard some of them quoted, asked who wrote them—and soon Realf was under her rather eccentric patronage in training to be under-manager of a family estate. He was well made and, though stubby, romantically handsome and seems to have got a young kinswoman of Lady Byron's with child and then run away from the problem and the job too. Eventually he was found in poor emotional shape living on what he could cadge from passers-by as a street singer in Southampton. When he had regained some stability his family sent him to the States. He worked awhile in New York City in what would now be called a settlement house, then went to Kansas as a free lance sending Abolition-slanted correspondence to several Northern papers. Like Hinton and Redpath, his journalist countrymen, he was soon a disciple of Old Brown's. The old man made him provisional Secretary of State in his projected mountain government. After the attack was postponed in 1858 Realf was sent to New York to scrape acquaintance with Forbes, who had never met him, and if possible, steal telltale papers in Forbes' possession; then go to England, raise money for the cause by lecturing on Kansas, and return to rejoin Old Brown's force before the great effort.

He did go to New York but he never approached Forbes. He did go to England, lecture principally on temperance—along with spiritualism a side interest of his—and return to the States but he never renewed contact with Old Brown. His motive for defecting cannot have been cowardice. He had seen as much shooting as the next man in Kansas and he was to have a good Civil War record. Enlisting in the ranks in 1862, he rose to be adjutant on the staff of a brigadier-general, was mentioned in dispatches and fought all through the Western campaign to the siege of Atlanta; after the war he was an officer in a Negro regiment. These military years were his stablest period. In the intervals his religious oscillations took him all the way from turning Catholic to joining the Shakers; he married three times, once bigamously; had prolonged psychic blackouts during which he would drop from sight, as he had at Southampton; varied lecturing with tramp journalism and finally committed suicide in San Francisco in 1878 to get away from a vindictive second wife—a miserable little story.

When summoned before the Mason Committee investigating the Harpers Ferry raid he testified with great candor as to why he had failed to participate.[21] Soon after reaching New York, he said, he had fallen on a book—*The Limitations of Human Responsibility* by Francis Wayland, president of Brown, then a great name in what was called "moral philosophy." It flatly denied and authoritatively condemned the Reformist-Puritan doctrines that it is sinful (or wrong) not to do incessantly everything you can to turn everybody else from sin (or wrongdoing); and that the individual conscience is God's voice and an infallible guide to what is wrong or sinful. This was not righteousness, said Wayland, but fanaticism.

"The [fanatic] feels that he *must* obey his conscience at all hazards . . . devote his whole intellectual and physical power to . . . the purpose to which he is urged by the voice of God, thus speaking in his bosom. But if unfortunately he have misinterpreted this voice, the whole power of the man is enlisted in the work of mischief. He bids defiance to human law, on principle. Consequences to himself not only, but specially to others, are as nothing. Opposition, by convincing him the more strongly of his own rectitude and the wickedness of others, only renders him the more ferocious . . ." It is easy to see how Realf came to apply this to Old Brown. Wayland moved on to say it was too much "taken for granted, that all duties belong to all . . . that every man, woman, and child is responsible for the discharge of every possible duty, and that every human being may urge this upon every other human being, under penalty of the infinite displeasure of the eternal God." This, of course, was exactly what Finney had taught Weld, who passed it on to the Seventy as reason for resisting any and all temptation to mind one's own business. Then, getting down to cases, Wayland showed how, though he personally considered slavery "a stain like a wound" on the nation, there were limits to what he or any other individual could or should do about it.

"We have a right to attempt to change Southern opinion . . . to show the master, by argument, that it is for his interest, and . . . his duty, to liberate his slaves . . . But we have no right to take any measures of which the natural tendency is to excite the slave to insubordination and civil war. We have a right to change the purposes of the master by *argument,* but . . . no right either to oblige him by our own *physical* force to change it, or to excite another person thus to oblige him . . . we are held responsible only for setting the truth before men. They have . . . as good a right to their ears as we have to our tongues . . . if they will not hear us, our responsibility is at an end . . . the indication is plain, that God does not mean to use *our* instrumentality in the affair. We must retire and leave the case in His hands, and turn our attention to the doing of good in some other way . . ."

Such mature-minded talk was new to a youngster probably reared among moral busybodies of Evangelical bent in England and then soaked in the *Liberator* and Theodore Parker in the States. No wonder that, as he told the Committee, it "set me pondering on a new train of ideas." Shaken and needing counsel, he confided some notion of Old Brown's scheme to a certain W. F. M. Arny, an agent of the National Kansas Committee who had befriended him in Kansas. Arny strongly advised him to get clear of any such project, go home to England, marry a nice girl and settle down. He was far too unstable for that program, of course. Within a year he had recrossed the Atlantic to Texas for personal investigation of what slavery was really like—and thence the Committee fetched him for his loquacious half hour in the witness' chair.[22] But he carried out the first part well enough to save himself to fight another day under better auspices.

No doubt it was not altogether Wayland's book that converted him. He may have already been ripening to hear that the whole ethico-religious basis of Old Brown's scheme was presumptuous; that nobody has the right violently to force on others his private idea of what wrongdoing is. He may have been in a downswing of zeal ever since he had visited Canada for the old man's "convention," for there he had found the actual habits and circumstances of the runaway slave colonies much inferior to what Abolitionist propaganda had led him to expect. But new insights may be valid though it requires a change of mood to arrive at them. Say that in mid-career Weld had altered enough to see the folly of laboring to destroy slavery in the same hate-minded spirit as that

of Abolitionist-hating slaveholders; and that Realf was fortunate to have this sober book so opportunely coincide with
one of his sanest phases, enabling him to see that there was
far more wilfulness than God's will in Old Brown. Both are
devastating comments on Abolitionism, but there is a special
relish to seeing ill-educated, flighty, half-baked little Richard
Realf making so much more sense than Old Brown's august
backers.

9 *The Secret Six*

"*What do you read, my lord? 'Words, words, words!' And what's in a word, my lord? Answer: corpses, millions of corpses. And the moral of that is, Keep your trap shut; or if you must open it, never take what comes out of it too seriously.*"
—ALDOUS HUXLEY, The Genius and the Goddess

CADMUS INDICTED

"*Thou God-maddened old man!*"
—MONCURE D. CONWAY on JOHN BROWN

Heywood Broun once wrote a column to the effect that people never look so foolish or do so much harm as when trying to act like somebody in a book or play. Illustrations of this harsh but valid point might well include Old Brown and most of his backers. It is not given to many to see such appalling consequences from literary-flavored antics.

Reading and writing were, in fact, a curse to the whole group. Their letters told too much. A mass of papers left at the farmhouse base in Old Brown's carpetbag implicated most of them as accessories before the fact to treasonable absurdity. But even more trenchantly the printed word—books, pamphlets, periodicals—had long been channeling their destinies into the ruts that the old man's wagon wheels cut in the dirt roads on the way to the Ferry. It had even dominated the uncultivated old martyr himself—militarily through the pathetically few writings about tactics that underlay his claims to expertness; intellectually through his early and always intimate acquaintance with the *Liberator*[1] and kindred inflammatory materials; indirectly through his poring over Plutarch and a life of Napoleon that were the only other reading matter known to have impinged on the Brown clan; and overwhelmingly through the Bible—the Browns' staple.

Old Brown could correct from memory slight deviations from any text. He knew the Bible as a Polynesian nobleman knew the roster of his ancestors, as Ionian bards knew the *Iliad;* but it was the alphabet and the printing press—Cadmus and Gutenberg—that brought him this stimulus. Garrison's equal intimacy with the same text particularly appealed to Brown; not a word but had that scriptural hang of the idiom, hence doubled and tripled effect. These things really are temperamental: From intimacy of the same order a third American of that generation, Abraham Lincoln, derived only a remarkable prose style and charity for practically all. Not being the same sort of self-dramatizer, Lincoln was not tempted to identify himself with Moses or the Man of Sorrows, as was the living martyr of Harpers Ferry as he sat in his cell dabbling in his own significance-to-be.

The specific sets of ideas in which paranoid-tending persons couch their need to dominate/suspect/hate/kill vary widely. Reared in a different family in our own time, Old Brown could have been a Red terrorist, an I.R.A. undergrounder, a Fascist hatemonger. But reared as he was, he poured his molten ego into the images and examples of what was, in that day, Holy Writ still unflawed. People calling him an Old Testament prophet—the bookish image oftenest used—had in mind the grim, hairy prophets in the illustrations of the family Bible. The parallel was apt: Those ferally shiny eyes, the reptilian thinness of those lips, that monotonous, remote intentness of discourse betokened a man who had incessantly pored and muttered and mused and prayed over all the texts calculated to make him as ruthless as Samson and as angry as Ezra denouncing Gentiles. Old Brown was smite-the-hearthen-hip-and-thigh-minded in a fashion all too well summed up by Mrs. Stowe:

" [Dred] had read of kingdoms convulsed by plagues; of tempest, and pestilence, and locusts; of the sea cleft in twain, that an army of slaves might pass through . . . of prophets and deliverers armed with supernatural powers raised up for oppressed people; had pondered on the nail of Jael, the goad of Shangar, the pitcher and lamp of Gideon; and thrilled with fierce joy as he read of how Samson, with his two strong arms, pulled down the pillars of the festive temple, and whelmed his triumphant persecutors in one grave with himself." Mrs. Stowe thought such primitive self-glorifying admirable and pertinent to Dixie's slave problem; and so did millions of her readers ripening to see Old Brown as a larger-than-life hero, even as he saw himself.

The Rev. James Freeman Clarke, an eminent Unitarian Abolitionist, called Old Brown "an Old Testament Christian." This abject paradox meant, of course, that the old man's spiritual home was the Old Testament, where he could continually snuff up the odor of blood righteously shed by the Chosen People—with whom New Englanders habitually identified themselves in their religious fantasies. And whereas it was the denunciations of the Prophets that Garrison most relied on, Old Brown leaned on the judges and kings of Israel, the men of God-sponsored action. But he could also feed his ferocity from the relatively benign New Testament. As he told Gerrit Smith and Sanborn of the plan that became the Harpers Ferry foray they raised one ob-

jection after another. To each his reply was the same; later
it issued from among his new whiskers with an authority
possible only to delusions of grandeur.

"If God be for us, who can be against us?" from the epistle
on which Calvinism is founded. He also liked to warn the
timid that "without blood there is no remission of sins,"
meaning, as they perceived shrinkingly and yet with stern
tinglings, that Old Brown would have to do some killing before the sin of slavery could pass away. His sense of his
Divine auspices "fascinated those who [met] it in spite of
themselves," wrote Gerrit Smith's official biographer. "The
discouragements fell into shadow. The moral aspect was
illuminated, the immoral aspects of disorder, violence, anarchy and murder were thrown into the background; and
the splendor of the anticipated deliverance cast a soft glow
over the path through which it was to be reached." That is
good indirect description of the influence exerted by meg-
alomaniacs over those tinged with the same emotional tendency. It also explains how normally humane people can be
got to yearn for bloody solutions of troublesome evils.

Old Brown's strong Biblical flavor must greatly have
strengthened his personal ascendancy over the Six, all reared
in a Bible-soaked time, two of them ministers of the Gospel
in a fashion. But that was only the beginning of how the
printed word shaped them to become the old man's zealous
tools. This brings up materials of quite another sort—novels
and poems that, without even mentioning Negro slavery,
nevertheless had a hand in creating this most bookish conspiracy in history. True, the Secret Six were steeped in the
great body of Abolitionist propaganda that was part of their
time. But in my serious judgment their special adherence to
Old Brown is not satisfactorily accounted for without reference to their special temperaments as stimulated by Scott,
Byron and their imitators.

Mark Twain had such a theory about Dixie, so the general
credit is his. He considered that "the debilitating influence

of [Scott's] fantastic heroes . . . romantic juvenilities . . . and . . . windy hum-buggeries" had much to do with Southerners' inability to keep their heads as the national crisis approached. He saw a deplorable connection between the mouthings about "Southron chivalry" that vitiated Southern judgment in the 1850's and the plume wavings and gauntlet throwings of Scott's medieval novels. My theory is that certain Northern elements compounded this by parallel obsession with Scott's sterner, earlier tales of the Scots Covenanters and English Roundheads of the 1600's—God-minded, zeal-and-steel militants contrasting picturesquely and not discreditably with silken, worldly characters. In this the North's taste was better. *Old Mortality* has much less of the bogus quality inseparable from the historical novel than, by my halidome, has *Ivanhoe* or *The Talisman*. But in any case prolonged exposure to the aura of Scott's bitterly Bible-mouthed zealots had well prepared men like the Six to identify them with Old Brown. Or say that Scott gave the Six, and others of like emotional bent, a ready-made, honorific vocabulary to admire Old Brown in, seeing him as Balfour of Burley reincarnated or as an astringently bracing throwback to Cromwell's New Model trooper. To realize the actual importance of such identifications between real persons and literary figures, consider Wagnerian opera and Nazi fantasies.

As to Old Brown these are no shadowy inferences. Members of the Six often spoke of their jayhawker hero in these identical bookish terms. They read too much, such men are dangerous. The clearest example is the Rev. Thomas Wentworth Higginson. It is only fair anyway to begin with him because he looked best in the frantic weeks after Harpers Ferry.

MOSS-TROOPERISM

*". . . the untamable gypsy element in me which gives me
instant sympathy with every desperate adventure."*
—T. W. HIGGINSON

Maybe it is important that Higginson was next to youngest
of the Six. Or maybe it means even more that, when he
found heroism incarnate in Old Brown, he was a well-ma-
tured man of thirty-five. His people were Brahmins—merchants, ministers, doctors, by no means all rich or even well-
to-do but of prestige coeval with the Bay Colony. Thomas
was proud to be tall, a vigorous swimmer, a muscular Christian eagerly leading Abolitionist mobs to take fugitive slaves
from the hands of the law. As colonel of the First South
Carolina Volunteers he made some 800 Negro "contra-
bands" from the isolated Sea Islands into an efficient combat
unit. His talents were versatile. At Harvard he had been a
promising mathematician; later he was a compelling if not
soul-searching preacher and later still a critic journalist with
a long and august post-Civil War career. His prose no longer
seems as distinguished as his quondam reputation implied,
but it was much better than his verse. His greatest contribution to literature lay in having a large hand in fostering the
eccentric genius of Emily Dickinson.

That called for faith in his own taste and judgment—a
thing always strong in him. He lost his first pulpit, in Newburyport, by outspoken Abolitionism in the teeth of the congregation's disapproval; then was "called" by a non-denominational, go-as-you-please church of "Jerusalem wildcats"
—a phrase that he had humor enough to prize—in Worcester, Mass., a hotbed of theological and social radicalism.
In that heyday of Reformism Higginson was particularly

choosy about his causes. He worked perfunctorily for "temperance" and zealously for women's rights, happy to omit "obey" when marrying Lucy Stone to her Henry; his letters and journals sound, in fact, as if he had been half in love with Lucy in an innocent way. But he could never stomach vegetarianism, non-resistance . . . could not actually be set down as a crank, though he was curiously willing to put up with cranks.

In that time New England parents above a certain level of literacy often read aloud to the family in the evening. Higginson's mother was only one of thousands who chose thus to steep their young in the Waverley Novels pretty much end to end. At the age of eleven Tom Higginson already owned his own copies of many Waverleys; his favorite was the strangely brittle *The Pirate* but he assimilated them all as intimately as a cow assimilates clover. Years later, asked by a Scottish scholar whether he had ever heard of Yarrow: "I could hardly help laughing . . . told him every educated American knew every place mentioned in Scott, Burns or the Border Minstrelsy." When he went to Kansas on Emigrant Aid business and he found himself crossing the "debatable ground"—a Scottish Border term—between Tabor, Iowa, and Nebraska City, he experienced, he said, "the sensations of a moss-trooper . . . delightful . . . there came to mind some thrilling passages from Mackay's 'Ballads of the Cavaliers and the Roundheads' . . . I could at that moment understand how Rob Roy, wishing to repay a debt . . . offered to take his benefactor's son back into the Highlands and 'make a man of him.' "

Such literary tags—usually from fiction, usually romantic fiction, preferably Scott—run through all he did as swearing does through some people's talk. When already father of a family and minister of a church, he wrote: "I never read of but one thing that came up to my idea of enjoyment, and that was the charge of the Six Hundred. All the rest of existence would I freely give for one such hour." To Wendell

Phillips he ascribed "highborn chivalrous courage . . . such as one fancies Montrose might have had." "General" Jim Lane reminded him of "a sort of Prince Rupert of humbler grade." He called James Montgomery, a somewhat more savory jayhawker, "a curious compound of the moss-trooper and the detective." It would have undone him to learn that by 1959 many literate Americans would need footnotes to identify "moss-troopers" as Scottish border guerrillas of the era that Scott so valued. The "gray beard and prophetic manner" of one of Higginson's company officers "always took me back to the Fifth Monarchy Men"—the most extreme Roundhead zealots of the English Civil War. And on first meeting Old Brown in 1858 he inevitably saw "a highminded, unselfish, belated Covenanter; a man whom Sir Walter Scott might have drawn." It was the highest praise that this fiction-distracted enthusiast knew. He was born too soon to discern that, supposing one must describe real people in artificially literary terms, Old Brown was created not by Scott but by Eugene O'Neill.

The cultivated Victorian's zeal for romantic violence was ill-advised but often sincere. "Chinese" Gordon was as brave as his pose demanded. Given the occasion, Higginson or Howe—the proved fighting men among the Six—would have charged down the throats of those Russian guns as gallantly as anybody in the Light Brigade. Their error was not fatuous yearning after deeds for which they would lack courage themselves but failure to develop adult approaches —particularly failure to suspect that poetry and fiction are poor lenses through which to view men and measures.

Even after Harpers Ferry the heady mixture of Abolitionism and Old Brown involved Higginson in fresh schemes with a strong flavor of Scott—or Cooper or Dumas *père*. He had long been one of a group maintaining the yacht *Flirt*[2] in Boston harbor ostensibly for hire but actually to "take [runaway] slaves from incoming vessels, or . . . to kidnap the claimant of a slave and keep him cruising . . . until his claim should be surrendered." Though assisting a few run-aways, the *Flirt* did no such kidnaping. But the notion revived in another form when Higginson, Lysander Spooner (a Boston lawyer and hot Abolitionist) and a young zealot named LeBarnes planned to charter a steam vessel, kidnap Governor Wise of Virginia and hold him at sea as hostage for Old Brown's neck. LeBarnes had a tug lined up. Only lack of ready cash prevented the attempt which, in the then alerted condition of Virginia, stood no chance of success, of course.

After the old man's death Higginson also sought to rescue those raiders awaiting trial. Montgomery[3] was fetched east to see what he could do as leader of a group of liberty-minded German exiles from the revolutions of 1848 whom Higginson had recruited. An aide of Montgomery's got committed to Charlestown jail as a drunk and talked it all over with the Harpers Ferry prisoners. They refused rescue because—this is as decent as it is strange—the plan probably meant killing the jailer, who had been kind to them.[4] Then Montgomery had to throw in his hand because heavy snow had made mountain travel difficult and tracking dangerously easy. Higginson, waiting in Harrisburg to move on command, was most reluctant to see the scheme dropped. Part of this must have been reluctance to see two turbulent young men hanged for doing what their elders and betters had assured them was God's work. But another reason may have been regret for a gesture so enticingly moss-trooperish.

Higginson's memoirs admitted that his boldness in rescuing slaves and backing Old Brown "did not come wholly from moral conviction but from . . . intrinsic love of adventure . . . boyish desire for a stirring experience . . ." This is intellectual honesty of an acute as well as a rare sort. He could not only describe his long-past self accurately but also refrain from calling it a young fool. It is unsporting to put such candid admissions in evidence against him. But the witness is the best possible, the testimony credible, the charge grave—and must be sustained. The eagerness of this able, vigorous, astute man deliberately to lob a fire bomb into the critically combustible Dixie of 1859 derived in considerable degree from callow "love of adventure" egged on by bookish romanticism.

The deliberateness is unmistakable, for his intellectual arrogance had fused with his romanticism. He was using Old Brown to bring on the splitting of the Union that he, T. W. Higginson, had long since decided was the best thing for his country. For thirteen years he had promoted "Disunionist" Abolitionism, openly pledged to use "whatever means may lie in my power to promote the Dissolution of the Union" because its main function, in his view and that of many extreme Abolitionists, was to help the South protect and spread slavery. His visit to Kansas in 1856 convinced him that slavery was a disease "too deep for cure without amputation." Gratifiedly he reported Kansas lacking "that spirit of blind superstitious loyalty to the U. S. Government which I feared to find . . . *the people of Kansas are just as ready to fight* the U. S. Government as the Missourians." He proposed to recruit in each free state a small private militia of fifty to a hundred pledged to invade Kansas at any time to support Free Staters against either Federal or Border Ruffian pressure, thinking it "essential . . . to involve every state in the war that is to be." Early in 1857 he worked closely with the Garrisonians in holding a convention to "consider the idea of disunion between Free and Slave States, as a practical problem that the times are pressing upon us."

Union-splitting talk was no novelty. For fifty years overanalytical minds had arrived at that point when pondering the potential meaning of persistent slavery. But by the late 1850's it had spread from the inner circles of pro- and antislaveryism to merchants, clergymen, politicians from whom European visitors often heard—and usually welcomed—pronouncements that the country was too unwieldy, its regional interests too diverse, for it to hold together much longer. The usual formula was three-ply: slave-and-cotton South; westward-creeping Middle West; industrial and maritime Northeast. The fission was thought of as occasioning little shock, the regions falling away from one another largely of their own weight, the new groupings legitimized by amendment to abrogate the common Constitution[5]—in any case probably without fighting. Horace Greeley was not alone in thinking it wisest to say "Erring sisters, depart in peace." Not even the rabid Garrisonians envisaged disunion by force; they were bound to Garrison's hobby of non-violence. The less rabid dreamed—when they considered ways and means at all—of the slaves' gradually buying their freedom or of gradual extinction of slavery state by state as had been done in the North. Only the Six and their slit-mouthed Gideon Balfour chose to try to precipitate matters by waging war against a state of the Union and capturing a Federal military installation. Such self-elected presumption is the egocentric's least ingratiating trait.

Of all the Six, Higginson was clearest about Union splitting's being surest cure for the nation's ills. If people hadn't the sense to see it his way, he would privately arrange to blow up the log jam and send the Union spinning downstream. True, there was only one word for it—the one that took Thompson and Anderson aback their last night on earth. Others avoided it: Sending Old Brown to J. M. Forbes, Dr. Howe called the old man's plan "what might perhaps seem at first to be treason." He did not explain why it was not treason first, last and all the time. But Higginson never bothered to gloss it over. Early in 1858 he had replied to one of Old Brown's regular appeals for funds: "I am always ready to invest money in treason, but at present have none to invest."

DR. GALAHAD

"Smile not, fair unbeliever!
One man, at least, I know
Who might wear the crest of Bayard
Or Sidney's plume of snow."
—J. G. WHITTIER ("The Hero", *i.e.* Dr. S. G. Howe)

Had Higginson never known Emily Dickinson or John Brown, few would care whether he ever existed. This cannot be said of Dr. Samuel Gridley Howe. The title page of Sanborn's book about him, written long after Harpers Ferry, calls him "The Philanthropist." That he was, if it is taken to mean "benefactor of mankind." "Lover of people" would not fit. Howe was no Abou ben Adhem. He readily seethed up into hatred, and sometimes his facile romantic-mindedness made him look silly. This was too bad because most of what he did was anything but silly. Toward the end of his career he organized the first statewide co-ordination of charities (in Massachusetts) and was high in the great Sanitary Commission that, anticipating the Red Cross, alleviated suffering in the Civil War. Earlier he boldly supported Horace Mann's reforms of teaching and public schools and Dorothea Dix's crusade against cruelty and squalor in insane asylums. Yet all this was secondary. In his own creative right, practically singlehanded, he founded constructive education of the blind and the feebleminded in America. To this day wherever people lacking sight or wits are intelligently helped, the influence of this ingenious, compassionate physician is still felt.

Improvising method by insight, trial and error; observing keenly; keeping in hand a savage temper in the interests of the handicapped, he made Boston's Perkins Institution (for the blind) and the Massachusetts School for Idiotic and

Above: The "Great House" (owner's residence) of Bryan Castle Estate, Jamaica. Owned by Bryan Edwards, M.P., planter and historian of Jamaica—and typical of the relative simplicity and informal, wide-verandahed design of such dwellings. *Institute of Jamaica.*

Below, left: Angelina (Grimké) Weld
Below, middle: Theodore Dwight Weld.
Below, right: Sarah M. Grimké
These engravings from daguerreotypes show Angelina, at age 39, in a costume that reflects her becoming a Quaker and remaining so until her marriage got her "read out of meeting"; Theodore at age 41, when he was most active in antislavery work; and Sarah at age 50. (From Garrison, *William Lloyd Garrison*)

A.

B.

C.

D.

E.

F.

THE SECRET SIX

A.   George Luther Stearns. *Library of Congress.*
B.   Dr. Samuel Gridley Howe. *Perkins School for the Blind, Watertown, Mass.*
C.   Theodore Parker (From Weiss, *Theodore Parker.*)
D.   Gerrit Smith. *Boston Public Library.*
E.   Franklin Benjamin Sanborn (From Sanborn, *Recollections of Seventy Years.*)
F.   Thomas Wentworth Higginson. *Boston Public Library.*

Feebleminded world-famous. His rehabilitation of blind and deaf Laura Bridgman made as much stir then as the case of Helen Keller in our time. He virtually rescued the child from drowning in nothingness. She and her preceptor ranked with Niagara Falls as a sight no eminent European visitor should miss. At least the first half of Chapman's assertion that this man, now fallen far out of the general ken,[6] "was one of the greatest of Americans and one of the best men who ever lived" was not absurd.

Achievement and personal harmony do not, however, always coincide. A highly catalytic man may be as stable as John Dewey or as dismaying as Rousseau. If Higginson's ailment was moss-trooperism, Howe's was derring-do-goodery, a Yankee Scottery combined with Byronistics. Sanborn's testimony reflected the same influences: ". . . the early years of the century invited romance and hazardous deeds. It was the age of . . . Byron . . . the Napoleon of the world of letters; of Scott, who inspired . . . chivalry . . . Of all the intellectual influences of his youth . . . Scott's was with Dr. Howe the most potent and the most intimate." And on the hat tree in his hallway hung the very helmet, gold-inlaid and azure-plumed, that Byron took to Greece. Thereby also hung a part of Howe's life explaining much of his affinity with Old Brown.

His father was a well-to-do Boston rope maker of sub-Brahmin social level married to a well connected beauty. Failure to collect for cordage supplied to the U. S. Navy in the War of 1812 so straitened the family resources that, this being before the day of work-your-way-through, only one son could go to college. The choice fell on Sam when he read aloud best of his brothers. At Brown, chosen because the Federalist odor of Harvard offended his father's nostrils, Sam was noted chiefly for monkeyshines, but then calmed down enough to graduate and go on to take a medical degree at Harvard. He never practiced in any regular fashion, having developed scruples against taking money for ministering to the sick and an ill-starred attachment for a girl of whom one knows only that she had blue eyes and married "another"—that anonymous Tertium Quid of nineteenth-century song and story. At this juncture Lord Byron, whose name for brilliance and wickedness had pervaded New England as much as anywhere, dramatized both himself and the current Greek war of independence by going to fight Turks. What with frustrated love, hero-worship, youthful restlessness—and no doubt good will for the struggling Greeks—off went Sam Howe in Byron's wake along with other young "Philhellenes" from all over the western world. The relative weight of the fourth factor is uncertain. Long afterward Howe wrote in a sort of echo of Higginson:

"I was impelled in early life to . . . [go] to Greece, rather by thoughtless indifference, perhaps ignorance of what course would have been profitable for me. Lacking prudence and caution, I followed an adventurous spirit." But then all his life Howe was exuberantly ready to risk his own and anybody else's neck, to exhaust himself and others for any purposes commendable in his eyes—the only admissible test. Let him choose the objective and every foot-pound of his great energy, every cell of his unusual brain was at the service of humanity. Phrenology, Polish refugees, hydropathy, the annexation of Santo Domingo, decency toward the insane—if it stirred Sam Howe up, he would see something done about it regardless; and it was odds-on that the world would be better for his arrogant zeal. If the objective be sound, he who thus pursues it with egocentric turbulence is preferable to him who does nothing. The risk is that the choice may be poor to pernicious, as in Howe's espousal of Old Brown's cause in consequence of his untrammeled Scottery.

He did himself great credit in Greece, where some other Philhellenes came sordidly to grief. After useful, plucky service as both fighter and surgeon he came home, wrote a hasty pro-Greek book about the struggle with Turkey, raised money for relief of war-harried Greeks and returned to manage its distribution. In canny anticipation of UNNRA methods he used relief supplies to hire refugee labor to improve the port of Aegina and create a model farm colony near Corinth. The new King of Greece made him a Chevalier of the Order of St. Saviour. Thenceforth his intimates, particularly his wife and Theodore Parker, called him "Chev," no doubt in fun. The honor was deserved, the eventual effect unfortunate. Chevaliers of any creation were rare in Boston. The conjunction of Byron's helmet—Howe had bid it in at a sale of the poet's effects—with a genuine if Levantine knighthood set plumes nodding, lances splintering and harem beauties languishing in his admirers' minds whenever they looked at him.

Never was man so loaded with plate-armor similes. Senator G. F. Hoar said that a visit from Dr. Howe was like a call from the Chevalier Bayard, Sir Philip Sidney or Richard I. James Freeman Clarke invoked Sir Lancelot and the Good Samaritan. Horace Mann mentioned Godfrey (de Bouillon, presumably) and Amadis de Gaul. Higginson called him "a natural crusader or paladin . . . in whom every call to duty took a chivalrous aspect." People talked like that back when Brian du Bois-Guilbert and "Roll on, thou deep and dark blue ocean, roll!" were household words in the same strata where Oedipus and existentialism would be trigger catchwords now. Even when catty about him, Howe's wife necessarily thought of trial by battle: "Chev's is one of those characters based upon opposition. While I always seem to work for an unseen friend, he always sees an armed adversary and arms himself accordingly."

He looked the part: tall, dark-haired, dashingly bearded, with keen blue eyes: "an Arab in figure and in horsemanship," wrote Sanborn, ". . . with a glowing color and a manner that bespoke energy tempered by inward courtesy." And he was intriguingly prone to "home on" trouble. Returning from Greece in 1830, he mingled exultantly with the Paris street revolution that ousted the Bourbons: "I knew it was none of my business, but I could not help joining in . . ." While studying in Paris next year he volunteered to administer American relief to Polish refugees in Prussia. His brisk but tactless approach to this mission got him some weeks of solitary confinement in a Berlin prison. Some of his friends believed that his unbecoming reaction to the news of Harpers Ferry reflected the abiding horror of imprisonment that this experience left with him.

Certified knightliness, dungeons, great good looks, worldwide renown . . . This distinguished bachelor of forty won the beautiful and vivacious Julia Ward, a redheaded, cultivated and witty toast of New York with a wealthy father and some money of her own. As the disparate chemistries of its attractive components reacted, this striking marriage disappointed them. Their daughter, who worshiped both, called it "the wedding of the northwest wind and the mountain torrent." Affection persisted; but Howe fretted because Julia's unearned income exceeded his salary at the Institute; tried to stop her publishing her verses even anonymously; and found it difficult to prevent her from taking him over as high-velocity wives of certain kinds sometimes take over preoccupied husbands. Julia found little interest in the Perkins Institution, where the highly specialized arrangements no doubt were trying; resented Chev's hostility to her writing, which relaxed only when he found her pen useful for change of pace in a virulent Abolitionist paper that he ran; and, between having babies, maintained guard against the considerable risk that her high-velocity spouse might take *her* over. "Life with a Comet-Apostle was not always easy," sighed her daughter biographers. To a sister about to marry, Julia wrote: "Marriage, like death, is a debt we owe to nature," and went on to describe Chev's return late from a good-cause party "quite intoxicated with benevolence."[7]

The ecstatic "Battle Hymn of the Republic" secured her an easy fame outlasting Chev's, but Julia had sometimes had stinging doubts of the wisdom of exhorting the Lord to loose the fateful lightning of His terrible swift sword. After visiting Nassau, Cuba and South Carolina the summer before Harpers Ferry she published her opinion that the Dixie Negro was "ugly as Caliban, lazy as the laziest of brutes, chiefly ambitious to be of no use to anybody" and "suggested . . . the unwelcome question whether compulsory labor be not better than none . . . Moral justice dissents from the habitual sneer, denunciation, and malediction, which have become consecrated forms of piety in speaking of the South." I do not know how she behaved on learning of Chev's involvement in the Harpers Ferry plan. But soon enough she was forgetting all the above and giving her sister the party line:

"No one knew of Brown's intentions but Brown himself and his handful of men. The attempt, I must judge insane, but the spirit *heroic*. I should be glad to be as sure of heaven as that old man may be, following right in the footsteps of the martyrs, girding on his sword for the weak and oppressed. His death will be holy and glorious—the gallows cannot dishonor him—he will hallow it."

Neither she nor Chev cared much about consistency; highly positive people seldom do. On the scene he wrote the rebel Greeks down as "ignorant, selfish, and thievish; none can equal them in deceit, & cunning; none surpass them in treachery." Years later he coolly gave all this the lie: "I found the Greeks kindly affectioned, trustful, grateful, and as far as my intercourse with them went, honest people." The first shows how abusive he could be;[8] the second is puzzling. It occurs in a long autobiographical letter to Horace Mann; maybe Howe was trying to live up to his reputation for universal benevolence.

"I do not like caution," said this Yankee knight-errant. "It betokens little faith in God's arrangements." This is plain in his hot Disunionism and hopes of widespread slave risings. When war came, he judged that within sixty days twenty to forty thousand volunteers could "plough through the South, & be followed by a blaze of servile war that would utterly and forever root out slaveholding and slavery." This hapless prediction shows another unfortunate result of his going to Greece. As a thoroughly brave man who had often smelled powder he considered himself rather expert in military matters. Visiting Morro Castle at Havana with Julia and the Parkers, he gravely analyzed the technical merits of the works, pointing out where besiegers would open trenches . . . When Old Brown laid his essential scheme before the Six, they naturally looked to Howe for his opinion, and he pronounced the plan feasible. Even after the disastrous fact he insisted that it had stood a fair chance of success. Maybe all the Six were so spellbound that they would have continued support for Old Brown anyway. "Without accepting Brown's plans as reasonable," Sanborn wrote, "we were prepared to second them merely because they were his." But this verdict of Howe's made certain that the old man could go on muddling and blending alternate plans while doling out to the Six just enough detail to keep them confused but openhanded.

Actually Howe's temperament preferred direct action, however misguided, to any wait-and-see approach. Soon after taking up Abolitionism he told a colleague that "some move of actual force" against slavery was overdue and, had he not just assumed "new duties" by marrying, he would have led it. Presently a Boston free Negro came to Howe showing good references and asking money for a fund to buy his slave daughter to prevent her being sold South. Under such circumstances most antislaveryites approved of this device, but the philanthropic doctor took very high ground—he would aid no such palliative, he said, but he would personally pay expenses for six people to go South and kidnap her into freedom. It cannot have been a pretext for avoiding giving. He often gave more than he could afford to causes that he approved of. But it remained true that this swash-

THE SECRET SIX 345

buckling gesture did nothing to keep the woman out of the trader's hands. Howe had much *ruat coelum* in him. Le ,Barnes went to him with a scheme to send Old Brown a Yankee lawyer to double as spy during the preliminaries to the trial with a view to giving him a better defense in any case and possibly to effecting a rescue. He was quite taken aback when Howe "threw cold water on the scheme" on the grounds that it was best to let the old man hang for the consequent "good effect on public opinion."

Yet he probably admired this man whom he proposed to sacrifice as much as anybody among the Six except Sanborn, describing him as "an honest, keen, and veteran backwoodsman . . . of the Puritan military order . . . an enthusiast, yet cool, keen, and cautious . . ." He was nearer truth when describing the old man as "Coleridge's Ancient Mariner . . . come to life." Old Brown did show the Mariner's obsessiveness; he was a "man forbid" exerting on the hesitant those relentless, will-sapping pressures with which paranoids are often adept. But the Mariner learned that "He prayeth best who loveth best/ All things both great and small . . ." Old Brown based on hatred—generalized hatred focused *a priori* by historical and cultural chance on slaveholders. This steady glow of pure emotion necessarily fascinated Howe, whose own "hatred of slavery and its works" his latest biographer calls "pathological."

It was a complex person, with the seizures of good will and brilliance as salient as the shrill rages and the adolescent posturings, and he puzzled his offspring too. "I do not remember his ever being irritable with any of us children," wrote his daughter, "yet he was not a patient man. He did not suffer fools gladly; he rent them in pieces and went on over the trampled bodies . . . *Impatient!* he springs into life at the word. And yet, I think of Laura Bridgman, and of the countless others for whom he toiled, without haste, without rest, year by year, his spirit fed as from some inexhaustible well of patience . . . Impatient? I draw my pen through the word. Then I hear his voice, quick, keen, incisive: 'Push on! push on! Fire away!' and I let it stand."

Shortly before he died he wrote to a close friend: "I am now the only surviving member of the gallant band of Philhellenes who fought for the freedom of Greece . . ." and signed himself "Sam'l G. Howe (Sometimes yclept the Chevalier)." On his coffin—I hesitate to include this detail but it apparently did not trouble his family—they laid a helmet and sword made of violets. No doubt Laura Bridgman, his own creation, knew the best of him. When he died, she went about taking people's hands and pressing into their palms in the code that he had invented and taught her: "I have lost my best friend."

PURITAN PROPHET

> *"Parker might . . . become Catholic, and then the world would have two Popes instead of one."*
>
> —JULIA WARD HOWE

Lydia Maria Child, the dean of lady Abolitionists, who knew Theodore Parker well, called him "the greatest man, morally and intellectually, that our country ever produced." He probably could not have been betrayed into open agreement but secretly he might have had small reason to demur.

While he taught school for a living at Watertown, Mass., and overworked at the languages and theology that would make him a highly learned man, he scorned fiction—except the Waverley Novels, from which he no doubt derived the same values as Higginson and Howe. He also felt a backhanded fascination with Byron. As minister marrying William and Ellen Crafts (a famous runaway slave couple in danger of recapture) he gave the groom a bowie knife and advised him to use it vigorously to defend their freedom— a gesture showing more Scottery than Christianity. So did his success in frightening slave catchers out of Boston by detailing for them just what violence they might expect from the Abolitionist mob if they remained in town to threaten the Crafts. He was proud of having written his sermons at this period with sword and pistol handy in an open drawer. But his basic picture of himself, though bookish, was less frivolous than Higginson's or Howe's, more like Old Brown's. Exultantly he wrote that a speech of his on a certain fugitive slave made him feel like "a Hebrew prophet. I have seldom risen so high . . . never thundered or lightened into such an atmosphere. I did not think of such words, they *came* . . . I did greater than I could counsel, far greater than I knew . . ."

Moses might have spoken thus after meeting Jehovah on Sinai; provided, that is, he were equally inclined to discuss matters. Old Brown might be Gideon or Joshua—Theodore Parker was Elijah before the priests of Baal, Nathan before David. It had once been and to some extent still was the prerogative of New England ministers, as of their prototypes, the English Puritan and Scots Presbyterian divines, to give kings, parliaments and peoples orders in the name of the Lord as had Samuel and Elisha. Parker could not let that function decay even if he had to maintain it singlehanded. "Not since the days of the Puritan theocracy," wrote Commager, "had any clergyman used so lordly a tone . . . He could tell all the politicians what to do and ignore the consequences." That requires a good conceit of oneself. In this respect too Parker was well fitted to be the philosopher of direct-action Abolitionism as well as a renowned religious heretic.

His self-assurance came of not Brahmin but yeoman background. His grandfather was the Captain John Parker who mustered the minutemen at Lexington in 1775. A musket there captured from a redcoat was grandson's most prized possession. Maybe a consequent faith in militia helped the Rev. Theodore Parker to take seriously Old Brown's private militia, whom the Virginia militia found so formidable in fact. Maybe Parker tended to identify Grandfather John— dead before Theodore was born—with this other plain, intrepid Yankee yeoman. But this is oversubtle. Say only that John Parker was militant and so was his scholarly grandson, as much at home in slave-rescuing mobs as in the pulpit, as ready to strike for the Lord's sake as were Barak and Samson, who were also judges in Israel, and much chagrined when a legal flaw robbed him of public trial for flouting the law of the land against aiding runaway slaves.

In the Yankee tradition of plain living and thinking as high as one can manage, he early embarked on an extreme Unitarianism and scholarship spiraling out widely from it. His professional reputation in Europe was high, a thing accorded few American scholars a century ago. His serene wife, whom he fondly called "Bearsie" because she had so delighted in the town bear of Berne, bore no children, which deeply distressed both; but he could also joke about it in an irreverent parody of the Shorter Catechism. Often far from stuffy, he amused Mrs. Howe, a great wit herself. He was as choosy as Higginson about "causes" and actually temperate about "temperance," a rare talent. He took great interest in the Brook Farm good-life colony of his intimate friend, George Ripley; but he was not moved to join it. Yet in his own way he was as hidebound and queer as any of the Six. For all his theological radicalism—conventional pulpits closed against him when he as good as denied the inspiration of the Bible—he saw nothing absurd in attributing the low dividends paid by British railroads to God's judgment on the stockholders for allowing trains to run on Sundays, a position that even Garrison reprehended. Extravagantly he professed to find only Benedict Arnold's treachery comparable to Daniel Webster's support of the Compromise of

1850. And, when pondering the gratuitous savagery of nature, he told himself in his private journal the prurient lie that he had personally seen one old squirrel hold down a young male while another old one chewed off the testicles.[9]

For lack of a church his admirers hired the Boston Music Hall for him to preach in. He drew many strangers too, for he was as much one of the sights of Boston as Bunker Hill. Stocky, bustly, with a snub "Socratic" face and a rustic air, he imposed himself on hearers by sheer intellectual and rhetorical vigor. As edited for print presumably by himself, his homilies show some of the ablest prose of a day when good Yankee prose meant Thoreau, Dana, Holmes. He was a hasty-pudding Burke, fond of giving a worthy idea a handsome setting and yet grittily relishing the sudden, small words. One way or another most of the Six wrote for publication. Higginson and Sanborn made careers of it. But Parker was the literary talent among them. It is too bad he died before he had set down his personal impressions of Old Brown; the recorded picture of the old man as it stands has too few such crosslights as he could have given it.

Parker's preaching skill supplied some of the most ringing statements of the "Higher Law" doctrine that rationalized both Old Brown's delusions and the infatuation of his backers. "There is no supreme law but that made by God; if our laws contradict that, the sooner . . . they are broken, why, the better." He did not originate this position but gave it very striking trappings. The next problem, of course, was: How may one learn the law of God on such specific matters as slavery and the laws against tampering with it? Though never quite explicit, the reply is always clear: Apply to the one-man, hieratic supreme court that, through God's inscrutable choice, with no merit attributed to the judge as such, consists of the Rev. Theodore Parker. He was commissioned the man who knew all about it, and when debates over the Fugitive Slave Law of 1850 offered clear occasion for the Higher Law doctrine, he applied it with cogent arrogance. I have pieced together the gist of it from speeches and sermons of his delivered between March, 1850, and April, 1851:

"The natural duty to keep the law of God overrides the obligation to observe any human statute . . . That you are morally bound to obey the statute, let it be never so plainly wrong and opposed to your conscience . . . is the most dangerous of false ideas . . . I have been amazed that they should dare tell us the law of God, writ on the heavens and in our hearts, never demanded we should disobey the laws of men! . . . Then it was old Daniel's duty at Darius's command to give up his prayer . . . John's and Peter's duty to forebear to preach Christianity . . . In the North the majority of men think that the law is subordinate to religion . . . that idea is the safeguard of the state and of the law . . . It will scourge every wicked law out of the temple of justice with iron whips, if need be . . . the law of God is a little greater than the statute of an accidental president, unintentionally chosen for four years . . . If this generation in America could believe that there was no law of God for you and me to keep . . . that would be a calamity which the nation would never recover from . . . No law higher than human will! . . . Who rules the State, and out of a few stragglers that fled here to New England . . . built up this mighty, wealthy State? Was it Carver and Winthrop? . . . Why, the boys at school know better! It was the eternal God whose higher law the Pilgrim and the Puritan essayed to keep . . .

". . . when you displace God from the throne of the world, and instead of his eternal justice, re-enact the will of the Devil, then you may keep slavery; keep it forever, keep it in peace. Not till then . . . By and by there will be a political party with a wider basis than the free soil party, who will declare that the nation itself must put an end to slavery in the nation; and if the Constitution of the United States will not allow it, there is another . . . that will . . .

the Constitution of the Universe . . . we shall reaffirm the
ordinances of nature and re-enact the will of God . . . it is
written on the iron leaf that it must come, come, too, before
long . . . There is no attribute of God which is not on our
side; because in this matter we are on the side of God." [10]

Thus the theologian skilled in God's attributes; the
stump speaker sneering at President Fillmore for doing his
sworn duty and misrepresenting for rhetorical effect the
president's part in lawmaking; the Yankee parochially sure
that, as Parker said elsewhere, New England was once "the
soul, although not the body" of America; the Puritan parson still resenting the separation of church and state and ar-
rogating to himself the functions of both oracle and Dutch
uncle. This stubby man with a steel-trap mind had on his
prophet's hat. The cabalistic symbols on it were the burning
bush, the martyr's crown and John Endicott's flag with St.
George's cross cut out of it, and there was a great deal of air
between his sanctified bare feet and the ground. And one of
the spirits he conjured up—naturally to his great satisfaction—was Old Brown, essentially a self-elected exponent of
the Higher Law acting out what such as Parker had been
demanding for a generation. Remember that reading Parker's sermons aloud was a conspicuous activity of Old Brown's
boys in training at Springdale.

At its height Parker's skill in vituperation reached Garrisonian levels; here he is on Northerners deputed to enforce
the Fugitive Slave Law: "I can look charitably upon thieves,
prowling about in darkness; on rum-sellers, whom poverty
condemns to crime; on harlots, who do the deed of shame
. . . I can pity the pirate, who scours the seas doing his
fiendish crimes . . . his sin is not so dreadful as that of a
commissioner in Boston who sends a man into slavery . . .
I cannot comprehend that in any man, not even in a hyena
. . . Forgive me, o ye wolves and hyenas! that I bring you
into such company . . . It has been said that the administration preferred low and contemptible men as their tools

. . . men cast off from society for perjury, for nameless crimes, and sins not mentionable in English speech . . . There are kennels of the courts wherein there settles down all that the law breeds most foul, loathsome, and hideous and abhorrent to the eye of day. There this contaminating puddle gathers its noisome ooze, slowly, stealthily, continually agglomerating its mass by spontaneous cohesion, and sinking by the irresistible gravity of rottenness into that abhorred deep, the lowest, ghastliest pit in all the subterranean vaults of human sin. It is true that Government has skimmed the top and dredged the bottom of these kennels of the courts . . . [but] Blame not the Government! It took the best it could get."

Such auto-intoxicated bawling naturally led him to dwell with ill-concealed relish on the possibility of bloody slave insurrection. In 1850 he said: "God forgive us our cowardice if we let it come to this, that three millions of human beings . . . degraded by us, must wade through slaughter to their inalienable rights." Only eight years later he was giving money to and otherwise aiding Old Gideon Balfour to bring on that very calamity, and writing to a woman friend: "I should like, of all things, to see an insurrection of the slaves." He thought it would fail but "it would do good even if it failed." Such grim willingness to tempt numerous young Abolitionists and thousands of Negro slaves to go and get massacred in a softening-up operation sounds more like a general staff or a Communist committee than like a professed disciple of a God of Love. Assume charitably that this thing grew on him as his dwindling physical powers exasperated a man accustomed to be tireless. When Old Brown struck, Parker was in Italy succumbing to the tuberculosis that had cropped up in his late forties. The news of Harpers Ferry made the old fires flare high. Though a failure, he wrote, the raid had shown "the weakness of the greatest Slave State . . . the worthlessness of her soldiery," and presaged the inevitable day when "The South must reap as she sows . . . a pretty crop . . . The Fire of Vengeance may be waked up even in an African's heart, especially when it is fanned by the wickedness of a white man; then it runs from man to man, from town to town. What shall put it out? The white man's blood!"

Ghastly talk; but then punitive-mindedness born of self-righteousness carried too far and gathering hatred too violently expressed was the Abolitionist's besetting sin, as Theodore Weld came to see; and the bloody-minded parson is a deplorably old story. Each fresh case, rightly regarded, is fresh occasion for wonder and, if you like, pity.

True, Parker had never been farther south than Washington, hence had few hampering impressions of apathetic slaves and civil slaveowners, hence could more readily assume a hangman's detachment and speak of Hayti-style servile uprisings, all screams and fire and mass blood lust, like a doctor of his day prescribing bleeding. But his exultance peeps through too plainly to allow this plea. Besides, first-hand knowledge did others of the Six little good. A visit to close relatives in Dixie as a young man had only temporarily perplexed Higginson by the contrast between actual conditions and those described in antislavery propaganda. Dr. Howe's difficulty was more recent. Only a few months before Harpers Ferry, Julia and he had been hospitably treated by several eminent South Carolina households; the experience left him rather shaken in his conviction that slave insurrection would be an admirable thing. But even so he had aided John Brown jr., in a last-minute campaign for funds and had sent Old Brown fifty dollars of his own within a few weeks of the actual raid. Such inconsistency was easy for men able to see whole groups of human beings, even their own countrymen, as generalized illustrations for books that had pleased them—prophets and unrighteous kings; moss-troopers; kidnaped African princesses; Covenanters and bloodhounds; Galahad and Simon Legree. In such cases Cadmus and Gutenberg have much to answer for.

LORD BOUNTIFUL

"Gerrit Smith . . . Bronson Alcott turned Maecenas."
—HENRY STEELE COMMAGER

Scott, Byron and Yankee now all disappear temporarily. Gerrit Smith's people were New York Dutch from Rockland County across the Hudson from Westchester. Older than Old Brown, eldest and most eccentric of the Six, Gerrit was born in 1797. His formative years antedated the full impact of Scott and Byron and, though literate and verbose, he was not genuinely bookish. Frothingham, his official biographer, was dismayed by the wateriness of his 1800-volume library: a little history, an obviously neglected collection of poets, "no drama, no fiction, no travel . . . [largely] religious literature, so called . . . sermons, homilies, commentaries . . . not the library of a cultivated, educated, or deeply thoughtful man."

Smith may be easiest of the Six to account for. I cannot fully explain how men of such bottom and intelligence as Howe's, Parker's and Higginson's could enroll under a banner so Bedlamite as Old Brown's, can only suggest emotional and literary factors that may have combined to that extraordinary end. The enigma remains, greater than the sum of its parts and occasion for salutary marveling. With Smith wonder, though still roused, is less intense. The figure he cut is still most familiar: the self-dramatizing millionaire addicted to causes, perhaps neo-Fascist, perhaps in guilt-assuaging subsidy of movements Reddish-to-Red; only in Smith's time the "down-with-us" impulse took other forms. Many wealthy persons manage to choose causes of reasonable quality to support and avoid more meretricious ones that better gratify the ego. But this calls for a stability and common sense that Gerrit Smith lacked.

Actual mental illness, again probably "in the family," also turns up here. His father gradually gave way to religious infatuations marked enough to cause grave concern even in that hell-obsessed time. Gerrit's elder brother was an eccentric problem drinker overtly psychotic toward his death. His younger brother was a lifelong psychotic. Gerrit himself was a pronounced hypochondriac[11] and shared his father's morbid terrors of damnation. Word of Harpers Ferry sent him into an emotional panic necessitating three months in an insane asylum. It looks as if he had merely had somewhat better luck than his brothers in the genetic draw. His campaigns against "dramshops" and for women's rights—and his adherence to Old Brown—may have betokened a minor version of what so disastrously ailed brother Peter and brother Adolph. Yet the bulk of his actions need not be referred to inchoate "insanity." His kind of zeal in a wide range of causes was common to many of his contemporaries within normal mental range; at least they had no such family histories and saw the inside of asylums only as philanthropic sightseers.

Always queer and growing queerer, Peter Smith, his father, founded a fortune just the same. He had a stage-struck period as a young clerk in New York, indeed acted minor parts professionally, but overcame the craving and went into the fur business with young John Jacob Astor. From the firm's trading store in Utica, catering largely to Indian trappers, Peter Smith embarked on extensive land speculation and presently severed the Astor connection.[12] He learned to buy tax-defaulted lands cheap, let the new taxes on them go to default again, then buy them in afresh for less than taxes due. This device, plus others more conventional, enabled him to build up a higgledy-piggledy empire of over a million acres concentrated in the Mohawk Valley and adjacent Adirondack wilderness. Southeast of Syracuse this

self-made patroon then founded a settlement named Peterboro round a large, wooden-columned manor house the lord
of which signed himself "Peter Smith of Peterboro." When
chronic "melancholia" moved him to hand the bulk of his
holdings over to Gerrit, he was worth some $400,000—then
a large fortune.

Gerrit grew up at Peterboro as self-centered squire of a
backwoods manor plagued by flighty relatives and nervous
ills. He attended nearby Hamilton College, of which he became a fitfully loyal and officious alumnus. Abolitionist-
Reformists usually saw one another as either godlike super-
men or fiends in human form, but Smith does really seem
to have been handsome and blandly charming when not in
one of his fits of snarling denunciation. Edmund Quincy
called this ingratiating young six-footer "one of the finest
specimens of a man, physically, morally and intellectually,
that I ever knew." Most of the Six were unusually tall, handsome men in contrast with Old Brown's middle-sized wiri-
ness. But they found it easy to look up to him anyway.

Smith's second wife—his first died soon after marriage—
loyally upheld his hands in his many doings and was duly
valued. When she came down to breakfast mornings, he
would gallantly announce, "Heaven has broken loose!" She
shared his morbid crotchets with sympathetic moanings and
soul searchings of her own, and joined in his espousal of the
Millerite end-of-the-world craze in the mid-1840's. She was
away from home when the faithful were supposed to assem-
ble on hilltops to ascend to heaven all at once, so Gerrit
wrote to her: "My dearly Beloved:—We have just had
family worship—perhaps for the last time. Today's mail
brought me . . . the extra Midnight Cry [a Millerite pa-
per]. It declares that the world will end at three tomorrow
morning. The Midnight Cry which came today says that
time may possibly continue until the 23d or even the 24th
. . . I know not, my dear Nancy, that we shall meet in the
air . . ." As his library showed he was almost professionally

religious, preaching lay sermons in local pulpits lacking ordained ministers and founding at Peterboro a free-wheeling, non-denominational congregation the unspoken credo of which was that Gerrit Smith was right on any topic that interested him.

That included a wide range. In his time he took up African colonization, compensated emancipation of slaves, direct-action Abolitionism, Sunday Schools, observing the seventh-day Sabbath, home missions, foreign missions, women's rights, prison reform, abolition of capital punishment, vegetarianism, the "peace" movement, the wars on rum and tobacco . . .[13] and found time to help create the Liberty Party and, as amateur politician, get elected to Congress in 1852. In Washington he gave lavish but cold-water dinners to his colleagues, Southerners as welcome as any, and advocated, among other striking measures, the abolition of the post office; prohibition in the District of Columbia; and stopping the rum issue in the U. S. Navy, a thing that took sixty years more and Josephus Daniels to accomplish. Maybe sensing that he was getting nowhere, he resigned before his term ended. All the while he managed his discontinuous kingdom, often with acumen like his acquisitive father's. Son's most valuable single holding—a large interest in the Oswego waterfront and the canal feeding it— was of his own shrewd purchase. By the time he met Old Brown his income was seldom under $60,000 a year.

His reputation for openhanded philanthropy made it a business merely to sort out the pleas for money that clogged every mail. He joked ponderously about how people thought him afflicted by "a pecuniary plethora that requires constant bleeding to assure health and vigor." By no means all this golden shower went to crackpots. Polish and Greek refugees, Irish famine victims got four-figured checks; the Oswego free library, $30,000. And even though susceptible to cranks he often said No for his own reasons, sometimes good, often absurd, but in any case retaining him the right to make up his own skittish mind. Honorably he paid the American Colonization Society a promised $3000 months after he had come to deplore its aims.

This independence of mind showed brightest after the Civil War when he, Horace Greeley and Cornelius Vanderbilt posted bond for Jefferson Davis and demanded that, after two years in prison, the man should be either tried or freed. He opposed attempts at "absolute prohibition" of alcohol as "unattainable . . . [and] ought to be unattainable," founding instead his own "Anti-Dramshop Party" to outlaw saloons as occasions of temptation. Yet he was hardly so liberal-intelligent as these schemes hint. He carried the principle of the best being the least government to the length of opposing public schools as well as post offices, canals and railroads. He agreed with most Reformists that moderate drinkers were pernicious because their ability to enjoy rum without disaster encouraged others to drink and perish. As confidently as Parker he wished government to be "the representative of God . . . drawing a line between religion and Civil Government . . . has brought this country to the very verge of ruin." Such mental habits readied him for Old Brown's plans to do what government's neglect of God's will had left unattended to.

What happened when this upstate Lord Bountiful tried to benefit his own village sounds like a Mark Twain satire. Unscrupulous lessees swindled him badly when he financed a "temperance" (*i.e.*, bone-dry) tavern to compete with the existing whiskified one. "He proposed to build and endow a public library . . . and the owners of desirable land sites were, all at once, misers, who held their ground at prices so exorbitant that the scheme was abandoned . . . He offered to erect a fountain on the common, and the jealousy of the residents, each of whom wanted it in front of his own house, caused a bitterness which the waters of Bethesda would not cure. He presented a town clock to the authorities, and they grew at once so parsimonious that he

was requested to provide a man to wind it up . . ." His
hyperbolic eagerness to lodge and feed all comers made his
household memorable. A guest recorded having dined one
day with "an Irish Catholic priest, a Hicksite Quakeress
minister, a Calvinistic Presbyterian deacon . . . two abolition lecturers, a Seventh Day Baptist, a shouting Methodist, a Whig pro-slavery member of Congress . . . And . . .
no one was neglected . . . [Smith] conversing with each
in such a sweet way as to disarm all criticism." Frothingham
sought to justify it all, even the corruption of Peterboro, on
the grounds that "the rules he practiced were laid down
by Jesus." But that hardly applied to the culminating quix-
oticism—support of Old Brown.

In middle age Smith sought earnestly to reduce his wealth
to nearer needle's-eye size and, as it happened, these attempts related to John Brown. To new and hot-Abolition-
ist Oberlin College Smith gave 21,000 undeveloped acres
of land in far western Virginia, now northwestern West Virginia. It was nominally slave territory and encumbered by
squatters who might never have heard of Gerrit Smith, but
eventually, it was hoped, "Christian tenants and free laborers"
would settle it. Now John Brown's father was a trustee of
Oberlin, and presently son John ought to survey the tract
for the college "with a particular view to settle my family on
it." In the end, after vacillation on both sides, nothing came
of the idea—except a month of "land-looking" that first
showed him the confusedly rugged trans-Ohio country
whence he derived the notion of a Maroon-type runaway
colony "in the mountains of Virginia." The Oberlin lands
were the other side of the Appalachians from Harpers Ferry,
but he always assured the Six that he had carefully studied
the very terrain where he planned to operate.

Soon Smith's land-ridden conscience forged another link
between him and Brown. In 1846 he gave some 140,000
acres, mostly in forty-acre parcels, to 3000-odd New York
free Negroes chosen by their own leaders as likely and de-

serving. The intent was admirable: to give them a fresh start and incidentally to qualify them to vote under New York's $250 property qualification. But the lands were mostly in the cold, sterile Adirondacks, few of the Negroes had the skills needed in semi-pioneering and, it was said, surveyors swindled them out of what good land was included. For a while, however, a Negro colony persisted in the Adirondacks and drew John Brown's attention. He visited the area in 1848 and proposed to Smith to settle the Brown clan there to train their Negro neighbors in better farming—an art in which Brown himself had not so far been oversuccessful. Secretly he hoped also to recruit Negroes for his violent if still vague antislavery schemes. In this he failed. But he did acquire the farm at North Elba, N.Y., eventually financed by Yankee admirers, that became his pre-Harpers Ferry headquarters.

This made Old Brown known to Smith just when the rich man's ideas were changing in an appropriate direction. Smith had long opposed violence against slavery and the incitement of slave risings. But as tempers heated up, his own included, he began to predict with diminishing dismay that "this infatuated nation will go on in its proslavery wickedness until her slavery has come to a violent and bloody end." By 1856 he allowed his $250 contribution to the Free-State cause to pay for rifles: ". . . there are instances in which the shedding of blood is unavoidable," said this backsliding "non-violence" man to A. A. Lawrence. "Hitherto I have opposed the bloody abolition of slavery," he wrote to a Syracuse paper. "But now when it begins to march its conquering bands into [Kansas] I and ten thousand other peace men are not only ready to have it repulsed with violence, but pursued even unto death, with violence." By mid-1857 he was dead ripe for Brown, writing to an Emigrant Aid zealot as to "our sacred work in Kansas . . . We must not shrink from fighting for Liberty—& if Federal troops fight against us, we must fight against them."

Already aware of Old Brown's plans in 1858, he warned Joshua Giddings, Abolitionist leader in Congress: "The slave will be delivered by the shedding of blood—and the signs are multiplying that deliverance is at hand"—meaning that he now knew his own mind and, like the Marxist or wave-of-the-future Fascist, sought actively to bring to pass what he wishfully took to be inevitable. After entertaining Old Brown and John jr. in April, 1858, he was "buoyant and hopeful" about the raid scheme. In August, 1859, he betrayed his vengeful relish in a most indiscreet letter to the Negroes of Syracuse. "The feeling among the blacks that they must deliver themselves gains strength with fearful rapidity . . . is it entirely certain that these [potential] insurrections will be put down promptly? telegraphs and railroads can be rendered useless in an hour . . . many who would be glad to face the insurgents would be busy in transporting their wives and daughters to places where they would be safe from the worst fate which husbands and fathers can imagine . . . but for this embarrassment Southern men would laugh at the idea of an insurrection . . . But trembling as they would for loved ones, I know no part of the world where so much as in the South, men would be likely in a formidable insurrection, to lose the most important time, and be distracted and panic-stricken."

Maybe Old Brown and Smith had discussed this. Yet I know no other indication that the Harpers Ferry plan relied on fear of rape to disorganize opposition. It may have been independently developed over the summer by the frantically Christian squire of Peterboro.

The man dismayed even his biographers. "Failure to agree with him was proof of bad judgment on the part of those less enlightened," wrote Harlow, the most scholarly and recent. "He lived too consciously in the world's eye," wrote Frothingham. "He was too large a figure in his own regard . . . his self-assurance proceeded from that reliance on the 'moral sense' which gives its possessor the much overrated, much abused prerogative of prophecy." That was much of what ailed Old Brown too, of course, and for that matter the rest of the Six. Smith may have shown this moral arrogance so very markedly because he had chosen ancestors tinged with mental illness almost as heavily as were Old Brown's. The other Five had less excuse for betting the future of thirty million of their countrymen on their own self-righteous and unsought judgment.

THE BEARDED ANGEL

> *". . . a merchant of Boston . . . one of the noblest in it."*
> —THEODORE PARKER introducing
> G. L. Stearns to Henry Ward Beecher

About the time Kansas began to bleed, George Luther Stearns, a well-to-do citizen of shipbuilding and rum-distilling Medford, Mass., a suburb of Boston, developed chronic bronchitis. His doctor advised him to grow a long beard as chest protector. Full-flowing beards were less common then than during and after the Civil War. The wavily luxuriant affair that thenceforth masked Stearns below the cheekbones made him conspicuous. But he often did as he pleased regardless of opinion—he even denounced the Demon Rum in Medford, proverbial home of the stuff—and persisted in this curious therapeutic device because it seemed to benefit him. His doctor may thus have contributed to the canonization of Old Brown. There is reason to believe that Stearns' magnificent hairiness was what led the old man to let his beard run to such Mosaic proportions when he needed disguise.[14]

This self-made magnate's gold thumb also played a large part. His was not a straight Horatio Alger story but the

Yankee variation with just the typical amount of whom-do-you-know re-enforcing earnest industry and astuteness at grasping opportunity. Stearns' father was a Medford obstetrician of good Bay State stock who ran a boys' school in the intervals of delivering babies. His wife's family connections included the opulently eminent Lawrences of Boston. Dr. Stearns died when the boy was eleven years old, and by the time he was fifteen young George had to start supporting himself—and learning the ways of commerce—by clerking in an uncle's store in Brattleboro, Vermont. Some years later family influence put him in a ship-chandlering warehouse on Boston's India Wharf. By obvious seriousness and agonizing zeal in improving his poor handwriting the boy did well, and also developed great physical strength from manhandling cables and casks of pork.

Presently he evolved a new way to produce linseed oil, one of the firm's staples and, still in his twenties, built a new type of oil mill. The necessary capital was raised half from a Medford deacon who wanted—and got—him as son-in-law, a quarter from the hesitant Boston relatives, and the final $5000 by a mortgage on the family house, his mother's principal asset. In three years the mortgage was cleared, the operation profitable. Later Stearns returned to chandlery in his old firm and prospered further; then he acquired New England rights to a patent for specially flexible lead pipe and did so well with it that he was personally clearing $15,000 to $20,000 a year—easily equivalent to $100,000 now. In a fit of middle-aged rashness he tried to corner the lead market and met disaster, facing bankruptcy and pondering suicide. But his solid reputation persuaded his creditors to give him time and, when the panic of 1857 struck, he was well enough re-established to help several who had thus helped him.

Long since he had bought an elaborately landscaped Medford house that he had admired as a boy. When it proved awkward to remodel for more room, he razed and replaced it with a pseudo-Tudor mansion that was one of the sights of Medford. He liked fine harness horses and drove them himself but scorned the show-off rich man's cult of racing trotters and pacers. He liked white wine but gave it up for consistency's sake when determining to support the "temperance" cause. He so delighted in the famous readings from Shakespeare given by Fanny Kemble, the Anglo-American actress, that he attended each of twelve straight performances, driving home from Boston after each. It is pleasant to think of the big, solemn, bearded man so innocently devoted to the most attractive woman of her day.

His first wife, the deacon's daughter, died within a few years.[15] His second was a well-connected niece of Lydia Maria Child, the lady Abolitionist, who disliked her aunt personally but shared her ideas. Her son's biography of his father makes Mary Stearns sound snobbishly flighty, an unreliable helpmeet who felt and said that lead pipe was vulgar. She had weeping fits when Stearns stayed late at the new oil mill to work out delicate details of processing. She nagged him about not entertaining more widely and for not dressing as richly as his presumed station called for. He took it all with a good temper that got him compared to Thackeray's Colonel Newcome. In certain matters, however, she stood with him, particularly in his many benevolences, and she took most zealously to Old Brown.

Stearns was already antislavery before he married her. His best friend in Medford was a local antislaveryite parson. The only three Medford votes for Birney on the Liberty Party ticket in 1840 were from Stearns, a local carpenter, and the watchman at the oil mill, an eccentric who loved to drink linseed oil. Stearns' most eminent friend was Charles Sumner, the pontifical slavery hater, who took him to the "Bird Club"—an antislaveryite group, including Dr. Howe, that dined weekly at Boston's famous Parker House. He once hid a runaway slave for a week under the floor of his own bathroom before smuggling him off to Canada; eventually he set him up as a barber on Harvard Square. Obviously such a man found the Emigrant Aid and Massachusetts Kansas Committees irresistible. He not only gave heavily to both but also personally pressed his own customers and business associates to give, and paid out of his own pocket for the $1300 worth of revolvers for Kansas that eventually found their way to Maryland with Old Brown. And, as his biographer son wrote, he and Old Brown met "like iron and magnet."

There is little direct Byronic Scottery here. Stearns' formidable mother had vowed to keep her house clear of poetical trash, and young George seems to have been no more bookish than Smith—after all, at formative periods he was too hard at work to cultivate literature. Maybe he picked up some secondary Scottery about Old Brown from Howe, Sumner and Emerson—whom Mary and he knew and idolized. But their passion for the old jayhawker was likelier one of those puzzling emotional-chemical affinities that can come over people under unrealized influences from deep-down analogies. The Stearns sons also took greatly to Old Brown, who talked with such offhand intimacy of soldiering. The eldest awedly asked "Captain Brown" to tell of himself as a boy—hence an invaluable third-person autobiographical sketch in which the old man actually dared to say that he had always "followed up with tenacity whatever he set about . . . hence . . . rarely failed in some good degree to effect the things he undertook." No hero-worshiping child was ever told a more outrageous if salutary lie, but no doubt the old man heartily believed it at the time.

Whether from craft or sentiment—he was capable of either—Old Brown made much of Mary Stearns. Laid up sick at Judge Thomas Russell's in Boston in 1858, he summoned her into town to hear the cross-grained, semi-paranoid "Old Brown's Farewell," and said: "Oh, if I could have the money that is smoked away during a single day in Boston, I could strike a blow that would make slavery totter from its foundations!" Proud to be handmaiden of what her son would call "a Cromwellian Ironside introduced in the nineteenth century for special purposes," she "drove home, thinking many thoughts . . . The splendor of spring sunshine filled the room when I awoke the next morning," and the luxurious charm of her environment made her "wish . . . to comfort and aid John Brown. It seemed not too much to sell our estate and give the proceeds to him for his sublime purpose. What if another home were not so beautiful?" And when Stearns woke, unaware that his wife was having a daydream straight out of an Abolitionist tract, "I told him my morning thoughts."

Thus urged to give up the premises that symbolized his rise from shy, needy boy to man of weight, this best-natured of husbands said gravely: "Perhaps it would not be just right to you and the children to do what you suggest; but I will do all I can in justice to them and you." After breakfast he took her into Boston to see Old Brown and guaranteed him up to $7000 to keep alive his plans for defending freedom in Kansas.[16] Mrs. Stearns offered to sell the carriage and horses, which might have fetched $1000 more, but apparently this sacrifice was not made. All in all, Stearns gave Old Brown far more than Smith in proportion to his ample but relatively smaller means. No doubt he felt well repaid when, on his last visit to Medford, Old Brown gave his benefactor the pearl-handled dirk that served as model for the pikes for which Stearns' money paid unbeknownst to him.

Actually the man hardly belongs among the Six. He did not have enough ego for their overweening society. He probably knew less of Old Brown's exact plans than Smith, Sanborn or Higginson. But if he who pays the piper fails not only to call the tune but to make sure no other is played . . . It is good business law that *qui facit per alium facit per se.*

THE YOUNGEST DISCIPLE

Bliss was it in that dawn to be alive,
But to be young was very heaven!

—WORDSWORTH

Frank Sanborn never had much money but his marked talent for hero-worship made him bulk large in Old Brown's story and among the Six. As undergraduate he annoyed the authorities of Harvard College by clamoring for leave to go into Boston Sundays to hear Theodore Parker instead of snoozing decently among his apathetic fellows in Holden Chapel. Aghast to find Parker's writings so rare at Harvard, he personally bought them out of his own slender purse for the library of the undergraduate Hasty Pudding Club of which he was conscientious secretary. His biography of Dr. Howe is a solicitous panegyric sticky with the writer's delight in having known such a man well. In later life he widely exploited having been neighbor and disciple of Emerson, Thoreau and Alcott in Concord, where he set up a coeducational private school financed by Judge E. R. Hoar to teach the children of "the more aristocratic portion of that community." And his successive writings about Old Brown are like what a devoted younger brother might have written about St. Paul or Judas Maccabeus.

Hero-worship is a hazardous hobby not to be entered into lightly. But it was much in vogue at the time, implicit in Byronic Scottery and recommended by Mr. Emerson's astringent friend Carlyle. By the age of twelve Frank had accumulated with his own money first the Waverley Novels complete, then Byron complete. Further preparing for Old Brown he browsed in his Calvinist grandfather's library at Hampton Falls, N.H. (where he was born in 1831), explor-

ing the heaven-flouting careers and bloody ends of Arch-
bishop Sharp, Grahame of Claverhouse and other accepted
monsters of the Scottish Reformation. Hear him about Kansas' troubles: "The annals of theft and murder and arson on
the Scotch border, around which Walter Scott and the older
ballad-makers cast an atmosphere of romance, were repeated
in ruder ways in these Missouri Marches, of which John
Brown and James Montgomery came to be the self-ap-
pointed wardens . . . Brown was of the unmixed Puritan
breed, and inherited from deacons and captains of Connecticut 'the sword of the Lord and of Gideon.' " With this romantic feeling for the harshest theology ever concocted went
a religiosity marked even for that day. At the age of eight
little Frank had read all the Bible word for word and preco-
ciously proclaimed himself a Universalist. After maturing
he shifted to the eccentric Unitarianism of Parker, Higginson
and James Freeman Clarke—hot Abolitionists all.

His pitiful love story reflects his tunnel-vision temperament and the emasculated ideals of his background. A cultivated bright girl of his own age named Ariana Walker came
to visit in Hampton Falls and saw great things in the tall,
bookish schoolboy. Their shy, slow and bookish romance led
to an engagement intentionally prolonged to allow him to
establish himself before a frugal, high-thinking marriage.
Then Ariana died of a strange neurological disease that had
often attacked her. Eight days before she died they were
married, both well aware that she could not live.[17]

Strange how things work out! It was Ariana's brother, an
Abolitionist who had known Old Brown in Springfield, who
sent the old man to Sanborn in early 1857, and so gave him
his mission in life. Within three months he assured Brown:
". . . should you fall in the struggle, I will take it on myself
to see that your family is made comfortable and your memory defended against any who attack it." He was already
neglecting his Concord school to act as part-time secretary
for an Emigrant Aid Committee. Now he took on new emo-

tional and clerical burdens as clandestine executive secretary of the Six. Whenever Old Brown appeared from among the mists of his growing delusions to ask for more "secret service" money, Sanborn persuasively shook down rich men like Smith, Stearns, A. A. Lawrence, and invariably added what few dollars he could spare himself. Once he even considered joining Old Brown's force training for Harpers Ferry. That did not work out, but he did fulfil the promise about memory defending. He earned his later living as able successor to Howe as head of the Massachusetts Board of State Charities; then as editorial writer for the Springfield *Republican;* then as lecturer and writer and a sort of tutelary genius of Concord, a living reminder of the days when all the saints and sages flourished and young Frank Sanborn knew them all. But all the while he was busiest at being Old Brown's henchman, body and soul, always writing another version of the biography, always more in awe of the destiny that had entwined his life with that of a bearded archangel. His loyalty survived even the discovery, forced on him by eventual new evidence, that Old Brown and some of his sons had lied in their teeth about their responsibility for the Pottawotomie Massacre.

Sanborn was not the most trenchant of the Six. Voluminously as Abolitionists recorded one another's ideas, appearance, sins and virtues, they set down little about this long, energetic youngster, handsome in a slightly womanish way. His record does not go beyond facile acceptance of the half-baked highmindednesses of the time. I see him as the type of well-intentioned Yankee—I think it persists—that goes all winter without an overcoat not from poverty but from a vague groping after the ascetically robust, striding with a righteous glow through clouds of its own shivering breath; in later life its unhatted hair is iron-gray (or snow-white) and spiky. He obviously had little humor. The most frivolous recorded detail is that, though on a dead sober Emigrant Aid mission, he danced most of the night at a ball in

Nebraska City. One wonders how the pioneer belles took the diffident good looks that Ariana had described to a *confidante* as like "the early portrait of Raphael"—a reference that not every man would include in his autobiography. On this trip he took a fancy to a strapping Kentuckian and was grieved presently to learn that he had joined a proslavery force and been killed in a Kansas skirmish. Old Brown would have said something short about one Amalekite the less, but his armor bearer was never so harsh. In view of his religious bent and the odor of dutiful benevolence about him, it is a pity that he escaped the pulpit. He would have preached charmingly. This career was once strongly suggested but Ariana said decidedly that he must not preach, he must go into literature and be the sort of writer that Mr. Emerson envisaged in *Representative Men*. And naturally that settled it.

A high respect for solemn advice even governed his behavior after news of Harpers Ferry came. All the Six were taken aback to hear that papers probably implicating them —nature of evidence, degree of involvement of each not known—had been found at Old Brown's farmhouse base. Sanborn went to Boston to consult John A. Andrew, an eminent Abolitionist lawyer soon to be governor of the state. Asked whether a closely implicated accessory of Old Brown's could be arrested and taken south as witness or principal, Andrew answered offhand that a certain obscure Federal statute made it quite possible. Sanborn walked direct from Andrew's office to the regular Portland boat en route to Quebec. Some while later he heard from Emerson that after further thought, Andrew had changed his mind. His new opinion was that a citizen of Massachusetts who had remained therein while aiding and abetting Old Brown's crime would have to be tried separately in Massachusetts.

A Yankee jury on such a case being quite a different thing from a Virginia jury, Sanborn yielded to Emerson's urgings and came home. But not for long. Presently a special com-

mittee of the U.S. Senate under Mason of Virginia went fishing in the Harpers Ferry record for ammunition useful
against the crescent Republicans. Obviously Sanborn would
be summoned before it to tell what he knew under oath. He
let Mason know that he would not come to Washington
partly because he preferred not to testify against others but
partly because he declined to risk the arrest, kidnaping or
mobbing implicit in crossing Maryland to reach Washington.[18] Mason offered a personal guarantee of safety. Sanborn
replied that, in view of how Senator Sumner had been
beaten half to death on the floor of the Senate by a proslavery Congressman, this was inadequate. The committee voted
his arrest as a contumacious witness—and again he went to
Quebec.

Toward spring he returned to Concord and his school, in
which Old Brown's two youngest daughters were now pupils
—tuition gratis, board paid by Stearns. One April evening
Sanborn answered a knock at his house door and admitted a
young man ostensibly asking charity but followed in by four
more strangers. One of them began to read aloud a Senate
warrant for Sanborn's arrest. The first words sent his housekeeper sister Sarah to screaming bloody murder out the back
door. The intruders handcuffed Sanborn and tried to hustle
him out to the closed carriage that had brought them. Six-
foot-four, young and strong, by bracing against the doorposts
and wriggling and digging in his heels, he made those few
yards take a long time—and Concord was rising to the
rescue. The three daughters of his blacksmith neighbor
scampered up and down pounding on doors. Judge Hoar
heard the row and, as prearranged, went to his desk and
began filling out a writ of *habeas corpus*. Sanborn's lawyer,
also a neighbor, ran up to the swirling mass the core of which
was his client, asked whether he desired such a writ, was answered pantingly "By all means!", dashed away and within
minutes was back waving it with Hoar's signature not yet
dry. In order to get the prisoner's flailing legs into the car-

riage door, one of the marshal's men, who had a beard, had pinioned the ankles. Sister Sarah, presumably still scream- ing, seized his beard and hauled so hard that the pain made him let go, and the legs resumed their kicking and sprawling. A young lady neighbor whipped up the carriage horse so that it started ahead and took the carriage with it away from the marshals and their captive . . .

The marshals refused to take notice of the writ, so the local sheriff created the bystanders a *posse comitatus* that, with a whooping rush, rescued Sanborn by force. Within a few days the marshal's men were arrested as kidnapers and eventually let go only on condition that they enlist in the Union army. If they survived the war, they had every right to tell their grandchildren that it had begun for them when they were playing their parts in the greatest hullaballoo Concord had seen since the redcoats' futile foray in 1775.

THE SORCERER'S APPRENTICES

> *"John Brown will mean little to those who do not believe that God governs the world and . . . makes his will known in advance to certain . . . prophetic, heaven-born men . . ."*
> —F. B. SANBORN

As fragmentary, slanted newspaper reports of Harpers Ferry came sputtering in, it looked as if the Six might have to pay dear for their puerilities. To some extent each had used Old Brown to scratch his private itches with and—this is a cardinal social sin—had taken his own emotional needs for those of the nation. The old man had now spelled out in action what had been really simmering behind that bitter face, what they had mistaken for a Scott character stepped right out of the printed page. He had shot down unarmed citi- zens, looted private dwellings, interfered with the mails,

sought forcibly to abrogate the Constitution, levied war on
the United States, and stupidly left behind him a mass of
papers incriminating God only knew whom-all. Quite a
genie to ooze out of their common bottle! No wonder most
of them were unbecomingly unnerved.

Sanborn's flustered actions have been described. Parker was
dying in Italy. Higginson's warning came when a customer
of a Worcester newsstand said, "Old Osawatamie Brown's
got himself into a tight place." Years later he professed to
have been unready for such news because his emotional stake
in Old Brown's plan had dwindled since the postponement
of 1858.[19] He had done little about the Browns' money rais-
ings in spring, 1859, because "It had all begun to seem to me
rather chimerical." Yet his surprise can hardly have been
total. Sanborn had let him know in June that Old Brown was
taking the field, and again early in October that recruits
were mustering somewhere. But Higginson's last address for
the old man was in northeastern Ohio, and he had assumed
that any action would occur on the western slope of the
Appalachians. The choice of Harpers Ferry, he insisted, took
him quite aback and suggested that repeated delays "had
somewhat disturbed the delicate balance of [Brown's]
mind."[20] He was the only one of the Six ever even to hint
that there was more pathology than inspiration in Gideon
Balfour. Nobody knows how much of this was hindsight.

That shattering autumn of 1859 Higginson refused to run
or even quibble. He never denied that he had supported Old
Brown well aware that his intentions were violently illegal
and that armed raiding of slave states was bound to entail
bloodshed. He made it clear that he saw no reason to flee the
country,[21] and that any legal process—subpoena from Virginia or the U. S. Senate, warrant from a Federal court taking up the treason issue—would find him in Worcester
prepared to answer for his actions. Practical impunity was
his reward for such intrepidity. Maybe neither prosecutors
nor politicking Senators wanted his sharp tongue reading

Abolitionist propaganda into the record of either trial or hearing. He was harsh about those of the Six who failed to follow his cool example, and they found it hard to forgive him for having made them look like fools by keeping his head. In view of his temperament it was probably his caustic integrity rather than cleverness that led him to the safest course. It annoyed him, in fact, when Mason neglected him while summoning Howe, Sanborn, Stearns and even Thaddeus Hyatt, the Emigrant Aid leader who was distinctly in the second echelon of Old Brown's backers. Within two years, however, Higginson could forget his chagrin by becoming the very pattern of that singular anomaly, the fighting parson, in a blue uniform with golden shoulder straps.

Stearns began badly, ended better. Howe and he were a day behind Sanborn in consulting John A. Andrew. Already less offhand, the lawyer searched authorities over the weekend and on Monday advised them that they could not be taken outside Massachusetts for trial for acts committed within the state—the finding that fetched Sanborn home the first time. But Howe and Stearns still feared lest Virginia ask Massachusetts for them as suspects or witnesses; the law officers of Massachusetts might differ with Andrew; and Governor N. P. Banks, who had a grudge against the Bird Club, might persuade himself that it was his duty to oblige Virginia. To avoid tempting him Howe and Stearns too went to Canada, staying until after Old Brown was hanged, Stearns returning first.[22]

Apparently this sharp contrast with Higginson's behavior convinced Mason that the pair were indispensable witnesses. They consulted Senator Sumner, who took the highminded position that it was their duty to testify—even to tell the whole truth. Both finally went to Washington—which annoyed Sanborn and Higginson—but neither was fool enough to follow Sumner's advice all the way. The usual comment on their testimony is that clumsy questioning enabled them to give false impressions without actually committing perjury.

I find it impossible not to see lying under oath in Stearns' replies about his entertaining John Brown jr. in late spring, 1859:

"*Q.* Did he speak of his father, and say where he was, or what he was engaged in? *A.* No, sir . . . *Q.* Was nothing said by young Brown of his desire to make collections in money for his father's use? *A.* Nothing whatever." Certainly Stearns' conscience must have streamed with apprehensive sweat as he explained:

"I understood John Brown . . . would take every opportunity to free slaves . . . I did not ask in what way . . . I furnished him with money . . . I did not ask him what he was to do with [it], nor did I suppose that he would do anything that I should disapprove . . . I should have disapproved if I had known of [the Harpers Ferry plan] . . ." But then he dropped casuistry and stood up to be counted in an abruptly candid fashion that must have made Senators Mason and Davis (Jefferson) regret having called him. "I have since changed my opinion," he went on. "I believe John Brown to be the representative man of this century, as Washington was of the last—the Harpers Ferry affair [one of] the great events of this age." The reference to Washington was absurd but the man's loyalty to his wife's and his small sons' hero was not. In 1863, as a Federal major recruiting Negro troops, he announced loudly in a Niagara Falls hotel for the benefit of a noisy Southerner that "I consider it the proudest act of my life that I gave old John Brown every pike and rifle he carried to Harpers Ferry."

Howe's position was poor before he took the stand. Within the previous year he had cooled off somewhat, as previously mentioned; had even had words with Old Brown about the morality of looting and horse stealing. He seems to have wobbled for months between the doctrine of might as well die for a sheep and the common sense conclusion for which his intelligence was reaching: that Old Brown had got too rich for his blood. On such insecure footing a stand like Higginson's was difficult. Anyway Harpers Ferry swept Howe off his feet. Two weeks before they hanged Old Brown he sent to the American press from Canada a "card"—a formal public statement—that set cocks crowing all through antislaverydom:

"Rumor has mingled my name with the events at Harpers Ferry . . . That event was unforeseen and unexpected by me; nor does all my previous knowledge of John Brown enable me to reconcile it with his characteristic prudence and his reluctance to shed blood, or to excite servile insurrection." Higginson called this downright "dishonorable." I do not know how he took Howe's testimony before the Mason Committee: "*Q.* In all your conversation or communication with Brown, had you ever . . . any intimation of an organized attempt or effort, on his part to be made, to produce an insurrection among the slave states of the South? *A.* Never." Those who have never been tempted to commit perjury to get out of a nasty scrape have small right to reproach a man so doing. In many contexts perjury is the least grave of felonies. But it does lack dignity.

Gerrit Smith was better off—or worse, depending on the point of view. When the news came, he had the wit to send his son-in-law to destroy incriminating correspondence in the hands of John Brown jr. and Sanborn; and to pack off to Europe his son's tutor, Edward Morton, who had attended certain enthralling meetings with Old Brown. Then Smith "went down under a troop of hallucinations . . . He [thought he] was an outcast; reduced to poverty . . . hunted for his life; [people] meant to carry him about the country in a cage and submit him to horrible tortures." Or "gentle as usual, but melancholy," this most gregarious man brooded in withdrawn silence or muttered about having to go to Virginia to vindicate Old Brown or suffer with him, it was never clear which. They tricked him into going peacefully to the asylum by telling him he was on his way to Harpers Ferry. Without impugning the good faith of the asy-

lum's staff one can say it was just as well thus to keep Smith
and the Mason Committee apart. Except possibly Sanborn,
he had been deepest in Old Brown's plans. Even normally
he was garrulous, unstable, flamingly self-righteous, and had
Mason got him on the stand, highly inconvenient things
might have come out. After his discharge a few months later
his recent history would have made it difficult to take his
testimony seriously and besides, by then it would have been
mistily harmless. For now he was erasing from his mind, or
rather refusing to stir up, all memory of connection with the
Harpers Ferry scheme. Frothingham, who had an astounding
grasp of psychology for the year 1877, was penetrating about
this:

"An enthusiast . . . at the same time a man of business
. . . In one case . . . all wings, in the other all eyes . . .
under [Brown's] influence . . . he surrendered uncondi-
tionally . . . At moments, his judgment hesitated, even
recalcitrated, but interposed no serious obstacle . . . On
emerging from the mental obscuration . . . the whole
scheme had vanished and become visionary . . . Then cool
reflection came in . . . The ill-judged nature of the plan
. . . made him wish he had never been privy to it . . . His
old horror of . . . violence as a means of redressing wrong,
resumed its sway . . . The man of business repelled the
association with the visionary . . . He set himself to . . .
reducing his alliance with the audacious conspirator to sentiments of personal sympathy and admiration . . . a desire
to persuade all others as well as himself of his innocence of
all complicity . . . a desire that became an importunate
demand as it was cherished."

Eight years afterward Smith still felt obliged to publish a
number of unnecessary lies about his relation to Brown.
Later he refused Sanborn's request for authentic details for
the historical record. He filed libel suits against newspapers
hinting that he was unscrupulously covering up, but never
forced the cases to trial. It would all be rather ridiculous, like

Howe's flounderings, if it were not so pitifully likely that mental disease underlay it. Yet in generously summing-up that astute biographer also implicitly described the too-familiar type of chronic haters who never crack up.

Smith, said Frothingham, "could never be accused of . . . deliberate, persistent, aimless unveracity. But he may have been capable of . . . thrusting into the background . . . things he did not choose should stand in front . . . in order that he might stand well with himself . . . Biography was to him more important than history . . . This was an infirmity." That is, he could not stand having to feel like a first-class fool, probably for the first time in his insulated life; and the strain of disillusion was so severe that he had to escape into the complete loss of touch with reality that had always been potential beneath his daily copings.

Thus he paid the most extreme penalty of any of the Six, because he alone among them had the honesty to admit, even if only implicitly, that Old Brown had made fools of them all. It is also ironical that the only one of the old man's backers to pay any legal penalty for the crime of suborning treasonable absurdity was Thaddeus Hyatt, who spent three months in prison for defying the Mason Committee's summons. But the most ironical touch of all is that as soon as his emotional equilibrium was restored, Smith went right back to knowing and preaching exactly what must be done about any religious, political or social problem that interested him. Barring his occasional episodes of lying about Old Brown, he spent the rest of his life exactly as if he had never been catastrophically wrong about Harpers Ferry and slave insurrections and had never been behind therapeutic bars.

"We must attack Slavery . . . in the Territories . . . in the District, and, above all, Slavery in the slave States . . . We must be aggressive, and kill the trunk, not maim the branches. When you attempt that, depend upon it the South will know you are in earnest."

—THEODORE PARKER (1858)

The flood of babble that followed Harpers Ferry in press and pulpit, bar and crossroads store, cast up some strange driftwood. Richard Realf, maybe harking back to confidences of Old Brown's, described the purpose of the raid as having been prophylactic—lest the slaves "overthrow [slavery] by a bloody war of extermination . . . to prevent the havoc and carnage which as [Brown] conceived, threatened the South . . . the same element . . . which would result in bloody excesses if not wisely and properly directed, might be made subservient to . . . high purposes of humanity, if . . . governing intelligence was at their side . . ." At certain phases of his private moon, when his antislavery passion was strong as ever but his hatred of slaveholders had temporarily ebbed, Old Brown might have worked it out so for an admiring hearer. It fits his confidence in the imminence of slave insurrection and in his own God-backed powers. At another phase, however, he might have agreed with the Rev. George B. Cheever of Brooklyn's Church of the Puritans—one of the most learned of Garrisonian name callers—who preached after Harpers Ferry that:

"It were infinitely better that three hundred thousand slaveholders were struck out of existence, than that four million human beings, with their posterity forever, should be . . . condemned to . . . a perpetual violation of God's law . . . forcible redemption, even by insurrection, would be a blessing, since [the slaveholders'] souls might be saved; but, continuing in this guilt, they must be shut out from Heaven; so that John Brown is in reality their greatest, kindest friend." This recalls the medieval ferryman saint who forcibly baptized lone heathen passengers in midstream and then drowned them overside to make sure they reached heaven before they could sin.

Misrepresentation of what happened at Harpers Ferry persuaded many Abolitionists that Southerners were white-livered as well as ill-organized. They noted how excessive was the force of militia on guard while the raiders passed through trial to the gallows, and how fear of attempted rescue augmented it during executions. It has been charged that Governor Wise kept so many under arms to dramatize the Northern threat. However that may be, it persuaded wishful Yankees that Dixie had the wind up to a cowardly degree. "We have seen the knees of a great slave state knocking together," the Rev. E. M. Wheelock told Boston, ". . . while wild and craven panic spread far and wide, from the slight skirmish of a single day, with less than a score of men . . ." A Garrisonian pamphleteer judged that the "assertion of . . . Miles of South Carolina, 'We are impregnable,'—betray[s] the depth and extent of their fear by the very attempt to conceal it . . ." Wendell Phillips impudently asserted ". . . there was not a Virginia gun fired at John Brown. Hundreds of well-armed Maryland and Virginia troops rushed to Harpers Ferry—and went away." This would have interested the seven raiders killed or mortally wounded before the Marines arrived. Whoever ghosted the account of the raid published in early 1861 by O. P. Anderson, one of those who escaped, wrote that ". . . the fight at Harpers Ferry . . . disproved the current idea that slaveholders will lay down their lives for their property . . . the cowards kept out of the way till danger was passed.[23]

This underestimate of the potential enemy was sinister. Even worse was the resulting new certainty that the non-slaveholding majority of Dixie whites, as alarmed by the thought of slave rebellion as any white-pillared planters, would support the proslavery zealot's war. No matter that while many Northerners were agreeing with Louisa May Alcott that Old Brown was "St. John the Just," many others, most Republican leaders among them, deplored the raid. Too many Southerners who had hoped that Southern Union splitters were just "talking for Buncombe" now wondered whether the fire-eaters weren't right after all. "The antislavery cause had gained a martyr," says A. T. Schlesinger, "but at the cost of convincing Southerners that the North was seething with violent designs." Further provocation from Yankees, such as Republican victory in 1860, would leave only the extremist program—secession—as shield against fanatic Abolitionism in a dozen violent or sinisterly insidious forms. Secession might well have come in the end, for Dixie's delusions of persecution were marked. But the Six could soon tell themselves that they had collectively done about as much to bring the boil prematurely to head as had Mrs. Stowe in writing *Uncle Tom's Cabin*[24] or Senator Douglas in introducing the Kansas-Nebraska Bill. None of the Six, except maybe Stearns, would have thought that grounds for reproach.

Meantime more and more Northerners edged toward seeing Old Brown in Beecher's terms: not for what he was—a self-frustrating absurdity or a mental invalid or both—but as a victim self-immolated to concentrate Divine and human notice on the antislavery cause. People came to speak of him as if, instead of killing several unoffending strangers and preparing to kill thousands more if they proved intransigent, he had laid down his life for the slave in a demonstration as peaceful as a hunger strike or an arduous pilgrimage. "St. John the Just" was barely within tolerable hyperbole. But hear Emerson: Old Brown "will make the gallows glorious like the cross." Thoreau: "He is not Old Brown any longer; he is an angel of light." Phillips: "John Brown is the impersonation of God's order and God's law, moulding a better future."

Parker did not live to see it. But others of the Six grew gratifiedly aware how the world—outside Dixie—was rallying to their private hero,[25] and how their small cryptic coterie within Abolitionism had called the psychological turn. The North never made up its collective mind, as Lincoln did, whether to save the Union or to free the slave was its major purpose in fighting. But in a muddily mystical way it did conclude that, as Andrew said, however dubious his scheme, Old Brown himself was basically right. Slavery being wrong—and God knows it was—whatever was against slavery must be right, and whatever was right was necessarily admirable. Such treacherous logic was necessary in order to blink the essential viciousness of Old Brown's ailing soul.

Epilogue: *The most dangerous -ism*

"Pity the portly man, pity the pious,
Pity the fool who lights the powder-mine,
They need your counterfeit penny, they will live long."
—BENÉT, John Brown's Body

On August 10, 1840, Parker and three Reformist cronies walked from Boston to Groton, Mass., to attend a convention of eccentrics with whom they felt sympathetic. On the way, as was fitting, they stopped at Concord to visit Emerson and Bronson Alcott, who joined the expedition. But a slight jar occurred when they called on "old Dr. Ripley, in his 90th year, who . . . admonished us of the evils of becoming *Egomites* . . ."—which Frothingham interpreted as meaning "self-sent men."[1] The old gentleman was wasting his reverend breath. Parker was only thirty but his destiny as chronic "egomite" was already plain on his forehead. He never felt misgivings such as those that removed Weld from active agitation. He was doomed instead smugly to share the schemings of the Six—those minor cases of self-sentness clustered round and under Old Brown like second-stage rockets helping him into third-stage orbit.

Those familiar with crackpot movements know the strong

affinities among their leaders. One self-sent agitator whips up hatred of Jews; another accuses boards of health of deliberately poisoning water supply through fluoridation; a third indicts the aluminum industry for knowingly spreading cancer by making aluminum saucepans; a fourth uncovers a Supreme Court conspiracy to "mongrelize" us . . . Targets vary but the ballistic fuels are the same: self-aggrandizement and hatred. Since people most approve those who act and sound most like what they yearn to act and sound like, hatemongers tend to mutual admiration and credulity. The Jew-baiter's paper prints anti-fluoridation articles; the aluminum crank addresses meetings of white trash called by Negro-haters. The individual cult leaders usually fall out as their lusts for power conflict; consider Garrison and colleagues. But in the meantime by exchanging mailing lists and other means of infection they develop a large body of eclectic adherents to a wide range of hate cults—people glad to cast their burdens of peevishness on self-sent prophets and more or less eager to believe in a "they" malignantly conspiring against health, morals or order.

The chosen target may actually have been or still be a public danger or nuisance. That has little to do with the crackpot's singling it out. McCarthyite anti-Communism is a prime example. There are many parallels among the Reformists of Old Brown's time and among their spiritual successors of today to whom "McCarthy" is anathema, usually for the wrong reasons. Too often they again embody the melancholy moral that the goodness of the cause does not guarantee responsibility or integrity in its adherents. Too many betray the abiding need of the crackpot of whatever stripe to appear more acute than others or more sensitive, better accepted on the side of the angels—hence better qualified to know what needs doing—hence privileged to force others to do it for their own good.

Recall Cheever's belief that Old Brown would have done the slaveowners a favor by forcing them to abandon slavery even if Hayti-style rape and massacre did keep most of them from admiring the results; or Redpath's eagerness to see all Negroes but one slaughtered if that one thus achieved freedom. Self-sent friends of man are often given to such Gestapo-style coldbloodedness. Twenty-five years ago I found my head swim on hearing a nationally famous philanthropist—just the man who would have been a hot Abolitionist, likely a Garrisonian, in Old Brown's day—chuckle fondly about the cozy candor with which Stalin had told him of his decision to starve *x* million peasants in order to secure Russia the moral and social benefits of collectivized farms. Yet under some circumstances this kind of cold blood warms up fast. The struggle for men's minds and hearts has an exasperating effect on the adrenal glands of crusaders joining the side of the angels without consulting the angels, and soon it turns into a struggle for their bodies too. First a hatred like Dr. Howe's for recalcitrant fools who presently begin to look and smell like knaves. Then wilder and wilder Parker- or Garrison-type denunciations of such knaves (or sinners). Then the wildest words reach a pure hater like Old Brown.

"It takes a crank to move the world," says the proverb. It is often maintained that self-sent men—the Cromwells, Robespierres, John Browns—are not only historically picturesque but also socially useful. Without such ruthlessness and self-righteousness, says this sentimental theory, salutary changes never come to pass. The shattering antics of the self-sent may leave society better off, as shock treatments may leave disturbed persons with better emotional integration; and so on. Actually these false analogies and this toleration of self-sentness show the same romantic irresponsibility as the Scottery of the Secret Six and "Southern chivalry." It is so exhilaratingly dramatic when the egomite cuts the Gordian knot and a whole civilization comes down by the run. Only carpers or second guessers point out that it would have left much less of a wreck unflaggingly to study the knot and try patiently to tease out its strands. To hear shouted with utter conviction the Garrisonian doctrine that God-and-one —meaning God-and-I—are a majority sets up a Promethean tingle in the faculty of egocentricity that all of us possess to some degree. But its social usefulness, never too high, has practically disappeared as western nations developed representative government and universal suffrage.

Jefferson had some reason to say that the Tree of Liberty needed regular irrigation with the blood of tyrants. During his formative years other ways to nourish it in hard times were inadequate. But presently extensive democratic franchises combined with high jealousy of civil rights to make it unnecessary—and, of course, inadvisable—for society further to run the appalling risks implicit in the kinds of violence that both reactionaries and reformers love. By Old Brown's time democracy had made the "sacred right of revolution" —changing the rules by violence, not by negotiation and peaceful adjustment—as anomalous as horseshoes on a locomotive. Egomites like Old Brown and the Six, and their opposite numbers in Dixie, could not perceive the force of this. Yet so long as Congress and most state legislatures were elected by wide suffrages; Congress retained power over the District of Columbia, the Territories and interstate commerce;[2] and the Constitution left open the power of amendment—all of which conditions held good when Old Brown struck Harpers Ferry—neither the Six nor any other antislaveryites had valid pretext for armed attack. The slaves, who lacked political rights and leverage, had every valid motive for any violence they could organize. But no white American had any business stirring them up to it.

The trouble was that orderly and probably protracted legislative nibbling at slavery could not answer the emotional necessities of hot Abolitionists. The impatience of the Six with the legislative approach and their insistence that Washington was the corrupt tool of slavery are too like the lynch mob's excuses for unilateral violence. In any case, during the crucial years between the Missouri Compromise of 1820 and Harpers Ferry the Abolitionists preferred to egg on the Americans of Charlestown, Mass., to hate the Americans of Charleston, S.C., rather than patiently and ingeniously to seek ways of avoiding having to use dynamite on the creeping fire of slavery. Similarly it better gratified the Dixie fire-eater to put a price on Garrison's head and pass votes of thanks to Preston Brooks for assaulting Charles Sumner than responsibly to explore possible ways gradually to rid Dixie of her cancerous "peculiar institution." Certain eminent and respected Southerners—George Wythe during the Revolution, St. George Tucker later—did broach schemes of gradual emancipation. After Nat Turner's rising the elements of Virginia's population least committed to slavery did come close to forcing a trial of some such scheme. But it was a little too late. King Cotton was rolling graspingly westward and Garrison had well begun the only thing he really accomplished—making it almost impossible for a Southerner to remain in Dixie and argue the case for getting rid of slavery.

Abolitionists too neglected opportunities that could never knock again, and let the nation flounder into civil war with most of the peaceable, democratic, constitutional avenues toward the possible extinction of slavery inadequately explored. They failed to follow up early schemes to see whether free labor might not raise cotton as efficiently as slave labor. They were lukewarm about movements to boycott slave-raised cotton and sugar[3]—a mighty weapon had it been used to optimum extent in both Britain and the States, yet it would hardly have exasperated Dixie more than Garrison was already doing. If as many persons had eschewed slave products between 1830 and 1860 as abstained from alcohol on organized moral principle, slavery would have been in grave trouble.

In 1839 J. Q. Adams introduced Constitutional amendments looking to gradual emancipation.[4] On the state level similar proposals came close to acceptance in the mid-1840's in Delaware and Kentucky. But Abolitionists were merely annoyed. By then they knew scornfully well that the only tolerable doctrine was literal "immediatism"—freeing all slaves overnight everywhere, both in Carolina rice swamps and on Missouri farms, after the fashion that had allegedly worked out so well in Antigua. As late as 1857 Elihu Burritt, a Reformist of stature,[5] had a remarkable seizure of common sense and agitated for Federal action to free the slaves and compensate their owners from the proceeds of the sale of still unoccupied Federal lands. This drew support from many eminent opponents of slavery but the only kiver-to-kiver Abolitionist among them was Gerrit Smith. His comrades were still too closely bound to British teachings that any such compensation was an obscenity; Garrison called it "paying a thief for giving up stolen property, and acknowledging that his crime was *not* a crime." The net result of this flawless logic was to leave slaves still enslaved and further to persuade their owner that antislaveryites were all bent on undermining property rights and insulting him at the same time.

Whether any such abortive schemes would have done well if tried in good faith is speculative. But Abolitionists' consistent scorn of them does suggest lack of primary interest in slave freeing. Or it may have come of the old trouble: It felt somehow hampering and disloyal to God to approach the problem in secular terms throughout, as if doubting that the walls of the slavery-Jericho would come duly tumbling down if only the righteous kept marching long enough and defying the heathen loudly enough. To start tunneling or building siege devices, as Adams and Burritt and others suggested, might seem, in God's eyes, like lack of faith. This same twist of mind allowed Old Brown to neglect proper planning before he struck.

Another clog on most Abolitionists—remember that Garrisonians were honorable exceptions—was failure to consider the Negro potentially equal to whites anywhere except in

the sight of God. Weld's Seventy often explained to mistrustful audiences that the Anti-Slavery Society "did not
wish [the slaves] turned loose, nor even to be governed by
the same Code of Laws which are adapted to intelligent
citizens." Parker glibly assured a friend that "in respect to
power of civilization, the African is at the bottom" and
pointed out what it meant about Negro mentality that
"nobody ever heard of a negro getting rich" in New England where several thousand of them enjoying freedom had
produced "none eminent . . . except [as] . . . a waiter."
Weld never got proper support for his doctrine that Abolitionism should give free Northern Negroes education
enough to show Dixie—and the color-minded North too—
what was in them, which would weaken the color bar by
attrition from below. True, most Abolitionists hoped to see
an end of the barbarities that propaganda like *Slavery As It
Is* persuaded them were daily visited on the majority of
Dixie's slaves. But their main concern was still the slaveholder's Heaven-defying and literally damnable hardness of
heart against God's manifest will. They craved to see that
haughty sinner on his broadcloth knees at the mourners'
bench confessing in agonized contrition—and if economic
ruin and social humiliation and even a glare of rape and
blood now and again went with it, serve him right.

> ". . . *social indignation* . . . *so frequently leads to the
> death of personal humility.*"   —JAMES BALDWIN

Since social crusaders often show a dash of self-sentness, that
element has handicapped the Negro's cause whenever and
wherever taken up. It certainly pervaded the misconceptions

persuading the Six that Old Brown made sense. The egomite is peculiarly prone to see only what suits his narcissistic requirements. With no uneasiness he can go on asserting that the Jews own the press of the United States right after somebody has clearly demonstrated that they own only a minor segment of it. His original statement remains true for him because he lusts for it to be true. His opposite number wires home to Moscow accounts of widespread starvation among the American depressed masses not altogether from cynical hope to give the boss what he wants; actually his own emotional debt to Marxist gospel convinces him that it must all be true even though it is so hard to find the evidence out here in the capitalist jungle. Be fair to the Six, however: the data that Abolitionism gave them to work with were often as misleading as their own judgment was warped.

Between gullibility and urge to believe, their load of Abolitionist stereotypes was really staggering: They actually saw the typical Southerner as a slightly acclimatized version of the swaggering, hard-drinking, callous West Indian proprietor of 500 Negroes—instead of the self-respecting, lean, ignorant, Bible-reading but somewhat intemperate Southern cotton farmer owning eight or nine slaves who really was typical. ". . . let them go and revel in their luxury and licentiousness," wrote a key Abolitionist of early Dixie threats to secede. They eagerly attributed to Dixie's slaveowners the West Indians' better-founded dread of St. Domingue-style risings: hence Old Brown's and their fatal belief that the slaves round Harpers Ferry or anywhere else would rally to any white man raising a standard to which the innocent and exploited might repair—with the event left somewhat presumptuously in the hands of God. Their illusions about the imminence of slave mutiny were about as ill-founded as were those of pre-World War II conservatives about the inevitable collapse of the Communist regime in Russia—or the sentimental fellow-travelers' conviction, often expressed by open-minded religious groups,

that day after tomorrow Big Brother would relax and the
Soviet Union become a Y.M.C.A. novel written by H. G.
Wells. There have always been a number of self-sent men of
familiar types among both Old Guard and sanguine parsons.

Geography too was treacherous, making melodrama out
of clinical problems. For the Six the bare word "Africa"
evoked a travel-folder paradise—a lovely, warm land spontaneously productive, rich with gold and primitive innocence; peopled with sleek black Nature's Noblemen doomed
to be snatched into degrading bondage by vicious whites
breaking into the Golden Age like rats into a nest of fresh
eggs; instead of the rowdy, frowsy, hand-to-mouth, venal
country of which the Ashanti and Dahomeyans were the
impressive but hardly innocent flower. The Abolitionism
that fed their hatred managed even to melodramatize the
foulness of the utterly foul Trade, ascribing principally to
lip-licking cruelty what often came, however hideously, of
mere callous custom. Then, as Washington's unlovely tenderness toward Dixie politicians encouraged the illicit Trade,
Union-splitting sentiment was deepened by disgust with a
national government so lax about honor and decency; and
hatreds flamed higher still when Dixie fire-eaters so shame-
lessly sought to revive slaving.

In time punitive-minded Abolitionists came almost to welcome news of growing frictions or fresh barbarities. Such
things justified the luxury of hatred and endorsed the acumen with which they had smelled out slaveholders' gamy
sinfulness. It followed that persons so acute and discriminating should use their talents boldly in so glorious a cause. Of
the Six, Higginson shows it all most clearly. He decided
with many others that only dissolving the Union could relieve Northerners from the sin of countenancing slavery.
Previous attempts at Union splitting, whether in New
England or South Carolina, for whatever purpose—and none
so righteous as his—had failed because nobody had begun
shooting when the time was ripe. Old Brown offered a sug-

gestively picturesque and timely means to get shooting started, and with really audacious self-confidence, Higginson seized the opportunity. And even though tactics changed at the last moment, his strategy was so sound that the effect he planned came to pass in spite of technical failure.

Here was essence of egomite. It could never occur to him to suspect that the sternly romantic figures out of Scott whom he saw in Old Brown had never been real anywhere, any time, were only energetic imaginings hung on historical lay figures. He could never hold his hand for a moment to ask himself when the American people had elected him thus to rig their future. He needed no ratification from mortals. He knew he was right, so he went ahead, and anybody asking for his credentials as stage manager for destiny would have got an answer that Old Brown knew by heart—that God and he were a majority and knew their business. Higginson really did have courage, and at first this looks like an example of it. But deeper probing makes it appalling arrogance and presumption. One would like to have seen his face when he was shown the Recording Angel's account of how, just to slake his own emotional thirsts, he exploited a sick old man self-deluded into confounding murderous impulses with God's will.

Last year Colonel Walter Williams, C.S.A., now sole survivor of all the blue and the gray, celebrated his 116th birthday by telling the press that the Civil War "was the final act of bitter people on both sides who wanted war . . . a minority, but they led the majority to war."

Self-sent men are still like that too.

Notes

PROLOGUE: *Immortality*

[1] In this book "Dixie" is used for concision in indicating the area of
the North American continent, in both the colonial and postcolonial
periods, that became the slaveholding states of 1850.

CHAPTER 1:   *The Blown Trumpet*

[1] A Rochester, N.Y., wool merchant who knew him well at this period
remembered Old Brown's "delusion that wool had never been properly
graded" as one evidence of his mental instability (Villard, *John Brown*,
595).

[2] Now the nickname for Kansans generally; then it meant a guerrilla-
looter and cattle and horse thief of the "Bleeding Kansas" period.

[3] For numerous professional soldiers this was true in still another sense.
Among regular officers involved in Kansas who attained prominence in
the Civil War were J. E. B. Stuart, John Sedgwick, E. V. Sumner,
Thomas J. Wood, Joseph E. Johnston.

[4] The evidence is in Villard, *John Brown* (1943 revision) and Malin,
John Brown and the Legend of Fifty-Six. The motive of this killing

may never be cleared up. It could be simple *lex talionis*. H. P. Wilson saw it as necessary part of a large-scale horse-stealing scheme. Old Brown and others sometimes represented it as required by the victims' threats against the lives of Free Staters. Jason Brown once hinted that the aim was to intimidate a Territorial court that included most of the victims among its officers. Old Brown once implied it was done on orders from "higher-ups," maybe the "Kansas Regulators," a shadowy secret order to which at least some of the clan belonged for a while. Most impudently the Bowery Theatre melodrama about John Brown by Kate Lucy Edwards produced late in 1859 suggested that the massacre was staged by proslaveryites in order to get the Browns into trouble.

[5] Redpath was soon mainland chief of a movement to settle American free Negroes in Hayti under auspices of the Haytian government. Eventually he left journalism, much for its good, and founded the first and eminently successful nationwide American "lecture bureau."

[6] These were Samuel Clarke Pomeroy, conspicuous in the Kansas troubles as a Free-State leader, eventually a U.S. Senator; Charles Robinson, "governor" of the Free-State mock-up government; James Henry Lane, Free-State militia organizer, later U.S. Senator. Old Brown's patronizing tone is specially cool since Lane had commanded volunteer regiments in heavy action in the Mexican War.

[7] A minor objective may have been to shock the South into carrying out her standing threat of secession, thus giving the North the occasion to "whip the South back into the Union without slavery" (Villard, *John Brown*, 56). This comes thirdhand, however, as what Salmon Brown's daughter recalled her father's telling of conversations between Old Brown and John jr. It may well be an apocryphal effort to make the old man appear a shrewd forecaster of what actually occurred.

[8] Remember the bayonets on poles ornamenting the Browns' war wagon at Lawrence. Old Brown's pike-mindedness may have come of his admirers' pike-mindedness, for the pike was the basic weapon of the seventeen-century army. Recent commentators, particularly Professor Malin in a private communication, point out that a standard pitchfork would have been more easily come by and as good or better for such use in domestic defense.

[9] Title to these arms had been assumed by G. L. Stearns as security for loans to a separate Kansas Aid committee. Some of its members were furious on learning that Old Brown had used them: Senator Henry Wilson, who had warned Howe to get them out of Brown's hands, said he hoped Stearns and Howe would hang for it. Sanborn wrote of this

ugly affair: "It is still a little difficult to explain . . . without leaving a suspicion that there was somewhere a breach of trust." (*Life and Letters,* 465.)

10 Much of the national confusion about Kansas was due to the number of newspapers relying on "letters" written on the spot by correspondents who were doubling in partisan warfare. Thus H. C. Pate, commanding the force that Old Brown captured at Black Jack, was correspondent of the St. Louis *Republican.* Realf, Redpath, Kagi and Richard J. Hinton simultaneously rode with Old Brown and sent stories regularly to their several papers.

11 The dedication reads: "TO CAPTAIN JOHN BROWN, Senior, of Kansas: . . . You have proven that the slaver has a soul as cowardly as his own 'domestic institution'; . . . I do not hesitate to urge the friends of the slave to incite insurrection, and encourage, in the North, a spirit which shall ultimate [*sic*] in servile and civil wars . . . You, Old Hero! believe that the slave should be aided and urged to insurrection . . ." (*Roving Editor,* iii-iv.) Then he says on p. 306: ". . . there are numbers of young men, trained to [guerrilla warfare] in the Kansas ravines . . . eager for an opportunity of avenging their slain comrades . . . in the . . . Carolinas and Georgia."

12 First the Ohio militia arms that Old Brown was allowed to take to Kansas in 1855; second, the Missourians' use of arms from the Federal arsenal at Liberty, Missouri (Wilson, *History,* II, 601; Villard, *John Brown,* 117); third, the Free-Staters' use of arms from the Iowa State arsenal (Hinton, *John Brown,* 55-6).

13 *John Brown,* 508-9, summarizes: "Brown's grandmother on the maternal side . . . six years in hopeless insanity . . . died insane . . . of [her] children, Brown's uncles and aunts, two sons and two daughters were intermittently insane . . . a third daughter had died hopelessly lunatic; [his] only sister, her daughter and one of his brothers were at intervals deranged . . . of six first cousins, two were occasionally mad, two . . . frequent commitments [to an asylum] . . . two more were at the time under close restraint . . ."

14 True, this was written for a boy of twelve. But the context obviously combines self-pity with aggressive self-assertiveness.

15 The actual total was twenty-two. Three stayed to guard the bulk of the arms at the farm, the rest made the attack under Old Brown. John Brown jr. stayed in Chambersburg, Penna., to forward arms and men.

16 This curious lad was grandnephew of Francis Jackson, militant Boston Abolitionist. He had spent the previous winter as interpreter for

Redpath in Hayti. The $600 was his from a small legacy; with it he went to Baltimore at Old Brown's behest to buy percussion caps for the carbines. A most innocent conspirator, he gave his right name to the store supplying them, had them sent to his hotel, and yet was so nervous about the storekeepers' obvious suspicions—they thought he was a Central American filibuster—that he forgot fifteen dollars' change and had to be run after with it. The considerable sum in gold found on Old Brown when he was captured was probably the balance of Meriam's contribution. He was one of the farm-guard detail, escaped with them, and returned to Hayti to work for a grandiose scheme to create a Negro nation taking in Dixie, the West Indies and part of South America. Later he returned to become a plucky but foolhardy officer in a Negro regiment. (Hinton, *John Brown*, 206-7; Villard, *John Brown*, 685; Mason Committee Report, 145-7.)

[17] *Harper's Weekly's* account pictures a short-barreled swivel gun as part of the raiders' armament but I can find no trace of it in the literature.

[18] Old Brown's conviction on all three went to the state Court of Appeals, which implicitly rejected the treason count but ruled that, however the issue might stand if taken alone, he should hang anyway on the other two convictions (Draper, "Legal Phases of the Trial of John Brown," *West Virginia History*, Jan., 1940). See also Morris, *Fair Trial*, 259 *et seq.*

[19] The association had a grim sequel: The blue-uniformed John Brown was drowned in line of duty in the Shenandoah River at Front Royal, not far upstream from Harpers Ferry (Kimball, "Origin of the John Brown Song," *New England Magazine*, December, 1889).

CHAPTER 2: *Sunny Fountains*

[1] A barracks warehouse for storing slaves being accumulated for sale to slave ships or for shipment on company account. The term is Spanish but slavers of many nations used it. Other terms, depending on locality, were "trunk" or "booth."

[2] The pre-French Revolution Frenchman's name for what has been called Hayti (or Haiti) since 1803. Columbus called the whole island Hispaniola. The eastern three-fourths of it, where influences were dominantly Spanish, came to be known as "Santo Domingo" after the capital. The western quarter, French-dominated after the late 1600's, used the French equivalent "St. Domingue." "San Domingo" is a version usually confined to English-speaking persons. "Hayti" is the earlier

of the two spellings; this book will use it though the official current usage is "Haiti," since we are concerned principally with the early days. "St. Domingue" will be used to mean "French colonial western Hispaniola."

3 Norman ships from Dieppe may have traded for ivory, etc., on the Gold Coast in the fourteenth century; this is supposed to account for the ancient Dieppois tradition of elegant carving in ivory. But the evidence is scanty, half-legendary, and suspected of having been concocted to bolster French claims in West Africa in Louis XIV's time.

4 The name is said to be a corruption of the Portuguese "Cabo Corse."

5 Now used as a penitentiary, Fort James housed Dr. Nkrumah during the prison term that he served for sedition, from which he was released to become first Negro native "leader of government business."

6 This does not necessarily imply that Assameni was not of substantial rank as rank went round Accra. Gold Coast "kings" were not infrequently rather poverty-stricken; and working for high-ranking white men, even in a fairly menial capacity, was not taken as reason for loss of social standing, as it might have been in some other cultures.

7 Internal evidence makes it very clear that Benezet and Wesley both relied heavily on *Astley's Voyages*, II-III, which contains Adanson.

8 Definition for purposes of this book: "Guinea" includes any Atlantic-facing African coastal region north of the Equator, plus more or less back country, from which significant numbers of Negro slaves were shipped to non-Portuguese America. This approximates Blake's Guinea extending from the Senegal River to Cape St. Catherine (*European Beginnings*, 7), as well as the most liberal definition in Donnan, *Documents* . . . It pretty well leaves out the coastal regions most infiltrated by Bantu elements and, by the same token, most of the area from which the Portuguese drew most of the slaves shipped to Brazil. This book has enough to do in the West Indies and North America without trying to refer more than incidentally to Brazilian matters.

9 Dr. Walter C. Lowdermilk, an authority on soil conservation, points out that, given the problem of raising food in tropical jungle "shifting cultivation" is about the only conceivable practical method. The answer, as he sees it, is to avoid forcing the nonliterate to use for agriculture lands better adapted to other uses.

10 Missionaries tell me that Islam is still spreading in West Africa partly because its allowing polygamy fits local ways better than Christan insistence on monogamy; and that its proselyting methods are often quite as militant as they are effective.

[11] Bovill, who knows as much as anybody of these misty matters, is positive about the site of Ghana's capital (*Golden Trade*, 68-9). He has taken seriously the possibility that the white founders were Jews strayed somehow into the Western Sudan (*Caravans*, 45). In view of all the speculation about the Lost Tribes, why has nobody tried to identify them with these African Jews?

[12] Caution: This does *not* mean that one does not find many tall-built or straight-nosed persons in the area. By now Gold Coasters are as mingled with cousin stocks as any other minor African ethnic group. A random-selected 500 Ashanti would, however, be readily distinguishable from a parallel group of 500 Kru or Mandingoes.

[13] One group of Upcountries pushed clear to the seacoast, becoming the Vai people settled on the present Liberia-Sierra Leone border back of Cape Mount. Alone among West Africans, they developed writing on their own—a long-ago Vai genius borrowed the basic notion from whites and created an original script to record the Vai speech.

[14] *I.e.*, Senegal, Dahomey and the Voltaic and Sudanese Republics. Shaw (*Tropical Dependency*, 16) and DuBois (*Black Folk*, 39) see Sudanese Negro cultures somewhat influenced by previously well developed Negro cultures upcountry from the Bights, *e.g.*, the Yoruba *et al*. Yet the germs of these cultures may have come from Egypt at some not too remote period. It will be centuries before these issues are rescued from wishful speculation.

[15] The progress of this corruption seems pretty plain in certain passages quoted in Blake, *European Beginnings*, 6-7, and *Europeans in West Africa*, I, 34, which cites early Portuguese speaking of "the Guineos of Gana." Bovill, *Golden Trade*, 119 *fn.*, much prefers to derive "Guinea" from Jenne, a later Sudanese commercial center of importance. Fage, *Introduction*, 45 *fn.* derives it from the Berber term for "Land of the Blacks."

[16] Other motives alleged: converting the heathen and at the same time taking in the rear the North African allies of the dwindling Moslems of Spain. But gold certainly bulked large from the beginning.

[17] The effort to by-pass the transdesert trade persisted for centuries, hampered by upcountry reluctance to see whites penetrate the areas producing slaves, gold, etc. When a suspicious chief on the Upper Niger asked Mungo Park the purpose of his second expedition, he replied: ". . . all the articles of value, which the Moors and people of Jinnie bring [here] are made by us [whites]. If you speak of a good gun, who made it? The white people. If you speak of a good pistol or

sword, or piece of scarlet . . . or beads or gunpowder, who made them? The white people. We sell them to the Moors; the Moors bring them to Timbuctoo and sell them to the people of Jinnie at a still higher price; and the people of Jinnie sell them to you . . . the king of the white people wishes to find out a way by which we may bring our own merchandise to you and sell you everything at a much cheaper rate." (*Travels*, 363-4.) A generation later Clapperton found the Arabs of the Western Sudan hostile because "They know well, if the native Africans were once acquainted with English commerce by way of the sea, their own lucrative inland trade would . . . cease." (Plumb, 258.)

[18] Gum arabic, still much used in pharmacy and industry, comes from certain West African acacia trees. The seventeenth century particularly valued it as indispensable in dyeing silks.

[19] A West African cardamon seed the vogue of which had disappeared in Europe by the middle of the eighteenth century. Some called it "grains of Paradise," hence "the Grain Coast" for what is now sea-coast Liberia.

[20] Dahomey and Benin seem to have been rather honorable exceptions in this. The old accounts insist that practically all slaves exported from these two kingdoms were criminals or war captives.

[21] The Negro slave as personal servant was so familiar in Europe by the early 1500's that, for safety in going to take his post as viceroy of the Netherlands, Don John of Austria traveled black-face, posing as a valet. The effect must have been curious for Don John had blue eyes (Motley, *Dutch Republic*, III, 153).

[22] Until the late 1600's brandy, not the traditional rum, was the slaver's standard trade spirits (Barbot, *Description*, 172). It was also the issue spirits of the Royal Navy until the West Indian interest got rum substituted in the late eighteenth century. In the nineteenth century squareface gin superseded both in the trade.

[23] W. E. Williams, *Africa and the Rise of Capitalism*, 9; a work further interesting for its frank attribution to Karl Marx of the view that Western capitalism was founded on Negro slavery, a theory that has had more notice than it probably deserves. It quotes Marx ("Misère de la Philosophie," *Collected Works*, Berlin, 1932, VI, 181): "Direct slavery is the pivot of bourgeois industry. Without slavery there is no cotton; without cotton there is no modern industry. It is slavery that has given value to universal commerce."

[24] "Ibos pend' cou' a yo' " ("Eboes hang themselves") was a French West Indian proverb (Moreau de St.-Méry, *Saint-Domingue* I, 31).

[25] Other spellings in the old books: Cromanty, Kromantyn, etc. All refer to a seaside settlement, site of the Dutch Fort Amsterdam, two miles east of the British trading fort at Anamabo. Both posts traded heavily with the local Fanti. "Koromantyn" etc., however, came to apply to slaves procured anywhere between Axim and Accra—the stretch of Gold Coast where the "slave castles" and their auxiliary posts were most concentrated. The nature of the trade implies much variation in the Negroes thus labeled. Exported "Koromantyns" could have included unlucky specimens of such local peoples as the Fanti, Fetu, Adom; or ditto from among the upcountry Ashanti and their vigorous neighbors; or war prisoners that the Ashanti caught far upcountry and traded down to the coast for salt, fish and European goods. Even so the bulk of Koromantyn slaves probably came from closely related peoples, justifying the physical and to some extent the psychological generalizations above.

[26] Fermented palm sap secured by cutting into the growing spathe of a palm near the top. Micronesians do the same with another kind of palm. I have never tried the stuff, being frightened away by tales of what its lively and variegated bacterial content can do to the outsider's enteric tract. In both the South Pacific and West Africa whites say that it is very powerful, particularly if drunk at maximum fermentation, and leaves a memorable hangover of the too-much-champagne variety. The Fanti had a specially heady palm wine that the traders called "Quaker" and spoke of with deep respect (Barbot, *Description,* 175). In respect to drinking the West Africans I have seen seem to me to have turned over a new leaf since the old days. Drunkenness, though not unknown, is no great problem in Accra, for instance, or so local white police have assured me. Yet natives are allowed any amount of drink they can pay for, from beer to whisky. Nor can their moderation be ascribed to lack of purchasing power. The Tahitian, whose per capita purchasing power can be no higher than the Gold Coaster's, also with unlimited access to wine and spirits, makes a childish sot of himself.

[27] I cannot explain why Senegalese boys were forced to a sort of self-cannibalism in swallowing the foreskin when cut off during circumcision (Barbot, *Description,* 62); maybe a quaint extension of the precautions common among the superstitious of burying or burning one's nail parings, hair combings, etc., lest enemies use them to prepare hostile spells.

[28] Rattrey, *Ashanti,* 47-50. This is the technical anthropological use of "totem"; see any good dictionary for its multiple layers of meaning.

Following the idea down logically, the Ashanti regarded adultery with a man outside husband's totem as far more serious than the same trespass with a totem comrade.

[29] Assorted instances: Little, *Mende,* 142; da Sorrento in Pinkerton, *Voyages,* XVI, 213; Barbot, *Description,* 242; Burton, *Mission,* II, 163; Bosman, *Description,* 420, calls it "wearing gilt horns."

[30] This obviously implies that, though it was not the prime motive, they made a profit on their investment. I do not know whether members of the syndicate had free use of the girl or had to pay regular fees into the common fund.

[31] This strange procedure usually involved some mutilation of the labiae to produce enlargement in an effect, said one witness, rather like a nanny-goat's udder (Dalzel, *History,* xviii). In one area the method was to let the parts be thoroughly gnawed by large biting ants. (Barbot, *Description,* 356.) As to motive, the above sounds to me like one of the familiar occasions when people have long forgotten the genuine reason for a peculiar custom and so provide for themselves and strangers a reason that sounds good enough but is not the original —whatever it was in this case I can't imagine.

[32] This does not imply that Haytian voodoo sacrifices men; it probably never did so in typical rites. When considering these things please observe the distinction between killing a man to propitiate a god likely to be pleased by the sacrifice of so valuable a thing (*i.e.,* Abraham and Isaac) and doing so to supply the ancestors in Deadland with proper service and prestige—Guinea's usual motive for killing prisoners and slaves. The two things may blur, of course, as historic ancestors grow vaguer and more august—the process that may have led to the demigods of Greece.

[33] The current cult of West African carving and sculpture, which goes along with current fascination with voodoo, is considered in an appendix to this book.

[34] In time such modifications may sink in to the point where a shogun or mayor of the palace takes over. Such a king was inevitably half the prisoner of his ministers and bureaucracy.

[35] Some such "kings" operating outside Africa were fakes. Lamb, the captured trader mentioned above, eventually took with him to America and treacherously sold as a slave one Tom, sent along with him to observe European ways for the King of Dahomey. After some years Lamb recovered Tom and took him to England, representing him as ambassador from Dahomey ". . . under which title he was generally re-

ceived; and several plays were performed for his black highness . . ." (Dalzel, *History*, 44-6.) After exposure he was sent back to Dahomey, where his knowledge of English enabled him to prosper as an interpreter.

36 A chief's special stool—actually a backless chair with a saucered seat adzed out of a single block of wood—was carried after him for ceremonial sitting and soon became symbol of his duties and prestige. Hence the West African terms "de-stooling" for deposition of a chief, and "stool" for the office of chief. After taking Kumasi the British could not find the Golden Stool and made a great fuss about it. Years later it was accidentally found during a road-building excavation; it had been secretly buried by devoted Ashanti, and was vandalized by low-class Ashanti for the bullion value of its priceless ornaments.

37 This is West African pidgin (Black English) for "wait a few minutes."

38 I am told that Haitian devotees of *voudun* used to take the salutes fired by foreign warships in Haitian ports as courtesies not to the secular government of Haiti but to the principal gods of the various *voudun* pantheons as infallible tokens of their power and prestige.

39 Whom he undoubtedly reckoned up by scores and hundreds instead of mere dozens. The above extracts are from Bowdich, *Mission*, one of the great books about West Africa; no references, since everybody who has access to it, with its beautiful illustrations, should read it all.

40 Three, in fact, Dahomeyan harems were guarded by eunuchs who were also killed to furnish part of the establishment of the ancestors in Deadland. (Burton, *Mission*, pp. 18-24.)

CHAPTER 3:   *The Middle Passage*

1 Depending on time of year, the southeast trades shift from well south of the equator to somewhat north of it.

2 These relatively light though bulky outward-bound ladings often made ballast necessary—hence much of the cut stone and Dutch brick in the old slave castles of the Gold Coast.

3 On the Gold Coast the annual payment for such a lease was called a "book"—a term transferred from the local "Black English" word for any printed or written paper which came soon to apply to any commercial or political agreement between whites and Negroes. The payments usually went to the holder of the local "stool," hence passed to a suzerain imposing himself by conquest. Thus the Ashanti insisted on

receiving the annual "book" for the fort sites at Elmina originally leased by the local stool to the Portuguese and then to the Dutch. Their title to it came from their having conquered the Elminas, hence taken over all attributes and assets of the Elmina stool.

4 Negroes accumulated on the coast for shipment were particularly subject to epidemic diseases, probably for the same reason that accounts for their devastating shipboard illnesses: in both environments they met viruses and bacteria of strains different from those to which they had become more or less immunized at home, though the diseases themselves were the same.

5 Some think that the "John Canoe" figure central in Jamaican Christmas pageantry recalls vague memories of the name of this Negro who so signally gave white men as good as he got. If so, this is another example of the strong Gold Coast influence persisting in Jamaica.

6 For a while c. 1700 a company chartered by the Elector of Brandenburg operated several posts on the Gold Coast. It was largely a front for Dutchmen trying to regularize their interloping activities by borrowing foreign auspices. Significantly the company headquarters were at Emden right across the river from Holland, and in time the Dutch bought out the Brandenburgers' forts in Guinea.

7 Phillips (Voyage, 233) was greatly taken by the method used by the Portuguese of St. Thomas to ward off "fluxes"; they advised him "every night, before I went to sleep, to wash clean, and dabble my fundament with luke-warm water for half or a quarter of an hour." It can have done little good against dysentery but at least it gave him something of a bath, a thing that the European in West Africa seldom resorted to.

8 In West Africa in 1953 it was interesting to see hatless Britons walking miles in the sun on the golf links.

9 These cozy relations sometimes lapsed: The captain of the slaver Thames wrote in 1776 of how: "About 3 weeks ago the [Danes and Dutch] . . . at Accra, and . . . their towns-people, went together at Logerheads and fought for 3 or 4 days . . ." (Donnan, Documents, III, 318).

10 The arrangement is not unique. Dutch and Canadian vessels in the West Indian trade did the same before World War II with deck crews working between Trinidad and the Bahamas. For record-keeping white pursers gave individual Kru men fancy names that they valued highly: In 1844 USS Truxtun shipped, among others, Tom Nimble, Jack Liverpool, Prince of Whales, Jack Never Fear, Pea Soup, Dandy Jim,

Tom Buzzard, John Crapeau, Half Crowbar; in 1849 USS *Yorktown's* complement included Jack Grappo, Poor Fellow and Tossa Dollar.

[11] Wool for West African wear sounds strange to us in the temperate zone. But Guinea nights can be chill, specially in the *harmattan* season, and the West African wants warmish garments at what we should consider rather high temperatures anyway. I remember the Kru boys on a coasting freighter pestering the stewards for *two* blankets apiece in latitude 4 N. No doubt this "thin bloodedness" is one reason why the Guinea Negro weaves his handsome cottons as thick as bath towels.

[12] An exception on the farthest fringe of Guinea: Lander found "a very coarse and inferior sort of gunpowder" made at a town near Busa on the Niger (*Journal*, I, 240).

[13] Much of the above still applies to West Africa. Anybody wanting the curious details, try my "World's Choosiest Customers," *Nation's Business,* May, 1953.

[14] The French iron (from Brittany) was in twenty-five pound bars. The English ones must have been much smaller (Barbot, *Description,* 44-5).

[15] Smallish species of the univalvular genus *Cypraeae*. Size seldom affected their value; only number on a string and number of strings was important. The value of these shells is said to derive, like the generic name, from the resemblance of the underside to the female pudenda.

[16] When Nathaniel Hawthorne was customs collector at Salem, Mass., he made a practice of personally checking the rum that "the Pingrees used to send out [to West Africa] for the negroes . . . with a test glass for spirits . . . into each cask, to prove its quality because he was determined the niggers should have good strong rum." (Sanborn, *Recollections,* 533.)

[17] As of 1680 Barbot thought exported slaves were mostly "prisoners of war, taken either in fight, or pursuit, or in the incursions they make . . . others stolen away by their own countrymen." (*Description,* 47.) Modify this with what Edwards found a century later (*History*, II, 121) from Africa-born slaves checked back on months later to see if their stories changed: Of twenty-five probably deserving credence, fifteen had been slaves sold for debt; five captured in petty wars probably amounting to slave raids; five kidnaped by Negro traders.

[18] John Wesley (*Thoughts on Slavery,* 9) was unable to accept the reality of such dealings in one's own offspring, commenting on Barbot's instances of same: "That their parents sell them is utterly false; whites, not blacks, are without natural affection!"

[19] In simpler cultures the "caboceer" (spellings vary) was an eminent member of the local council of elders which advised or dominated the "king" or sometimes ruled without any specific head. The word always implies rank and important activity in war, government or both.

[20] The evidence is sketchy but it does seem that slaves unsalable because of poor condition, stoppage of trade or glutted markets were sometimes killed to prevent costly upkeep; see Edwards, *History*, III, 132; Murray, *Letters*, 253; M'Queen, *West India Colonies*, 88; Kingsley, *West African Studies*, 511. Concentration of these data in the period after most Western nations had outlawed the Trade may mean that it happened oftener in that even less scrupulous time.

[21] The effect on the slave trade of the gradual Moslemization of Africa which still goes on was complex. Arab traders down from the desert were the backbone of the pre-white Trade that educated Guinea to export slaves. But Moslem missionaries of the 1700's in Sierra Leone managed much piecemeal suppression of local slaving in the upcountry villages where their influence took hold (Utting, *Story*, 64).

[22] Wirth and Goldheimer (in Klineberg, *Characteristics*, 259) have a suggestion on this point: ". . . the excessively long time that slave coffles often required to reach the coast may have led to overestimation of the distance from which slaves were brought."

[23] Sierra Leone and Hayti both have small lively movements to erect these local pidgins into written languages with defined syntax and hopes of bodies of literature of their own. The parochial nationalism of such schemes is obviously deplorable. Such pidgins may be temporarily useful to begin the education of illiterate masses with, and both places are saddled with just that. But in the long run the Sierra Leonean or Haytian must make his way into the outside world's ideas as well as techniques—things that such sub-languages too often cannot convey. Here is a sample of each as formulated by a local dark-skinned enthusiast; Sierra Leone "Creole" first:

"Dis pickin day go school but de school day far away. E got get for pass wan tone way den say na debul tone, but any tem way dis pickin reach near dis tone, nah da ten day e kin tire pass all. Wan particlar day e so tire dat e say make are sidom blow lillie bit . . ."

Then Haytian "Creole": "A la tracas mesanmis! Gain oun grand beurrier qui voyagé Jeremie pour decrasser toute beurre que habitants ap batté lan bouetille . . ."

[24] When slaving in the Bights ships usually prepared elaborately for a probably lengthy stay by sending down the yards and topmasts and

with them building a temporary "house" roofed with native mats to shelter the entire deck, making it very hot and stuffy below decks for the slaves being accumulated there (Falconbridge, *Account,* 5-7).

[25] Large-bore short muskets mounted on swivels set in a ship's rail or the bows of a boat, charged with small shot, highly destructive at close range.

[26] The definition of "ton" and the manner of calculating it changed frequently while the Trade existed, so only the roughest comparisons are possible from one century to another. The period covered by the above figures is, however, short enough to allow rational comparison.

[27] This was a serious fire hazard, of course, necessitating rules that no slave could smoke belowside. In a ship lying "slaving" off Anamabo a sentry caught a woman slave smoking in the 'tweendecks and went at her so menacingly that she panicked and threw away her lighted pipe —starting a fire that got into the magazine and blew up the ship with most of her slaves and crew (Donnan, *Documents,* II, 316-7).

[28] Abolitionists often used a tale of a slaver with cargo and crew all thus blinded meeting another slaver at sea in the same predicament. The standard version is in Dow, *Slave-Ships,* xxviii, *et seq.*—an unlikely story implausibly told and I am unable to take it seriously.

[29] Such comparisons are hampered by the curious way Spanish and French and sometimes other slavers reckoned slave numbers: The basis was the "pieze d'Inde" or "pièce d'Inde" in which a normal-sized male, fit slave counted one "pièce." So did a couple of boys of twelve, say; or a fit young woman with a small child; three fit middle-aged men might count as two such "pièces." So a French slaver rated at 300 "pièces" might have from 350 to 400 slaves actually on board (Donnan, *Documents,* I, 106; IV, 638-9).

[30] Royal Navy officers sometimes shipped slaves in His Majesty's ships on convoy duty between Africa and the Caribbean, presumably without official permission (Donnan, *Documents,* II, 463-6).

[31] *Travels,* 328. In dealing with this book one must bear in mind that Bryan Edwards ghosted it from Park's journals and other papers after the great explorer had died with his boots on; and that, valuable as his own writings are, Edwards was basically a realistic apologist for slavery. In this context, however, his views on American slavers can be more useful than Park's could be, since Edwards was well acquainted with the whole feel of the Trade, as reflected in the West Indies and England, and had long made it a practice to ask all kinds of questions about slavery of anybody anywhere likely to know something.

³² Spears, *American Slave Trade,* 19, quoting Samuel Hopkins. A tax of £3 per slave imported was earmarked for paving the streets of Newport (Donnan, *Documents,* III, 113)—probably the first and last place in this world or the next ever to be paved with ill intentions.

³³ Actually the Yankee's principal contribution to New World slavery lay in his function as supplier, in direct trade to the West Indies, of the lumber, saft fish and draft animals without which slavery could never have grown great in either British or French islands.

³⁴ Pinckard (*Notes,* I, 227-38) visited an American slaver watering at Barbados en route to Savannah with 130 slaves, mostly in their teens, and was most favorably impressed with their apparent cheerfulness and good condition, the cleanliness of their quarters and the length of time that they had been allowed on deck during the voyage. A few had even been trained to help work the vessel and otherwise take on crew's functions. Note, however, that the youthfulness of the cargo was exceptional, making it much easier to keep them controlled; and that even so the ship had had a mutiny on the Coast, in which the master and mate were killed and several hands severely wounded.

³⁵ An obvious parallel to the French-Spanish "pièce d'Inde" system (cf. p. 406, note 29) and naturally subject to the same abuses.

³⁶ It should be noted that Royal Navy provisions were so poor in this same period that midshipmen sometimes cooked and ate ships' rats, which were said to be fairly tasty once the taboo was surmounted—and given a boy's appetite. They were called "midshipman's rabbit."

³⁷ Edwards, a source to be taken seriously, doubted the actual existence of this belief (*History,* II, 104-6). Yet numerous early references make it clear that, though Negroes from Peoples A or B might reject it, those from C, D and E were well convinced of it; see, for instance, Donnan, *Documents,* I, 401, and Pinckard, *Notes,* I, 273-5. The belief sometimes included the notion that mutilation would prevent posthumous return to Africa. So Captain Snelgrave, making an example of a slave-mutineer, had him decapitated instead of shot or hanged in view of all other slaves on board to make it clear that there would be no Africa for him or anybody else attempting another mutiny at the risk of death (*New Account,* 183-4).

³⁸ Liverpool owners had a pretty custom of naming slavers after their wives, daughters and, no doubt, sweethearts: *Betsy, Peggy, Saucy Sally,* that sort of thing. The ladies probably took it for a compliment.

³⁹ One hopes that each was served out a tot of rum before going below to the stinks again. Note that privateer tactics stressed close quarters

and boarding in overwhelming force for hand-to-hand combat rather than gun duels between ships. A privateer charged her guns with chain shot and canister to sweep an enemy's decks and cut up her rigging to keep her from manoeuvering to escape boarding, rather than try to batter her hull and smash her spars.

[40] Consider also that, at this time, Italian emigration to South America was also very heavy. The populations of the two areas concerned compare thus: That of West Africa in the period 1400-1800 is thought to have hovered round 20,000,000; that of Italy in 1901 was somewhat above 32,000,000, in 1911 more than 34,000,000. But reflect too that the vast bulk of Italian emigration to the New World came from south of Rome, where cities were smaller and population scantier, so that the areas actually subject to major "depopulation" would have had populations of very much the same order, with West Africa higher if there was a discrepancy.

CHAPTER 4:   *U.S.S.* Frustration

[1] Combe, *Tour,* II, 139. Findings as to Cinquez were: "a well-made man of 24 to 25 years of age. His head rises high above the ear, particularly in the regions of Self-Esteem and Firmness . . . Destructiveness is large, but not excessive. Benevolence and Veneration are well marked . . . The middle perpendicular portion, including Comparison and Eventuality, is decidedly large. Individuality is full. The temperament seems to be nervous-bilious. This size and form of brain indicate considerable mental power, decision, self-reliance, prompt perception, and readiness of action." All of which could, of course, have been deduced from Cinquez' history without feeling his head at all. The only thing to be taken seriously in all this is the seriousness with which phrenology was taken then, before it sank to the level of a gypsy gimmick. The "nervous-bilious," by the way, means not that Cinquez was suffering from psychogenic jaundice but that his disposition combined the sensitive with the aggressive.

[2] It seems to have been the Duke of Wellington who first suggested that the sharp lines of the illicit slaver implied worse overcrowding. The notion was spread by Laird's widely read book on his explorations in the 1830's: "Instead of the large and commodious vessels which it would be to the interest of the slave-trader to employ, we . . . forced him to use . . . American clippers of the very worst description . . . every quality being sacrificed for speed." (In Buxton, *African Slave Trade,* 158-9.)

³ Thus Buxton (*African Slave Trade,* 135-6) dwelt on the slaver *Eleanor's* 135 slaves/60 tons; and the *Deux Soeurs'* 132 slaves/41 tons, which is about pre-1808 New England style. Commodore Hotham (Denman, *Slave Trade*) set the prevailing ratio in illicit slavers at about three slaves per ton; mortality at 5%, which very probably reflects greater speed. Again changes in methods of calculating tonnage make these figures ambiguous in comparison with earlier ratios.

⁴ *Wanderer* was 95' in the keel, beam 26'; she loaded some 400 slaves her first voyage, some 600 her second (Spears, *American Slave-Trade,* 199). *Brooks'* lower deck (roughly same as length of her keel) was 100' long, beam 25'; she was legally rated to carry 450 slaves but once landed 646 in Jamaica, which must mean she had loaded over 700. (Williams, *Liverpool Privateers,* 385-6.) C. A. L. Lamar once figured on loading no more than 2000 slaves in a 1750-ton steamer (*North American Review,* 454).

⁵ The other, of course, was the antislavery Northwest Ordinance.

⁶ These details largely from Spears, *American Slave-Trade,* 199-208. The New York Yacht Club tells me that Spears was wrong in identifying a painting of a *Wanderer* in the Manhattan clubhouse as the old slave smuggler; this is a later vessel of the same name, always popular with yacht owners. I think there is another error in the press rumors (in Cole, *Irrepressible Conflict,* 76) that the *Wanderer's* second voyage landed slaves in Texas.

⁷ A close cousin of L. Q. C. Lamar, the Southern politician recently celebrated by Senator Kennedy. He had imagination or effrontery, depending on point of view: He actually applied for U.S. clearance for a voyage to bring Africans to the States as "apprentices," aping French and British schemes of that sort. He planned to buy a steamer, fit her with Paixhan guns and a crew of gentleman-adventurers, and blow out of the water antislaving patrol vessels that she couldn't run away from. He was also hopeful of getting Henry J. Raymond of the New York *Times* to accept a challenge to a duel resulting from some of the harsh things the *Times* said about his activities.

⁸ This was a South Seas term for nominally indentured but usually kidnaped or purchased "labor" procured for guano digging in the Peruvian islands, work in Queensland sugar plantations, etc.—and a foul trade in its own right. Martin may have been an old South Pacific hand.

⁹ Details from Roche, *Historic Sketches,* and Foster's account kindly lent me by Mr. Leo W. Brown of Mobile. Slavers making successful

voyages were often thus burned, presumably for some reason connected with destroying evidence that an admiralty lawyer would understand better than I do. It was expensive but the profits were so high that even a new ship could pay for herself and much to spare in a single trip.

[10] Remember that the value of the dollar was then four or five times what it is today. Sometimes seamen got so much per head of slaves landed alive.

[11] The final scale of Royal Navy rewards to personnel of ships making good prize of slavers was: £4 per ton of ship condemned; £5 per head for slaves landed alive in Sierra Leone or the West Indies; £2/10 for those captured in slavers but dying during the voyage to the landing depot (Mathieson, *Great Britain and the Slave Trade*, 35).

[12] Soulsby *(Right of Search, 47 fn.)* calls exaggerated DuBois' classic statement *(Suppression, 162)* that "the American slave-trade . . . came to be carried on principally by United States capital . . . in United States ships . . . under the United States flag." The major capital was likely to be Latin-American and the United States flag and papers were used only to ward off search by non-American, usually British, cruisers. Turnbull *(Travels, 141)* had some reason to believe that some, probably not much relatively, British capital went into the illicit Trade.

[13] The father of these Orders in Council was James Stephen, admiralty lawyer and author of *War in Disguise* (1807), which lent his great weight to bitter feelings against Americans' and others' opportunism in disguising contraband shipments to France. He was also an eminent antislaveryite and the last man wishing to do anything calculated to discourage suppression of the Trade; but that was the long-run effect.

[14] The judge in U.S. *vs.* Darnaud (alien captain of the *Grey Eagle* slaver, Spanish-financed in the Cuban Trade) went into the matter with rather dizzying thoroughness: "Slave vessels sail with two or three, or four captains. One captain clears her in a United States port, and swears he is a United States citizen. Another belonging to a different country, in connection with the first, when she arrives at the coast of Africa receives the slaves on board. Another, after the slaves are received, takes charge of them and commands the vessel, and makes one of the former captains the doctor, mate, steward, or something else. Another delivers the slaves on shore. This is done . . . to enable the vessels to seek the protection of a flag which the cruiser hailing them will . . . regard . . . when an American cruiser comes in sight, the

Portuguese or Spanish flag is run up, and the false Portuguese or Spanish papers are produced. In the present instance, when a British cruiser hove in sight, the American flag was run aloft . . . and when the flag was seen the cruiser went off." (Catterall, *Judicial Cases,* IV, 215.)

15 The last such violation of which I find record was in 1864, when the *Reindeer,* obviously American-owned and proving obviously to be a slaver, was seriously damaged in a squall in latitude 31°N. while bound for West Africa and sought safety in Newport. She was seized by the U.S. marshal, who had no political reason to hesitate, with the Civil War so far advanced, but what disposal was made of her and her crew I do not know.

16 Actually an American court was probably first in the field, in 1821 before Britain included the principle in reciprocal-search treaties with other powers: USS *Alligator* had seized and sent to Boston on suspicion of slaving the American-built but French-registered *Jeune Eugénie.* She carried no slaves when seized, claimed to be a palm-oil trader, but was obviously expecting company, black and lots of it. She had rice and water enough to last her crew of nineteen for some years, and was fitted with grating useless except in slavers. The court agreed with the prosecution that she was a slaver but, since she did seem genuinely to be property of a Guadeloupe firm, turned her over to a French consul "to be dealt with according to his own sense of duty and right." (Catterall, *Judicial Cases,* IV, 497.)

17 This is one of the few times when this book touches on the Trade between East Africa and the Americas. North America and the West Indies got some but relatively very few of these slaves from Madagascar, Mozambique, etc.; they went mostly to Brazil. At no time was the number shipped to any New World area of the same order as that coming out of Guinea or Angola.

18 *Truxtun* log in National Archives. The *Spitfire's* crew seem to have included more Americans than was usual in slave smugglers even under U.S. registry: Peter Florrey (master), Ferdinand Waltz, William Otten, William Turner, Frederick Emmers, Antonio de Mijo, Ebenezer Jackson. De Mijo was very probably the Spanish supercargo front.

19 Spears (*American Slave-Trade,* 151) found that in six of the years from 1843 to 1857 the West Africa Squadron was under eighty guns even in theory. During this period the Royal Navy's opposite number squadron averaged 140 guns in spite of the Crimean War. The U.S. Navy averaged four ships on duty; the Royal Navy, eighteen. Some of the most illustrious old ships—*Constitution, Constellation, United*

States—served as flagship of the American Squadron. The Perry who opened up Japan had two West African commands and enjoyed neither. USS *Somers* was returning from taking dispatches to USS *Vandalia* off West Africa when she had that notorious mutiny. USS *San Jacinto*, Commander Wilkes, was homeward bound from this duty when she took Mason and Slidell off that British mail steamer. Commodore Josiah Tatnall, USN, who aided a British attack on Korea on the theory that "Blood is thicker than water" and then distinguished himself in the Confederate Navy, knew the West African station as well as Commodore Andrew Foote, USN, whose river gunboats helped so much in cutting the Confederacy in two.

[20] Cass' attitude toward the right of search sounds almost pathological. But it did produce one of the most successful pieces of casuistic eloquence ever to ornament American history when he shouted: "Our flag is to be violated to see if it has been abused!" (Soulsby, *Right of Search*, 114.)

[21] It occurs to me that this may have been the trick that cajoled Captain Gordon into showing American colors on the *Erie*. The ship's log mentions no such thing, but then that would hardly be expected. The logs of U.S. Navy ships on the West Africa station sometimes do mention using British colors but never explain why.

[22] This seems to have been her original name, after the tradition of pretty names for slavers. *Black Joke* was originally *Henriquetta* (says Lloyd, *Navy*, 71) or maybe *Henri Quatre* (says Utting, *Story*, 123), which seems likelier. The second name is a puzzle too. A *Black Joke* landed slaves in South Carolina in 1764 (Donnan, *Documents*, IV, 400), and a grim name for a slaver.

[23] No doubt the wide discrepancy in armament tempted the slaver to have a try. Lloyd (*Navy*, 70-3) says the action was fought at close range, making it even more impressive, since one would have expected the *Black Joke* to keep away and exploit the superior range of her long gun. On the West India station HMS *Monkey*, with nothing but a single long gun, beat a fourteen-gun slaver (Turnbull, *Travels*, 26). *Fair Rosamond* had only one carronade and a six-pounder field piece trundled here and there on deck as occasion suggested.

[24] In the 1850's, very late in the game, slavers began to use fair-sized steamers to neutralize this advantage.

[25] When Spanish slavers did not name their ships after their womenfolk, they liked cheerful abstractions: *Feliz, Amistad, Felicidade.*

26 A special hero of the Preventive Squadron was Surgeon McKinnel of HMS *Sybille* who drank a wineglass of black vomit from a yellow fever patient to disprove the theory that the disease was contagious (Lloyd, *Navy*, 134-5).

27 In 1817 the Asantehene wrote to the governor of Cape Coast: "I will thank you to impress on the King of England that I have sworn not to renew the war on the Fantees out of respect to him . . . I hope therefore he will . . . consider if he cannot renew the Slave Trade, which will be good for me [and] let all foreign vessels come to the coast to trade . . ." (Bowdich, *Mission*, 149-50.)

CHAPTER 5:   *The Curse of Cane*

1 Since ninety-five of a hundred cultural factors originally involved must have been the same, this is a strange situation. I know of no satisfactory accounting for it and doubt that one can ever be found by this late date. For a sample of Jamaican speech as locally printed for local readers: "Im wanted to know how im diden si mi pan di bus . . . Mi no was ridin mi motor cycle behind sah! . . . Mi would like to know which part you was too . . ." (Jamaica *Times*, January 12, 1957.)

2 In terms of the time this really was not absurd. Canada was utterly undeveloped and largely unexplored. Martinique's position in the chain of islands was highly strategic for wind ships, and British planters had flooded in slaves and made it a most valuable property during a recent wartime occupation.

3 Slaves separated after surviving the Middle Passage together usually retained a high sense of comradeship. In their meager, rootless universe the term "shipmate" carried great emotional meaning; I find this a strangely poignant detail (Edwards, *History*, II, 94; Walsh, *Notices*, II, 184).

4 The large British islands, particularly Jamaica, somewhat heightened these discrepancies by smuggling Negroes out for sale in the Spanish islands. It remains true, however, that while slavery lasted, no important West Indian island under any national auspices achieved more than bare maintenance of its numbers.

5 Hans Sloan (*Voyage*, xlviii) says British planters of the 1600's bought "wives in proportion to their Men lest the Men should wander to neighboring plantations." Ligon (*History*, 46-7) confirms this for Bar-

bados c. 1660. Later planters thought it paid better to buy mostly men.

6 Tetanus of the newborn is still serious in both West Africa and the West Indies, no doubt because soils are still impregnated with the organism and midwives are still lax about hand washing. Note, however, that in spite of this hazard, West Indian populations continue rising to an alarming extent.

7 Worthy Park estate had nine births a year average among 350-odd slaves; ratio of live births to miscarriages 9/2 (Phillips, "A Jamaica Slave Plantation"). He also cites a Grenada surgeon's estimate that one slave baby in three died in its first three months. Dixie had infant mortality of the same order, so lack of pregnancies as well as miscarriages must be responsible for the difference between the two areas. True, in many Dixie situations field labor for women was only occasional; whereas in both Louisiana and the West Indies sugar plantations demanded it consistently.

8 Edwards (*History*, II, 176) estimated that some 10,000 West Indian slaves of the driver-houseman-craftsman stratum had several recognized "wives" apiece. The ladies probably did not consistently avoid enjoyment of other men, however, so this did not much affect their total number of opportunities to conceive. Raynal (*History*, V, 280-1) naïvely failed to take this into account when assuming that, since men slaves outnumbered women, the extra men were forced to continence.

9 Mathieson (*British Slavery*, 105-9) uses slave smuggling after 1809 as a principal explanation of Dixie's population increase. Actually the scale of it cannot possibly have been large enough to make serious difference in view of the above considerations. This is only one detail showing that Mathieson's knowledge of Dixie conditions may not have been adequate for judging such issues properly. What his comments finally boil down to, however, is that the large-plantation system imposed by sugar culture was probably the principal villain— which is unquestionably sound. The Louisiana sugar planters, historically close to the French colonials of heavily brutalized St. Domingue, also had trouble growing their own replacement slaves. So did some South Carolina rice planters, on whose places conditions were notoriously inhumane (Stampp, *Peculiar Institution*, 297). But sugar was not inevitably a man-killing crop. The Georgia low country had at least one humane and fairly fecund sugar plantation; see my *Goodbye to Uncle Tom*, p. 107.

10 Here used as in the West Indies, meaning "colonial-born." A St. Domingue-born white grandee was as much as "Creole" as his estate-born slave; one spoke of "Creole horses," a "Creole table" if locally made.

11 St. Kitts was actually first but remained a highly minor outpost of empire shared with the French until sugar cane from Barbados gave it a rich future.

12 Cf. Macmillan, *Warning*, 66-7. Handlin (*Race and Nationality*, 25) maintains that lack of room in any given island, preventing offers of land ownership as inducement to migrate, helped to check the growth of white population in the Islands; whereas Dixie had plenty of land to offer. He associates this with the eventual lower status of physical labor in the Islands as compared with Dixie; whence he derives, among other things, the special savageries of Island slavery. This certainly adds an interesting item to the list of factors maybe involved; it must also include the special inhumanities associated with large slave plantations; the economics of sugar; the specially poor quality of whites sent to the West Indies . . .

13 An exception might be Australia, now intelligent and enterprising in spite of having begun with the kinds of human discards earlier sent to the West Indies and the mainland colonies. But beginning in the 1830's Australia received many nondelinquents—youths looking for a chance, depressed but decent rustics and proletarians—heavily diluting the first mass of transported convicts.

14 The estates supporting the College worked 300-odd slaves under supervision of the Society for the Propagation of the Gospel—an anomaly much celebrated by antislaveryism (Edwards, *History*, II, 41); the slaves are said to have been neatly branded with "Society" as identification. Others were thus guilty: the Jacobin friars owned slaves on Martinique (Labat, *Voyage*, I, 515); the Moravian mission on St. Croix owned a plantation and presumably slaves to work it (Ramsay, *Essay*, 164).

15 Nowadays this significant use of the word "home" is strongest in Crown colonies, next strongest in New Zealand, next in Australia, next in the West Indies, hardly to be found in Canada.

16 Honorable exceptions were "Monk" Lewis and Sir William Young, both of whom have been cited above. Lewis' second trip to the Islands caused his death—of yellow fever on the return voyage. His will required future owners of his estates to visit them at least every three years for at least three months.

[17] This was the terminology of Jamaica and the Windwards. Elsewhere the overseer was called "manager" and the bookkeeper "overseer." (Mathieson, *British Slavery*, 61 *fn.*; J. Stephen, *Slavery*, I, 47, *fn.*)

[18] Mathieson (*British Slavery*, 103 *fn.*) says it was the smaller West Indian estates that treated the slaves worse. This may have something in it. Few or none would have been small enough for real personal master-slave relations.

[19] Stampp (*Peculiar Institution*, 330-1) points out that, though discipline was harsher and work harder on big gang-labor plantations, they also offered the slave the social advantages of great after-hours freedom from observation and general opportunity to work out his own life his own way. True enough; but this advantage was probably more than wiped out by the stultifying effect of isolation and lack of cross-cultural stimulus.

[20] Or "quildive," obviously cognate to "killdevil." Modern Haytians call raw rum "clairin"; in the Windwards I have heard it called "soldiers' rum." For reasons that I cannot learn French brandy was the issue spirits of the Royal Navy until, late in the 1700's, West Indian pressure got rum admitted as replacement (Ragatz, *Fall*, 165-6; 313). This ran counter to the mercantile ideas of the day and must have been inconvenient during long wars with France. There is a legend, by the way, that the rich flavor of the Demerara rums issued in today's Royal Navy comes of soaking Cayenne pepper and old sea boots in them as they age. The French West Indies were discouraged by their government from making rum, in order to favor the home brandy distiller. Sold to Yankee traders instead of being distilled, French molasses became the mainstay of New England's rum industry and one of the minor causes of friction that led to the Revolutionary War (Burn, *West Indies*, 69).

[21] There was much prurient talk about West Indian slaveowners "washing their families white" by incestuously begetting whiter and whiter offspring on their own mixed-blood daughters and granddaughters. No doubt there were rare instances of such goings-on but it can hardly have been part of the general pattern.

[22] James Stephen (*Slavery*, I, 31-2; 55) denies this marked cruelty among mixed-blood owners; he offers no evidence, just denies it. He knew Barbados and St. Kitts pretty well and must be taken seriously, but he is the only informed man to assert any such thing.

[23] Not that the ideal was always attained. Most sizable plantations occasionally bought supplementary staples. Some hard-driving Dixie

planters thought it best to follow the West Indian system and buy staple provisions from the farmers of the Middle West. But autarchy was the approved objective and a well run place often came near it.

[24] The old accounts show a few exceptions: Gildersleeve, an Abolitionist but probably reliable, saw Georgia slave women at work "with no other covering than a few filthy rags fastened above the hips . . ." (Weld, *Slavery*, 41.) Asa Stone was very definite about having seen "in the heat of the day . . . forty or fifty [Louisiana slaves] in a gang, men and women promiscuously together, naked as they were born," though they admitted having clothes available ("General Treatment . . . ," II, 30). This was sugar country, of course, and maybe further evidence of general lower standards on sugar plantations.

CHAPTER 6: *The Spartacus Complex*

[1] One such area is often called "The Land of Lookbehind" because, says legend, the commanders of troops operating against Maroons thereabouts put their men two to a horse, one facing backward for better observation in watching for signs of ambush.

[2] At least two Maroon hill settlements persist in Jamaica today. Enterprising tourists sometimes visit them. The people themselves, it appears, are hardly distinguishable from other upcountry Jamaican Negroes, but some vestiges of the old proud ways, even some of the old language, are said to linger beneath the visible surface.

[3] The latest instance of this peculiarly horrible "exemplary punishment" that I can find was the hanging of a slave ringleader in chains on Dominica in 1784 (J. Stephan, *Slavery*, I, 309-10).

[4] This hyperacute color consciousness is evident in the fact that St. Dominigue developed a terminology expressing degrees of racial mixture far more elaborate than that of any other slave culture; Moreau de Saint-Mery (*Description*, I, 71-5) lists them interminably: "mulâtre, quarteron, métif, mamelouque, quarteronné, sang-mêlé, griffe, sacatra, marabou . . ."

[5] For a significant parallel note G. M. Young's statement (*Victorian England*, 214 *fn.*) that the color bar between English and East Indians was very weak at first but "grew firmer as easier communications brought women in increasing numbers to India."

[6] Generalizations about West Indian slavery as it affected world opinion need not obscure local variations. By and large the best of it seems to have been the Danish regime in the Virgin Islands; next, the Spanish

regime in Cuba, Puerto Rico and Santo Domingo, notable for humane provisions for freedom-buying and for maintaining a majority of whites; Cuba's sugar boom after Waterloo badly damaged the beneficent system there. Observe that, though Martinique and Guadaloupe were no paradises for slaves, they were consistently better than St. Domingue.

[7] This syncretion seems much to have accelerated after Haytian freedom. Catholic lore came in with the French missionaries, of whom some, like Father Labat, were able. But slaves' contacts with them were meager and Catholic leverage on them minor, unlike that of the Dissenting missionaries in such islands as Antigua and Jamaica.

[8] For several intervals Haytian governments broke Spanish control of the eastern two-thirds of Hispaniola and nominally or actually ran the whole. But there was never much future in attempts to blend French big-estate and Spanish sloppy-ranching traditions. The story of Hayti's agony can be understood well enough without reference to matters outside her present boundaries.

[9] In 1838 the American Anti-Slavery Society sent two agents to Hayti to secure data showing Negro capacity for self-government. Their report was never published presumably because what they saw in Hayti failed to support the thesis (Barnes & Dumond, *Weld-Grimké Letters*, II, 663 *fn*). In 1819 British antislaveryites encouraged Christophe to negotiate with Americans hoping to send freed slaves or free-born Negroes to Hayti; his death aborted the scheme (Griggs, *Christophe . . . 68*). Benjamin Lundy personally took several parties of newly freed slaves there in the 1820's and 1830's. The notion revived in the late 1850's; Redpath, Old Brown's windy ally, was involved, visiting Hayti twice; the second time his companion was F. J. Merriam, the young enthusiast who joined Old Brown just before Harpers Ferry. The scheme involved Episcopalian Negro missionaries. The hierarchy thus founded in Hayti is now a lively constructive force in a place badly needing such. Otherwise the scanty migration ended in disillusion and has left traces only in certain family names surviving among the élite. (Leyburn, *Haitian People*, 261-2; et al.)

[10] Whittier put this favorite theme of Bourne's rather juicily into verse in his apostrophe to Toussaint:

> "*And on the night-air, wild and clear,*
> *Rose woman's shriek of more than fear;*
> *For bloodied arms were round her thrown,*
> *And dark cheeks pressed against her own!*
> *Then, injured Afric! for the shame*

Of thy own daughters, vengeance came
Full on the scornful hearts of those,
Who mocked thee in thy nameless woes,
And to thy hapless children gave
One choice—pollution or the grave! . . ."

Works, III, 17

It is sometimes hard to understand why the Society of Friends persist in taking credit for Friend Whittier.

[11] Believers in the ever-present-menace theory of slave risings in Dixie often excuse the scantiness of the record by adducing Southern reluctance to publicize sporadic incidents. True, many small local troubles, often the equivalent of impromptu strikes, may have been hushed up to avoid giving other slaves ideas. But journal keepers and letter writers with no thought of publication would have had no motive for omitting news of such painful interest, and scholars find very little mention of such episodes in surviving papers.

[12] Epilepsy is clinically associated with eccentricity often near the psychopathic. Vesey's case sounds as if his disease had changed its nature as he aged: the fits may have ceased to occur but the psychic lesion remained and deepened, furthering his change from smiling, docile servant to domestic tyrant and dreamer of vengeful, self-aggrandizing dreams.

[13] Abolitionists usually knew the Vesey story well; quite possibly this is what gave Old Brown the notion of arming rebel slaves with pikes.

[14] This must have been residue from the Revolution and the War of 1812, during which Royal Navy commanders did persuade a good many slaves to come aboard for transport to freedom in Nova Scotia or the West Indies. Visitors to Trinidad (*e.g.,* Coleridge, Kingsley) in the early and mid-1800's found survivors of these emigrants. Another group turned up at Samana Bay, in what is now Santo Domingo, and were still distinguishable from the rest of the population only a generation ago.

[15] Mrs. Dorothy Heyward's play based on the Vesey incident, *Set My People Free,* was produced by the Theatre Guild in 1948 with Canada Lee in the cast, running only thirty-six performances. Its alterations of fact, maybe necessary for dramatic purposes, mar the feral grimness of the actuality and—inevitably—make Vesey treacherously kidnaped from Africa by white men.

[16] Verbatim from Turner's first-person confession said to have been freely given, taken down in his presence and read to him for approval. His admirers and detractors agree to take it as substantially correct;

certainly its spirit is appropriately paranoid. The examiner must have tricked it up with bookish rhetoric, however; Turner was intelligent and a famously eloquent preacher but it is highly unlikely that he knew any such words as "hieroglyphic."

[17] Like the Jamaica slaves who, armed and mustered to go fight Tackey's rebels, touched their caps to master and marched off to join Tackey but without hurting a hair of master's head (Long, *History*, pp. 447-62). It was not true that, as Higginson sillily wrote (*Atlantic Monthly*, August, 1861) the slaves were "all swift to transform themselves into fiends of retribution." On the Whitehead place, for instance, only three out of forty went with Turner (Blackford, *Mine Eyes*, 25-7).

[18] There may possibly have been some connection between Turner's ideas and the call for Negro slave rebellion issued not long before in a most inflammatory pamphlet, *Walker's Appeal*, published by David Walker, a free Negro of Boston, some copies of which were are known to have got into Virginia, North Carolina and Tennessee. Turner would probably have done all he did, however, if Walker had never existed.

[19] This does not include the curiously few cases of whites (Seth Concklin, John Fairfield, Alexander Ross *et al.*) penetrating Dixie to persuade slaves to take the Underground Railroad. It does include Boxley's private rebellion in Virginia in 1816 (Aptheker, *Slave Revolts*, 255) and the Murrell episode of 1835 (Coates, *Outlaw Years*, 169-301; Nye, *Baker's Dozen*, 116-37).

[20] Thus it makes great play with a really silly bit of melodrama about two Negro men slaves on St. Kitts, intimate friends, who both fell in love with the same slave girl so passionately that they killed her to make sure that neither enjoyed her to the exclusion of the other, and then both committed suicide over her dead body. Presented by Raynal as sober fact, this tale actually comes out of Addison's *Spectator*, No. 215, where its validity is most airily vouched for as from such a source that the author has "no manner of reason to suspect the truth of it." The anecdote became a favorite of antislaveryites. Kotzebue worked it almost verbatim into his Abolitionist flavored *Die Negersklaven*.

[21] Contemporary pictures show Forrest retaining his mustache and goatee for all roles, regardless of incongruity, except that of Metamora, the noble savage Indian, who apparently held out for being smooth shaven. How Forrest worked this out in day-to-day repertory acting I do not know.

[22] The eighteenth-century biography of Mrs. Behn, including most of what is known of her, is said to be spurious. Her text mentions a Surinam "tiger" the size of a heifer and depicts Negroes blushing, which leaves room for doubting she ever visited Surinam. Two data are reliable, however: she was daughter of a barber, though claiming gentle birth, and was buried in Westminster Abbey (Baker, *Novels of Aphra Behn,* viii-ix).

[23] Of which Mrs. Behn, whose own morals were probably no better than they should be, had the usual low opinion: "Rogues and renagades, that have abandoned their countries for rapine, murder, theft and villainies." (Baker, *Novels of Aphra Behn,* xiii-iv.)

[24] Dr. Moseley (*Treatise,* 197) said that he had inspected Jack's Obeah equipment as shown to him by Reeder's comrades: it consisted of the end of a goat's horn filled with a mixture of grave dirt, the blood of a black cat and human fat; also a bag containing a cat's foot, a pig's tail and a slip of kidskin parchment marked with characters in human blood. The doctor, the most detailed source on Jack, does seem to have been in Jamaica at the time. But he may not have been the most reliable of witnesses; certainly one would like to ask him what analysis available in 1781 made it so sure that the fat and blood were human.

[25] This further betrays how little these dramatists knew of the actualities of West Indian slavery. A Jamaican slave even suspected of hoping to rape his owner's wife would have had nothing to look forward to but a very painful and probably lingering death.

[26] "Transpontine" because such stuff was the staple of the cheap, popular theaters on the Surrey side of the Thames, hence across bridges from the dearer—and presumably more dignified—houses of London proper. Such melodramas became a self-contained school of half-baked drama, like soap opera or Grade B Westerns. Stevenson's "Penny Plain . . ." gives the flavor.

CHAPTER 7: *A Man and a Brother*

[1] The geography is muddled Park, and names that Park used crop up here: Daisy for the King of Kaarta, for instance. Note that Jack is sometimes called Karfa on the stage; and that *Karfa* was sometimes the main title of the piece in the billing; this is the name of the kindly slave trader who befriended Park.

[2] Thus in *Philip* Thackeray has a caricature of the kneeling Negro used to discredit a touched-with-the-tarbrush West Indian candidate

for a seat in Parliament. In *Martin Chuzzlewit* Mark Tapley refers to it as a matter of universal acceptance when identifying for Martin the former slave hired to carry their baggage in New York.

3 One of these inconveniences was soon manifest. For many of the thousands of Negroes in England thus suddenly enabled to leave master if they chose and deprived of the capital value that made it to master's interest to maintain them, the decision was a mixed blessing. The genuine misery among the resulting little clumps of free Negroes in the great towns of England moved Sharp and others years later to found Sierra Leone colony as refuge for them.

4 "Should we [antislaveryites] address ourselves to the public at large? . . . It may inflame the world against the guilty, but that is not likely to remove the guilt. Should we appeal to the English nation in general? That also is striking wide. As little would it avail . . . to apply to the parliament. So many things, which seem of greater importance, lie before them, that they are not likely to attend to this." (*Thoughts on Slavery,* 19-21.)

5 Nelson's tone was typical: ". . . neither in the field nor in [Parliament] shall [West Indian] rights be infringed while I have an arm to fight in their defence or a tongue to launch my voice against the damnable, cruel doctrine of Wilberforce and his hypocritical allies . . . who would certainly cause the murder of all our friends and fellow-subjects in the Colonies." (Knutsford, *Macaulay,* 258 *fn.*) Colonel Banastre Tarleton of American Revolution fame was also hot anti-antislavery. General Burgoyne, the loser at Saratoga, voted against the Trade. Otherwise brass on the antislavery side consisted of two undistinguished major-generals and three Royal Navy captains; but antislavery witnesses at Parliamentary inquiries usually included numerous ratings and some junior officers.

6 Two in the *Tartar,* one in the *Amelia,* both under command of a Captain Frazer who, shipping men told Clarkson, was the only slaver captain who had not long deserved hanging; Falconbridge confirmed that he was humane. The fourth voyage was in the *Alexander,* which Falconbridge and his mate both described independently as a genuine floating hell.

7 Eventually Clarkson found a partial answer to all this: a wealthy M.P. conspicuous in the antislavery cause named Whitbread undertook to relieve hardships resulting from these retaliations.

8 The rather fatuous flavor of the *Amis des Noirs* is clear in la Fayette's reaction to hearing that Mirabeau had this plan: such a speech from

that man might accomplish its purpose, he said, "yet I regret he has taken the lead in it. The cause [of antislaveryism] is so lovely that even ambition . . . is too impure . . . not to sully it. It should have been placed in the hands of the most virtuous man in France . . . la Rochefoucauld." (Clarkson, *History*, II, 99-133.)

9 La Fayette even accepted an honorary commission as commanding general of the putative armed forces of St. Domingue's *affranchis*.

10 Its lovely oval library (see sketch in Forster, *Marianne Thornton*, opp. p. 19) was designed by William Pitt for his friend Henry.

11 The quickest way to get the feel of Evangelicalism is to read George Eliot's *Scenes of Clerical Life*, especially "Janet's Repentance."

12 The tract, *The Washerwoman of Finchley Common*, so conspicuous in *Vanity Fair*, comes of Miss More's famous *Shepherd of Salisbury Plain*.

13 Whatever it may mean, the first generation of British antislaveryites included a strangely high proportion of men from either Scotland or the North Country: Macaulay, Ramsay, Stephen, Grant all were Scots; Brougham virtually so. Sharp was from Durham, Wilberforce from Yorkshire.

14 Dickens paid his respects to the successors of the Clapham Sect in his reproaching John Jarndyce of *Bleak House* with overtoleration of circles where "Benevolence took spasmodic forms . . . charity was assumed, as regular uniform, by loud professors and speculators in cheap notoriety . . . adulatory of one another, and intolerable to those . . . anxious quietly to help the weak from falling rather than with a great deal of bluster and self-importance to raise them up a little way when they were down." He may also have been thinking of the notorious fecklessness of the Wilberforce household—Cousin William's wife was devout and earnest but a poor manager—in the dirt and confusion surrounding Mrs. Jellyby as she promoted that benevolent settlement at Borioboola Gha on the banks of the Niger. Certainly her schemes reflect Buxton's ill-fated Niger project of the 1840's.

15 Samuel Johnson made the same point—about the only one on which he and Paine could conceivably have agreed. At about the same time the notion of Divine retribution for slavery was strongly set forth by General James Oglethorpe, the high-minded founder of Georgia and crusader against press gangs: "The ruins of Babylon," he wrote to Granville Sharp in 1776, "Memphis and Tyre are strong mementoes to a Paris, a London, and a Lisbon, of the retributions paid to those who fat their luxuries on the labour of wretched slaves." (Hoare, *Sharp*,

156.) Early American antislaveryites, such as the Rev. Dr. Samuel Hopkins and Dr. Benjamin Rush held similar views.

[16] Zachary Macaulay, who knew plantation management firsthand, was aghast at learning that government had included elimination of the overseer's whip as an item in this schedule of reforms. He knew the symbolical value of the whip in both West African and colonial terms and feared that, if it disappeared by government fiat, the slaves would jump to the conclusion that absolute freedom had been granted and would become uncontrollable.

[17] Wilberforce and his colleagues did what they could, as veteran politicians, to make advantage for antislaveryism out of the East India Company's hopes that antislavery measures would cripple West Indian sugar and cotton—which, in spite of antislaveryites' assurances to the contrary, was exactly what came of Emancipation. It was good antislavery propaganda as well as good logrolling to promote abstinence from West Indian sugar and rum in favor of East Indian products. Economic determinists often suggest that all this connects with the presence of several men among the Saints with close ties with the East India Company. Particularly Dr. Eric Williams, now premier of Trinidad, has done an adept Marxist's best to derive the success of British antislaveryism primarily from such influence plus the dwindling importance of the West Indies relative to other parts of the Empire. That such leverages existed is extremely likely. But, as often happens when Marxists depend on the naïve psychology of the cult, the emphases are far off balance.

[18] Though hot against slavery in his writings on America, Dickens preferred to satirize British antislaveryism: "O my young friend," said Mr. Stiggins, the unctuous splinter-sectarian, to Sam Weller, "who else [than Sam's scoffing father] could have resisted the pleadings of sixteen of our fairest sisters . . . to subscribe to our noble society for providing the infant negroes in the West Indies with flannel waistcoats and moral pocket handkerchiefs?" The elder Weller, it appeared, had merely "sat and smoked his pipe and said the infant negroes were— what did he say the infant negroes were?' 'Infant humbugs,' said Mr. Stiggins, deeply affected."

[19] This account of Thompson follows G. Stephen, *Antislavery Recollections*, 50-2, rather than May, *Recollections*, 109-112. Stephen was unkind about Thompson, in describing how he did badly in Parliament because he lacked the indicated gentlemanly background, but he was on hand when the Committee hired the man and directed his English activities. May's information probably came wholly from

Thompson and has many suspect details. The question how he could afford costly elocution lessons on his wages may have a hint of solution: Anti-Abolitionists in the States published intimations that he had been in trouble for embezzlement in England as a youth. In a letter to Angelina Grimké he confessed that he had somehow made unauthorized use of eighty pounds "entrusted to my care. I need say nothing of my temptations or intentions at the time." Anyway it was "a grievous wrong" that he had since made right by repayment, plus seventy pounds more from a sense of moral obligation, and "My former master is now my friend." (Barnes & Dumond, *Weld-Grimké Letters*, II, 775-6.)

CHAPTER 8: *Borrowed Plumage*

[1] To avoid verbal clutter, from here on this book uses "Abolitionism" to mean *American* organized antislavery agitation as distinguished from such activity elsewhere. "Emancipationism" will mean only the post-Waterloo British movement avowedly looking to full freedom for all slaves in the British Empire.

[2] In view of Bourne's general unsavory tone, it is not surprising that he was also a leader in the Catholic-baiting of the time and author of *Lorette, the History of Louise, Daughter of a Canadian Nun, Exhibiting the Interior of Female Convents*. But then in a slightly less lip-licking way, the same was true of, among others, the Rev. Dr. Lyman Beecher and Elijah Lovejoy, the Abolitionist martyr of Alton, Ill.

[3] Here is a constitutional curiosity. Islands with their own elected legislatures (*i.e.,* Jamaica, St. Kitts, Barbados . . .) retained much the same relation to the Crown and Parliament that Virginia and Massachusetts had in 1774. Their case for resisting being legislated for without being allowed to send representatives to Parliament could have been identical. But three things made a great difference: The matter came up forty-six years later; the white populations of such islands was far too small for any revolutionary purpose; and throughout the struggle against the Trade and slavery, the West Indies had, and everybody knew they had, a powerful and effective bloc of votes and immense leverage in both Houses.

[4] Birney did better than most: "If a man were hired to kill a den of venomous snakes, it would show that he was insane if he jumped into the den." (Birney, *Birney,* 370.) But he would look little better if all he did was to stand on the edge out of reach and scream at them.

Keep in mind, of course, that, as champion of antislaveryism in northern Alabama and then Kentucky, Birney had earned his spurs several times over.

5 Barnes, *Anti-Slavery Impulse,* traces the close relation between this prevalent equation of slaveholding with sin and the doctrines, methods and personalities of C. G. Finney's Great Revival of the 1820's and so on. The book makes an unimpeachable case. It may be suggested, however, that even had there been no Great Revival, had Tappan, Weld, Leavitt *et al.* never applied its terms and methods to promote antislaveryism, American antislaveryites might well have picked this approach up from the British preceptors on whom they always leaned. The whole thing is well spelled out in the writings of Wesley, Newton, Clarkson and James Stephen, all antedating Finney. It is very difficult to keep King Charles' head out of this book.

6 She often attended Abolitionist meetings in and about Boston and talked interminably from the platform, discussing the Bible and anything else that came into her head, attributing most evils to "the capitalists." Meticulous respect for free speech caused the Garrisonians to let her talk whenever possible. But once, when three of their leaders felt it necessary to carry her out of the hall, she gigglingly told the audience that, whereas Christ had only one jackass to carry him she had three (Johnson, *Garrison,* p. 332).

7 Noyes taught that special virtue attached to more or less promiscuous intercourse (but only if utterly voluntary) which long training enabled the male partner to prolong almost indefinitely without orgasm; or so they said. Noyes thought of it as combining birth control with an erotic sacrament never allowed to degenerate into either culminating lust or the specifically prohibited sin of Onan.

8 "Temperance" alone might challenge this. But some Reformers doubted the intrinsic sinfulness of tippling; whereas I know of nobody conceivably classed as Reformer who was not antislavery.

9 It was applied to Old Brown and not inaccurately. He showed very few signs of general interest in "causes." He was anti-tobacco, perhaps partly from thrift, and his guerrilla companies had rules against alcohol, but that was partly good judgment and partly the respectability of the day.

10 E.g., Barnes *Anti-Slavery Impulse* (1933); Barnes and Dumond, *Letters of Theodore Dwight Weld* (1934); Nye, *William Lloyd Garrison . . .* (1955).

[11] Founded in 1816 by eminent men such as Henry Clay, James Monroe, Francis Scott Key, the American Colonization Society and its several state branches (*e.g.*, New York, Maryland, Ohio, Mississippi) drew support and funds from many early antislaveryites such as the Tappans, Gerrit Smith, Lyman Beecher. It aimed to colonize free Negroes in West Africa (1) to free them from the handicaps imposed on them by color prejudice in the States; (2) to create foci of legitimate trade in West Africa to wean the area away from slave trading; (3) to show Negroes could take care of themselves; (4) to encourage freeing of slaves by providing a sound future for freed Negroes; (5) to rid the South of free Negroes as potential enticers of runaways and fomenters of revolt. In the 1820's the movement was strongly attacked, specially by Charles Stuart, as distraction from the Immediatist cause. In 1832 Garrison, drawing much from Stuart's work, published his *Thoughts on Colonization,* which accused the Society of hypocritically hoping to keep up the price of slaves by removing surplus Negroes from the South and of being futile anyway, since it could never export even the annual increase in Negro population. The latter point was indisputable; otherwise Abolitionist attack on the movement and its sponsors was often fantastically abusive. As it gradually lost acceptance many supporters—*e.g.*, Smith, Weld, Birney, the Tappans—dropped it in the early 1830's.

[12] Knapp seems to have been an excellent printer and, while it lasted, highly loyal to Garrison. But he was also given sporadically to drink and, as years passed, the relation became less and less edifying with threatening letters to Garrison hoping to raise money for a suffering family . . .

[13] Notable exceptions: Weld, Birney (less definitely), Thaddeus Stevens . . . But only Garrisonians thought that seeing the Negro as a potentially equal human being was essential to right antislavery feeling. May once told some Boston anti-antislaveryites: ". . . we Abolitionists are not so foolish as to . . . wish that ignorant Negroes should be considered wise . . . vicious negroes . . . considered virtuous, poor negroes . . . considered rich . . . All we demand is that negroes shall be permitted, encouraged, assisted to become as wise, virtuous, and as rich as they can, and be acknowledged to be just what they have become, and be treated accordingly." (*Recollections,* 29.)

[14] And often conveyed such delusions to his clique. In 1835 Mrs. Child, reflecting his reaction to the burning of antislavery papers in Charleston, wrote to Mrs. Loring from Brooklyn, N.Y., that she wouldn't dare cross to Manhattan, where it was like "the French Revolution . . . Private assassins from New Orleans are lurking at the corners of the

streets to stab Arthur Tappan . . . large sums are offered for anyone who will convey Mr. [George] Thompson into the slave states . . . He is almost a close prisoner in his chamber." A brother-in-law of Garrison's was also writing that "there are those in Boston who would assassinate [Thompson] in broad daylight." (Garrison, *Garrison*, II, 490-1.)

15 J. G. Birney's biographer son, who saw plenty of anti-Abolitionist rioting as a youth, rightly deplored the militants' tendency to make these occasions sound much more numerous and far more violent than they actually were. Serious injury was very rare indeed; and he estimated that in Ohio, at the height of the trouble, hardly one meeting in a hundred was disturbed (Birney, *Birney*, 230-3).

16 Most of them went to provide a student body for Oberlin College and took some of Beecher's faculty along. Oberlin immediately became famous for admitting women and Negroes as well as for being a hotbed of Abolitionism and a developing station on the Underground Railroad.

17 Son Frederick also became a distinguished lawyer and jurist as a member of the Ohio Supreme Court. He wrote *The Nature and Tendency of Free Institutions,* which Barnes (*Anti-Slavery Impulse,* 270) called "the most penetrating criticism of abolitionist doctrine that I have found in contemporary literature."

18 Whittier managed to stay in the good graces of Friends by leaving the room before the actual ceremony began.

19 Lucy Stone was an early and pretty consistent bloomer wearer. Sarah and Angelina adopted it late, toward the end of the farm period, as better suited than trailing skirts for country life, but were never very militant about it (Birney, *Grimkes,* 281-2).

20 The wife of Marcus Spring, head of this colony, went to Charlestown to nurse Old Brown in jail. While there she promised Hazlitt and Stevens that their bodies would find graves at the colony. The burials were duly made in the spring of 1860 after some trouble with local anti-Brown rowdies. There is no record of what Weld thought of Old Brown's exploit. Sarah much admired it; she called him "the John Huss of the United States" and wrote to a friend: "Last night I went in spirit to see the martyr. It was my privilege to enter into sympathy with him . . . to feel his past exercises, his present sublime position." (Birney, *Grimkés,* 282.)

21 Redpath said that Realf's testifying made him "dead to honor" and prophesied that he would play "the part of Judas" well. Ambrose

Bierce professed to take most seriously the three sonnets that Realf left to justify his suicide: "Here lies a great soul killed by cruel wrong . . ." is the only line in them in which I can see much significance, and that is clinical. Realf had victimized Bierce, as he had other editors previously, by selling him as new verses some of his that had already appeared elsewhere (McDevitt, *Bierce . . . Realf*, 6-9).

[22] As witness he received over $600 in traveling and *per diem* expenses. It is an especially curious detail of the Old Brown story that soon after leaving Washington, Realf met two of the fugitives from Harpers Ferry in Cleveland and gave them several hundred dollars of this money of the Senate's to help them escape outside Federal jurisdiction.

CHAPTER 9: *The Secret Six*

[1] Whether it was Garrison's influence or not, Old Brown seems to have had a period of "non-resistance" convictions. Dr. Arny, who claimed to have known him in western Virginia c. 1839-40, told the Senate investigation of 1860 about the old man's non-resistance Abolition talk of that time (Mason Committee, 72). And there was an earlier bit of gossip about his taking a threshing without striking back in his tanning days in Pennsylvania because he claimed to cleave to non-resistant principles (*McClure's Magazine*, January 1898, pp. 278-82). To whatever extent it was real, such feeling could not forever resist his aggressive temperament.

[2] In an 1896 letter (Siebert Papers, Houghton Library) Higginson called this craft *Maria* and described how information about fugitives on shipboard was obtained through a Negro woman going out in a boat to sell fruit and pies to incoming ships' crews.

[3] After all the hifalutin talk and fine print about Old Brown it is refreshing to come on Mrs. Montgomery's summary of the Abolitionist Free Stater's position in its basic terms as she saw them: "I do get plumb tired of being shot at but I won't be druv out." (Villard, 350.)

[4] The boys here took their lead from Old Brown, who had given this same reason for refusing a previous projected rescue. But the old man by then actively craved being hanged; whereas these youngsters stood to gain little by martyrdom and to lose a great deal.

[5] Early in 1861 Congressman Vallandigham of Ohio (later a Copperhead leader) introduced a proposed Constitutional amendment setting up separate divisions of the Senate and Electoral College to give a veto on selection of presidents, ratification of treaties, etc., to each of four

semi-autonomous sections of the nation: North, South, West, and Pacific Coast (*Dict. Am. Biog.*).

6 Even so it is amazing that a professional historian dealing with Old Brown in 1924 (*American Mercury,* March, 1924) should have identified Howe with Elias Howe, inventor of the sewing machine.

7 In her final phases, when she was an American institution, much as Mrs. Eleanor Roosevelt is now, Mrs. Howe refused to admit that she had ever said, when her eye caught the name of Boston's Charitable Eye and Ear Infirmary: "Oh! I did not know that there was a charitable eye or ear in Boston!" (Richards *et al., Julia Ward Howe,* 129.) The above account of the marriage is on my own responsibility; the data come mostly from standard biographies of both parties, the most recent being Tharp, *Three Saints and a Sinner;* Schwarz, *Samuel Gridley Howe.* I doubt if either author would agree with all of it. I omit as, in my judgment, impertinent the prolonged episode late in Dr. Howe's career that unworthily involved him in corruption-flavored schemes to take over Santo Domingo. It seems to me that only senility can explain the worse aspects of this business, hence it has little to do with the essential Howe who went to Greece and taught Laura Bridgman and backed Old Brown.

8 An able biographer calls both Howe and his intimate, Charles Sumner, "patronizing when agreed with, but wild with rage, contemptuous, and vituperative when opposed . . . Everyone who disagreed with them they characterized as maliciously inspired, and incapable of ever acting in good faith on any matter." (Schwarz, *Howe,* 149.)

9 The American Museum of Natural History advise me that this is one form of a familiar bit of folklore of which no proof known to them has ever been brought; they think it may have arisen either from the great reduction in size of squirrel testicles after the breeding season or from observed damage actually due to botfly. My interest in it comes not so much from distress for the squirrels as from wondering what it may mean about Parker that he so embroidered the old tale. He could be really glib about Jews: ". . . their intellect . . . sadly pinched in those narrow foreheads . . . cruel, also . . . I doubt not that they did sometimes kill a Christian baby at the Passover . . . also lecherous; no language on earth . . . so rich in terms for sexual mixing . . . What mouths they have!—full of voluptuousness; only the negro beats them there . . ." (Frothingham, *Theodore Parker,* 467.) This smells as if the late Josef Goebbels had just passed by. But a century ago such irresponsible absurdities about ethnic groups were common

among educated persons of greater latitude of spirit than Parker's; so, one may add, was a sort of innocent anti-Semitism such as that shown by Thackeray and Dickens.

10 Higginson, a mere journeyman at best, saw fit to patronize Parker as stylist (*Contemporaries*, 51). I do not put forward the extracts in this text as adequate samples of Parker's best writing. Try this from his *Experience as a Minister:* "It is not for me to say that there is no limit to the possible attainments of man's religious or other faculties. I will not dogmatize where I do not know. But history shows that the Hercules' pillars of one age are sailed through the next, and a wide ocean entered on, which in due time is found rich with islands of its own, and washing a vast continent not dreamed of by such as slept within their temples old, while it sent to their very coasts its curious joints of unwonted cane, and even elaborate boats, wherein lay the starved bodies of strange-featured men, with golden jewels in their ears."

11 One of his more definite complaints was hemorrhoids; Angelina Grimké once gave him a horse chestnut and assurance that to carry it in his pocket would relieve this trouble (Harlow, *Gerrit Smith*, 36).

12 When the panic of 1837 found Gerrit Smith most dangerously over-extended in credits to land purchasers, Astor lent Peter Smith's son a huge sum to tide over with (Frothingham, *Gerrit Smith*, 89).

13 Reformism was often much of a family matter on both sides of the Atlantic: Elizabeth (Cady) Stanton, women's rights leader, was Gerrit Smith's first cousin. His second wife's sister married J. G. Birney, the Alabama slaveholder-Abolitionist. His daughter Elizabeth (Miller) helped create the "Bloomer" garb of baggy trousers and smock promoted by Mrs. Amelia Bloomer and Lucy Stone. All, of course, showed the Abolitionist symptom of the syndrome.

14 Stearns, *George Luther Stearns*, 101, states this without further elaboration. Evidence or not, it is a nice detail.

15 Four of the Six—Smith, Higginson, Stearns, Sanborn—lost their first wives early. This is no sinister coincidence; it merely indicates the hazards of being a woman in even the upper strata of the America of the mid-1800's.

16 Sanborn (*Life & Letters*, 510) had it from Mrs. Stearns that Stearns gave Brown a check for $7000 then and there; Russell confirmed it (Stearns, *Stearns*, 159). F. P. Stearns had good reason, however, to believe that the paper then changing hands was some sort of open letter

of credit authorizing Brown to draw on Stearns from time to time for sums totaling $7000.

17 He did not remarry until 1862, when he espoused a cousin, Louisa Augusta Leavitt. It is very strange that his autobiography says nothing whatever about Louisa, though painfully full about Ariana. This may somehow be connected with Sanborn's later sense of guilt about not having fought in the Civil War, since the 1862 marriage may somehow have kept him out of uniform. Still our forebears of that day did not have our ideas about military service for all being indicated in a crisis, other things being equal.

18 This may not have been altogether convenient pretext. Montgomery Blair, one of the shrewdest public men of his time, took this risk seriously in advising Old Brown's counsel (Hinton, *John Brown,* 372).

19 Soon after Harpers Ferry Higginson suggested for his own epitaph: "The only one of John Brown's friends and admirers who was not frightened by the silly threats of Hugh Forbes into desiring that year's delay which ruined the enterprise." (Higginson, *Higginson,* 199-200.)

20 Soon after Harpers Ferry Higginson spoke with Charles P. Tidd, who had escaped with the farmhouse garrison. He told Higginson that Harpers Ferry was "the only mistake Brown ever made" and "attributed it, as now [*i.e.,* the 1890's] generally assigned to a final loss of mental balance from overbrooding on one idea." (Higginson, *Yesterdays,* 228-9.) Tidd died of disease in 1862 in the Federal army.

21 So far as I know Higginson was not mentioned in the papers left at the farmhouse base; his name first cropped up in Realf's testimony for the Mason Committee. Yet poor as Virginia's intelligence work was, it was rightly taken for granted that both state and Federal authorities knew Higginson was deep in the thing.

22 Much later Mrs. Stearns maintained that her husband would never have gone to Canada at all if Howe had not besought him for his company, representing himself as "in delicate health and constitutionally subject to violent attacks of nervous headaches" and likely to go insane under the strain of the aftermath of Harpers Ferry unless he got away and Stearns went along to look after him. Her account of all this (Hinton, *John Brown,* 726) is rather ambiguous, however, and, sparing the lady's presence, she was not the most reliable of witnesses.

23 A news story of a Harpers Ferry sentry causing a night alarm by firing on a stray cow set Redpath versifying—a bad habit of his:
"No wizard's hand to raise a band
    Of patriots long since dead need we,

To keep our flag and take the brag
  Out of the Southern chivalry.
Ah, no! To save that fragile form,—
  The Union,—or to lull the storm
Of Civil Wars when they impend,
  A simple course I recommend:
Crush the Slave States? With blood imbrue them?
  No! drive a herd of oxen through them."

(Echoes, 300)

The actual incident is confirmed in Harper's Weekly, Dec. 13, 1859, and Avery, Capture and Execution.

[24] The significance of this disastrous book is developed in my Goodbye to Uncle Tom (1956).

[25] Outside the circle of professed Abolitionists Victor Hugo committed the greatest absurdity about Old Brown: After hearing a rumor that the execution had been postponed, he wrote an open letter to the London press demanding clemency for him; he did not explain how publication in England would further that end. The letter describes Old Brown's trial in terms confusing the original arraignment with the actual trial and accusing the court of condemning Old Brown and three followers to death after only forty minutes' deliberation; it mentions two utterly apocryphal cannon set up in court "with an order to the jailer to shoot the prisoners in case of an attempted rescue"; and has an inimitable Hugo flourish toward the end: ". . . something more terrible than Cain slaying Abel—it is Washington slaying Spartacus." The particular beauty of it all is that Hugo was so little familiar with what he was talking about that his draft manuscript of the letter calls his hero "Georges Brown." (Princeton University Library Chronicle, Winter, 1953, pp. 94-6.)

EPILOGUE: The Most Dangerous -Ism

[1] Parker's journal actually interprets this as taken by him to mean "men who claimed a divine mission for themselves." (Weiss, Parker, 125.) The sense is much the same, and Frothingham is crisper.

[2] The Federal government's power over the District slave trade was sometimes denied by Southerners, yet it was readily swallowed in return for Northern concessions in the Compromise of 1850.

[3] Minor efforts to this end continued off and on from the 1780's right up to the Civil War on both sides of the Atlantic. In the States it got farthest among Quakers.

4 I have no notion that, inflamed as things were by 1839, these amendments ever stood a chance of going to the states for ratification. The
point, however, is the Abolitionists' slavish dogmatism in denying them
support, if only as a means of propaganda. Consider too that it eventually required constitutional amendment after the Civil War permanently and universally to free American slaves.

5 Known as "the learned blacksmith," this self-made Yankee was prominent in the "peace movement" and in agitation for cheaper transatlantic postage, a minor Reform popular because of its hands-across-
the-sea promise of better international relations.

APPENDIX

1 A technique thought to have come, however indirectly, from Egypt
to Guinea. Wax is molded into the desired shape over a clay core, then
the wax is coated with a clay shell, leaving a small hole at top leading
to the uppermost wax and another at bottom leading out from the
nethermost wax. Molten metal poured in at top melts the wax pro-
gressively downward till all has run out at the bottom. For very small
castings no cores are needed.

2 This word is much to be mistrusted, of course, but it is still too much
used to be suppressed, particularly in such contexts as this. Take it
here as meaning: "Pertaining to a culture that has yet to develop the
art of writing and the extensive utilization of non-muscular power."
It should not be used, though it often is, to imply an idyllically spontaneous simplicity of ways of doing. Its other fault is that, unless
carefully limited as above, it falsely implies the old primitive/bar-
baric/civilized social evolution that now needs such heavy modification.

3 Within limits this process probably has some validity, of course. The
cult of Japanese art, for instance, did a good deal for Western painting late in the nineteenth century. There may be a useful analogy in
the anthropological theory that cultures receive a sort of "hybrid vigor"
stimulus when impinged on by alien cultures for considerable periods.
We have already noted above the Negro kingdoms of the upper Niger
as possible instances of this. But there is also great justification for the
cumulative harshness of Gorer's comment: "In common with most
people today I find a great deal of negro sculpture extremely stimulating and satisfying aesthetically; the strange compositions, distortions,
and symmetry . . . revolutionized the European conception of painting and sculpture in the first decade of this century; but I am certain
that for the negroes these qualities, with the possible exception of

symmetry, were entirely accidental and irrelevant; their chief object
was to communicate as vividly as possible. As for the 'abstract art'
which was evolved from it—the academic cul-de-sac which, after three
years of exciting scientific discoveries became a refuge for frightened
but pretentious decorators with no idea beyond a pattern—and which
was fathered on to the unfortunate negro, such an idea had never
occurred to them." (*Africa Dances,* 309.)

4 "Primitive Art" in *Encyclopaedia of Social Sciences*. Kroeber distin-
guishes, however, between "truly primitive arts growing up in isolation
or in contact only with others of the same kind, and derivative peasant arts . . . more or less dependent on civilized ones . . . [including]
most of the so-called primitive arts of Asia, Malaysia and Africa . . ."
which last are believed to reflect to some extent ancient Mediterranean, Mohammedan and Egyptian influences. "An unlettered people
can occasionally achieve an art of high distinction on such foundations,
as witness the bronzes of Benin . . . the wood-carvings . . . in the
Congo. But this seems to be the exception." One can pretty well assume
anyway that the Benin bronze caster and the Congo carver had no
glimmering of the supra-craftsmanship ideals of the Western "artist."
But, skill and feeling being what they are, the Benin craftsman's work
could be and often was superior to that of the yearning Western
botcher.

5 The specific sources quoted from in this appendix are:
    Shapiro, *Art News,* March, 1946.
    Kroeber, "Primitive Art," *Encyclopaedia of Social Sciences.*
    Adam, *Primitive Art.*
    Gorer, *Africa Dances.*

Works consulted

In the interests of the general reader, who understandably dislikes a text peppered with reference numbers, this book relies for specific acknowledgment of sources on informal mention in the text or exact identification of material in the chapter notes immediately preceding this section. Beyond that the following check list will indicate the scope of investigation underlying the book. It does not by any means list everything read but is meant primarily to aid people who may want to get better acquainted with the background of the people or issues treated. Items of particular general interest or particularly worth reading for enjoyment are marked with an asterisk. Specialists in the fields here touched on will have all this at their fingertips anyway.

Adams, Charles Francis. *Richard Henry Dana: A Biography*. Boston, Houghton, Mifflin and Company, 1891.
Adanson, Michel. *A Voyage to Senegal* . . . With Notes by an English

Gentleman, who resided some Time in that Country. (In Pinkerton, *Voyages & Travels,* XVI.)

Alexis, Stephen. *Black Liberator: The Life of Toussaint Louverture.* Translated from the French by William Sterling. London, Ernest Benn, n.d. [1949].

American Anti-Slavery Society. *Declaration of Sentiments of the* . . . Adopted at the Formation of said Society . . . 1833. [Penny Tracts. Number One.] New York, Published by the . . . , n.d. [1844].

[*Amistad.*] *The African Captives. Trial of the Prisoners of the* . . . New York, Published . . . at 143 Nassau Street, 1839.

Anderson, Osborne P. *A Voice From Harper's Ferry* . . . *With Incidents Prior to and Subsequent to Its Capture by Captain John Brown and His Men.* By . . . one of the number. Boston, Printed for the Author, 1861.

Anonymous. "The West Indies as They Were and Are," *Edinburgh Review,* April, 1859.

Anti-Slavery Record, The. Vols. I, II, III, for 1835-6-7. New York, Published for the American Anti-Slavery Society.

Aptheker, Herbert. *American Negro Slave Revolts.* New York, Columbia University Press, n.d. [1943].

Arnould, Sir Joseph. *Memoir of Thomas, First Lord Denman,* formerly Lord Chief Justice of England. London, Longmans, Green, and Co., 1873.

Avey, Elijah. *The Capture and Execution of John Brown. A Tale of Martyrdom.* By . . . Eye Witness. Elgin, Ill., Brethren Publishing House, n.d. [1906].

Bach, Marcus. *Strange Altars.* Indianapolis, The Bobbs-Merrill Company, n.d. [1942].

Baker, Ernest A., ed. *The Novels of Mrs. Aphra Behn.* With an Introduction by . . . London, George Routledge & Sons, Limited, 1905.

Barbot, John. *A Description of the Coasts of North and South Guinea* . . . by . . . Agent-General of the Royal Company of Africa, and Islands of America, at Paris. (In Churchill, *Voyages,* V.)

* Barnes, Gilbert Hobbs. *The Antislavery Impulse. 1830-1844.* New York, D. Appleton-Century Company, n.d. [1933].

——— and Dwight L. Dumond, eds. *Letters of Theodore Dwight Weld, Angelina Grimké Weld and Sarah Grimké. 1822-1844.* New York, D. Appleton-Century Company, n.d. [1934].

Bartlett, David W. *Modern Agitators: or, Pen Portraits of Living American Reformers.* New York, Miller, Orton & Mulligan, 1855.

Beecher, Catherine E. *An Essay on Slavery and Abolitionism, with*

Reference to the Duty of American Females. Second edition. Philadelphia, Henry Perkins, 1837.

[Benezet, Anthony.] *A Caution and Warning to Great Britain, and Her Colonies.* N.P., n.d. [Philadelphia, 1766].

—— *A Short Account of That Part of Africa, Inhabited by the Negroes.* The Second Edition with large Additions and Amendments. Philadelphia, W. Dunlap, 1762.

—— *Some Historical Account of Guinea.* Philadelphia, Joseph Cruikshank, 1771.

Birney, Catherine H. *The Grimké Sisters. The First American Women Advocates of Abolition and Women's Rights.* Boston, Lee and Shepard, 1885.

Birney, William. *James G. Birney and His Times: The Genesis of the Republican Party with Some Account of Abolition Movements in the South before 1820.* New York, D. Appleton and Company, 1890.

Blackwell, Alice Stone. *Lucy Stone: Pioneer of Women's Rights.* Boston, Little, Brown, and Company, 1930.

Blake, John W. *European Beginnings in West Africa. 1454-1578.* A survey of the first century of white enterprise in West Africa, with special emphasis upon the rivalry of the Great Powers. London, Longmans, Green and Co., n.d. [1937].

—— ed. *Europeans in West Africa, 1450-1560. Documents to illustrate the nature and scope of Portuguese enterprise in West Africa.* Translated and edited by . . . London, The Hakluyt Society, 1942.

Blake, William O. *The History of Slavery and the Slave Trade, Ancient and Modern.* Compiled from Authentic Materials by . . . Columbus, Ohio, H. Miller, 1860.

Booth, Charles. *Zachary Macaulay: His Part in the Movement for the Abolition of the Slave Trade and of Slavery.* An Appreciation by . . . London, Longmans, Green and Co., 1934.

Bosman, William. *A New and Accurate Description of the Coast of Guinea.* Written originally in Dutch by . . . Chief Factor for the Dutch at the Castle of St. George d'Elmina. (In Churchill, *Voyages,* V.)

Boteler, Alexander R. "Recollections of the John Brown Raid," *Century Magazine,* July, 1883.

[Bourne, George.] *Picture of Slavery in the United States of America.* Middletown, Conn., Edwin Hunt, 1834.

Bourret, F. M. *The Gold Coast: A Survey of the Gold Coast and British Togoland. 1919-1946.* London, Oxford University Press, 1949.

Bovill, E. W. *Caravans of the Old Sahara. An Introduction to the History of the Western Sudan.* Published for the International Institute of African Culture and Languages. London, Oxford University Press, 1933.

*—— *The Golden Trade of the Moors*. New York, Oxford University Press, 1958.

* Bowdich, T. Edward. *Mission from Cape Coast Castle to Ashantee . . . By . . . Conductor*. London, John Murray, 1819.

Bradford, Gamaliel. *Damaged Souls*. Boston, Houghton Mifflin Company, 1923.

[Bridge, Horatio.] *The Journal of an African Cruiser . . . By an Officer of the U.S. Navy*. Edited by Nathaniel Hawthorne. Aberdeen, George Clark and Son, 1849.

Brown, Salmon. "My Father, John Brown," *Outlook,* January 25, 1913.

Burn, W. L. *The British West Indies*. London, Hutchinson's University Library, 1951.

Burtis, Mary Elizabeth. *Moncure Conway. 1832-1907*. New Brunswick, Rutgers University Press, 1952.

* Burton, Richard F. *A Mission to Gelele, King of Dahome*. London, Tinsley Brothers, 1864.

Buxton, Charles. *Memoirs of Sir Thomas Fowell Buxton, Baronet. With Selections from his Correspondence*. Edited by his son . . . , Esq. Philadelphia, Henry Longstreth, 1849.

Buxton, Thomas Fowell. *The African Slave Trade and Its Remedy*. London, John Murray, 1840.

Canot, Theodore. *Adventures of An African Slaver*. His Own Story as Told in the Year 1854 to Brantz Mayer. Now Edited with an Introduction by Malcolm Cowley. New York, Albert & Charles Boni, 1928.

Carroll, Joseph Cephas. *Slave Insurrections in the United States: 1800-1865*. Boston, Chapman & Grimes, n.d. [1938].

* Cary, Joyce. *Britain and West Africa*. Revised Edition. London, Longmans, Green and Co., n.d.

*—— *The Case for African Freedom*. Searchlight Books. No. 11. London, Secker & Warburg, 1941.

Catterall, Helen Tunnicliff. *Judicial Cases Concerning American Slavery and the Negro*. Washington, D.C., The Carnegie Institution of Washington, 1926 . . . 1936.

* Cave, Hugh B. *Haiti: Highroad to Adventure*. New York, Henry Holt and Company, n.d. [1952].

Chadwick, French Enson. *Causes of the Civil War. 1859-1861*. The American Nation: A History. Vol. 19. New York, Harper & Brothers, n.d. [1906].

Chambers, Jennie. "What A School-Girl Saw . . . ," *Harper's Magazine,* CIV, pp. 311-18.

Channing, William Ellery. *Slavery*. Boston, James Monroe and Company, 1835.

Chapman, John Jay. *Learning and Other Essays*. New York, Moffatt, Yard and Company, 1910.

—— "William Lloyd Garrison." (In *The Selected Writings of . . .* Edited with an introduction by Jacques Barzun. New York, Farrar, Straus and Cudahy, n.d. [1957].)

Cheever, George B. *The Guilt of Slavery and the Crime of Slaveholding, Demonstrated from the Greek and Hebrew*. New York, 1860.

Child, David Lee. *The Despotism of Freedom*. A Speech at the first anniversary of the New England Anti-Slavery Society. Boston, Published by the Boston Young Men's Anti-Slavery Association, n.d. [1834].

Child, Lydia Maria. *An Appeal in Favor of that Class of Americans Called Africans*. Boston, Allen and Ticknor, 1833.

—— *The Right Way the Safe Way*. Proved by Emancipation in the British West Indies, and Elsewhere. New York, Published . . . at 5 Beekman Street, 1860.

Chinard, Gilbert. *l'Exotisme Américain dans la Littérature Française au XVIe Siècle d'aprés Rabelais, Ronsard, Montaigne, etc.* Paris, Librairie Hachette et Cie., 1911.

Clarke, James Freeman. *Anti-Slavery Days*. New York, J. W. Lovell Company, 1884.

—— *Memorial and Biographical Sketches*. Boston, Houghton, Osgood and Company, 1878.

Clarkson, Thomas. *The History of the Rise, Progress, & Accomplishment of the Abolition of the African Slave-Trade, by the British Parliament*. First American, from the London edition. Philadelphia, James P. Parke, 1808.

Coffin, Joshua. *An Account of Some of the Principal Slave Insurrections . . . in the United States and elsewhere, during the last two centuries*. New York, Published by the American Anti-Slavery Society, 1860.

Cole, Arthur Charles. *The Irrepressible Conflict. 1850-1865. A History of American Life*, Vol. VII. New York, The Macmillan Company, n.d. [1934].

Coleridge, Henry Nelson. *Six Months in the West Indies*. Fourth Edition with Additions. London, Thomas Tegg, 1841.

Commager, Henry Steele. *Theodore Parker*. Boston, Little, Brown, and Company, 1936.

Coupland, Reginald. *The British Anti-Slavery Movement*. The Home University Library. London, Thomas Butterworth, n.d. [1933].

———— *Wilberforce. A Narrative.* Oxford, at the Clarendon Press, 1923.

———— "William Wilberforce," *Encyclopaedia of Social Sciences,* XV.

Craven, Avery. *The Coming of the Civil War.* Second Edition Revised. N.P., The University of Chicago Press, n.d. [1957].

———— *The Repressible Conflict. 1830-1861.* University, Louisiana, Louisiana University Press, 1939.

Cugoano, Ottobah. *Thoughts and Sentiments on the Evil and Wicked Traffic of the Slavery and Commerce of the Human Species . . . by . . .* a native of Africa. London, 1787.

Curti, Merle. *The Learned Blacksmith: The Letters and Journals of Elihu Burritt.* New York, Wilson-Erickson, 1937.

Daingerfield, John E. P. "John Brown at Harper's Ferry," *Century,* June, 1885.

Dalzel, Archibald. *The History of Dahomey . . .* By . . . Formerly Governor at Whydah, and Now at Cape-Coast-Castle. London, T. Spilsbury and Son, 1793.

Davis, H. P. *Black Democracy. The Story of Haiti.* New York, Lincoln MacVeagh-The Dial Press, 1928.

Davy, John. *The West Indies Before and Since Slave Emancipation . . . founded on notes and observations collected during a three years' residence.* London, W. & F. G. Cash, 1854.

de-Graft-Johnson, J. C. *African Glory. The Story of Vanished Negro Civilization.* New York, Praeger, n.d. [1955].

Denman, [Joseph]. *The Slave Trade, the African Squadron, and Mr. Hutt's Committee.* By the Hon. Captain . . . R.N. London, John Mortimer, n.d.

Dodds, John Wendell. *Thomas Southerne, Dramatist.* Yale Studies in English, LXXXI. New Haven, Yale University Press, 1933.

Donnan, Elizabeth. *Documents Illustrative of the History of the Slave Trade to America.* Washington, D.C., Carnegie Institute of Washington, 1930.

Douglass, Frederick. *The Life and Times of . . .* Written by Himself . . . With an Introduction by the Right Hon. John Bright, M.P. Third Edition. London, Christian Age Office, 1884.

* Dow, George Francis, ed. *Slave Ships and Slaving.* With an Introduction by Capt. Ernest H. Pentecost. Salem, Marine Research Society, 1927.

Dowd, Jerome. "The African Slave Trade," *Journal of Negro History,* January, 1917.

Drake, Richard. *Revelations of a Slave Smuggler . . .* With a Preface by his Executor, Rev. Henry Bard West, of the Protestant Home Mission. New York, Robert M. De Witt, n.d. [1860].

Draper, Daniel C. "Legal Phases of the Trial of John Brown," *West Virginia History,* January, 1940.

Dresser, Amos. *The Narrative of . . . with Stone's Letters from Natchez . . . and Two Letters from Tallahassee, relating to the treatment of slaves.* New York, Published by the American Anti-Slavery Society, 1836.

Du Bois, W. E. Burghardt. *Black Folk Then and Now. An Essay in the History and Sociology of the Negro Race.* New York, Henry Holt and Company, n.d. [1939].

―――― *John Brown.* American Crisis Biographies. Philadelphia, George W. Jacobs & Company, n.d. [1909].

―――― *The Suppression of the African Slave Trade in the United States of America. 1638-1870.* New York, The Social Science Press, 1954.

* Dumond, Dwight Lowell. *Antislavery Origins of the Civil War in the United States.* Foreword by Arthur Schlesinger, Jr. N.P., The University of Michigan Press, n.d. [1939].

―――― ed. *Letters of James Gillespie Birney, 1831-1837.* The American Historical Association. New York, D. Appleton-Century Company, n.d. [1938].

Dunham, Katherine. *Journey to Accompong.* New York, Henry Holt and Company, n.d. [1946].

Dykes, Eva Beatrice. *The Negro in English Romantic Thought, or A Study of Sympathy for the Oppressed.* Washington, D.C., The Associated Publishers, 1942.

Dyson, Zita. "Gerrit Smith's Efforts in Behalf of Negroes," *Journal of Negro History,* October, 1918.

* Edwards, Bryan. *The History, Civil and Commercial, of the British Colonies in the West Indies.* Third Edition, with Considerable Additions. London, John Stockdale, 1801.

Eaton, Clement. "A Dangerous Pamphlet in the Old South," *Journal of Southern History,* August 1936.

―――― *A History of the Old South.* New York, The Macmillan Company, n.d. [1949].

Easton, David K. "The Guianas," *Focus,* November, 1957.

Ellis, George W. *Negro Culture in West Africa. A Social Study of the Vai-Speaking People.* Introduction by Frederick Starr, Curator of Anthropology in the University of Chicago. New York, The Neale Publishing Company, 1914.

* Esquemeling, John. *The Buccaneers of America.* Edited by William Swan Stallybrass . . . [with] an Introductory Essay by Andrew Lang.

Third Impression. Broadway Translations. London, George Routledge & Sons, Ltd., n.d.

Fage, J. C. *An Introduction to the History of West Africa.* Cambridge, at the University Press, 1955.

* Fairchild, Hoxie Neale. *The Noble Savage. A Study in Romantic Naturalism.* New York, Columbia University Press, 1928.

Falconbridge, Alexander. *An Account of the Slave Trade on the Coast of Africa.* London, Printed by J. Phillips, 1788.

Fladeland, Betty. *James Gillespie Birney: Slaveholder to Abolitionist.* Ithaca, Cornell University Press, n.d. [1955].

Fletcher, F. T. H. "Montesquieu's Influence on Anti-Slavery Opinion in England," *Journal of Negro History,* XVIII, 414-26.

Filler, Louis. "Parker Pillsbury, an Anti-Slavery Apostle," *New England Quarterly,* September, 1946.

Foner, Phillip S. *Business & Slavery. The New York Merchants and the Irrepressible Conflict.* Chapel Hill, The University of North Carolina Press, 1941.

Foote, Andrew H. *Africa and the American Flag.* New York, D. Appleton & Co., 1854.

* Forster, E. M. *Marianne Thornton. A Domestic Biography.* New York, Harcourt, Brace and Company, n.d. [1957].

Fortes, M., and E. E. Evans-Pritchard, eds. *African Political Systems.* London, Oxford University Press, 1940.

Foust, Clement E. *The Life and Dramatic Works of Robert Montgomery Bird.* New York, The Knickerbocker Press, 1919.

* Frothingham, Octavius Brooks. *Gerrit Smith: A Biography.* New York, G. P. Putnam's Sons, 1878.

——— *Theodore Parker: A Biography.* Boston, James R. Osgood and Company, 1874.

Froude, James Anthony. *The English in the West Indies: or, The Bow of Ulysses.* New York, Charles Scribner's Sons, 1892.

Garrison, Wendell Phillips. *The Preludes of Harper's Ferry.* Reprinted from the *Andover Review,* December, 1890. N.P., n.d.

[———] *William Lloyd Garrison. 1805-1879. The Story of His Life Told by His Children.* Boston, Houghton, Mifflin and Company, n.d. [1885].

Gide, André. *Voyage au Congo. Carnets de Route.* Paris, Librairie Gallimard, n.d. [1927].

* Gorer, Geoffrey. *Africa Dances. A Book About West African Negroes.* London, Faber & Faber, n.d. [1935].

Greeley, Horace. *Recollections of a Busy Life.* New York, J. B. Ford & Company, 1868.

Greene, Laurence. *The Raid. A Biography of Harpers Ferry.* New York, Henry Holt and Company, n.d. [1953].

Grégoire, Henri. *De la Littérature des Nègres.* Paris, Chez Maradan, Librairie, 1808.

Griggs, Earl Leslie, and Clifford H. Prator, eds. *Henry Christophe and Thomas Clarkson: A Correspondence.* Berkeley and Los Angeles, University of California Press, 1952.

—— *Thomas Clarkson: The Friend of Slaves.* London, George Allen & Unwin, Ltd., n.d. [1936].

[Grimké, Angelina.] *Letters to Catherine E. Beecher, in reply to an Essay on Slavery and Abolitionism, addressed to . . .* Revised by the Author. Boston, Printed by Isaac Knapp, 1838.

Grinnell, Joseph Busnell. *Men and Events of Forty Years.* Autobiographical Reminiscences of an active career from 1850 to 1890. Boston, D. Lothrop Company, n.d. [1891].

Hailey, Lord. *An African Survey: A Study of Problems Arising in Africa South of the Sahara.* London, Oxford University Press, 1938.

Hakewill, James. *A Picturesque Tour of the Island of Jamaica . . .* by . . . [the] author of the "Picturesque Tour of Italy." London, Hurst and Robinson, 1825.

Hakluyt, Richard, ed. *The Principal Navigations, Voyages, Traffiques & Discoveries of the English Nation.* Everyman's Library. London, J. M. Dent & Co., n.d.

Hale, William Harlan. *Horace Greeley: Voice of the People.* New York, Harper & Brothers, n.d. [1950].

* Halévy, Elie. *A History of the English People in 1815.* London, Penguin Books, Limited, n.d. [1937].

[Hamilton, J., jr.] *An Account of the Late Intended Insurrection Among a Portion of the Blacks in This City.* Published by Authority of the Corporation of Charleston. Charleston, A. E. Miller, 1822.

Hamilton, James Cleland. "John Brown in Canada," *Canadian Magazine,* December, 1894.

* Handlin, Oscar. *Race and Nationality in American Life.* Boston, Little, Brown and Company, n.d. [1957].

Hanks, Charles E. "A 'Blackbirder' that Flew the Burgee of a Famous Yacht Club," *Yachting,* October, 1946.

Harlow, Ralph Volney. *Gerrit Smith: Philanthropist and Reformer.* New York, Henry Holt and Company, n.d. [1939].

Helps, Sir Arthur. *The Conquerors of the New World and Their Bondsmen. Being a Narrative of the Principal Events which led to Negro Slavery in the West Indies and America.* London, William Pickering, 1848.

·———— *The Spanish Conquest in America and Its Relation to the History of Slavery and to the Government of Colonies.* A New Edition edited with an Introduction, Maps and Notes by M. Oppenheim. London, John Lane, 1904.

Henriques, Fernando. *Family and Colour in Jamaica.* With a Preface by Meyer Fortes, M.A., Ph.D., Professor of Social Anthropology, Cambridge University. London, Eyre & Spottiswoode, 1953.

* Herskovits, Melville J. *Dahomey: An Ancient West African Kingdom.* New York, J. J. Augustin, 1938.

———— *Life in a Haitian Valley.* New York, Alfred A. Knopf, 1937.

———— and Frances S. *Rebel Destiny. Among the Bush Negroes of Dutch Guiana.* New York, Whittlesey House, 1934.

———— and Frances S. *Trinidad Village.* New York, Alfred A. Knopf, 1947.

Higginson, Mary Potter Thacher. *Thomas Wentworth Higginson: The Story of His Life.* Boston, Houghton Mifflin Company, 1914.

Higginson, Thomas Wentworth. *Army Life in a Black Regiment.* New York, Longmans, Green, and Co., 1896.

———— "A Charge with Prince Rupert," *Atlantic Monthly,* June, 1859.

———— *Cheerful Yesterdays.* Boston, Houghton Mifflin and Company, 1898.

———— *Contemporaries.* Cambridge, the Riverside Press, 1900.

———— "Nat Turner's Insurrection," *Atlantic Monthly,* August, 1861.

———— *Travellers and Outlaws. Episodes in American History.* Boston, Lee and Shepard, 1889.

———— "William Lloyd Garrison," *Century,* August, 1885.

Hinton, Richard J. *John Brown and His Men. With Some Account of the Roads They Travelled to Reach Harper's Ferry.* New York, Funk & Wagnalls, 1894.

Hoare, Prince. *Memoirs of Granville Sharp, Esq. . . . with observations on Mr. Sharp's Biblical criticisms,* by the Right Rev. the Lord Bishop of St. David's. London, Henry Colburn and Co., 1820.

Hosmer, William. *The Higher Law, in its Relations to Civil Government: with particular reference to Slavery, and the Fugitive Slave Law.* Auburn, Derby & Miller, 1852.

* Howard, C., ed. *West African Explorers.* Selections Chosen and Edited by . . . With an Introduction by J. H. Plumb. The World's Classics. London, Oxford University Press, n.d. [1951].

Howe, George. "The Last Slave-Ship," *Scribner's,* July, 1890.

Howe, Julia Ward. *Memoir of Dr. Samuel Gridley Howe . . . with other memorial tributes.* Boston, Published by the Howe Memorial Committee, 1876.

———— *Reminiscences: 1819-1899*. Boston, Houghton, Mifflin and Company, 1900.

* ———— *A Trip to Cuba*. Boston, Ticknor and Fields, 1860.

[Howe, Samuel Gridley.] *Proceedings at the Celebration of the One Hundredth Anniversary of the Birth of . . . November 11, 1801*. Boston, Wright & Potter Printing Company, 1902.

———— *The Refugees from Slavery in Canada West*. Report to the Freedmen's Inquiry Commission. Boston, Wright & Potter, 1864.

Hughes, Sarah Forbes, ed. *Letters and Recollections of John Murray Forbes*. Boston, Houghton, Mifflin and Company, 1899.

Huntley, Sir Henry Veer. *Seven Years' Service on the Slave Coast of Africa*. London, Thomas Cautley Newby, 1850.

Jackson, Henry Rootes. *The Wanderer Case: The Speech of Hon. . . . of Savannah, Ga*. Introduction by Bill Arp. Atlanta, Ga., Ed Holland, Publisher, n.d.

Jarrett, H. Reginald. "Sierra Leone," *Focus*, December, 1957.

Jay, William. *An Inquiry into the Character and Tendency of the American Colonization, and American Anti-Slavery Societies*. Third Edition. New York, Leavitt, Lord, & Co., 1835.

Jenks, Leland H. "The John Brown Myth," *American Mercury*, March, 1924.

Jobson, Richard. *The Golden Trade, or a Discovery of the River Gambra, and the Golden Trade of the Aethiopians*. Set down as they were collected on travelling parts of the yeeres 1620 and 1621 . . . London, the Penguin Press, n.d. [1932].

Johnson, Oliver. *William Lloyd Garrison and His Times . . .* With an Introduction by John G. Whittier. New, Revised, and Enlarged Edition. Boston, Houghton, Mifflin and Company, 1882.

Johnston, Sir Harry H. *The Opening Up of Africa*. New York, Henry Holt and Company, n.d.

Karsner, David. *John Brown, Terrible Saint*. New York, Dodd, Mead & Company, 1934.

Keller, Allan. *Thunder at Harper's Ferry*. Englewood Cliffs, N.J., Prentice-Hall, Inc., 1958.

Kimball, George. "Origin of the John Brown Song," *New England Magazine*, December, 1889.

Kimble, George. "Resources of the Tropics: I, Africa," *Focus*, December, 1952.

Kingsley, Charles. *At Last: A Christmas in the West Indies*. London, Macmillan and Co., 1892.

* Kingsley, Mary H. *West African Studies*. London, Macmillan and Co., Ltd., 1899.

Klingberg, Frank J. *The Anti-Slavery Movement in England. A Study in English Humanitarianism.* New Haven, Yale University Press, 1926.

Knutsford, Viscountess. *Life and Letters of Zachary Macaulay.* By his granddaughter . . . London, Edward Arnold, 1900.

Korngold, Ralph. *Citizen Toussaint.* Boston, Little, Brown and Company, 1944.

—— *Two Friends of Man. The Story of William Lloyd Garrison and Wendell Phillips and Their Relationship with Abraham Lincoln.* Boston, Little, Brown and Company, 1950.

* Labat, Jean-Baptiste. *Voyage aux Iles de l'Amérique (Antilles). 1693-1705.* Avant-Propos de A. t'Serstevens. Editions Dichartre, Paris, n.d. [1931].

[Lamar, C. A. L.] "A Slave-Trader's Letter-Book," *North American Review,* November, 1886.

Land, Mary. "John Brown's Ohio Environment," *Ohio State Archaeological and Historical Quarterly,* January, 1948.

Lander, Richard and John. *Journal of an Expedition to Discover the Course and Termination of the Niger: with a Narrative of a Voyage down that River to its Termination.* Second Edition. London, Thomas Tegg & Son, 1838.

Landor, Walter Savage. "Romilly and Wilberforce." (In *Imaginary Conversations,* Second Series. Dialogues of Sovereigns and Statesmen. Boston, Roberts Brothers, 1885.)

Lawrence, William. *Life of Amos A. Lawrence.* With Extracts from his Diary and Correspondence. Boston, Houghton, Mifflin and Company, 1899.

Lawrence, William Beach. *Visitation and Search: or, An Historical Sketch of the British Claim to Exercise a Maritime Police over the Vessels of all Nations.* Boston, Little, Brown and Company, 1858.

* Lewis, M. G. *Journal of a West India Proprietor 1815-17.* Edited with an introduction by Mona Wilson. Boston, Houghton, Mifflin Company, 1929.

* Leyburn, James G. *The Haitian People.* New Haven, Yale University Press, 1941.

* Ligon, Richard. *A True and Exact History of the Island of Barbados.* London, Printed for Humphrey Moseley, 1657.

Lloyd, Arthur Young. *The Slavery Controversy. 1831-1860.* Chapel Hill, The University of North Carolina Press, 1939.

Lloyd, Christopher. *The Navy and the Slave Trade. The Suppression of the African Slave Trade in the Nineteenth Century.* London, Longmans, Green and Co., n.d. [1949].

Locke, Mary Stoughton. *Anti-Slavery in America from the Introduction of African Slaves to the Prohibition of the Slave Trade (1619-1808)*. Radcliffe College Monographs No. 11. Boston, Ginn & Company, 1901.

[Long, Edward.] *The History of Jamaica, or General Survey of the Ancient and Modern State of That Island*. London, T. Lowndes, 1774.

Lovejoy, Owen. *The Barbarism of Slavery*. Speech of Hon. . . . of Illinois. Delivered in the U.S. House of Representatives, April 5, 1860. Washington, D.C., Buell & Blanchard, n.d.

[Macaulay, Zachary.] *The Slave Colonies of Great Britain; or A Picture of Negro Slavery Drawn by the Colonists Themselves*. London, Printed for the Society for the Mitigation and Gradual Abolition of Slavery Throughout the British Dominions, 1825.

MacInnes, C. M. *England and Slavery*. N.P., Arrowsmith, n.d. [1934].

Mackenzie-Grieve, Averil. *The Last Years of the English Slave-Trade: Liverpool 1750-1807*. London, Putnam & Co., Ltd., n.d. [1941].

Maclay, Edgar Stanton. *A History of the United States Navy from 1775 to 1901*. New York, D. Appleton & Company, 1918.

* Macmillan, W. M. *Warning from the West Indies*. A Tract for the Empire. Harmondsworth, Penguin Books, n.d. [1938].

Macy, Jesse. *The Anti-Slavery Crusade. A Chronicle of the Gathering Storm*. The Chronicles of America. Vol. 28. New Haven, Yale University Press, 1919.

Madden, Richard Robert. *A Twelvemonth's Residence in the West Indies, during the Transition from Slavery to Apprenticeship*. Philadelphia, Carey, Lea and Blanchard, 1835.

Malin, James C. *John Brown and the Legend of Fifty-Six*. Philadelphia, The American Philosophical Society, 1942.

—— "The John Brown Legend in Pictures," *Kansas Historical Quarterly*, November, 1939.

Manning, Edward. *Six Months on a Slaver. A True Narrative*. New York, Harper & Brothers, 1879.

Martineau, Harriet. *The Martyr Age of the United States*. Boston, Weeks, Jordan & Co., 1839.

—— *Retrospect of Western Travel*. London, Saunders & Otley, 1838.

Mathieson, William Law. *British Slave Emancipation: 1838-1849*. London, Longmans, Green and Co., 1932.

—— *British Slavery and Its Abolition*. London, Longmans, Green and Co., 1926.

—— *Great Britain and the Slave Trade. 1839-1865*. London, Longmans, Green and Co., 1929.

May, Samuel J. *Some Recollections of Our Antislavery Conflict.* Boston, Fields, Osgood, & Co., 1869.

McDevitt, William. *Ambrose Bierce on Richard Realf.* San Francisco, Recorder-Sunset Press, 1948.

M'Queen, James. *The West India Colonies: the Calumnies and Misrepresentations Circulated against them* . . . Examined and Refuted by . . . London, Longman, Hurst & Co., 1825.

Mellor, George R. *British Imperial Trusteeship: 1783-1850.* London, Faber and Faber Limited, n.d. [1951].

Michael Angelo of Gattina, and Denis de Carli of Picenza. *A Curious and Exact Account of a Voyage to Guinea, in the Years 1666 and 1667.* (In Pinkerton, *Voyages,* XVI.)

Moreau de St.-Méry, L. E. *Description Topographique, Physique, Civile, Politique et Historique de la Partie Française de l'Isle de Saint-Domingue.* A Philadelphie, Chez l'Auteur, 1797.

Morel, Edmund Dene. *The Black Man's Burden.* Manchester, the National Labour Press, Ltd., n.d. [1920].

Morella, Jerome. *A Voyage to Congo* . . . *in the Year 1682.* (In Pinkerton, *Voyages,* XVI.)

Morley, John. *Diderot and the Encyclopaedists.* London, Macmillan & Co., 1897.

Morris, Richard B. *Fourteen Who Stood Accused from Anne Hutchinson to Alger Hiss.* New York, Alfred A. Knopf, 1952.

Moseley, Benjamin. *A Treatise on Sugar. With Miscellaneous Medical Observations* . . . Second Edition, with considerable additions. London, Printed by John Nicholls, 1800.

Moses, Montrose J. *The Fabulous Forrest. The Record of an American Actor.* Boston, Little, Brown, and Company, 1929.

Mottram, R. H. *Buxton the Liberator.* London, Hutchinson & Co., n.d.

Mozley, Geraldine, ed. *Letters to Jane from Jamaica. 1788-1796.* London, Published for the Institute of Jamaica, n.d.

Munro, Wilfred Harold. *Tales of an Old Sea Port: A General Sketch of the History of Bristol, Rhode Island.* Princeton, Princeton University Press, 1917.

Murray, Amelia M. *Letters from the United States, Cuba and Canada.* New York, 1856.

Newhall, Fales Henry. *Funeral Discourse Occasioned by the Death of John Brown of Ossawottamie* . . . *preached at Roxbury, Dec. 4* . . . Boston, J. M. Hewes, 1859.

Newton, John. *An Authentic Narrative of Some Remarkable and Interesting Particulars in the Life of* . . . *in a Series of Letters to the Rev. Mr. Haweis.* New York, Evert Duykinck, 1806.

—— *Thoughts Upon the African Slave Trade*. London, Printed for J. Buckland, 1788.

Nichols, Alice. *Bleeding Kansas*. New York, Oxford University Press, 1954.

[Nugent, Lady.] *Lady Nugent's Journal: Jamaica One Hundred and Thirty Eight Years Ago*. Reprinted from a Journal Kept by Maria, Lady Nugent, from 1801 to 1815. London, Published for the Institute of Jamaica, 1939.

Nye, Russel B. *A Baker's Dozen. Thirteen Unusual Americans*. East Lansing, Michigan State University Press, n.d. [1956].

*—— *Fettered Freedom. Civil Liberties and the Slavery Controversy. 1830-1860*. East Lansing, Michigan State College Press, 1949.

*—— *William Lloyd Garrison and the Humanitarian Reformers*. The Library of American Biography. Boston, Little, Brown and Company, n.d. [1955].

Olivier, Sydney Haldane, Baron. *Jamaica: The Blessed Island*. London, Faber & Faber, 1936.

Owens, William A. *Slave Mutiny. The Revolt on the Schooner Amistad*. New York, The John Day Company, n.d. [1953].

Paine, Thomas. "African Slavery in America." (In *Life and Writings of* . . . Edited by Daniel Edwin Wheeler, II, 105-12.)

Pares, Richard. *War and Trade in the West Indies: 1739-1763*. Oxford, at the Clarendon Press, 1936.

Park, Mungo. *Travels in the Interior of Africa*. Edinburgh, Adam and Charles Black, 1860.

Parker, Robert Allerton. *A Yankee Saint: John Humphrey Noyes and the Oneida Community*. New York, G. P. Putnam's Sons, 1935.

Parker, Theodore. *The Collected Works of* . . . Edited by Frances Power Cobbe. London, Trübner & Co., 1863.

Parry, J. H. and P. M. Sherlock. *A Short History of the West Indies*. London, Macmillan & Co., 1956.

Perkins, A. J. G., and Theresa Wolfson. *Frances Wright, Free Enquirer. The Study of a Temperament*. New York, Harper & Brothers, 1939.

Phelps, Amos Augustus. *Lectures on Slavery and Its Remedy*. Boston, Published by the New-England Anti-Slavery Society, 1834.

* Phillips, Thomas. *A Journal of a Voyage Made in the Hannibal of London, Ann. 1693, 1694, from England, to* . . . *the Coast of Guinea* . . . (In Churchill, *Voyages,* VI.)

Phillips, Ulrich Bonnell. "A Jamaican Slave Plantation," *American Historical Review*, April, 1914.

Phillips, William A. "Three Interviews with John Brown," *Atlantic Monthly*, December, 1879.

Pillsbury, Parker. *Acts of the Anti-Slavery Apostles,* Concord, N.H., 1883.

Pinckard, George. *Notes on the West Indies: written during the expedition under the command of the late General Sir Ralph Abercromby.* London, Longman, Hurst, Rees, and Orme, 1806.

Pitman, Frank Wesley. *The Development of the British West Indies. 1700-1763.* New Haven, Yale University Press, 1917.

———— "Slavery on British West India Plantations in the Eighteenth Century," *Journal of Negro History,* October, 1926.

Princeton University Library Chronicle, XIV, No. 2, Winter, 1953. "Victor Hugo."

Ragatz, Joseph Lowell. *The Fall of the Planter Class in the British Caribbean. 1763-1833.* New York, The Century Co., n.d. [1928].

Ramsay, James. *An Essay on the Treatment and Conversion of African Slaves in the British Sugar Colonies.* London, James Phillips, 1784.

Rattray, Robert Sutherland. *Ashanti.* Oxford, at the Clarendon Press, 1923.

Raynal, Abbé [Guillaume Thomas François]. *A Philosophical and Political History of the Settlements and Trade of the Europeans in the East and West Indies . . .* Newly translated from the French, by J. O. Justamond. London, Printed for W. Strahan, 1783.

Realf, Richard. *Poems by . . . Poet, Soldier, Workman.* With a Memoir by Richard J. Hinton. New York, Funk & Wagnalls Company, 1898.

———— *Richard Realf's Free-State Poems. With Personal Lyrics Written in Kansas.* Edited, with Historical Notes, by Col. Richard J. Hinton. Crane & Company, Topeka, Kansas, 1900.

Redpath, James. *Echoes of Harper's Ferry.* Boston, Thayer and Eldridge, 1860.

———— *The Public Life of Captain John Brown . . . with an Auto-Biography of His Childhood and Youth.* Boston, Thayer and Eldridge, 1860.

———— *The Roving Editor: or, Talks with Slaves in the Southern States.* New York, A. B. Burdick, 1859.

Richards, Laura E., and Maud Howe Elliott. *Julia Ward Howe. 1819-1910.* Boston, Houghton, Mifflin Company, 1915.

Richards, Laura E., ed. *Letters and Journals of Samuel Gridley Howe. The Greek Revolution.* With notes and a preface by F. B. Sanborn. Boston, Dana Estes & Company, n.d. [1906].

———— *Samuel Gridley Howe.* By his Daughter . . . New York, D. Appleton-Century Company, 1935.

Richman, Irving B. *John Brown Among the Quakers, and Other Sketches.* Des Moines, The Historical Department of Iowa, 1894.

Rigaud, Odette M. "The Feasting of the Gods in Haitian Vodun," *Primitive Man,* January and April, 1946.

Roberts, W. Adolphe. *Jamaica: The Portrait of an Island.* New York, Coward-McCann, Inc., n.d. [1955].

Roche, Emma Langdon. *Historic Sketches of the South.* New York, The Knickerbocker Press, 1914.

Saddler, Harry Dean. *John Brown: The Magnificent Failure.* Philadelphia, Dorrance & Company, n.d. [1951].

St. John, Sir Spenser. *Hayti: or, The Black Republic.* London, Smith, Elder, & Co., 1884.

Sanborn, Franklin Benjamin. *Dr. S. G. Howe, The Philanthropist.* American Reformers Series. New York, Funk & Wagnalls, 1891.

—— ed. *The Life and Letters of John Brown, Liberator of Kansas and Martyr of Virginia.* Boston, Roberts Brothers, 1885.

—— *Recollections of Seventy Years.* Boston, The Gorham Press, 1909.

* [Schaw, Janet.] *Journal of a Lady of Quality; being the Narrative of a Journey from Scotland to the West Indies . . . in the years 1774 to 1776.* Edited by Evangeline Walker Andrews, in Collaboration with Charles McLean Andrews. New Haven, Yale University Press, 1922.

* Schlesinger, Arthur M. *The American as Reformer.* Cambridge, Harvard University Press, 1951.

Schlesinger, Arthur M. jr. "The Causes of the Civil War," *Partisan Review,* October, 1949.

Schwarz, Harold. *Samuel Gridley Howe, Social Reformer.* Cambridge, Harvard University Press, 1956.

—— "Samuel Gridley Howe as Phrenologist," *American Historical Review,* April, 1952.

* Seldes, Gilbert. *The Stammering Century.* New York, The John Day Company, n.d. [1926].

Shaw, Flora L. (Lady Lugard). *A Tropical Dependency: An Outline of the Ancient History of the West Sudan with an Account of the Modern Settlement of Northern Nigeria.* London, James Nisbet & Co., 1905.

Sloan, Sir Hans. *A Voyage to the Islands Madera, Barbados, Nieves, St. Christophers and Jamaica.* London, Printed by B.M. for the Author, 1707.

* Smith, Abbott Emerson. *Colonists in Bondage. White Servitude and Convict Labor in America. 1607-1776.* Chapel Hill, University of North Carolina Press, 1947.

Smith, William. *Voyage to Guinea . . .* By . . . Esq., Appointed by the Royal African Company to survey their Settlements, make Discoveries, &c. The Second Edition. London, Printed for John Nourse, 1745.

Snelgrave, William. *A New Account of Some Parts of Guinea, And the Slave-Trade.* London, Printed for James, John, and Paul Knopton, 1734.

Soulsby, Hugh G. *The Right of Search and the Slave-Trade in Anglo-American Relations. 1814-1862.* Series LI. Number 2. The Johns Hopkins University Studies in Historical and Political Science. Baltimore, The Johns Hopkins Press, 1933.

Southey, Thomas. *Chronological History of the West Indies.* London, Printed for Longman, Rees, Brown, and Green, 1827.

Speers, John R. *The American Slave-Trade: An Account of Its Origin, Growth and Suppression.* New York, Charles Scribner's Sons, 1900.

Spilsbury, F. B. *Account of a Voyage to the West Coast of Africa; performed by His Majesty's Sloop* Favourite *in the Year 1805.* London, Richard Phillips, 1807.

* Stampp, Kenneth M. *The Peculiar Institution. Slavery in the Ante-Bellum South.* New York, Alfred A. Knopf, 1956.

Stearns, Frank Preston. *Cambridge Sketches.* Philadelphia, J. B. Lippincott Company, 1905.

———— *Sketches from Concord and Appledore.* New York, G. P. Putnam's Sons, 1895.

———— *The Life and Public Services of George Luther Stearns.* Philadelphia, J. B. Lippincott Company, 1907.

Stephen, Sir George. *Antislavery Recollections: in A Series of Letters addressed to Mrs. Beecher Stowe.* London, Thomas Hatchard, 1854.

[Stephen, James.] *The Dangers of the Country,* by the Author of War in Disguise. London, J. Butterworth, 1807.

———— *England Enslaved by Her Own Slave Colonies.* An Address to the Electors and People of the United Kingdom. Second Edition. London, Hatchard and Son, 1826.

———— *The Slavery of the British West India Colonies Delineated, as it exists both in law and in practice.* London, Joseph Butterworth and Son, 1824. *Ibid.* Vol. II: London, Saunders and Benning, 1830.

Stephen, Sir James. *Essays in Ecclesiastical Biography.* Second Edition. London, Longman, Brown, Green, and Longman, 1850.

Stuart, Charles. *Immediate Emancipation . . . An Outline for It, and Remarks on Compensation.* Second American Edition. Newburyport, Published by Charles Whipple, 1838.

Stoddard, Theodore Lothrop. *The French Revolution in San Domingo*. Boston, Houghton Mifflin Company, 1914.

Stowe, Harriet Beecher. *Men of Our Times; or Leading Patriots of the Day*. Hartford, Conn., Hartford Publishing Company, 1868.

Sturge, Joseph. *A Visit to the United States in 1841*. Boston, Dexter S. King, 1842.

—— *Horrors of the Negro Apprenticeship System in the British Colonies, as detailed at the public breakfast given by the citizens of Birmingham to . . . June 6, 1837*. Edinburgh, W. Oliphant & Son, 1837.

—— and Thomas Harvey. *The West Indies in 1837; being the Journal of a Visit . . . undertaken for the purpose of ascertaining the actual condition of those islands*. Second Edition. London, Hamilton, Adams, and Co., 1838.

Stutler, Boyd B. "The Hanging of John Brown," *American Heritage*, February, 1955.

—— "John Brown and the Oberlin Lands," *West Virginia History*, April, 1951.

Sypher, Wylie. *Guinea's Captive Kings: British Anti-Slavery Literature of the XVIIIth Century*. Chapel Hill, University of North Carolina Press, 1942.

Taussig, Charles William. *Rum, Romance, and Rebellion*. New York, Minton, Balch & Company, 1928.

[Taylor, Sir Henry.] *Autobiography of . . . 1800-1875*. London, Longmans, Green and Co., 1885.

Tharp, Louise Hall. *Three Saints and a Sinner. Julia Ward Howe, Louisa, Annie and Sam Ward*. Boston, Little, Brown and Company, n.d. [1956].

* Thomas, Benjamin P. *Theodore Weld: Crusader for Freedom*. New Brunswick, Rutgers University Press, 1950.

Thomas, Charles W. *Adventures and Observations on the West Coast of Africa, and Its Islands*. New York, Derby & Jackson, 1860.

Thompson, George. *Lectures of . . . Also, a brief History of His Connection with the Anti-Slavery Cause in England*, by Wm. Lloyd Garrison. Boston, Published by Isaac Knapp, 1836.

Tuckerman, Bayard. *William Jay and the Constitutional Movement for the Abolition of Slavery*. New York, Dodd, Mead & Company, 1893.

Turnbull, David. *Travels in the West. Cuba; with Notices of Porto Rico and the Slave Trade*. London, Longman, Orme, Brown, Green, and Longmans, 1840.

Udal, J. S. "Obeah in the West Indies," *Folk-Lore*, XXVI, 1915, pp. 255-95.

United States Senate: 36th Congress, 1st Session: Report of Committees No. 278. June 15, 1860 . . . "Report. The Select Committee of the Senate appointed to inquire into the late invasion and seizure of the public property at Harper's Ferry . . ."

Utting, F. A. J. *The Story of Sierra Leone*. London, Longmans, Green and Co., n.d. [1931].

Vandercook, John. *Black Majesty*. New York, Harper & Brothers, 1928.

Vaux, Roberts. *Memoirs of the Life of Anthony Benezet*. Philadelphia, Published by James P. Park, 1817.

Villard, Oswald Garrison. *John Brown: 1800-1859. A Biography Fifty Years After*. [Revised Edition.] New York, Alfred A. Knopf, 1943.

von Holst, Hermann. *John Brown*. Edited by Frank Preston Stearns. Boston, Cupples and Hurd, 1889.

Walsh, R. *Notices of Brazil in 1828 and 1829*. Boston, Richardson, Lord and Holbrook, 1831.

Ward, W. E. *A Short History of the Gold Coast*. Fourth Edition. London, Longmans, Green, and Co., n.d. [1949].

* Warren, Robert Penn. *John Brown: The Making of a Martyr*. New York, Payson & Clarke, Ltd., 1929.

* Weiss, John. *Life and Correspondence of Theodore Parker*. New York, D. Appleton & Company, 1864.

* Welch, Galbraith. *North African Prelude. The First Seven Thousand Years*. New York, William Morrow & Company, 1949.

[Weld, Theodore Dwight.] *American Slavery As It Is: Testimony of a Thousand Witnesses*. New York, American Anti-Slavery Society, 1839.

———— *The Bible Against Slavery* . . . The Anti-Slavery Examiner, No. 5. New York, Published by the American Anti-Slavery Society, 1838.

———— *The Power of Congress over the District of Columbia* . . . The Antislavery Examiner, No. 5 [*sic*]. New York, Published by the American Anti-Slavery Society, 1838.

Wesley, John. *Thoughts on Slavery*. N.P., n.d. [1774].

Whiteley, Henry. *Three Months in Jamaica in 1832: comprising a residence of seven weeks in a sugar plantation*. London, J. Hatchard and Son, 1833.

Williams, Eric. *Capitalism and Slavery*. Chapel Hill, University of North Carolina Press, 1944.

———— *The Negro in the Caribbean*. Washington, D.C., The Associates in Negro Folk Education, 1942.

Williams, Gomer. *History of the Liverpool Privateers . . . with an*

Account of the Liverpool Slave Trade. London, William Heinemann, 1897.

Williams, James. *Narrative of the Cruel Treatment of . . . a Negro Apprentice in Jamaica.* Glasgow, Printed by Aird & Russell, 1837.

Williams, Samuel H. *Voodoo Roads.* Wien, Verlag für Jugend und Volk, n.d. [1949].

Williams, Wilson E. *Africa and the Rise of Capitalism.* Howard University Studies in the Social Sciences, Vol. I, No. One. 1938.

* Wilson, Edmund. *Red, Black, Blond and Olive: Studies in Four Civilizations: Zuni, Haiti, Soviet Russia, Israel.* New York, Oxford University Press, 1956.

Wilson, Henry. *History of the Rise and Fall of the Slave Power in America.* Boston, James R. Osgood and Company, 1874.

Wilson, Hill Peebles. *John Brown, Soldier of Fortune.* A critique. Boston, The Cornhill Company, n.d. [1918].

Wilson, J. Leighton. *The British Squadron on the Coast of Africa.* By . . . an American Missionary in the Gaboon River. With Notes by Captain H. D. Trotter, R.N. London, James Ridgway, 1851.

Wish, Harvey. "American Slave Insurrections Before 1861," *Journal of Negro History,* July, 1937.

—— "The Revival of the African Slave Trade in the United States 1856-1860," *Mississippi Valley Historical Review,* March, 1941.

—— "Slave Disloyalty under the Confederacy," *Journal of Negro History,* October, 1938.

Wolf, Hazel Catherine. *On Freedom's Altar: The Martyr Complex in the Abolition Movement.* Madison, University of Wisconsin Press, 1952.

* Woodward, C. Vann. *The Strange Career of Jim Crow.* New York, Oxford University Press, 1955.

Wyndham, The Hon. H. A. *The Atlantic and Slavery.* Problems of Imperial Trusteeship. A Report in the Study Group Series of the Royal Institute of International Affairs. N.P., Oxford University Press, 1935.

* Young, G. M. *Victorian England: Portrait of an Age.* Garden City, Doubleday & Company, 1954.

Appendix

It would greatly have astonished Old Brown's admirers to hear that their cultivated great-grandchildren would learn to regard the heathen images of Dahomey and Benin with the same parrotish reverence that the 1850's accorded to the works of Canova and Thorwaldsen. West Africa traders had sometimes marveled at the high craftsmanship of Guinea textiles and the virtuosity in "lost-wax" [1] techniques that produced the gold, brass and bronze castings of the great Guinea kingdoms. But the outlandishly proportioned results necessarily struck Hiram Powers' contemporaries as not only ugly but also unsuccessful. This spared the Abolitionist the temptation to urge the Negro's cause, as has been done in our day, on the grounds that his "primitive" [2] carvings and sculptures were of immensely significant quality.

A layman may sometimes say with innocent baldness what experts hint at: in this case that there is a good deal of the Emperor's New Clothes about current views of primitive, and particularly West African, art. For certain anthropologists find a crucial difference between the approach to his work of the craftsman-maker of a fine West African carving and that of the self-conscious European artist who has borrowed certain West African design conventions for use as provocative *clichés;* the simplest example is Modigliani's delight in the fish mouth, ski-jump nose and slit eyes of the West African ritual mask. ". . . the 'art' in primitive art," says Shapiro, "is a process of discovery by Europeans," and the primitive artist knows no tradition of "a self-conscious form of individual expression . . . seeking to impart a personal message or to express himself in a peculiarly individual style . . . In primitive society there are no 'artists'—only craftsmen who occupy a functional role in the culture and work only in established modes."

That is, when Picasso stirs West African ingredients (as he has distortingly perceived them) into a design, he is like a sculptor hoping to make something validly new by substituting soap for stone. He may thus arrive at a new and interesting kind of surface texture. But he has—if it matters, and in Picasso's case it probably does—also broken completely with the purpose of the man who made that cake of soap. What *he* had in mind was hand washing. From West African conventions as to the shapes of carved faces Modigliani sought a fresh European view of shapes and depths.[3] But what the Ivory Coast carver intended was an object practically useful in religious maneuvers—a tool for influencing gods or ancestors; or in ornamenting a building—a tool for manifesting prestige; and sometimes the two purposes mingled. Both of them reflected persisting needs, so the carver worked, with only slight and often half-inadvertent variations, in long-standing conventions—stiff pose, emphasis on sexual traits, enlarged heads—familiar to him since he first set tool to wood.

"It is doubtful," says Kroeber, ". . . whether modern art can borrow more than an occasional stimulus or suggestion from primitive art . . . the difference in basis of form, feeling and objective is probably too great to allow any successful transfer." [4] Reinhard Adam says: ". . . a purely aesthetic approach [to primitive art] restricted to formal qualities, is inadequate," and suggests that knowledge of the primitive religions concerned is needed for sound appreciation. "Picasso's primitiveness is quite definitely his own 'Picassian primitiveness' . . . obviously not spontaneous, like the productions of a South Sea Islander or an African, but the outcome of a more or less complicated intellectual process. Imitating the mere primitiveness of primitive art is like rejecting all modern comforts and acquisitions and going back to caves and skins." That fairly defines one element in the misguidedness of certain trends in today's art. It means at least that, in order to draw bison as gloriously well as Neolithic man, you need not go lie on your back in a cave. Nor need you expect that, though you have the luck to be a great draftsman, your bison will have the same style or the primitive draftsman's emotional approach. After all, put Michelangelo in that same working position and you get the Sistine frescoes instead of the bison.

Necessarily the primitive craftsman's working conditions, whether of tools or ideas, affect his end product in fashions that trip up Western seekers after significance. Adam quotes a teacher artist working sympathetically with West Africans in West Africa using West African conventions who wrote of a certain critic's enthusiasm for the "cubism" of Negro sculpture: "If only he were here and could realize that his 'cubism' is simply due to the deep shadow in which every sensible [African craftsman] works . . . one has to work in simple shapes if one is to see anything at all—he would not have written this pathetic nonsense." This anthropologist deduces that the stiff styling of the arms in many Guinea figurines comes at least partly from working with naturally cylindrical pieces of wood. A facial expression that Westerners may assume is meant to arouse fear—or maybe an awesome mystical inscrutability—may actually intend, he says, "an entirely different attitude, maybe no emotion at all." And that last, of course, is the hardest thing for the Western enthusiast to accept. Gorer observed in West Africa that large dance masks cause wearers to bend their heads well forward: ". . . when masks are placed flat on a shelf or against a wall [as in Western displays] the perspective is usually distorted; they should be looked at about thirty degrees out of the perpendicular . . . at this angle many apparent distortions— long noses and small mouths, for instance—regain their proportions." Ah there, Modigliani!

The believer in special "primitive" aptitudes is disconcerted by Adam's further statement: ". . . there exists only a limited number of primitive works of art of really outstanding quality . . . there is also a bad primitive art, pieces of mediocre workmanship, and others of no aesthetic merit at all." It follows from this that one body of "primitive" art can excel another in the intangible qualities making up whatever "aesthetic merit" may be as well as in the concrete achievements of what we know craftsmanship is. That is, though both cultures enjoyed the same blessings of illiteracy, relative lack of non-muscular power and non-self-conscious spontaneity of aesthetic approach, the carvings of the Northwest Indians were far superior in both craftsmanship and what we Westerners see as aesthetic style to those of the Marquesans only a few thousand miles to the southward. These distinctions hold good even within closer ethnic groupings: the New Zealand Maori, brother Polynesians of the Marquesans, were far greater craftsmen and achieved much finer "aesthetic" effects. And closer home for this book, the merits of those recently discovered Yoruban portrait bronzes are, though just as primitive in the defined sense, higher than as well as different from those of later work from the same general area. Yet it was such later work, particularly the crudely roughed-out, workaday carvings of the backwoods Ivory Coasters and other equally underprivileged West Africans that certain European romantics chose whereon to stand when prying the artistic world off balance.

This is written in the inscrutable presence of certain ceremonial masks that I personally acquired on the Liberia-French Guinea border. To judge from the alarm of a local Negro who saw them in my possession, they ooze supernatural meaning. In their own style they are good specimens. Their owner knows something of their function in bush life and is aware that there probably cannot be a supra-cultural "art" with standards objectively pertinent across cultural-historical lines. Yet he cannot dissuade himself from the opinion that the body of "primitive art" that these masks well represent is essentially inferior to corresponding achievements of equal or greater "primitive" origin in Siberia, say, or the American Northwest. Could such things conceivably be measured, the typical quality of Eskimo carvings would far outstrip that of the West African work that Europe knew at that crucial period forty and fifty years ago—the stuff that still makes up the vast bulk of the evidence. It was strange that, in singling out West African art for use as aesthetic catalyst, the Western world chose something second-rate. But these things happen. It was noted previously in this book that mutually alien cultures in contact often borrow some of each other's worse features.[5]

Index

Abolitionist Movement, U.S.; abolition of slave trade, 154-155, 164, 256; American Antislavery Society, 50, 286, 288-291, 294-295, 308, 310, 313, 315, 316, 318, 389; *Amistad* case, 152-154; anti-abolitionist activity. *See* Kansas, New England, South; antislave trade activity. *See* Slave trade; and John Brown. *See* Brown, John; Colonization Movement, 303, 305, 307, 309, 313, 357, 358; disunion agitation, 305, 307, 336-337, 343, 360-361, 380-381, 391-392; fictional writings, 45-46, 231-232, 234, 235-236, 243, 282, 315, 320, 329, 381; fugitive slave aid, 20, 26, 152-154, 296, 332, 334-335, 346-348, 364-365; Garrison faction. *See* Garrison; influence on British movement, 281, 286-288; in Kansas. *See* Kansas; motivation to direct action, 21, 51, 152-153, 181, 202, 206-207, 217, 220-221, 229-230, 278, 290, 291, 294, 343-344, 361, 379, 386, 390, 391; New England Antislavery Society,

Abolitionist Movement *(cont.)* 310, 311; newspapers. *See Genius, Liberator, New York Tribune;* Quakers in. *See* Quakers; reaction to Harpers Ferry raid, 379-382; and Reform Movements, 297-300, 316, 356, 357; religious motivation, 49-51, 267, 288, 294-295, 313, 315, 324-325, 347, 349-351, 379-380; roots: in British movement, 6, 154, 182-183, 188-189, 205, 208, 278, 285, 286-290, 293-294, 297, 303, 310, 312; in Europe, 232-234, 247, 286, 296; in U.S., 164, 251, 296-300 and the Seventy, 313-314, 316, 317, 324, 389; on slavery, 7-8, 26, 49-51, 105-106, 182, 205, 304, 313, 315, 317, 352-353, 379-380, 389-391; in South. *See* South; tactics, 221-222, 229, 289-295, 296-297, 313-317, 334-335, 386-389; views on Negro, 6, 62, 75, 153, 235-236, 243-244, 388-389, 391
Accra, Ghana, 60, 116, 118
Adams, Charles Francis, 297

Adams, John Quincy, 289, 292, 315, 387, 388
Adirondacks Negro colony, 21, 359
Affranchis, 215; deputation to French Assembly, 262-263; role in St. Domingue uprising, 217-220
African art, 459-463 (appendix)
Agency Committee, 280-285, 288, 313
Agoma. *See* Negroes, West African
Alcott, Bronson, 367, 383, *quoted*, 18
Alcott, Louisa May, 381
Aldridge, Ira, 242-243
Amelia and Eleanor, slaver, 147
Amelia Island, 157
American Antislavery Society. *See* Abolitionist Movement, U.S.
American Colonization Society. *See* Abolitionist Movement, U.S.
American Revolution, 203, 267
American Slavery As It Is (Weld), 315, 389
Amistad uprising, 131, 152-154, 215
Anderson, Harpers Ferry raider, 40, 42, 337
Anderson, O. P., 380, *quoted*, 380
Andrew, John A., 32, 370, 374, *quoted*, 32
Angola, Portuguese West Africa, 165, 179
Antigua, B.W.I., during slavery, 187, 196, 204, 205, 213-214, 283, 388
Arabs in Guinea, 68, 70, 71, 72, 124
Arawak Indians, 72, 207, 208
HMS *Ardent*, 171
Argus, privateer, 156
Arny, W. F. M., 325
Ashanti. *See* Negroes, West African
Ashanti, Kingdom of, 102; modern-day, 97-98
Ashburton, Lord, 172

Babington, Thomas, 265
Baltic, states in slave trade, 165
Baltimore, 303
Baltimore clippers, in illegal slave trade, 156, 161, 167, 185
Bance, island of, 53
Banks, Gov. N. P. of Massachusetts, 374
Bantu. *See* Negroes, West African
Baptists, English, antislavery activity, 271, 275, 278

Barbados, B.W.I., estate conditions, 196, 197, 198, 199, 200, 215; slave conditions, 184, 185, 186, 196, 207; as slave market, 109, 141, 185; quality of settlers, 189, 190, 192
Barbot, John, 118, 124, 127, *quoted*, 81-82, 86-87, 89, 103-104, 117, 146
Barracoons, 54, 55, 114, 176, 179
Barry, slaver captain, 111
"Battle Hymn of the Republic" (Howe), 342
Baxter, Richard, 106, *quoted*, 106
Beecher, Catherine, *quoted*, 291
Beecher, Henry Ward, 24, 381, *quoted*, 44
Beecher, Lyman, 304, 315, quoted, 291-292
Behn, Aphra, 237-238, 239
Benezet, Anthony, antislavery propagandist, 62, 63, 73, 185, 247, 253, 256, 286; *quoted*, 62, 267
Benin, Kingdom of, 66, 86, 89, 93, 102-103, 104, 110, 359
Bight of Benin. *See* Benin
Bights, 89, 120, 133, 172
Bird Club, abolitionist group, 364, 374
Birney, James G., 270, 288, 299, 301, 313, 314, 319, 364
HMS *Black Joke*, 177
Blackstone, Sir William, 248-249
Blackwell, Henry, 321, *quoted*, 320
Bonaparte, Napoleon, 218
Booth, Junius Brutus, 240
Border Ruffians, 14-15, 16, 336
Boston, abolitionist activity in, 308, 317, 347, 349, 367; as slaver port, 141, 163
Bourne, George, 49-50, 51, 105, 288, *quoted*, 50, 105, 221
Bowdich, T. Edward, *quoted*, 98-100, 101
USS *Boxer*, 173
Brandenburg, in slave trade, 117
Brazil, origin of sugar trade, 185; as slave market, 154; in slave trade. *See* Slave trade
Bridgman, Laura, 339, 345, 346
Brissot, Jacques Pierre, 261
Bristol, England, as slaver port, 142, 164, 259
Bristol, R.I., as slaver port, 53, 141

Britain, in gold trade, 70-71; trading posts, 59, 60, 68, 77, 116, 118; in slave trade. *See* Slave trade
British Admiralty, 174, 176
British Antislavery Movement: abolition of slavery and slave trade. *See* British Parliament; alliance with French, 260-264; antislave trade activities. *See* Slave trade; fictional writings, 236-244, 245-246, 272-273, 276, 285; influence on American abolitionists. *See* Abolitionist Movement, U.S.; influences on, 208, 220, 247, 276-278, 281, 286-288; organizations, 246, 253, 254, 260, 280-281, 284; Parliamentary activities. *See* British Parliament; and religious groups. *See* Clapham Sect, Dissenters, Evangelical Movement, Quakers; religious motivation, 251-252, 255, 257-258, 264, 267-271; splitting of forces, 280-284; tactics, 182, 246, 253, 254, 272-276, 278-285, 290; test cases, 247-250
British Parliament: antislavery activity in, 253-256, 261, 265, 267, 269, 270-271, 274, 275-276, 278-280, 281-284, 289-290, 293; emancipation laws, 154, 233, 281, 283-284, 286; inquiries into slave trade, 112, 254; proslavery activity in, 176, 255, 261-262, 271, 274, 279; Parliamentary Reform, 251, 270, 278-279, 282, 290; outlawing of slave trade, 255-256, 267-268
British Royal Navy, on antislave trade patrol, 155, 164-168, 169, 171-173, 174-180; sentiment on slave trade, 258-260, 262
British West Indies: absentee landlords, 194-197, 215; banning of slave trade to, 164, 188, 255-256; caste system, 201-202, 216; emancipation of slaves. *See* Slaves; estate life, 194, 197-201; Negro white ratio, 195-196; persecution of antislaveryites, 225, 275, 278, 282; plans for slave emancipation, 233, 274-276, 278-280, 282, 293; post-emancipation, 283-284, 293-294, 315, 388; proslavery bloc in Parliament, 255, 271, 274-275, 279; quality of settlers,

British West Indies (*cont.*)
190-194, 202; resistance to emancipation, 273-275, 279-280, 283, 290; slave activity. *See* Slaves; slave treatment. *See* Slaves; as slave market, 77, 109, 135, 138, 141, 147, 148, 268; sugar economy, 185, 196, 209, 273, 274-275
Brook Farm, 348
Brooke, slaver, 148
Brooks, slaver, 156
Brougham, Charles, 280, 281-282, *quoted,* 281
Brown, Florilla, 13
Brown, Frederick, 13-14, 17, 30
Brown, Jason, 13-14
Brown, Jeremiah, 30
Brown, John: as Abolitionist hero, 3-5, 7, 10, 44-46, 47, 275, 312, 329, 343, 367, 380, 381-382; activities in Kansas, 5, 14, 16-19, 25-26, 29; burial in Adirondacks, 3, 4, 9-10, 46; capture, 41-42; claim to divine inspiration, 21, 30, 32, 44, 330; conjectures on sanity, 11, 26, 30-33, 43, 48, 258, 328, 373; described, 5-6, 10-11, 12, 19-20, 29-30, 32, 44-45, 46, 48, 309-310, 334, 345, 356; early life, 9-14; hanging, 3, 5, 44-46, 374, 376; Harpers Ferry raid, 5, 9, 34-42, 352, 379; indictment, 42-43; influence of readings, 20, 22, 24, 47-51, 182, 295, 301, 311, 328; plan for mountain colony, 21-22, 23, 26, 32, 33, 36, 37, 212, 322-323, 325, 359; plans and preparation for raid, 20, 22-27, 29, 33-34, 37, 206-207, 322-323, 325, 329-330, 344, 351, 353, 360-361, 365-366, 369, 375, 377; private militias, 5, 17-18, 23-25, 26, 33-42, 322-324, 348, 351, 365, 369, 380; *quoted,* 19, 21, 22, 26, 32, 40, 44, 46, 48, 311, 330, 365-366; rewards for capture, 5, 25-26; and the Secret Six. *See* Secret Six; "Spartacus" inspiration, 22, 207, 232; trial, 5, 30, 42-46, 345, 370; writings, 31, 47-48, 365-366
Brown, Captain John, 9
Brown, John, of 2nd Massachusetts Infantry, 46-47
Brown, John Jr., 13-14, 16, 17, 27, 30, 353, 361, 375, 376

Brown, Oliver, 14, 33, 35, 39, 40-41, 46
Brown, Owen (father of John), 9-10, 11, 13, 20, 312, 313, 359
Brown, Owen (son of John), 13-14, 37
Brown, Ruth. *See* Thompson, Ruth
Brown, Salmon, 13-14, 29, *quoted*, 29-30
Brown, Watson, 38, 40, 42, 46
Bruce, Commander, 171
Bryant, William Cullen, 297
Buchanan administration, 43, 158
Buffum, Arnold, 288
Burke, Edmund, 255, 263, 264, *quoted*, 254
Burritt, Elihu, 388
Buxton, Sir Thomas Fowell, anti-slavery leader, 271, 276, 283, 284, 289, 310; and Clapham Sect, 269; *quoted*, 269, 271, 280
Byrd, Col. William, *quoted*, 188, 211-212
Byron, Lady, 322
Byron, Lord, 330, 339, 340, 346, 367; influence on Secret Six, 302, 330

Cady, Daniel, 320, quoted, 320-321
Cape Coast, 59, 60, 66, 77, 118
Cape Coast Castle, 59, 144
Caribs, 192, 200
Cary, Joyce, *quoted*, 65
Cass, Lewis, 173
Catharine, slaver, 167-168, 170
Channing, W. E., 297, *quoted*, 293
Chapman, John Jay, *quoted*, 3, 306, 339
Chapman, Maria Weston, 288
Charleston, S.C., 226; as slaver port, 111, 164
Charlestown, slaver, 140-141
Charlestown, W. Va., site of John Brown's trial, 3, 42-46, 335
Cheever, Rev. George B., 379, 384, *quoted*, 379-380
Child, Mrs. Lydia Maria, 346, 364, *quoted*, 346
Church of England, 194, 251, 266, 271, 276, 278
Civil War, 26, 321, 338; slavery agitation as cause, 4, 15, 298, 392
Clapham Sect, 251, 253, 264-267, 268-269, 277

Clare uprising, 144
Clarke, Rev. James Freeman, 341, 368, *quoted*, 329
Clarkson, Thomas, 256-263, 265, 282, 286, 288, 310, *quoted*, 257, 267, 269
Clotilda, slaver, 160
Code Noir of Louis XIV, 216, 233
Commodore McDonogh, privateer, 155-156
Commodore Perry, privateer, 155-156
Compromise of 1850, 290, 307, 348-349
Concord, Mass., as Reform center, 8, 367, 369, 371-372, 383
Condorcet, Marquis de, 261, 263
Congo River, as slave center, 161-162
Congo tribes. *See* Negroes, West African
Cook, John, 33, 34, 39
Copeland, John A., 38-39
Coppoe, Edwin, 42
Coromanti. *See* Negroes, West African
Corrie, W. G., 158, 159
Covenanters, 331, 334
Cowper, William, 276, *quoted*, 272
Crafts, Ellen and William, 346-347
Creoles, 188, 216
Criterion, privateer, 156
Crofton, Commodore, 180
Cuba, 343; as slave market, 152, 154, 161, 163, 166-167, 179, 185; in slave trade. *See* Slave trade; sugar economy, 169, 185
Curaçao, Dutch West Indies, 109, 144

Dahomey, Kingdom of, 67, 77, 87, 88, 93, 94, 95-96, 102-104, 116, 123, 124, 129, 130, 391; modern day, 77
Dana, Richard Henry, 297, 349, *quoted*, 302
Danish, African trading posts, 60-61; in slave trade. *See* Slave trade
Davis, Jefferson, 196-197, 358, 375
De Bolas, Juan, Maroon leader, 208
Declaration of the Rights of Man, 217, 263
Demerara, B.W.I., 275
Denman, Commander, 175-176, 179
Dickinson, Emily, 332, 338
Diderot, Denis, 232
Dissenters, 251, 267, 271, 276, 279; in Jamaica, 225, 278, 282

HMS *Dolphin,* 167-168
Dominica, B.W.I., 189, 194
Douglas, Stephen A., 157, 381
Douglass, Frederick, 22, 26
Dred: A Tale of the Great Dismal Swamp (Stowe), 231-232, 236, 243, *quoted,* 329
Dred Scott Decision, 249
Dutch, in African trade, 124, 125; trading posts, 58, 59, 60, 68, 114-115, 116, 117, 118; in slave trade. *See* Slave trade
Dutch West India Company, 60
Dutch West Indies (Guiana), slaves, activity and treatment of. *See* Slaves

East India Company, 114, 265, 282
Eboes. *See* Negroes, West African
Edwards, Bryan, M.P., 76-77, 126, 197, 222, *quoted,* 76-77, 139, 198-199, 222
Elmina, Gold Coast slave center, 58, 59-60, 114-115, 118, 119
Emerson, Ralph Waldo, 7, 365, 367, 370, 383, *quoted,* 12, 381
Emigrant Aid Societies, 15, 333, 360, 365, 368, 369, 374
England. *See* Britain, British
Erie, slaver, 168, 173
Europeans, in Africa: advent, 66, 67, 71-73, 74, 79-82; quality of, 111-112, 116-117, 163; relations with natives, 56-57, 59-60, 76, 80, 85, 86, 88, 94-95, 108, 130; rivalry among, 60, 114-115, 116; trading company posts, 52, 54, 57-59, 60, 67-68, 98, 114-120, 138, 142, 175, 176
Evangelical Movement, 251-253, 254, 264-267, 268, 269-270, 271
Eyeo, African kingdom, 131

HMS *Fair Rosamond,* 175, 177
Falconbridge, Alexander, 259
Fanti. *See* Negroes, West African
HMS *Fantome,* 176
Felicidade, slaver, 178
Fernando Po, Bights, 172, 178-179
Ferrers uprising, 145-146
Fetu, African tribe, 66
Finney, Charles Grandison, 312-313, 320, 324
Flirt, Abolitionist yacht, 334-335

Flushing, England, slaver port, 111, 141
Forbes, "Colonel" Hugh, 24-25, 26, 33, 43, 323
Forbes, John Murray, 7, 337
Forest Negroes. *See* Negroes, West African
Forrest, Edwin, 235-236, 240
Forster, E. M., 266, *quoted,* 253, 265, 268-269
Foster, William, slaver captain, 160
Fox, Charles, 253, 255, 267, 271
France, abolition of slavery in F.W.I., 284; antislavery activity, 232-234, 236, 247, 260-264, 277; in slave trade. *See* Slave trade
Franklin, Benjamin, 287, 296, 297
Free Negroes: In B.W.I., 196. *See also* Maroons; in F.W.I., *See Affranchis, Marrons;* in North, 20, 22, 301, 304, 344, 389; in South, 226; caste systems, 201-202, 215-216; in Civil War, 26, 332, 375; colonies. *See* Adirondacks, Liberia, Ontario, Sierra Leone
Free-Staters, 14-19, 336, 360
French Revolutions: of 1789, 217, 254, 261, 262, 263-264; of 1830, 279; of 1848, 284, 342
French West Indies: absentee landlords, 215; antislavery bloc in French Assembly, 262-263; caste system, 202, 215-216; emancipation of slaves, 284; estate life, 199-200; proslave trade lobby in Paris, 261-263; quality of settlers, 190, 202; St. Domingue Uprising. *See* Hayti; slave activity and treatment. *See* Slaves; as slave market, 54, 109, 130, 147; sugar economy, 185, 215, 217
Frothingham, O. B., 359, 383, *quoted,* 354, 361-362, 377, 378, 383
Fugitive Slave Act, 20, 181, 349, 351

Gaboon. *See* Negroes, West African
Gabriel, leader of Virginia slave conspiracy, 223, 225, 226, 227, 229
Gallinas River, 163, 172, 175, 179
Gambia, British West Africa, 65, 118
Gambia River, 64, 110
Garrison, William Lloyd, 296, 299,

Garrison, William Lloyd (*cont.*)
300-311, 348; disunion agitation,
305, 307, 311, 336-337; faction, 291,
292, 300-302, 309-311, 314, 336, 337,
384, 387, 388; and Grimké sisters,
316-318; *quoted,* 47, 221, 264, 291,
294, 301, 302, 304, 305, 306-307
Genius of Universal Emancipation,
303
Germany, in African trade, 53, 119;
in slave trade, 53
Ghana, Empire of (Ghanata), 68-70,
71, 73
Ghana, Republic of, 68, 69-70, 77, 96,
132
Giddings, Joshua, 314, 319-320, 361
Gold Coast, in gold trade, 72, 74, 115,
123, 125; peoples, 67, 78-79, 83-84,
88, 93-94, 95; in slave trade, 57, 74,
116, 119, 123, 150, 179
Gold trade, 57-58, 67, 70-75, 109, 115,
118, 119, 121 122, 124, 125
Gordon, Sylvanus, slaver captain, 168
Goree, slave trade center, 51, 52-55,
56-57, 61, 80, 114, 119
Grain Coast, 87, 120, 125, 127, 145
Grain Trade, 72, 122, 125
Grant, Charles, 265
Greek war of independence, 339-341,
343-344, 346, 357
Great Dismal Swamp, 207, 224, 228
Greeley, Horace, 20, 337, 358
Green, Lieut. Israel, USMC, 40, 41
Green, Shields, 42
Grégoire, Abbé, *quoted,* 57, 234
Grenville, William Wyndham, 255,
263
Grimké, Angelina. *See* Weld, Ange-
lina Grimké
Grimké, Archibald and Francis, 319
Grimké, Sarah, 316, 319, 320
Gromettoes, 119
Guadeloupe, F.W.I., 54, 109, 215
Guinea, 53-104, 105-151, 178-180; Eu-
ropean accounts of, 61-62, 65, 66,
72; flora and fauna, 64-65; geog-
raphy, 63-65; origin of name, 70
Guinea Negroes. *See* Negroes, West
African
Guinea trade, 54-63, 67-68, 70-73, 106,
108, 111, 115, 122-125, 132, 175-176;
conditions in, 123-126; *see also*

Guinea trade (*cont.*)
Slave trade, Gold trade, Grain
trade, Ivory trade, Palm-oil trade

Hannibal, slaver, 138
Harpers Ferry, Va., 3, 28-29
Harpers Ferry raid, 34-42, 183, 310,
337, 375, 386; imprisonment and
trial of raiders, 42-46, 335; investigation of. *See* Mason Committee;
public reaction to, 206-207, 372,
379-382
Hausa, 76
Hawkins, John, 107
Hayti, Rebellion, 22, 121, 207, 210,
212, 216-218, 219, 222-223, 277; foreign intervention, 218, 222, 353; influence on slaves in South, 222, 223,
225, 226, 227; post-rebellion conditions, 65, 188, 202, 218-219, 220, 277-
278; pre-rebellion. *See* St. Domingue
Henry I, of Hayti, 219, 220, 277
Dos Hermanos, slaver, 171-172
Heyrick, Elizabeth, *quoted,* 270
Higginson, Thomas Wentworth, 332-
337; abolitionist and religious
views, 332, 336-337, 368, 391-392; influences, 333, 353, 354; as member
of Secret Six, 7, 366; *quoted,* 21, 33,
306, 310, 332, 333, 334, 335, 336,
337, 341; reaction to Harpers Ferry
raid, 331, 373-376; in Reform
causes, 333, 348
Hispaniola, 72, 207, 217
Historical Account of Guinea (Benezet), 256-257
Hoar, Judge E. R., 367, 371
Holmes, Oliver Wendell, 349, *quoted,*
47
Honduras, 207, 209
Hopkins, Samuel, 285, 287
Howe, Dr., observer on slaver, 161-
163
Howe, Julia Ward, 342-343, 344, 348,
353, *quoted,* 341, 343, 346
Howe, Dr. Samuel Gridley, 338-346,
353, 369; as member of Secret Six,
7, 334, 337; *quoted,* 340, 343, 344,
345, 346; reaction to Harpers Ferry
raid, 345, 374; testimony before
Mason Committee, 374, 375-376, 378

Huguenots, 190, 287
Hyatt, Thaddeus, 7, 374, 378

Inman, Commodore, USN, 173
Ivory Coast, 81, 108, 125, 127
Ivory trade, 67, 72, 73-74, 75, 79, 108, 109, 121, 122, 123, 125

Jackson, Francis, 300
Jacobins, 197, 222, 263, 264, 278-279
Jacques I, of Hayti, 219
Jamaica, B.W.I., estate conditions, 184, 194, 195, 196, 197, 215; Dissenters in, 282; quality of settlers, 190, 191, 192, 193, 194, 202; resistance to emancipation, 274-275, 290; slave activity and treatment, 77, 121, 182, 185, 186, 187, 189, 206, 208-211, 212, 213, 216, 233, 240-241, 245, 284; as slave market, 130, 135, 141; Spanish in, 208
Jay, William, 300
Jayhawkers, 13, 23, 25, 47, 334
Jefferson, Thomas, 386, *quoted,* 224
Jemmy, leader of South Carolina slave uprising, 224
Jervis, Admiral John, 258
Jobson, Richard, *quoted,* 71, 72, 74, 81, 82
John Brown's Body (Benét), 4
"John Brown's Body," 46-47, *quoted,* 47
Jonathan case, 248
Jones, Jonas, 28
Judson, judge in *Amistad* case, 153-154

Kagi, John Henry, 23, 37
Kansas, opening of, 13; slavery agitation in, 6, 13-19, 25, 29, 322, 323, 333, 336, 360, 362, 365, 366, 368, 370
Kansas Committees, 15, 325, 365
Kansas-Nebraska Bill, 13, 381
Kenutcky, slaver, 170
King William, slaver, 147
Kingston, Jamaica, 111, 147
Knapp, Isaac, 303-304
Knibb (Baptist ministers), 278
Kru. *See* Negroes, West African

Labat, Father, 56, 197, 199, *quoted,* 200

Lafayette, Marquis de, 35, 236, 261
Lagos, slave center, 53
Lamb, Bulfinch, 87-88, *quoted,* 88
Lane, James Henry, 19, 334
La Rochefoucauld, Duc de, 261
La Rochelle, France, slaver port, 165
Laurens, Henry, 133, *quoted,* 133
Lawrence, Amos A., 7, 15, 360, 363, 369
Lay, Benjamin, 287
LeBarnes, 335, 345, *quoted,* 345
Lee, Col. Robert E., 40, 41, 49
Lewis, "Monk," 187, 199, 201, *quoted,* 187
Libby, Cyrus, slaver captain, 170
The Liberator, 20, 48, 221, 301, 304-311, 313, 316, 325, 328; first printed, 229, 296, 303-304; quoted by Southern editors, 292, 307
Liberia, 120; free Negro colony in, 161, 173
Liberty Party, 314, 364
Ligon, Richard, 84, *quoted,* 83-84, 183
Lincoln, Abraham, 3, 308, 328, 382
Liverpool, center of British slave trade, 111, 141, 142, 164, 176, 259, 260
London, 142
Loring, Ellis Gray, 300
L'Ouverture, Toussaint, 193, 218-219, 225, 232, 234, 236, 277
Lowell, James Russell, *quoted,* 298, 309
Lundy, Benjamin, 303

Macaulay, Zachary, 265-266, 282, 288
Mali (Melle), Empire of, 69-70, 73
Mandingoes. *See* Negroes, West African
Mann, Horace, 338, 341, 343
Mansfield ruling, 249, 250
Maroons, colony on Jamaica, 77, 208-210, 211, 213, 214, 233; uprising, 210-211; repatriated to Sierra Leone, 211
Marrons, fugitive slave colony on St. Domingue, 216-217, 218
Martin, slaver captain, 159
Martinique, F.W.I., economy, 185, 215; as slave market, 54, 147; treatment of slaves, 203, 205
Mary Ann, slaver, 163-164

Maryland militia at Harpers Ferry, 39, 40, 41, 380
Mason, George, 193, 370, 374, 375, 376
Mason Committee, investigation of Harpers Ferry raid, 323, 325, 370-372, 373-377, 378
Mason-Dixon Line, 193, 291
Matson, Commander, RN, 176
Mauritius, B.W.I., 268
May, Rev. Dr. Samuel J., 221, 300, 306, *quoted*, 221, 300, 306
Mende. *See* Negroes, West African
Meredith, Commander, RN, 175, 176
Meriam, Harpers Ferry raider, 34
Methodism, 62, 276, 281; antislavery stand, 106, 247, 271
Middle Passage, 110, 135, 138, 140, 144, 151, 177, 185
Middleton, Sir Charles, 258
Millerites, 319, 356
Milner, Isaac, 251
Mirabeau, Comte de, 262
Missouri, 14-18, 25-26
Missouri Compromise, 296, 387
USS *Mohican*, 168, 172, 173
Monroe, James, 166, 223, 224
Montesquieu, Baron de, 247
Montez, Pedro, 152-154
Montgomery, James, 32, 334, 335, 368
Morgan, Sir Henry, 192-193
Morton, Edward, 376
Moslems, in African trade, 72, 73-74, 106-107; ruling Gold Coast, 63, 68-69
Mosquito Indians, 207, 209
Mulattoes, in Africa, 76, 88, 108, 119, 134, 207; in B.W.I., 199, 200, 201, 202, 207; *see also Affanchis*, Quadroons

Nancy, slaver, 113, 135
Nantes, France, as slaver port, 111, 141, 165
Napoleonic Wars, 155, 165, 166, 179, 210, 255, 264, 268
Narborough uprising, 145
Necker, Jacques, 261
Negroes, West African, during Guinea trade: customs and institutions, 78-92, 98-100, 102-104, 122, 129; cultural influences, 63, 67, 70; described by whites, 60, 65, 66, 67, 70,

Negroes, West African (*cont.*)
73, 76-84, 86-91, 93-95, 98-104, 132; diseases, 64, 66, 112, 115; economy, 64-65, 70-75, 88; ethnic distinctions, 75-77; government, 93-96, 98-102, 150, 237; physical appearance, 76, 83; polities. *See* Ashanti, Benin, Dahomey, Eyeo, Ghana (Ghanata), Mali (Melle), Songhai, Whydah; settlements, 65; slavery among, 58, 73-75, 85, 107; tribes: Agoma, 88; Ashanti, 58, 69, 70, 84, 85, 95, 96, 97-104, 123, 129, 179, 180, 391; Bantu, 76, 77; Congo, 77, 158, 215; Coromanti, 69, 77, 113, 209, 213, 215; Eboes, 77, 139, 213, 214, 215, 226; Fanti, 67, 69, 116, 119; Fetu, 66; "Forest Negroes," 69, 73; Fula, 76, 243; Gaboon, 79, 140; Hausa, 76; Kru, 76, 80, 85, 120; Liberian, 123; Mandingoes, 69, 76, 77; Mende, 81, 152-154, 213, 215; Papaw, 77; Quaqua, 83, 108; Senegal, 66, 79, 82, 127; Temne, 211; Whydah, 83, 86, 87, 89, 136; Yoruban, 123
tribal migrations, 65, 67, 76
Nelson, Admiral Horatio, RN, 258
New England, Antislavery Society, 310-311; in slave trade, 106, 107-108, 141-142
New York City, as Abolitionist center, 296, 300, 303, 308, 318, 323; as slaver port, 163, 168, 169
New York Tribune, 20
Newby, Dangerfield, 38
Newport, R.I., as slaver port, 111, 141, 146
Newton, John, 129, 130, 140, 252, 254, 264, *quoted*, 122, 129-130
Niger River, center of Guinea trade, 64, 70, 71, 72, 81, 124, 130, 140
Nigeria, West Africa, 124, 132
Nkrumah, Kwame, 60
Noble, slaver captain, 148
HMS *North Star*, 177-178
Northwest Ordinance, 296
Nugent, Lady, *quoted*, 201, 202

Obeah, slave religion, 213, 214, 215, 217, 241
Oberlin College, 13, 38, 312, 359

Oneida Institute, 313
Ontario (Canada West), free Negro colonies, 25-26, 37, 364
Oroonoko (Behn), 237, 239; *dramatized*, 239-240, 242, 243
Osawatomie, Kan., 17, 19

Paine, Lieut., USN, 171
Paine, Thomas, 264, 267, 287
Palmerston, Lord, 174
Palm-oil trade, 121, 163, 180
Papaws, African tribe, 77
Park, Mungo, 54, 130, 140-141, 142, 245; *quoted*, 65, 141
Parker, Captain John, 347-348
Parker, Theodore, 346-353; influences on, 346-348; as member of Secret Six, 7, 354, 373, 382, 383; as preacher, 24, 347, 348-349, 351-352, 373; *quoted*, 349, 350-353, 362, 379, 389; reaction to Harpers Ferry raid, 352-353
Perfect uprising, 113
Philadelphia, as abolitionist center, 286, 296, 316; as slaver port, 163
Phillips, Thomas, *quoted*, 125, 136-137, 138
Phillips, Wendell, 300, 302, 306, 308, 311, 333-334, *quoted*, 306, 308, 311, 380, 381-382
A Picture of Slavery (Bourne), 50
Pilgrim, slaver, 139
Pitt, William, as antislave trade leader in Parliament, 251, 253, 254, 255, 261, 262, 263, 267, 271, 284
Plymouth, England, as slaver port, 112
Pomeroy, Samuel Clarke, 19
Popo, Guinea, 126
Pongo River, center of illegal trade, 171, 173, 179
Porpoise, slaver, 170
Portland, Maine, as slaver port, 163, 168
Porto Novo, Guinea, slave center, 126
Portugal, African trading posts, 58, 114-115, 116-117; in gold trade, 57-58, 71-72, 74, 78, 123-124; in slave trade. *See* Slave trade
Pottawatomie Massacre, 16-17, 369
HMS *Prometheus*, 175

Quadroons, 200, 201
Quakers, American, abolitionist activities, 222, 247, 297, 299-300, 303, 316
Quakers, British, antislavery activities, 247, 253, 254, 257, 258, 263, 265, 267, 271, 275, 276, 280, 284, 287
Quaqua, African tribe, 83, 108
Queen Elizabeth, slaver, 111

Rainbow uprising, 145
Ramsay, James, 265-266, 274
USS *Raritan*, 170
Raynal, Abbé, 232-234, 247, 261, 263, 286
Realf, Richard, 24, 322-326, 379, *quoted*, 379
Rebecca, slaver, 161-163
Redpath, James, 18-19, 27, 45, 221, 298, 322, 385, *quoted*, 45, 221-222
Reform movements in U.S., 297-300, 313, 316, 332, 383-384, 389; education, 299, 338; humane societies, 299, 338; peace movement, 299, 303, 333, 357; prison reform, 299, 357; temperance, 299, 302, 313, 323, 333, 348, 355, 357, 358, 362; universal suffrage, 298; women's rights, 299, 316, 317, 320, 333, 355, 357
Republican Party, 24-25, 314, 319, 321, 371, 381
Rhode Island, center of U.S. slaving, 141, 142
HMS *Rifleman*, 180
Ripley, George, 348, 383
Rodney, Admiral George Brydges, 258
Royal African Company, 118, 138
Ruffin, Edmund, 23
Ruiz, Jose, 152, 153
Runaway slaves. *See* Slaves
Russel, Lord, 174

Sahara, 71, 74
St. Domingue, F.W.I., antislave trade bloc in French Assembly, 262-263; caste system, 202, 215-216; pro-slave trade lobby in Paris, 263; quality of settlers, 190; Uprising. *See* Hayti; as slave market, 54, 136; sugar economy, 185, 215
St. Jan, slaver, 144

St. Kitts, B.W.I., 185, 192, 200
St. Thomas Island, Portuguese West Africa, 117, 138, 207, 212
St. Vincent, B.W.I., 139, 194, 203, 207
Salem, Mass., as slaver port, 141
Sanborn, Ariana Walker, 368, 370
Sanborn, Franklin Benjamin, 338, 349, 367-372, 376; as member of Secret Six, 7, 21, 329-330, 345, 366, 369, 376, 377; *quoted*, 341, 344, 368; reaction to Harpers Ferry raid, 370-372, 373, 374
Sanborn, Sarah, 371-372
Santo Domingo, Spanish West Indies, 207, 340
Scott, Sir Walter, as influence on Secret Six, 302, 330, 331, 333, 334, 335, 339, 354, 365, 372, 385, 392
Secret Six: advocacy of violence, 6, 51, 181, 290-291, 336-337, 343-344, 352, 358, 360, 381, 386-387, 391; implication in Harpers Ferry raid, 327, 370-371, 374-377, 378; influences on, 49-50, 182, 243, 295, 306, 311, 330-334, 339-340, 346-347, 364, 365, 367-368, 390, 392; and John Brown, 6, 21, 24-25, 27, 34, 51, 206, 243, 311, 327-328, 329-332, 334, 335, 337, 343-345, 348, 351, 356, 358-362, 364-366, 368-378, 382, 383, 390-392; members, 7; motivations, 347, 348, 351, 356-357, 368, 383-386, 389-392; social status, 6-7, 300, 332, 333, 347-348, 354, 356, 362-363; views on slavery, 6, 49-50, 182, 206, 351-353, 391
Sekondi, Gold Coast, 58, 59-60, 114
Seminole Indians, 208
Senegal River, in Guinea trade, 64, 71, 72, 76, 95, 110, 123, 126
Senegalese. *See* Negroes, West African
Seven Years War, 148, 203
The Seventy. *See* Abolitionist Movement, U.S.
Sewall, Samuel, 300
Seward, Senator William H., 25
Shama, Gold Coast, 57-58
Sharp, brother of Granville, 248
Sharp, Granville, 247, 248-249, 250, 253, 256, 257, 265, 287-288, *quoted*, 245
Sierra Leone: description, 65, 117; free Negro colony, 129, 211, 250,

Sierra Leone (*cont.*)
287-288; modern-day, 89, 122, 132; peoples, 81, 120, 152, 211; slave patrol station, 171, 172, 175, 177-178; slave area, 112, 128, 144, 152-153
The Six. *See* Secret Six
Slave Coast, as area of slave procurement, 74, 126, 129-130, 132, 150, 215; trading forts, 114; wars, 120
Slave trade: arguments for, 134, 156; centers in Africa, 52-55, 57-60, 63, 110, 114-120, 126, 129, 130, 150, 179; centers in West, 111, 141, 142, 163, 164; competition, 52, 54-60, 115, 116; effect on Africa, 150-151; hazards, 52, 68, 77, 107-108, 112-114, 115-116, 117; illegal, 152-181; inception and causes, 71-73, 74-75, 107, 109, 110, 120-121; intra-African, 73-75; methods of procuring slaves, 54, 55, 57, 58, 73, 105-109, 114, 126-131; mortality of slaves, 110, 111, 139, 143, 149; native traders, 56-57, 60, 67, 79, 107-108, 114, 115, 117, 127-132, 133, 155, 176, 179-180; natives employed in, 119-120, 128, 129, 132; number of slaves shipped, 149-150; outlawed, 153-155, 164-166, 255-256, 267, 268; participants: Baltic states, in illegal, 165; Brandenburg, 117; Brazil, 117, 165, in illegal, 155, 170, 180; Britain, 53-54, 55-57, 58-60, 68, 72, 86, 107, 111-112, 115, 116, 139, 141, 142, 145, 147, 148; Cuba, 117, in illegal, 152-155, 167-168; Denmark, 53, 60-61, 117, 142; France, 53-54, 55-57, 72, 77, 111, 115, 116, 127, 139, 141, 142, 147, 148, 165, 268, in illegal, 165; Germany, 53; Italy, 117; Latin American states, 155, 165; Netherlands, 53-54, 58, 59, 68, 72, 111, 115, 139, 142, 144; Portugal, 53, 58, 72, 74, 107, 114, 116, 117, 165, in illegal, 155, 165-166, 177; Spain, 53, 72, 107, 116-117, 152-154, 157, 165, 268, in illegal, 155-156, 158, 161-163, 166-167, 171-172; Sweden, 117; U.S., 106, 107, 117, 140-142, 144, 146, 148, in illegal, 154-172
policy on, and enforcement of ban

Slave trade (*cont.*)
against: British, 154-155, 161-162, 164-180; Dutch, 154; French, 154, 165, 173, 261; Latin Americans, 165-166; Portuguese, 154-155, 160, 162, 165-166; Spanish, 154-155, 165-166, 167; U.S., 153-154, 159, 164-174, 180-181
principal markets, 54, 109, 110, 130, 141, 154, 157, 158, 161, 163, 164, 165, 166-167, 186: profitability, 116, 121; quality of whites in, 111-112, 116-118, 131, 134, 144-145; regulation of, 135, 139, 142, 254, 262; routes. *See* Slaving ships; sentiment and activity against: British, 106, 127, 129, 246, 253-265, 267-268, 271-273; French, 260-264; U.S., 105-106, 109, 133, 149, 156, 157, 391
sentiment and activity for: British, 124, 255, 258, 260-261, 271, 274, 279; French, 261, 263; U.S., 157-158, 172
Slaves: Abolitionist views of. *See* Abolitionist Movement, U.S., British Antislavery Movement; codes regulating treatment, 139, 183-184, 216, 233; emancipation of: in B.W.I., 154, 188, 281-284, 293-294, 315, 388; in F.W.I., 218, 284; in U.S., 284
fugitive: in Britain, 247-249; in B.W.I., 214-215, 240-241, 245; in U.S. North, 20-21, 25, 332, 334-335, 346-348, 364-365; in U.S. South, 315
colonies: in B.W.I., 77, 207-214, 216, 224; in Dutch Guiana, 208, 212, 233; in F.W.I., 216-218; in Portuguese West Africa, 207, 212; in U.S. South, 207-208, 212, 332
mixed-blood, 199, 200-202, 215; religions, 82, 90, 92, 213-215, 216, 217, 219, 225, 241; slave English, 184; treatment: in B.W.I., 148, 182-189, 196, 203-205, 273-274, 283, 284; in Dutch Guiana, 132, 186, 216; in F.W.I., 182, 185, 189, 203, 205, 215-217, 263; in slave trade, 54, 55-56, 109-113, 125, 132-149, 156, 162, 177-178, 180, 186, 259, 262;

Slaves (*cont.*)
in U.S. South, 50-51, 183-184, 185, 187-189, 191, 196-197, 204-205, 211-212, 224-225, 227, 315, 316
uprisings: aboard slavers, 55-56, 113, 131, 144-146, 152-154, 207; in U.S. South, 121, 207, 212, 222-230, 235-236; in B.W.I., 121, 206, 209-210, 212-215, 275, 278; in F.W.I. *See* Hayti
Slaving ships, conditions on, 55-56, 110-113, 117, 132-148, 156, 162, 177-178, 180, 258-259, 262; in illegal trade, 152-180; routes, 109-110
Smith, Gerrit, 354-362; influences on, 320-321, 354-356, 365; as member of Secret Six, 7, 329-330, 354, 362; *quoted*, 356, 360; reaction to Harpers Ferry raid, 298, 355, 376-378
Smith, John, Baptist Missionary, 275
Smith, Nancy, 356
Smith, Peter (father of Gerrit), 355-356
Smith, Peter (brother of Gerrit), 355
HMS *Snapper*, 175
Société des Amis des Noirs, 261, 263, 277
Somerset, James, 249
Songhai, Kingdom of, 69-70
South: abolitionist activities in, 7-8, 15, 23, 157-158, 181, 188, 202-203, 288, 291, 293, 296, 303, 307, 308, 315, 387-388, 391; caste system, 184, 201-202; economy, 6, 184-185, 191-197; fear of Negro uprisings, 206-207, 211-212, 222, 225, 229-230, 380, 381, 390; growth of antagonism toward Abolitionism, 7-8, 291-293, 380-381, 387, 391-392; in illegal slave trade. *See* Slave trade; plantations, 196-197, 200-201; proslave trade sentiment. *See* Slave trade; proslavery agitation in Kansas, 14-19; quality of settlers and slaveholders, 189-190, 191, 193, 202; reaction to Harpers Ferry raid, 4, 207; secessionist sentiment, 307, 381, 390, 391; slave activity and treatment. *See* Slaves
South Carolina, slave treatment, 183-184, 187-188, 224; slave uprisings, 207, 224-227

Southey, *quoted*, 276
Spain, in gold trade, 72; in slave trade. *See* Slave trade
Spanish colonies. *See*, Cuba, Hispaniola, Jamaica, Santo Domingo
Spartacus, 22, 207, 232, 235-236, 240-243
Spitfire, slaver, 171-172
Spooner, Lysander, 335
Stanton, Elizabeth Cady, 320
Starry, Dr., 36, 38, 39
Stearns, Dr. (father of George), 363
Stearns, George Luther, 362-366, as member of Secret Six, 7, 19, 365-366, 369, 371, 374-375; *quoted*, 366; reaction to Harpers Ferry raid, 374; testimony before Mason Committee, 374-375
Stearns, Mary, 364, 365, 366, *quoted*, 366
Stephen, George, 280, 283, 289, 297
Stephen, James, 265-266, 267, 280, *quoted*, 127, 146-147, 268
Stevens, Aaron, 23, 24, 38, 39, 42
Stone, Lucy, 320, 333
Stowe, Harriet Beecher, 231, 301, 305, 329, 381, *quoted*, 305
Stuart, Lieut. J.E.B., 40-41
Stuart, Charles, 281, 288, 297, 312, 313, *quoted*, 281
Sturge, Joseph, 280, 281, 283-284, 288-289, 294, 297
Sumner, Senator Charles, 364, 365, 371, 374, 387
Surinam, Dutch Guiana, slaves in, 182, 208, 212, 216, 233, 237-239
Sweden in slave trade, 117

Tackey, leader of Jamaican conspiracy, 213, 214, 229
Tappan, Arthur, 288, 300, 303, 316
Tappan, Lewis, 300, 316
Taylor, Stewart, 39
Teignmouth, Lord, 265
Télémaque. *See* Vesey, Denmark
Temne, African tribe, 211
Thomas uprising, 113
Thompson, George, 264, 281-282, 288-289, 297, 305, 308
Thompson, Henry, 14, 42, 337
Thompson, Ruth, 13
Thompson, William, 38, 39

Thomson, Francis, 276
Thoreau, Henry David, 7, 19, 349, 367, *quoted*, 13, 381
Thornton family, 251-252, 264-265
HMS *Tigris*, 162
Tigris, slaver, 168
Timbuctoo, Guinea, 68, 71
Tomboy, leader in Antigua plot, 213-214, 225
Tories, 251, 254
Tortuga, F.W.I., 190, 192
Trinidad, B.W.I., amelioration measures, 274; quality of settlers, 194; slave uprising, 214, 215
USS *Truxtun*, 171-172, 173
Tubman, Harriet, 26
Turner, Nat, 227-229, 230, 231, 234, 235-236, 387

Uncle Tom's Cabin (Stowe), 236, 282, 291, 315, 320, 381, *quoted*, 52
Underground Railroad, 20, 26, 296
Unitarians, 329, 348, 368
U.S. Congress: abolition of domestic slave trade, 290; Abolitionist activity in, 314, 315, 361; antislavery pressure on, 289, 290; extent of jurisdiction over slavery, 290-291, 386, 391; work towards gradual emancipation, 387
U.S. Constitution, 43, 254, 337, 386
U.S. Government, enforcement of antislave trade laws. *See* Slave trade
U.S. Navy, on antislave trade patrol, 164-165, 168, 169, 170-173, 178, 180-181
U.S. Senate, investigation of Harpers Ferry raid, 323, 325, 370-377, 378
U.S. troops, at Harpers Ferry, 39, 40, 41, 42, 380; in Kansas, 15, 17, 336
USS *United States*, 173

Vanderbilt, Cornelius, 358
Veloz, slaver, 177
Venn, Rev. Mr. John, 265
Vesey, slaver captain, 226
Vesey, Denmark, 224, 225, 226-227, 229
USS *Vincennes*, 162
HMS *Viper*, 161-162
Virginia: abolitionist sentiments, 229, 288, 296, 387; Gabriel's Conspiracy

Virginia (*cont.*)
of 1800, 222-224, 225; militia at Harpers Ferry, 40, 41, 348, 380; prosecution of John Brown, 5, 42-46, 345, 370, 374, 376; slave activity and treatment in, 207, 212, 223-224, 227, 249; as slave market, 141; Nat Turner uprising, 227-230, 236, 387
HMS *Vixen*, 162
Volta River, 64, 71, 125-126, 179
Voodoo, 82, 90, 92, 216-217, 219

Wade, Benjamin, 314
Walker, Amasa, 300
Walker, William, 158
Wanderer, slaver, 156, 158-159, 161, 164
HMS *Wanderer*, 175-176
War of 1812, 10, 155-156, 166, 339
Ward, Julia. *See* Howe, Julia Ward
Washington, Col. Lewis, 9, 35, 36, 38, 41
USS *Washington*, 153
HMS *Water Witch*, 168
Waverley novels (Scott), 333, 346, 367
Wayland, Francis, 323
Webster, Daniel, and Compromise of 1850, 348; and Webster-Ashburton Treaty, 172
Wedgwood, Josiah, 288
Weld, Angelina Grimké, 316-319, 320, *quoted*, 317
Weld, Theodore Dwight, 311-321, as propagandist, 188, 288, 301; *quoted*, 316, 320; and the Seventy, 313-314, 317, 389; withdrawal from active agitation, 319-321, 325-326, 353, 383
Wesley, John, 73, 247, 253, 257, 286, *quoted*, 62, 105, 106, 129
West Africa, present-day, 53-54, 57-58, 63, 70, 89, 92, 96-98; in slave trade. *See* Guinea, Slave trade
West Indies, 189; abolition of slavery. *See* Slaves; absentee landlords, 194-197, 215; antislavery pressures on, 222, 262-263; caste systems, 201-202,

West Indies (*cont.*)
215-216; economy, 169, 185, 186, 191, 196, 200, 203, 209, 215, 273, 274-275; estates, 194, 197-201; native Indians, 72, 189, 192, 200, 207-208; Negro/white ratio, 195-196; post-emancipation conditions, 188, 218-219, 220, 277-278, 282-284, 293-294, 315, 388; proslavery pressure on home governments, 254, 261, 263, 271, 274-275, 279; quality of settlers and slaveowners, 189-194, 202; as slave market, 55, 110, 129, 134, 142, 165; slaves, activity and treatment. *See* Slaves; *see also* British West Indies, Cuba, Dutch Guiana, French West Indies, Hayti
Western Reserve, 10, 290
Whigs, 253
Whiteley, Henry, 282, 284
Whittier, James Greenleaf, 45, 234, *quoted*, 45-46
Whydah, Kingdom of; 67, 76, 116; as slave center, 124, 129, 132, 160; tribes. *See* Negroes, West African
Wilberforce, William, antislave trade leader in Parliament, 253-256, 260, 261, 264, 269, 271, 277, 280, 289, 296, 310; and Clapham Sect, 264-265; founding of Sierra Leone, 250; influences on, 251-253, 258; *quoted*, 133, 254-255; writings, 288
William and Jane, slaver, 56-57
Williams case, 284
Wilson, Senator Henry, 24-25
Wise, Gov. Henry A. of Virginia, 43, 335, 380
Woolman, John, 284-285
Wordsworth, William, 234, 276
Wren, Percival C., 63
Wright, Fanny, 288
Wright, Henry C., 317, 318
Wythe, George, 193, 387

Yoruban tribe, 123

N

NO'